JOHN WILLIS'

DANCE WORLD

1974

Volume 9

JOHN WILLIS'

DANCE WORLD

1974

Volume 9
1973-1974 SEASON

CROWN PUBLISHERS, INC.
419 Park Avenue South
New York, N.Y. 10016

TO

ERIK BRUHN

internationally acclaimed as one of the greatest male classic dancers of all times. His retirement, after a twenty-six-year career, saddened everyone in the world of dance, but left beautiful memories of his unique virtuosity.

Eleanor D'Antuono and Ivan Nagy in "Coppelia"
American Ballet Theatre

CONTENTS

EDITOR: JOHN WILLIS
Assistant Editor: Stanley Reeves
Staff: Raymond Frederick, Frances Harwood, Robert Maldonado,
Jack Moore, Don Nute, Evan Romero
Staff Photographers: Lyn Smith, Van Williams

DANCE COMPANIES ON BROADWAY

LYCEUM THEATRE
Opened Tuesday, February 5, 1974*
Chimera Foundation for Dance presents:

NIKOLAIS DANCE THEATRE

Choreography, Sound Score, Costume and Lighting Design by Alwin Nikolais; Technical Director, Robert Keil, Jr.; Technician, Howard Nelson; Audio-Visual Technician, Mark Goodman; Production Coordinator, Ruth Grauert; Technical Director for this engagement, Sander Hacker; Manager, Peter Obletz

COMPANY

Lisbeth Bagnold, Rob Esposito, Stevan Iannacone, Janet Katzenberg, Lynn Levine, Suzanne McDermaid, Gerald Otte, Gladys Roman, Jessica Sayre, James Teeters, Fred Timm

REPERTOIRE

"Suite from Sanctum," "Tower from Vaudeville of the Elements," "Divertissement," "Tent," "Somniloquy," "Scenario," "Foreplay" PREMIERES: "Cross-Fade" on Tuesday, Feb. 5, 1974; "Scrolls" on Friday, Feb. 8, 1974.
General Managers: NR Productions
Press: Merlin Group, Sandra Manley
Stage Manager: Robert Keil, Jr.

*Closed Feb. 17, 1974 after limited engagement of 15 performances.

Oleaga, Caravaglia Photos

"Scenario" Top Left: "Tent"

"Scrolls" Top: "Cross-Fade"

"Somniloquy" (*Oleaga Photo*)   Top: Group Dance from "Sanctum"
NIKOLAIS DANCE THEATRE

"Somniloquy" (*Oleaga Photo*)   Top: "Foreplay" (*Markatos Photo*)

NIKOLAIS DANCE THEATRE

LYCEUM THEATRE
Opened Tuesday, February 19, 1974*
Chimera Foundation for Dance presents:

MURRAY LOUIS DANCE COMPANY

Artistic Director-Choreographer, Murray Louis; Technical Director, James Van Abbema; Assistant Technical Director, David Anderson; Costume Director, Frank Garcia; Production Coordinator, Ruth Grauert; Manager, Peter Obletz; Supervising Designer James Tilton

COMPANY

Murray Louis, Michael Ballard, Richard Haisma, Helen Kent, Anne McLeod, Robert Small, Marcia Wardell, and Special Guest Artist Phyllis Lamhut

REPERTOIRE

"Interims" (Foss), "Hoopla" (Los Canarios), "Personnae" (Free Life Communication), "Proximities" (Brahms), "Continuum" (Corky Siegel Blues Band-Alwin Nikolais), "Index (to necessary neuroses . . .)" (Oregon Ensemble)
PREMIERES: Tuesday, February 19, 1974 "Porcelain Dialogues" (Peter I. Tchaikovsky, Murray Louis; Lighting, Alwin Nikolais; Costumes, Frank Garcia) performed by Michael Ballard, Richard Haisma, Helen Kent, Robert Small, Marcia Wardell; *NY premiere* Thursday, Feb. 21, 1974 of "Scheherezade, a dream" (Rimsky-Korsakov-Alwin Nikolais-Free Life Communication, Murry Louis, Lighting, Alwin Nikolais; Costumes, Frank Garcia) danced by the company in two acts with intermission

* Closed March 3, 1974 after limited engagement of 14 performances.

Caravaglia Photos

"Continuum"   Top Left: "Hoopla"

"Porcelain Dialogues" (also top)

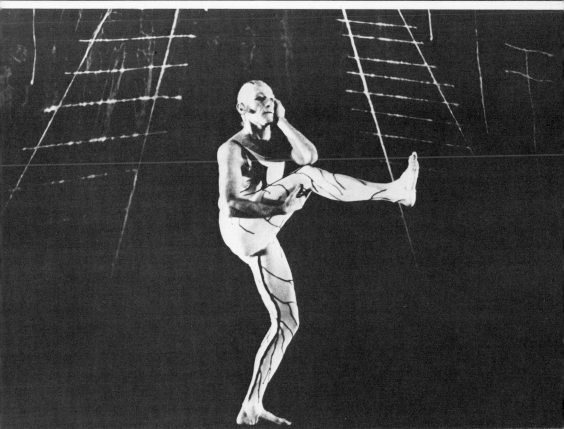

Murray Louis in "Index" Top: "Index" (*Caravaglia Photos*)
MURRAY LOUIS DANCE COMPANY

MARK HELLINGER THEATRE
Opened Monday, April 15, 1974*
The Martha Graham Center of Contemporary Dance (Ron Protas, Executive Director) presents:

MARTHA GRAHAM DANCE COMPANY

Artistic Director-Choreographer, Martha Graham; Associate Artistic director-Regisseur, Robert Powell; Conductor, Robert Irving; Associate Conductor, Stanley Sussman; Settings, Isamu Noguchi, Arch Lauterer, Dani Karavan, Fangor; Lighting, Jean Rosenthal, William H. Batchelder; Maquillage, Jeffrey Navarro; Production Supervisor, William H. Batchelder, General Manager, NR Productions

COMPANY

Takako Asakawa, Phyllis Gutelius, Yuriko Kimura, Robert Powell, Ross Parkes, William Carter, David Hatch Walker, Diane Gray, Judith Hogan, Janet Eilber, Peggy Lyman, Tim Wengerd, Mario Delamo, Daniel Maloney, Peter Sparling, Lucinda Mitchell, Diana Hart, David Chase, Carl Paris, Armgard von Bardeleben, Bonnie Oda, Elisa Monte, Holly Cavrell, Susan McGuire, Eric Newton, Sherry Linn
GUEST ARTISTS: Pearl Lang, Jean Erdman, Christina Asher (soprano), John Ostendorf (bass-baritone)

REPERTOIRE

Introduction and Technique Demonstration with Miss Graham and company, "Excerpts from Clytemnestra, Appalachian Spring, Cave of the Heart, Deaths and Entrances, and Diversion of Angels," "Seraphic Dialogue" (Dello Joio), "Circe" (Hovhaness), "Appalachian Spring" (Copland), "Clytemnestra" (El-Dabh), "El Penitente" (Horst), "Diversion of Angels" (Dello Joio), "Deaths and Entrances" (Johnson), "Embattled Garden" (Surinach), "Letter to the World" (Johnson), "Night Journey" (Schuman), "Errand into the Maze" (Menotti)
PREMIERES: Friday, April 19, 1974 "Chronique" (Carlos Surinach, Martha Graham; Text from "Chronique" by St. John Perse; Set, Fangor; Lighting, William H. Batchelder; Narrator, John Ostendorf; Guitarist, Donald Frost; Conductor, Lewis Stewart; Revised version of "Mendicants of Evening" with new score and choreography) danced by Peggy Lyman, William Carter, Phyllis Gutelius, Tim Wengerd, Yuriko Kimura, Ross Parkes, Diane Gray, Takako Asakawa, David Hatch Walker, and Lucinda Mitchell, Bonnie Oda, Judith Hogan, Diana Hart, Elisa Monte, Sherry Linn, Mario Delamo, Eric Newton, Peter Sparling, David Chase
Saturday, April 27, 1974 "Holy Jungle" (Robert Starer, Martha Graham; Set, Dani Karavan; Lighting, William H. Batchelder; Conductor, Robert Irving) with Diane Gray, Janet Eilber, William Carter, David Hatch Walker, Judith Hogan, Armgard von Bardelben, Phyllis Gutelius, Peggy Lyman, Bonnie Oda, Mario Delamo, Tim Wengerd, Daniel Maloney, David Chase, Eric Newton
General Manager: Cynthia Parker
Press: Tom Kerrigan
Stage Managers: Howard Crampton-Smirth, Anne McKey

* Closed May 4, 1974 after limited engagement of 21 performances, and one student performance.

Martha Swope Photos

Top Left: Judith Hogan, David Hatch Walker, Janet Eilber in "Holy Jungle"

Peggy Lyman, William Carter
in "Chronique"

**Ross Parkes, Phyllis Gutelius, Eric Newton
in "Deaths and Entrances"**

William Carter, Peggy Lyman in "Chronique"
Top: Yuriko Kimura, Pearl Lang, Takako Asakawa
the three "Clytemnestras" for the season

Peggy Lyman, Ross Parkes, Daniel Maloney
Yuriko Kimura in "Embattled Garden"

MARTHA GRAHAM DANCE COMPANY

Pearl Lang in "Letter to the World" Top Left: Takako Asakawa in
"Cave of the Heart" Right: Mario Delamo, Diane Gray in "Seraphic Dialogue"
MARTHA GRAHAM DANCE COMPANY

**William Carter, Phyllis Gutelius in "Appalachian Spring" Top Left: Diane Gray
in "Night Journey" Right: Takako Asakawa, David Hatch Walker in "Seraphic Dialogue"**
MARTHA GRAHAM DANCE COMPANY

Diane Gray, David Hatch Walker, Ross Parkes in "Night Journey"
MARTHA GRAHAM DANCE COMPANY

ANTA THEATRE
Opened Tuesday, April 16, 1974*

DANCE THEATRE OF HARLEM

Directors-Producers, Arthur Mitchell, Karel Shook; Co-Producer, Hal deWindt; Assistant Director, Myrtha Rosello; General Administrator, M. Phyllis Butcher; Business Manager, M. J. Plimpton; Conductor-Piano Soloist, Tania Leon; Guest Conductors, Henry Lewis, Kermit Moore; Concertmaster, Gerald Tarack; Assistant General Manager, Robert Frissell; Lighting Designer, Paul Sullivan; Costumes, Carl Michell, Zelda Wynn; Music Director, Tania Leon; Ballet Master, William T. Scott, Jr.; Wardrobe Mistress, Yvonne Stoney; Music Coordinator, Earl Shendell

COMPANY

Lydia Abarca, Karen Brown, Laura Brown, Brenda Garratt, Yvonne Hall, Virginia Johnson, Laura Lovelle, Susan Lovelle, Gayle McKinney, Melva Murray-White, Shenikwa Nowlin, Sheila Rohan, Ronda Sampson, Roslyn Sampson, Karen Wright, Gerald Banks, Roman Brooks, Homer Bryant, Ronald Perry, Walter Raines, Paul Russell, Allan Sampson, William Scott, Samuel Smalls, Derek Williams, Joseph Wyatt

REPERTOIRE

"Fete Noire" (Shostakovich, Arthur Mitchell), "Le Corsaire" (Drigo, Karel Shook after Chabukiani), "Dougla" (Arranged by Tania Leon, Geoffrey Holder), "Holberg Suite" (Grieg, Mitchell), "Biosfera" (Marlos Nobre, Mitchell), "Forces of Rhythm" (Traditional-Contemporary, Louis Johnson), "Concerto Barocco" (Bach, Balanchine), "Agon" (Stravinsky, Balanchine), "Rhythmetron" (Nobre, Mitchell), "Design for Strings" (Tchaikovsky, John Taras), "Tones" (Leon, Mitchell)
N.Y. PREMIERES: "Wings" Tuesday, April 16, 1974 (Benjamin Britten, Louis Johnson; Costumes, Carl Michell; Lighting and Projections, Paul Sullivan), "Caravansarai" Thursday, Apr. 18, 1974 (Santana, Talley Beatty; Costumes, William Pennington; Lighting, Paul Sullivan), "Haiku (A Dream for Brown Eyes)" Tuesday, Apr. 23, 1974 (Tania Leon, Walter Raines; Costumes, Walter Raines; Lighting, Gary Fails), "Ancient Voices of Children" Thursday, Apr. 25, 1974 (George Crumb, Milko Sparemblek; Costumes, Milko Sparemblek; Lighting, Gary Fails; Sculpture, Bill Sullivan)
General Manager: Norman Rothstein
Company Mangers: Richard A. Gonsalves, Lorenzo James
Press: Merle Debuskey, Susan L. Schulman
Stage Managers: Gary Fails, Steven Terry, Jerome King, Ramdeo

* Closed Apr. 28 after limited engagement of 16 performances.

Martha Swope Photos

"Haiku" Top Left: Melva Murray-White in "Ancient Voices of Children" Below: "Ancient Voices of Children"

Walter Raines, Virginia Johnson in "Tones"
Top: Paul Russell, Virginia Johnson, Homer Bryant
in "Holberg Suite"

Derek Williams, Gayle McKinney, Homer Bryant
in "Forces of Rhythm"

Paul Russell, Laura Brown in "Le Corsaire" Top Left: "Concerto
Barocco" Right: Melva Murray-White, Joe Wyatt in "Ancient Voices of Children"
DANCE THEATRE OF HARLEM

"Agon" Above: "Fete Noire"
Top: "Rhythmetron"

"Holberg Suite"
Above: "Forces of Rhythm"

DANCE THEATRE OF HARLEM

DANCE COMPANIES AT LINCOLN CENTER

ALICE TULLY HALL
June 5–10, 1973*

LOUIS FALCO DANCE COMPANY

Artistic Director-Choreographer, Louis Falco; Associate Directors, Jennifer Muller, Juan Antonio; Managing Director, Carl Hunt; Music Director, Burt Alcantara; Lighting Director, Richard Nelson; Artistic Adviser, William Katz; Production Assistant, Nancy Golladay; Stage Manager, Suzanne Egan

COMPANY

Louis Falco, Jennifer Muller, Juan Antonio, Georgiana Holmes, Matthew Diamond, Mary Jane Eisenberg

REPERTOIRE

"The Moor's Pavane" (Purcell, Limon), "Rust—Giacometti Sculpture Garden" (Burt Alcantara-Pete Klaus Meyer, Jennifer Muller), "The Sleepers" (Louis Falco), "Caviar" (Vertical Burn, Falco), "Huescape" (Schaefer-Lasry-Baschet, Falco), "Nostalgia" (Collage, Jennifer Muller), "Soap Opera" (Alcantara, Falco)
PREMIERES: "Avenue" (Vertical Burn, Louis Falco; Costumes, William Katz; Lighting, Richard Nelson) on Tuesday, June 5, 1973; "Tub" (Burt Alcantara, Jennifer Muller; Costumes, Christina Ham; Lighting, Richard Nelson) on Wednesday, June 6, 1973; "Twopenny Portrait" (Burt Alcantara, Louis Falco; Decor and Costumes, Victor Paul; Lighting, Richard Nelson) on Thursday, June 7, 1973.

* The company performed May 21–26, 1974 with Angeline Wolf added to the cast, and presented three *premieres*: "Biography" (Burt Alcantara, Jennifer Muller; Costumes, Melissa Greenberg; Lighting, Beverly Emmons), "Storeroom" (Kirk Nurock, Louis Falco; Decor and Costumes, Victor Paul; Lighting, Beverly Emmons) both on May 21, 1974; "Speeds" (Burt Alcantara, Jennifer Muller; Costumes, William Katz; Lighting, Richard Nelson) on May 22, 1974.

Jack Mitchell Photos

Top Right: "Tub" Below: "Caviar"

**Louis Falco, Georgiana Holmes in
"Twopenny Portrait"**

"The Sleepers"
(*Bela Szabo Photo*)

METROPOLITAN OPERA HOUSE
Opened Tuesday, June 26, 1973.*
S. Hurok presents:

BOLSHOI BALLET
and
Bolshoi Dance Academy

Director General, Kiril Molchanov; Artistic Director, Yuri Grigorovich; Artistic Director American Tour, Alexander Lapauri; Tour Director, Yuri Pribegin; Production Manager, Vladimir Pogodin; Stage Technician, Chuck Renaud; Dance Coordinator, Simon Semenoff; Balletmaster, Maxim Martirosyan; Conductors, Vakhtang Paliashvili, Georgi Zhemchuzhin; Balletmistress, Lidia Khlustova; Director of the Bolshoi Dance Academy, Sofia Golovkina; Lighting, Gilbert V. Hemsley, Jr.

COMPANY

PRINCIPALS: Raissa Struchkova, Nina Sorokina, Marina Leonova, Ludmila Semenyaka, Yelena Riabinkina, Nadezhda Pavlova, Yelena Cherkasskaya, Svetlana Kolyvanova, Irina Kholina, Tamara Varlamova, Nicolai Fadeyechev, Maris Liepa, Yuri Vladimirov, Shamil Yagudin, Vyacheslav Gordeyev, Alexander Godunov, Vilen Galstyan, Bladimir Nikonov, Vladimir Romanenko, Yuri Griboriev, Yuri Papko, Sergei Radchenko
SOLOISTS: Tatiana Domashevskaya, Ella Maslennikova, Yelena Matveyeva, Natalia Pozdnyakova, Maya Kruchkova, Valentina Savina, Inna Kharlamova, Ludmila Vlasova, Semon Kaufman, Isander Khmelnitski, Anatoli Danilychev, Oleg Rachkovski, Mikhail Messerer, Leonid Bolotin, Leonid Kozlov, Nicolai Fyodorov, Vladimir Anisimov
with full corps de ballet, and symphony orchestra, and students of the Senior, Intermediate, and Junior grades of the Bolshoi Dance Academy

REPERTOIRE

"Ballet School" (Glazounov-Tchaikovsky-Rachmaninoff-Glinka-Gliere, Maxim Martirosyan) performed by the students of the dance academy at every performance, "Chopiniana" (Chopin-Glazounov, Mikhail Fokine), "Highlights," "Giselle Act II" (Adam, Perrot-Petipa), "Walpurgis Night" "Don Quixote Excerpts," "Swan Lake Act II"

Company Manager: David Bines
Press: Sheila Porter, Edward Parkinson, John Gingrich
Stage Manager: Spencer Mosse

* Closed July 22, 1973 to tour, after limited engagement of 32 performances.

Judy Cameron Photos

Right: Nina Sorokina, Yuri Vladimoriov

**Shamil Yagudin in
"Walpurgis Night"**

**Nina Sorokina
in "Flames of Paris"**

25

"Giselle" Top Left: Nadezhda Pavlova Right: Marina Leonova

BOLSHOI BALLET

Ludmila Semenyaka in "Swan Lake"
Top: "The Awakening of Spring"

Nicolai Fadeyechev

BOLSHOI BALLET

"Swan Lake" Top Left: Raissa Struchkova   Right: Nina Sorokina, Yuri Vladimirov in "Flames of Paris"

BOLSHOI BALLET

"Paquita" Top Left: Maris Liepa in "Giselle"
Right: Irina Kholina
BOLSHOI BALLET

NEW YORK STATE THEATER
Opened Tuesday, July 3, 1973.*
Ballet Theatre Foundation (Sherwin M. Goldman, President) in association with City Center of Music and Drama (Norman Singer, Executive Director) presents:

AMERICAN BALLET THEATRE

Directors, Lucia Chase, Oliver Smith; Principal Conductor, Akira Endo; Conductor; David Gilbert; Regisseurs, Dimitri Romanoff, Enrique Martinez; Ballet Mistress, Patricia Wilde; Resident Lighting Designer, Nananne Porcher; Technical Coordinator, George Bardyguine; Production Assistant, Dana Bruce

COMPANY

PRINCIPALS: Paolo Bortoluzzi, Eleanor D'Antuono, Michael Denard, Carla Fracci, Cynthia Gregory, Ted Kivitt, Natalia Makarova, Ivan Nagy, Terry Orr, John Prinz, Sallie Wilson, Gayle Young
SOLOISTS: Karena Brock, William Carter, David Coll, Ellen Everett, Ian Horvath, Jonas Kage, Keith Lee, Daniel Levins, Bonnie Mathis, Dennis Nahat, Marcos Paredes, Zhandra Rodriguez, Christine Sarry, John Sowinski, Marianna Tcherkassky, Martine van Hamel
CORPS DE BALLET: Buddy Balough, Amy Blaisdell, Fernando Bujones, Christine Busch, Richard Cammack, Betty Chamberlin, Mona Clifford, Beverly Colvin, Warren Conover, Deborah Dobson, Jan Fisher, Carol Foster, Rory Foster, Ingrid Fraley, Nanette Glushak, Rodney Gustafson, Kim Highton, Kenneth Hughes, Marie Johansson, Susan Jones, Rhodie Jorgenson, Dennis Marshall, Jacquelyn Marshall, Sara Maule, Ruth Mayer, Jolinda Menendez, Hilda Morales, Janet Popeleski, Giselle Roberge, Richard Schafer, Janet Shibata, Frank Smith, Clark Tippet, Gaudio Vacacio, Charles Ward, Denise Warner, Patricia Wesche, Maria Youskevitch, and apprentices Charles Maple, Cathryn Rhodes

REPERTOIRE

"Petrouchka" (Stravinsky, Fokine), "At Midnight" (Mahler, Feld), "The River" (Ellington, Ailey), "Swan Lake" (Tchaikovsky, Blair after Petipa-Ivanov), "Jardin aux Lilas" (Chausson, Tudor), "Etudes" (Czerny, Lander), "Some Times" (Ogerman, Nahat), "Variations for Four" (Keogh, Dolin), "Romeo and Juliet" (Delius-Dorati, Tudor), "The Maids" (Milhaud, Ross), "Giselle" (Adam Blair after Coralli-Perrot), "Pillar of Fire" (Schoenberg, Tudor) "Unfinished Symphony" (Schubert, Van Dyke), "Graduation Ball" (Strauss, Lichine), "La Sylphide" (Loewenskijold, Bruhn after Bournonville), "Undertow" (Schuman, Tudor), "Don Quixote Pas de Deux." "Monument for a Dead Boy" (Boerman, Van Dantzig), "Intermezzo" (Brahms, Feld), "Billy the Kid" (Copland, Loring) "Mendelssohn Symphony" (Mendelssohn, Nahat), "Scherzo for Massa Jack" (Ives, Lubovitch), "Theme and Variations" (Tchaikovsky, Balanchine), "Three Virgins and a Devil" (Respighi, deMille), "Fancy Free" (Bernstein, Robbins), "The Moor's Pavane" (Purcell-Sadoff, Limon)
PREMIERES: "Diana and Acteon" (Cesare Pugni, Rudolf Nureyev after Agrippina Vaganova; Costumes, Marcos Parades; Conductor Akira Endo) on July 3, 1973 with Eleanor D'Antuono and Ted Kivitt (a pas de deux)
"Polyandrion" (Aaron Copland, Tomm Ruud) featuring Karena Brock, Terry Orr, Dennis Nahat on July 6, 1973
"TALES OF HOFFMAN" (Jacques Offenbach-John Lanchbery Peter Darrell; Scenery and Costumes, Peter Docherty; Lighting Nananne Porcher; Conductor, Akira Endo) on July 12, 1973—a full-evening ballet for the company, featuring Cynthia Gregory Jonas Kage.

General Manager: Daryl Dodson
Company Manager: Phillipe de Conville
Press: Judi Jedlicka, Ginny Hymes, Irene Shaw
Stage Managers: Jerry Rice, Paul Nickel, Boyd Staplin

* Closed Aug. 12, 1973 after 48 performances. Opened winter season on Tuesday, Jan. 8, 1974 at City Center 55 Street Theater and closed Feb. 3, 1974 after 32 performances.
New members of the company were Elizabeth Ashton, Kevin Haigen, Melissa Hale, Linda Kuchera, and Sandall Whitaker
Additions to the repertoire were "Apollo" (Stravinsky, Balanchine) "Harbinger" (Prokofiev, Feld), "Dark Elegies" (Mahler, Tudor), a new production of "Divertissements from Napoli" (Paulli-Helsted Gade, Hans Brenaa after Bournonville), "Coppelia" (Delibes, Martinez), "La Fille Mal Gardee" (Hertel, Romanoff), and on Jan. 15 1974 the *World Premiere* of "Three Essays" (Charles Ives' Orchestral Set No. 2, Lar Lubovitch) for the company.

Judy Cameron Photos
Top Left: Natalia Makarova, Ivan Nagy in "La Fille Mal Gardee"

Ted Kivitt, Eleanor D'Antuono in "Napoli"
Above: Cynthia Gregory, Jonas Kage in "Apollo"

Terry Orr, Marianna Tcherkassky in "Billy the Kid"   Daniel Levins, Gayle Young in "The Maids"
Top: Natalia Makarova, Ted Kivitt in "Coppelia"

Karena Brock, John Sowinski, Jonas Kage, Christine Sarry, Bonnie Mathis, David Coll in "Intermezzo" Top Left:
Marcos Paredes, Bonnie Mathis in "Harbinger" Right: Cynthia Gregory, Gayle Young in "Dark Elegies"

AMERICAN BALLET THEATRE

Eleanor D'Antuono, Fernando Bujones in "Don Quixote"
Top: Ivan Nagy in "Les Sylphides"

Marcos Paredes, Sallie Wilson in "Pillar of Fire"

AMERICAN BALLET THEATRE

Dennis Nahat, Ruth Mayer, Christine Sarry, Sallie Wilson in "Three Virgins and a Devil" Top Left:
Cynthia Gregory, Ivan Nagy in "Paquita" Right: Eleanor D'Antuono, Ted Kivitt in "Theme and Variations"
AMERICAN BALLET THEATRE

Keith Lee, Ivan Nagy, Sallie Wilson in "The Moor's Pavane" Top Left: Fernando Bujones,
Terry Orr, Buddy Balough in "Fancy Free" Right: Terry Orr, Christine Sarry in "Graduation Ball"
(*Bil Leidersdorf Photo*)

AMERICAN BALLET THEATRE

NEW YORK STATE THEATER
Opened Tuesday, November 13, 1973*
The City Center of Music and Drama presents:

NEW YORK CITY BALLET

Director, Lincoln Kirstein; Ballet Masters, George Balanchine, Jerome Robbins, John Taras; Musical Director-Principal Conductor, Robert Irving; Associate Conductor, Hugo Fiorato; Costume Execution, Karinska; Assistant to Ballet Masters, Rosemary Dunleavy

COMPANY

PRINCIPALS: Anthony Blum, Jean-Pierre Bonnefous, John Clifford, Jacques d'Amboise, Allegra Kent, Gelsey Kirkland, Sara Leland, Peter Martins, Kay Mazzo, Patricia McBride, Francisco Moncion, Helgi Tomasson, Violette Verdy, Edward Villella, Karin von Aroldingen

SOLOISTS: Gloria Govrin, Susan Hendl, Deni Lamont, Robert Maiorano, Teen McConnell, Marnee Morris, Shaun O'Brien, Frank Ohman, Susan Pilarre, Carol Sumner, Robert Weiss

CORPS: Muriel Aasen, Merrill Ashley, Debra Austin, Tracy Bennett, James Bogan, Bonita Borne, Victoria Bromberg, Maria Calegari, Stephen Caras, Victor Castelli, Hermes Conde, Bart Cook, Gail Crisa, Richard Dryden, Penelope Dudleston, Daniel Duell, Gerard Ebitz, Renee Estopinal, Nina Fedorov, Elise Flagg, Wilhelmina Frankfurt, Jean-Pierre Frohlich, Judith Fugate, Kathleen Haigney, Gloriann Hicks, Linda Homek, Richard Hoskinson, Dolores Houston, Elise Ingalls, Sandra Jennings, William Johnson, Deborah Koolish, Catherine Morris, Peter Naumann, Colleen Neary, Alice Patelson, Elizabeth Pawluk, Delia Peters, Bryan Pitts, Terri Lee Port, Lisa de Ribere, Christine Redpath, David Richardson, Donna Sackett, Paul Sackett, Stephanie Saland, Lilly Samuels, Marjorie Spohn, Marilee Stiles, Carol Strizak, Richard Tanner, Nolan T'Sani, Sheryl Ware, Heather Watts, Garielle Whittle, Sandra Zigars

REPERTOIRE

(All choreography by George Balanchine except where noted) "Afternoon of a Faun" (Debussy, Robbins), "An Evening's Waltzes" (Prokofieff, Robbins), "Brahms-Schoenberg Quartet" (Brahms) "The Cage" (Stravinsky, Robbins), "The Concert" (Chopin, Robbins), "Concerto Barocco" (Bach), "Cortege Hongrois" (Glazounov), "Dances at a Gathering" (Chopin, Robbins), "Danses Concertantes" (Stravinsky), "Dim Lustre" (Strauss, Tudor), "Divertimento from Le Baiser de la Fee" (Stravinsky), "Donizetti Variations" (Donizetti), "Don Quixote" (Nabokov), "Duo Concertant" (Stravinsky), "Firebird" (Stravinsky, Balanchine-Robbins), "Four Bagatelles" (Beethoven, Robbins), "Goldberg Variations" (Bach, Robbins), "Harlequinade" (Drigo), "Irish Fantasy" (Saint-Saens, d'Amboise), "La Source" (Delibes), "La Valse" (Ravel), "Liebeslieder Walzer" (Brahms), "Monumentum Pro Gesualdo" (Stravinsky), "Movements for Piano and Orchestra" (Stravinsky), "Orpheus" (Stravinsky), "Pas de Deux" (Tchaikovsky), "Prodigal Son" (Prokofieff), "Pulcinella" (Stravinsky, Balanchine-Robbins), "Scenes de Ballet" (Stravinsky, Taras), "Scherzo Fantastique" (Stravinsky, Robbins), "Scherzo a la Russe" (Stravinsky), "Scotch Symphony" (Mendelssohn), "Serenade" (Tchaikovsky), "Serenade in A" (Stravinsky, Bolender), "Stars and Stripes" (Sousa-Kay), "Stravinsky Violin Concerto" (Stravinsky), "Swan Lake" (Tchaikovsky), "Symphony in C" (Bizet), "Symphony in Three Movements" (Stravinsky), "Tarantella" "Song of the Nightingale" (Stravinsky, Taras), "Tchaikovsky Concerto #2" (Tchaikovsky), "Tchaikovsky Suite #2" (Tchaikovsky, d'Amboise), "Tchaikovsky Suite #3" (Tchaikovsky), "Valse-Fantaisie" (Glinka), "Watermill" (Ito, Robbins)

Martha Swope Photos

Top right: Helgi Tomasson, Patricia McBride in "Dybbuk"
Below: Helgi Tomasson in "Dybbuk"

* The scheduled opening on Nov. 13, 1973 was cancelled when the 83 dancers went on strike demanding a guarantee of work or pay for the full season. The strike lasted for 25 days, and performances did not begin until Dec. 6, 1973 with "The Nutcracker." The season ended Feb. 17, 1974 after 39 performances of "The Nutcracker" and 48 performances in repertory.

The company opened its spring season Tuesday, April 30, 1974 and gave 72 performances, closing June 30, 1974. Added to the repertoire were: "Agon" (Stravinsky), "Allegro Brillante" (Tchaikovsky), "A Midsummer Night's Dream" (Mendelssohn), "Bugaku" (Mayuzumi), "Divertimento No. 15" (Mozart), "Illuminations" (Britten, Ashton), "In the Night" (Chopin, Robbins), "Jewels" (Faure-Stravinsky-Tchaikovsky), premieres of "The Dybbuk Variations" (Leonard Bernstein, Jerome Robbins; Scenery, Rouben Ter-Arutunian; Costumes, Patricia Zipprodt) on Thursday, May 16, 1974; "Saltarelli" (Vivaldi, Jacques d'Amboise; Costumes and Scenery, John Braden; Lighting, Ronald Bates) on Thursday, May 30, 1974; "Bartok No. 3" (Bartok, John Clifford; Costumes, Ardith Haddow) on Thursday, May 23, 1974; "Variations pour une Porte et un Soupir" (Pierre Henry, George Balanchine; Decor, Rouben Ter-Arutunian; Lighting, Ronald Bates) on Thursday, Jan. 17, 1974.

Jacques d'Amboise, Allegra Kent in "Scotch Symphony"
Above: Jacques d'Amboise, Gloria Govrin
in "Firebird" Top Left: Jean-Pierre Bonnefous,
Gelsey Kirkland in "Four Bagatelles"

"Stars and Stripes" Top: Kay Mazzo, Jean-Pierre
Bonnefous in "Don Quixote"

Debra Austin in "Bartok No. 3" Top: Anthony Blum, Sara Leland in "Bartok No. 3"
NEW YORK CITY BALLET

John Clifford, Karin von Aroldingen in "Variations pour une Porte et un Soupir"
Top: Karin von Aroldingen in "Variations pour un Porte et un Soupir"
(Martha Swope Photos)

Merrill Ashley in "Saltarelli" Top Left: Gloria Govrin, Frank Ohman in
"Western Symphony" Right: Francis Sackett, Christine Redpath in "Saltarelli"

NEW YORK CITY BALLET

Sara Leland and company in "The Concert" Top Left: Jean-Pierre Bonnefous, Violette Verdy and (top right) Gelsey Kirkland, Helgi Tomasson in "Four Bagatelles"
NEW YORK CITY BALLET

Edward Villella (also top right) in "Watermill"
Top Left: Helgi Tomasson in "Symphony in Three Movements"

Lynda Yourth, John Clifford in "Danses Concertantes"
Top: Bart Cook, Bryan Pitts, Gelsey Kirkland in "Scherzo Fantastique"
NEW YORK CITY BALLET

ALICE TULLY HALL

December 17–21, 1973

Lincoln Center for the Performing Arts, Con Edison, and Performing Arts Foundation present:

THE ALLNATIONS COMPANY

Producer, Herman Rottenberg; Artistic Director, Rick Ornellas; Technical Director, Chuck Golden; Stage Managers, Bob Rottenberg, Meli Zinberg

COMPANY

Ronnie Alejandro, Pierre Barreau, Larry Bianco, Richard Clairmont, Asha Coorlawala, Jose Coronado, Linda Cuneo, Ashi Devi, Natasha Grishin, Noel Hall, Lee Harper, Sachiyo Ito, Robert Owen Jones, Sun-Ock Lee, Robin McCabe, Katya Majewska, Sumiko Murashima, Barbara Neiss, Rick Ornellas, Maldwyn Pate, Joyce Pierre-Louis, Marti Ramona, Elaine Shapiro, Gertrude Sherwood, Simion Timlichman, Ching Valdes, John VanBuskirk, Nancy Wilmarth, Tina Yuan

PROGRAM

Liberia: "Welcome Chant," "Fanga," Wales: "Y Gwcw," "Croen Y Ddafad Felen," Mexico: "Sandunga," "El Colas," Russia: "Ukrainian Dance," "Medley of Russian Songs," "Gypsy Dance," Jamaica: "Jamaican Pepper Pot," Korea: "Farmer's Dance," "Mask Dance," "Temple Dance of Five Drums," United States: "American Dance Suite," "Square Dance," "Mississippi Soft Shoe," "The Charleston," "Shaft," Philippines: "Wine Drinking Song," "Bamboo Stick Dance," "Season's Greetings"

Allnations Company

Emily Frankel

ALICE TULLY HALL

Friday, January 4, 1974

Matthews/Napal Ltd. in association with Dancehouse Inc. presents:

EMILY FRANKEL
in
MAHLER'S FIFTH SYMPHONY

Choreographed by Norman Walker; Director, Philip Lawrence; Costumes, Ben Benson; Tapes, Jon Black; Stage Manager, Owen Ryan; Press, Don Westwood

JUILLIARD DANCE ENSEMBLE

Production Director, Martha Hill; Production Supervisor, Joe Pacitti; Stage Manager, Lee Shlosberg; Costume Supervision, Guus Ligthart; Wardrobe Mistress, Peggy Schierholz; Rehearsal Assistants, Lance Westergard, Billie Mahoney, Gary Masters, Jennifer Scanlon; Administrative Assistant for Production, Mary Chudick; Pianist, Pawel Checinski

PROGRAM

"Come, Come Travel with Dreams" (Alexander Scriabin, Anna Sokolow; Costumes, Guus Ligthart; Lighting, Snowdon Parlette) a *premiere* with Pierre Barreau, Ann Crosset, Robert Swinston, William Belle, Linda Spriggs, Tsueh-Tung Chen, Richard Caceres, Dian Dong, Andrew Roth, Anthony Ferro, Jaynie Katz, Mercie Hinton, Gregory Mitchell, Mary Lou Fager, Jane Hedal, Joyce Herring, Dianne Hulburt, Nancy Mapother, Patrice Regnier, Shelley Washington

"Night of the Four Moons with Lone Shadow" (George Crumb, Kazuko Hirabayashi; Projections, Robert Yodice; Costumes, Kazuko Hirabayashi, Guus Ligthart; Lighting, Joe Pacitti; Conductor, Peter Leonard) a *premiere* with Teri Weksler, Jennifer Douglas, Christopher Pilafian, Robert Swinston, Richard Caceres, Anthony Ferro, Dianne Hulburt, Susan Osberg, Shelley Washington, Janice Carp, Ann Crosset, Nancy Mapother, Linda Spriggs, Gregory Cary, Barry Weiss, Colette Yglesias

"A Choreographic Offering" (Bach, Limon; Restaged by Daniel Lewis) with Roxolana Babiuk, Daryl Bratches, Janice Carp, Ann Crosset, Dian Dong, Jennifer Douglas, Virginia Edmands, Joyce Herring, Penny Hutchinson, Nancy Mapother, Linda Spriggs, Catherine Sullivan, Shelley Washington, Teri Weksler, Colette Yglesias, David Briggs, Richard Caceres, Anthony Ferro, Christopher Pilafian, Andrew Roth, Robert Swinston, Phillip Bond

Jane Rady, Johan Elbers Photos

Top Right: "Come, Come Travel with Dreams"

"Night of the Four Moons" Above: "Come, Come Travel with Dreams"

**"Choreographic Offering"
Above: "Night of the Four Moons"**

HARKNESS BALLET

Artistic Director, Rebekah Harkness; General Manager, J. B. Cerrone; Musical Director-Conductor, Samuel Krachmalnick; Ballet Masters, Perry Brunson, Vicente Nebrada, Norman Walker; Technical Director, Tony Tucci; Assistant General Manager, Patricia Sinnott; Assistant Technical Director, Ro Cunningham; Company Pianist, Mark Richards.

COMPANY

Christopher Aponte, Manola Asensio, Darrell Barnett, Miguel Companeria, Clara Cravey, Linda DiBona, Helen Heineman, Chris Jensen, Miyoko Kato, Tanju Tuzer, Jeanette Vondersaar, Zane Wilson, Glen Alan, Laura Bail, Linda Bogsrud, Raymond Bussey, Anitra Fevola, Albert Forister, Raymondo Fornoni, Mindy Gars, George Giraldo, Trudi Hirsch, Cynthia Jones, Patricia Machette, Eric McCullough, Susan McKee, Rod McQuilliams, Roberto Medina, Manuel Molina, Francisco Morales, Kay Preston, Berthica Prieto, Deleah Shafer, Dana Shwarts, Gary Snider, Jannis Stenger, Dale Talley, DeAnne Tomlinson, Rory Woodmansee

REPERTOIRE

"Percussions for Six Men" (Schubert, Nebrada), "Sebastian" (Menotti, Nebrada), "Souvenirs" (Barber, Bolender), "The Brood" (Schaeffer, Kuch), "Firebird" (Stravinsky, Macdonald), "Time Out of Mind" (Creston, Macdonald), "Le Corsaire" (Drigo, Martin-Viscount), "Schubert Variations" (Schubert, Nebrada), "Three Preludes" (Rachmaninoff, Stevenson), "Night Song" (Hovhaness, Walker), "Canto Indio" (Chavez, Macdonald)
NY PREMIERES: "Ceremonials" April 9, 1974 (Ginastera, Norman Walker), "Gemini" Wednesday, Apr. 10, 1974 (Mahler, Nebrada)
WORLD PREMIERES: "Ballade" Wednesday Apr. 10, 1974 (Faure, Norman Walker), "Shadows" Thursday, Apr. 11, 1974 (Debussy, Nebrada), "Bergamasca" Saturday, Apr. 13, 1974 (Respighi, Helen Heineman), "The Lottery" Tuesday, Apr. 16, 1974 (Stravinsky, Brian Macdonald; Based on Shirley Jackson's short story), "Rodin—Mis en Vie" (Michael Kamen, Margo Sappington), "Memories" Thursday, Apr. 18, 1974 (Chopin, Vicente Nebrada)
Press: Judi Jedlicka
Stage Manager: Joseph Ellison
* Closed April 21, 1974 after limited engagement of 14 performances. The former Colonial Theatre was converted by Mrs. Harkness into the first New York theatre designed specifically for dance, and will be the home for her company.

Bil Leidersdorf Photos

Left and Above: Clara Cravey in "Rodin . . ."

Clara Cravey, Glen Allen, Zane Wilson
in "The Lottery"

"The Lottery"

"The Brood" Above: "Night Song" Top:
Jeanette Vondersaar, Tanju Tuzer in "Firebird"

Susan McKee, Helen Heineman, Christopher Aponte
in "Sebastian" Above: "Percussion for 6" Top: Manolo
Asensio, Tanju Tuzer in "Le Cosaire"

Patricia Machette, Tanju Tuzer in "Firebird"
Top: "Souvenirs"
HARKNESS BALLET

METROPOLITAN OPERA HOUSE
Opened Tuesday, April 23, 1974*
S. Hurok presents:

NATIONAL BALLET OF CANADA
with
RUDOLF NUREYEV

Artistic Directors, Celia Franca, David Haber; Associate Artistic Director, Betty Oliphant; Resident Producer, Erik Bruhn; Music Director-Conductor, Aubrey Bowman; Assistant Conductor, John Goss; Concert Masters, Jesse Ceci, Isabel Vila; Ballet Master, David Scott; Ballet Mistress, Joanne Nisbet; General Manager, Gerry Eldred; Production Director, Dieter Penzhorn; Resident Scenic Artist, Georg Schlogl; Assistant to the Artistic Directors, David Walker; Resident Ballet Master, Daniel Seillier; Dance Coordinator, Simon Semenoff

COMPANY

PRINCIPALS: Vanessa Harwood, Mary Jago, Karen Kain, Nadia Potts, Veronica Tennant, Frank Augustyn, Winthrop Corey, Tomas Schramek, Sergiu Stefanschi, Hazaros Surmeyan

SOLOISTS: Victoria Bertram, Andrea Davidson, Linda Maybarduk, Sonia Perusse, Wendy Reiser, Robert Denvers, Jacques Gorrissen, Charles Kirby, Andrew Oxenham

CORPS: Yolande Auger, Maria Barrios, Josephine Baurac, Carina Bomers, Deborah Castellan, Gerre Cimino, Katherine Collingwood, Christy Cumberland, Ann Ditchburn, Norma Fisher, Loretta French, Lorna Geddes, Kathryn Joyner, Jennifer Laird, Daphne Loomis, Cynthia Lucas, Gloria Luoma, Esther Murillo, Patricia Oney, Katherine Scheidegger, Kristine Soleri, Mavis Staines, Barbara Szablowski, Kathleen Trick, Charmain Turner, Valerie Wilder, Jane Wooding, Ronald Alexander, Brian Armstrong, Richard Bowen, Daniel Capouch, John Carrell, Victor Edwards, David Gornik, Stephen Greenston, Nicholas Hilferink, James Kudelka, Michael Natinzi, Michael McKim, Bill Meadows, Thomas Nicholson, Constantin Patsalas, David Roxander, Eric Weichardt

REPERTOIRE

"The Sleeping Beauty" (Tchaikovsky, Nureyev after petipa), "Les Sylphides" (Chopin, Bruhn) "Flower Festival at Genzano Pas de Deux," "Le Loup" (Dutilleux, Petit), "Giselle" (Adam, Bruhn), and the *NY Premiere* of "Don Juan" (Gluck-de Victoria, John Neumeir; Decor and Costumes, Filippo Sanjust; Lighting, Gil Wechsler; Narration, Ralph Richardson; Conductor, George Crum)

Company Manager: John H. Wilson
Press: Sheila Porter, Lillian Libman, John Gingrich
Stage Managers: Norm Dyson, Ernest Abugov, Lawrence Beevers
* Closed May 5, 1974 after limited engagement of 16 performances.

Sergiu Stefanschi, Karen Kain, Rudolf Nureyev in "Don Juan" Top: Mary Jago, Rudolf Nureyev in "Don Juan"

Vanessa Howard in "Cool City"

Tomas Shramek, Gerre Cimino in "Sleeping Beauty"
Top: Veronica Tennant, Rudolf Nureyev in "Sleeping Beauty"

Veronica Tennant, Tomas Schramek Top Left: Winthrop Corey, Karen Kain
Right: Winthrop Corey, Vanessa Harwood in "Le Loup"

NATIONAL BALLET OF CANADA

Karen Kain, Mary Jago, Sergiu Stefanschi, Nadia Potts
Top: Mary Jago in "Les Sylphides"
NATIONAL BALLET OF CANADA

"Giselle" Top Left: Karen Kain
Right: Veronica Tennant, Rudolf Nureyev in "Giselle"
NATIONAL BALLET OF CANADA

METROPOLITAN OPERA HOUSE
Opened Tuesday, May 7, 1974*
S. Hurok presents:

ROYAL BALLET

Founder, Ninette de Valois; Founder-Choreographer, Frederick Ashton; Director, Kenneth MacMillan; Associate Director, Peter Wright; Music Director, Ashley Lawrence; Ballet Master, Desmond Doyle; Conductors, Anthony Twiner, Emanuel Young; Regisseur, Henry Legerton, Ballet Mistress, Jill Gregory; Press, Vivien Wallace; Technical Manager, Tom Macarthur; Wardrobe Mistress, Joyce Wells; Dance Coordinator, Simon Semenoff.

COMPANY

GUEST ARTIST: Rudolf Nureyev
PRINCIPALS: Elizabeth Anderton, Deanne Bergsma, Michael Coleman, Lesley Collier, Laura Connor, Vergie Derman, Anthony Dowell, Desmond Doyle, Leslie Edwards, Ronald Emblen, Alexander Grant, Stanley Holden, Ann Jenner, Nicholas Johnson, Desmond Kelly, Gerd Larsen, Donald MacLeary, Monica Mason, Merle Park, Georgina Parkinson, Jennifer Penney, Derek Rencher, Brian Shaw, Antoinette Sibley, Wayne Sleep, Alfreda Thorogood, Diana Vere, David Wall
SOLOISTS: David Adams, David Ashmole, Petrus Bosman, Sandra Conley, David Drew, Wayne Eagling, Adrian Grater, Carl Myers, Ria Peri, Marguerite Porter
CORYPHEES: Christine Aitken, Christopher Carr, Meryl Chapell, Rosalind Eyre, Peter Fairweather, Graham Fletcher, Garry Grant, Dennis Griffith, Sally Inkin, Anthony Molyneux, Suzanna Raymond, Brigid Skemp, Rosemary Taylor, Hilary Tickner, Julie Wood, Christine Woodward, Anita Young
ARTISTS: Carolyn Abbott, Joanna Allnatt, Elizabeth Alpe, Lynda Ambler, Sally Ashby, Anthony Conway, Michael Corder, Belinda Corken, Derek Deane, Jacqueline Elliott, Wendy Ellis, Wendy Groombridge, June Highwood, Lynn Hollamby, Julian Hosking, Judith Howe, Jennifer Jackson, Robert Jude, Gillian King, Susan Lockwood, Barbara Lower, Ross MacGibbon, Andrew Moore, Linda Moran, Ian Owen, Beverley Parker, William Perrie, Sally Powell, Mark Silver, Jacqueline Tallis, Heather Walker, Rosalyn Whitten, Pippa Wylde

REPERTOIRE

"Manon" (Massenet, Kenneth MacMillan) a *NY premiere*, "Swan Lake" (Tchaikovsky, Petipa-Ivanov; Additional Choreography, Ninette de Valois, Frederick Ashton), "La Bayadere" (Minkus, Nureyev after Petipa), "La Fille Mal Gardee" (Herold-Lanchbery, Ashton), "Romeo and Juliet" (Prokofiev, MacMillan), "Apollo" (Stravinsky, Balanchine), "Symphonic Variations" (Frank, Ashton), and NY *premieres* of "Pavane" (Faure, MacMillan), "Walk to the Paradise Garden" (Delius, Ashton)

Company Manager: John H. Wilson
Press: Sheila Porter, John Gingrich
Stage Managers: Jeffrey Phillips, Bruce Percival

* Closed May 26, 1974 after limited engagement of 24 performances.

Anthony Dowell, Antoinette Sibley in "Manon"
(also top right)

Antoinette Sibley, David Wall
in "Manon"

David Wall, Merle Park in "Walk to Paradise Garden" Top Left: Antoinette Sibley,
Anthony Dowell in "Pavane" Right: Merle Park in "Swan Lake"

THE ROYAL BALLET

Alexander Grant in "La Fille Mal Gardee" Top: "Swan Lake"
THE ROYAL BALLET

Donald MacLeary, Georgina Parkinson
in "Romeo and Juliet" (also top)

Antoinette Sibley, Anthony Dowell
in "Romeo and Juliet"

58   **THE ROYAL BALLET**

Ann Jenner, Donald MacLeary, Jennifer Penney,
Merle Park in "Symphonic Variations"

"La Bayadere" (also above)

THE ROYAL BALLET

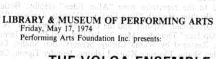

LIBRARY & MUSEUM OF PERFORMING ARTS
Friday, May 17, 1974
Performing Arts Foundation Inc. presents:

THE VOLGA ENSEMBLE

Larry Bianco
Natasha Grishin
Simon Timlichman

PROGRAM: "Trepak," "Korobushka," "Metelitza," "Pereplyas,"
"Medley of Moldavian Melodies," "Uzbek Dance," "The Gypsies,"
"Dances from Poland," "Marichka," "Darumadar," "Man's Dance
from Transylvania," "Songs from the 'Shtetl'," "Tale of the Bumble-
bee," "Russian Songs and Dances"

The Volga Ensemble

DANCE COMPANIES AT CITY CENTER
Norman Singer, Executive Director

CITY CENTER 55 STREET THEATER
Opened Wednesday, October 10, 1973*
Foundation for American Dance in association with City Center of Music and Drama presents:

CITY CENTER JOFFREY BALLET

Artistic Director-Choreographer, Robert Joffrey; Assistant Director-Choreographer, Gerald Arpino; General Administrator, William Crawford; Music Director, Seymour Lipkin; Assistant Conductor, Sung Kwak; Assistant Administrator, Molle Regan; Lighting Designer, Thomas Skelton, Jennifer Tipton; Ballet Master, Basil Thompson; Assistants to Mr. Joffrey, William Leighton, Scott Barnard; Administrative Assistant, Edith Jerell; Production Assistants, Philip Pena, Stan Ware

COMPANY

Charthel Arthur, Eileen Brady, Diana Cartier, Francesca Corkle, Donna Cowen, Starr Danias, Ann Marie DeAngelo, Erika Goodman, Jan Hanniford, Alaine Haubert, Nancy Ichino, Denise Jackson, Krystyna Jurkowski, Janey Kawaguchi, Pamela Nearhoof, Diane Orio, Beatriz Rodriguez, Trinette Singleton, Christine Uchida, Rebecca Wright, Adix Carman, Gary Chryst, Richard Colton, Donn Edwards, Robert Estner, Tom Fowler, Larry Grenier, Phillip Hoffman, Christian Holder, Jeffrey Hughes, Ted Nelson, Russell Sultzbach, Paul Sutherland, Robert Talmage, Burton Taylor, Robert Thomas, Edward Verso, Dennis Wayne, Glenn White, William Whitener, Jonathan Watts (Guest Artist)

REPERTOIRE

"Weewis" (Walden, Sappington), "Interplay" (Gould, Robbins), "Reflections" (Tchaikovsky, Arpino), "Facade" (Walton, Ashton), "Le Beau Danube" (Strauss, Massine), "Sacred Grove on Mount Tamalpais" (Ralph, Arpino), "Petrouchka" (Stravinsky, Fokine), "Jive" (Gould, Feld), "Secret Places" (Mozart, Arpino), "Grand Pas Espagnol" (Moszkowski, Harkarvy), "The Green Table" (Cohen, Jooss), "Confetti" (Rossini, Arpino), "Kettentanz" (Strauss, Arpino), "Trinity" (Raph-Holdridge, Arpino), "Square Dance" (Corelli-Vivaldi, Balanchine), "Moves" (Robbins), "Parade" (Satie, Massine), "Cakewalk" (Gottschalk-Kay, Boris), "Chabriesque" (Chabrier, Arpino), "Nightwings" (LaMontaine, Arpino)
PREMIERES: (Company) "The Dream" on Wednesday, Oct. 10, 1973 (Felix Mendelssohn-Bartholdy, Frederick Ashton; Adapted from Shakespeare's "A Midsummer Night's Dream"; Directed and Staged by John Hart; Scenery and Costumes, David Walker; Lighting, Thomas Skelton; Conducter, Seymour Lipkin); "The Moor's Pavane" Saturday, Oct. 13, 1973 (Henry Purcell, Jose Limon; Costumes, Pauline Lawrence; Staged by Jennifer Scanlon; Lighting, Thomas Skelton; Conductor, Seymour Lipkin) with Christian Holder, Burton Taylor, Jan Hanniford, Beatriz Rodriguez (World) "Remembrances" Friday, Oct. 12, 1973 (Richard Wagner, Robert Joffrey; Set, Rouben Ter-Arutunian; Costumes, Willa Kim; Lighting, Jennifer Tipton; Conductor, Seymour Lipkin; Pianist, Stanley Babin) with Francesca Corkle, Jonathan Watts, Jan Hanniford, Donna Roll, and company; "As Time Goes By" Wednesday, Oct. 24, 1973 (Franz Josef Haydn, Twyla Tharp; Costumes, Chester Weinberg; Conductor, Seymour Lipkin) with Beatriz Rodriguez, Eileen Brady, Adix Carman, Pamela Nearhoof, Burton Taylor, William Whitener, and company
Company Manager: Delores S. Smith
Press: Isadora Bennett, Robert Larkin, Rima Corben, Penney Finkelman
Stage Managers: Dan Butt, Jon Garness

Herbert Migdoll Photos

Top Right: Christian Holder, Burton Taylor, Beatriz Rodriguez, Jan Hanniford in "The Moor's Pavane"

* Closed Nov. 4, 1973 after 31 performances. Opened spring season Wednesday, March 6, 1974, and closed March 31, 1974 after 3_ performances. Gregory Huffman and James Dunne returned t_ the company, and Eileen Brady and Glenn White were on leav_ of absence.
Added to the repertoire were "After Eden" (Hoiby, Butler "Abyss" (Richter, Hodes), "Viva Vivaldi!" (Vivaldi, Arpino), "Va_ entine" (Druckman, Arpino), and the *Company Premiere* of "N.Y Export, Op Jazz" Thursday, Mar. 21, 1974 (Robert Prince, Jerom_ Robbins; Restaged by Wilma Curley; Scenery, Ben Shahn; Co_ tumes, Ben Shahn, Florence Klotz, Lighting, Jennifer Tipton; Con_ ductor, Robert Rogers)
On Friday afternoon, Nov. 2, 1973, JOFFREY II COMPAN_ (Director, Jonathan Watts; Associate, Sally Brayley) performed th_ *company premiere* of "Butterflies Can't Live Here Any More," (Ba_ tok, Norbert Vesak) and *world premieres* of "Mother's Mozart '73 (Mozart, Wilma Curley; Costumes, Patton Campbell), and "Kno_ ville: Summer of 1915" (Samuel Barber, Norbert Vesak) with Co_ chita Blazquez, David Cuevas, Michelle Hamilton, Jerel Hildin_ Carol Messmer, Philip Jerry, Sharon Pedersen, Andrew Levinso_ Nancy Thuesen, Stephen Shaw, Jody Wintz, Rick Wakal

"New York Export, Op. Jazz" (also top)

Larry Grenier, Rebecca Wright in "The Dream" Top Left: Paul Sutherland, Francesca
Corkle in "Remembrances" Right: Burton Taylor in "The Dream" (*Herbert Midgdoll Photos*)
CITY CENTER JOFFREY BALLET

Robert Thomas, Christian Holder   Trinette Singleton, Gregory Huffman in "Viva Vivaldi!"
in "The Green Table" Top: "As Time Goes By"

CITY CENTER JOFFREY BALLET

"Facade" Top Left: Gary Chryst in "Trinity" Right: Donna
Cowen, Gregory Huffman in "Secret Places" (*Herbert Migdoll Photos*)
CITY CENTER JOFFREY BALLET

"Interplay" Top: **"Parade"**
(Herbert Migdoll Photos)
CITY CENTER JOFFREY BALLET

65

CITY CENTER 55 STREET THEATER
Opened Tuesday, November 6, 1973*
The National Ballet Society (Mrs. Richard Riddell, President) in associa-
tion with City Center of Music and Drama (Norman Singer, Executive
Director) presents:

THE NATIONAL BALLET

Directors, Frederic Franklin, Ben Stevenson; General Manager,
Ralph Black; Conductors, Ottavio deRosa, Bruce Steeg; Lighting
Designer, Jennifer Tipton; Ballet Master, Hiller Huhn; Wardrobe,
Catherine Gentilucci, Patricia Sorrell

COMPANY

PRINCIPALS: Christine Knoblauch, Michelle Lees, Carmen
Mathe, Kirk Peterson, Dennis Poole, Fredric Strobel
SOLOISTS: Diane Duffy, Charlene Gehm, Susan Frazer, Hiller
Huhn, Jonathan Kelly, Edmund LaFosse, Kevin McKenzie, Robert
Petersen, Andrea Price, Judith Rhodes
CORPS: Leslie Andres, Dean Badolato, Stephen Baranovics, Sergio
Cal, Benjamin Caref, Judith Carlson, Nancy Davis, Nadine Froh-
lich, Deidre Grohgan, Jennifer Holmes, Linda Kintz, Eve Leyman,
Suzanne Longley, Alfredo Martin, Rosemary Miles, Dorio Perez,
Krissy Richmond, Abigail Rigby, Lauren Rouse, Susan Smith,
Christine Spizzo, Elizabeth Wade

REPERTOIRE

"Water Study" (Doris Humphrey), "Graduation Ball" (Strauss, Li-
chine), "Raymonda" (Glazounov, Balanchine-Danilova), "Eaters of
Darkness" (Britten, Gore), "Sleeping Beauty" (Tchaikovsky, Ste-
venson after Petipa)
NY PREMIERES: "Bartok Concerto: (Bartok, Ben Stevenson),
"Courante" (Bach, Stevenson), "Jungle" (Badings, Rudi Van Dant-
zig), "Harlequinade Pas de Deux" (Drigo, Stevenson), "La Es-
meralda Pas de Deux" (Pugni, Jules Perrot)
Company Manager: Harry Baernstein III
Press: Robert Larkin
Stage Manager: Anthony Clarke
* Closed No. 11, 1973 after limited engagement of 8 performances.
Sunday, Nov. 11 was a gala benefit performance with guest artists
Margot Fonteyn, Desmond Kelly, Arlene Francis, Patsy Kelly,
Julie Newmar, Paulette Goddard, Gwen Verdon appearing in a
special version of "Aurora's Wedding," and Olga Ferri from the
Teatro Colon Buenas Aires made her NY debut in "The Dying
Swan," Galina Samsova and Andre Prokovsky danced "Le Cor-
saire Pas de Deux." "Pas de Quatre" was danced by Ben Steven-
son, Dean Badolato, Fredric Strobel, and Hiller Huhn.
On June 12, 1974 it was announced that the National Ballet was
suspending activities because of financial difficulties.

"Bartok Concerto"

Kirk Peterson in "Bartok Concerto"
Top Left: Christine Knoblauch, Kirk Peterson
in "Harlequinade"

Dennis Poole, Michelle Lees Top Left: Carmen Mathe
Right: Hiller Huhn, Suzanne Davis, Michelle Lees in "Sleeping Beauty" Below:
Galina Samsova, Andre Prokovsky in Gala Benefit(*Louis Peres Photo*)

Margot Fonteyn, Desmond Kelly in Gala Benefit(*Louis Peres Photo*)
Top: Christine Knoblauch in "Graduation Ball"
NATIONAL BALLET

CITY CENTER 55 STREET THEATER

Opened Tuesday, November 13, 1973*
The City Center of Music and Drama (Norma Singer, Executive Director)
in association with Sheldon Soffer presents:

INBAL DANCE THEATRE OF ISRAEL

Founder-Artistic Director, Sara Levi-Tanai; Administrative Director, Gila Toledano; Wardrobe Mistress, Rina Erez; Associate Producer, John Hebel; Coordinator, Geri Bernstein; Production Assistant, William Hendrickson; Assistant Producer, Molly King; Lighting, Rafi Cohen

COMPANY

Mordechai Abramov, Ilana Cohen, Tami Cohen, Nissim Garame, Malka Haghbi, Aviva Haziz, Shlomo Haziz, Rachel Mori, Zion Nurel, Moshe Romen, Aharon Shikarchi, Sara Shikarchi, Drora Yakobovitz, Menashe Yakovian, Moshe Yizhak-Halevi, Zadok Zuberi (Singer)

REPERTOIRE

"The Loom" (Ovadia Tuvin, Sara Levi-Tanai), "Jar" (Avraham Amzaleg, Sara Levi-Tanai), "Hora" (Mordechai Zeira, Sara Levi-Tanai), "Nimrod and the Coat" (Albert Piamenta, Rina Sharet), "Women" (Yemenite Oriental Melodies, Sara Levi-Tanai), "The Pearl and the Coral" (Menachem Avidom, Sara Levi-Tanai), "Carry Us to the Desert" (Ovadia Tuvia, Sara Levi-Tanai)

General Manager: Mary Lou Tuffin
Company Managers: Moshe Yizhak-Halevi, Ward Pinner
Press: Merle Debuskey, Patricia McLean Debuskey, Barbara Carroll
Stage Managers: Raphael Cohen, Moshe Cohen
* Closed Nov. 18, 1973 after limited engagement of 8 performances.

Mula & Haramaty Photos

Ilana Cohen, Shlomo Haziz in "The Pearl"
Top Right: "Nimrod"

Sara Shifarchi in "The Jar"
Above: "The Loom"

CITY CENTER 55 STREET THEATER
Opened Tuesday, November 27, 1973.*
City Center of Music and Drama (Norman Singer, Executive Director)
presents:

ALVIN AILEY CITY CENTER DANCE THEATER

Artistic Director-Choreographer, Alvin Ailey; Musical Director, Howard Roberts; Production Manager, William Hammond; Ballet Mistress, Fiorella Keane; Ballet Master, Dudley Williams; Costumes, Ursula Reed, Margie Tobin, Carl Moore, Bea Feitler, Rouben Ter-Arutunian, Charles D. Tomlinson, A. Christina Giannini, Judy Dearing, Ves Harper; Lighting, Chenault Spence, Nicola Cernovitch, Shirley Prendergast, Tom Skelton; Decor, Rouben Ter-Arutunian, Ming Cho Lee, A. Christina Giannini, Ves Harper; Business Manager, Nancy Shannon; Administrative Assistant, Susan Palmer

COMPANY

Judith Jamison, Mari Kajiwara, Linda Kent, Dana Sapiro, Estelle Spurlock, Sylvia Waters, Sara Yarborough, Tina Yuan, Masazumi Chaya, Hector Mercado, Michihiko Oka, John Parks, Kenneth Pearl, Kelvin Rotardier, Clive Thompson, Dudley Williams, Nerissa Barnes, Ulysses Dove, Melvin Jones, Christa Mueller, Edward Love, Elbert Watson, Donna Wood, Peter Woodin
SPECIAL GUEST ARTISTS: Leon Bibb, Brother John Sellers, Arthur C. Thompson, Jeanne Faulkner, Walter Turnbull, the Howard Roberts Chorale

REPERTOIRE

"Hidden Rites" (Patrice Sciortino, Alvin Ailey), "According to Eve" (George Crumb, John Butler), "Masekela Langage" (Hugh Masekela, Ailey), "The Lark Ascending" (Ralph Vaughan Williams, Ailey), "Love Songs" (Leon Russell-Jeremy Wind-Leonard Bleecher-Bobby Scott-Bobby Russell, Ailey), "Dance for Six" (Antonio Vivaldi, Joyce Trisler), "Rainbow 'Round My Shoulder" (Arranged by Robert de Cormier and Milton Okun from the collection of John and Alan Lomax, Donald McKayle), "Revelations" (Traditional, Ailey), "Streams" (Miloslav Kabelac, Ailey), "Nubian Lady" (Kenneth Barron, John Parks), "Icarus" (Matsushita, Lucas Hoving), "Metallics" (Kenneth Barron-Henry Cowell, Paul Sanasardo), "Cry" (Coltrane-Nyro-Voices of Harlem, Ailey), "Kinetic Molpai" (Jess Meeker, Ted Shawn)
COMPANY PREMIERES: "Carmina Burana" (Carl Orff, John Butler) on Tuesday, Nov. 27, 1973, and "Missa Brevis" (Zoltan Kodaly, Jose Limon) on Tuesday, Dec. 4, 1973.
General Manager: Ivy Clarke
Company Manager: John Scott
Press: Meg Gordean, Howard Atlee, Clarence Allsopp
Stage Managers: William Burd, Donald Moss
* Closed Dec. 16, 1973 after 24 performances. Returned for 24 additional performances from Tuesday, May 14 through June 2, 1974. Additions to the company were Clover Mathis, Cynthia Penn, Warren Spears, and Ballet Master Ali Pourfarrokh. Additions to the repertoire were "Blues Suite" (Traditional, Ailey), "Spirituals" (Traditional, Janet Collins), "Congolese Wedding" (Traditional, Pearl Primus), "Fanga" (Traditional, Primus), and PREMIERE of "Canticle of the Elements" (Bach-Villa Lobos, Janet Collins) on Tuesday, May 21, 1974.

Fred Fehl Photos

Top Left: Judith Jamison, Dudley Williams, Kelvin Rotardier in "Icarus" Below: Clive Thompson, Tina Yuan in "Hidden Rites"

Sara Yarborough, Hector Mercado
in "According to Eve"

Judith Jamison in "Carmina Burana" Top: "Missa Brevis"
(*Fred Fehl Photos*)

"Streams" Top Left: Judith Jamison in "Cry"   Right: "Masekela Langage"
(*Fred Fehl Photos*)
ALVIN AILEY CITY CENTER DANCE THEATER

John Parks, Sara Yarborough in "Blues Suite"
(*Luis Peres Photo*)   Top: Sara Yarborough, Clive Thompson
in "The Lark Ascending"

Mari Kajiwara, Hector Mercado in
"Rainbow 'Round My Shoulder"
(*Fred Fehl Photos*)

ALVIN AILEY CITY CENTER DANCE THEATER

**Sylvia Waters, Dudley Williams in "Metallics" Top Left: John Parks, Clive Thompson in
"Kinetic Molpai" Right: Judith Jamison in "Nubian Lady"**(*Fred Fehl Photos*)

ALVIN AILEY CITY CENTER DANCE THEATER

"Revelations" (also above and top) Top: Linda Kent,
Hector Mercado (*Rose Mary Winckley Photo*)

Judith Jamison in "Revelations"
(*Fred Fehl Photos*)

ALVIN AILEY CITY CENTER DANCE THEATER

CITY CENTER 55 STREET THEATER
Opened Tuesday, December 18, 1973.*
S. Hurok presents:

BALLET FOLKLORICO OF MEXICO

General Director-Choreographer, Amalia Hernandez; Director, Norma Lopez Hernandez; Artistic Coordinators, Guillermo Keyes-Arenas, Pedro Munoz-Zuno; Choral Arrangements, Luis Sandi, Dr. Ramon Noble; Costumes, Dasha, Delfina Vargas, Luis Alaminos; Scenery, Robin Bond, Delfina Vargas, Luis Alaminos; Lighting, Louisa Guthman, Edmundo Arreguin; Administrator, Jose Juan Parades; Stage Director, Leonardo Pelaez; Assistant Artistic Coordinator, Jose Villanueva; Wardrobe Master, Mario Sosa.

COMPANY

Guillermina Lopez, Teresa Minguet, Violeta Jimenez, Elsa Garcia, Esther Vizcarra, Elisa Reyes, Patricia de Lima, Concepsion Morales, Maria Carmen Cardenas, Rosalinda Torres, Elia Macias, Eva Morales, Leticia Cazares, Silvia Mena, Brisa Guilarte, Ana Tapia, Flor de Azalea Gasca, Jose Villaneuva, Pedro Rodriquez, Jose Luis Gasca, Fernando Castillo, Efren Tello, Francisco Cruz, Nestor Castelan, Juan Jose Burgos, Eduardo Velasquez, Jorge Garduno, Jesus Carreon, David Rodriguez, Jose Santacruz, Mario Garcia, Emilio Ceron, chorus of 26, and 16 musicians

PROGRAM

"Chiapas," "Songs and Dances of Michoacan," "The Revolution," "Fiesta in Veracruz," "The Tarascans," "Wedding in the Huasteca," "Dance of the Deer," "Serenade," "Guadalajara," and U.S. *Premiere* of "Los Concheros" (Dance of the Shells)
Company Manager: Kurt Neumann
Press: Sheila Porter, Lillian Libman
Stage Manager: Louisa Guthman
* Closed Jan. 6, 1974 after limited engagement of 24 performances.

Right: "Guadalajara"
Top: "Los Concheros"

"The Tarascans"

"La Bamba"

CITY CENTER 55 STREET THEATER
Tuesday, February 5, 1974*
S. Hurok presents:

TRINIDAD CARNIVAL BALLET
and Steel Band

Founder-Artistic Director, Aubrey Adams; Choreographer, Eugene Joseph; Lighting, Henry Beard; Costumes, Aubrey Adams, Eugene Joseph; Art Pieces, Ian Ali; Dance Coordinator, Simon Semenoff

PROGRAM

"The Village—Grande Riviere," "Trinidad All Stars Steel Band," "Folk Choir and Musicians," "Can Can Creole Dance," "The Mighty Duke, Kelvin Pope," "The King Sailor Dance." "Drumology," "Dance Ambakaila—Carnival Dance"

Company Manager: Irving Sudrow
Press: Sheila Porter, John Gingrich
Stage Manager: Osmond Noel

* Closed Sunday, Feb. 10, 1974 after limited engagement of 8 performances.

Kelvin Pope
("The Mighty Duke")

CITY CENTER DOWNSTAIRS
February 22–25, 1974
The Jose Limon Dance Foundation presents:

JOSE LIMON DANCE COMPANY

Artistic Director, Ruth Currier; Co-Managers, Mary Jane Ingram, Judith Hankins; Production Manager, John Toland; Lighting Design, Jennifer Tipton; Technical Director, Jane Youtt

COMPANY

Clay Taliaferro, Rob Besserer, Robyn Cutler, Ronald Dunham, Laura Glenn, Fyland Jordan, Gary Masters, Fred Mathews, Carla Maxwell, Aaron Osborne, Marjorie Philpot, Jennifer Scanlon, Louis Solino, Risa Steinberg, Ann Vachon, Nina Watt

REPERTOIRE

"Homage to Federico Garcia Lorca" (Sylvestre Revueltas, Anna Sokolow; Poetry, Garcia Lorca; Costumes, Jose Coronado) a NY premiere, "Orfeo" (Beethoven, Limon), "The Exiles" (Schoenberg, Limon), "Choreographic Offering" (Bach, Limon), "The Moor's Pavane" (Purcell, Limon), "Carlota" (Jose Limon), "La Malinche" (Lloyd, Limon), "Brandenburg Concerto No. 4" (Bach, Doris Humphrey-Ruth Currier), "Concerto Grosso in D Minor" (Jose Limon), "The Unsung" (Jose Limon), "There Is a Time: (dello Joio, Limon), "The Winged" (Johnson, Limon), "Dances for Isadora" (Chopin, Limon), "The Emperor Jones" (Villa-Lobos, Limon)

Michael Greenberg Photos

Right: Clay Taliaferro in "The Emperor Jones"

Carla Maxwell in "Carlota"
Above: "There Is a Time"

Jennifer Scanlon in "The Moor's Pavane"
Above: "La Malinche"

CHARLES WEIDMAN
and
THEATRE DANCE COMPANY

EXPRESSION OF TWO ARTS THEATRE
Performances on weekends for 48 weeks during the season
Artistic Director-Choreographer, Charles Weidman; Administrative Assistant, Dennis Kear; Sound, Paul Spong; Stage Manager, Lee Hopkins; Costumes, Charles Weidman, Janet Towner; Lighting, Patrika Brown

COMPANY

Charles Weidman, Janet Towner, Barry Barychko, Robert Kosinski, Karen Mullin, Elyse Chaskes, Jerianne Heimendinger, Catlin Cobb, Pamela Valente, Dennis Kear, Debbie Carr, Irene Porretto, Nina Cohen, Joenine Roberts, Max Schufer

REPERTOIRE

"Adagio for Strings," "Opus 51," "Fables for Our Time" (Miller), "Christmas Oratorio" (Bach), "Lynchtown" (Engel), "Letter to Mrs. Bixby" (Hindemith-Nowak), "Easter Oratorio" (Bach), "St. Matthew's Passion" (Bach), "A House Divided" (Lionel Nowak), "Gymnopedies Suite" (Satie), "Melmillo," "Soledad," "Brahms Waltzes," "Dialogue—Situation Two" (Bloch)

Andy Sealfon Photos

**Right: Dennis Kear, Janet Towner
in "St. Matthew's Passion"**

**"A House Divided" Above: Barry Barychko,
Debbie Carr in "Adagio for Strings"**

**Charles Weidman
in "A House Divided"**

CHOREOGRAPHERS THEATRE
ChoreoConcerts & Critiques

NEW SCHOOL FOR SOCIAL RESEARCH
Director, Laura Foreman; Administrative Coordinators, Donna Moore, Jane D. Schwartz; Lighting Designer, Cheryl Thacker; Stage Manager, Rachel Lampert; Electrician, Nancy Offenhauser; Sound, Hank O'Neal; Special Technical Assistant, Charles Hyman; Graphics, John Anthes; Program Coordinators, Laura Foreman; Discussion Coordinators, Richard Bull, Robert Dunn, Raymond Johnson, Phyllis Lamhut; Production Assistants, Mara Greenberg, Martha Hudson, Reenie Linden, Gregory Parisek, Philip Tietz

October 9, 1973
PROGRAM I: (all premieres) "Decimal Banana" (Choreography, Gus Solomons, Jr.; Lighting, Ruis Woertendyke; Costumes, Eva Tsug) danced by Mr. Solomons, Santa Aloi, Ruedi Brack, Ben Dolphin, Randall Faxon, Douglas Nielsen; "Moment" (Cage) choreographed and danced by Phyllis Lamhut; "East—To Nijinsky" (Joseph Tal) choreographed and danced by Manuel Alum; "Body Music" (Fred Simpson, Beverly Brown; Costumes, Philip Hipwell) danced by Beverly Brown, Bill Kleinsmith

October 16, 1973
PROGRAM II: (all premieres) "Nevada" choreographed and performed by Douglas Dunn; "Delay" (Messian, Robert Dunn) danced by Peggy Hackney, Janis Pforsich; "Reflections on the French Revolution" choreographed and danced by Carolyn Lord; "Daguerreotype" choreographed by Sara Shelton who also danced it with Jude Morgan

October 23, 1973
PROGRAM III: (all premieres) "Mini-Quilt" (Traditional Irish, Elizabeth Keen; Film, Kirk Smallman) danced by Jennifer Donohue, Elizabeth Keen, Patty Kozono, Dalienne Majors, Christopher Pilafian, Roger Preston Smith; "Rope Dance I" (Elina Mooney) danced by Joan Finkelstein, Theodora Yoshikami; "Bentwood Piece" (Beethoven, Janet Soares) danced by Carol-Rae Kraus; "Landmark I" (Barnes-Liebert-Mitchum-Reich, Raymond Johnson) danced by Ellen Bryson, Johanna Murray, Patricia Ross, Joyce Zyznar, Carter McAdams, John Magill, Thom Scalise, Tom Schmitz

October 30, 1973
PROGRAM IV: (all premieres) "Crossover" (Sally Bowden) performed by Jenny Ball, Sally Bowden, Jacques Brouwers, Scott Caywood, Barbara Gardner, Carolyn Lord, Charles Stanley; "Transit Gloria" (Bach, Stuart Hodes) danced by Michael Aiken, Kim Arrow, Barbara Boyle, Ellen Ducker, Stuart Hodes; "Performance" (John Watts, Laura Foreman-John Watts) performed by Kanji Haruta, Timothy Haynes, Sybil Huskey, Judi Pisarro, Nancy Salmon, Satoru Shimazaki, Graciela Torino, David Varney, John Watts; "9.16666" (Richard Bull-Lou Grazzi-Duvid Smering-Bill Casals-Jody Shayne, Richard Bull; Lighting, Fred Kraps; Costumes, Sharron Kraps) danced by Kathleen Barnett, Oxanne Bond, Peter Bertini, Sherry Chornay, Leslie Creamer, Kayla Dove, Sharon Glazer, Sandra Handelman, Roy Pottruck, Tanya Williamson (The New York Chamber Dance Group)

Milton Oleaga Photos

Patty Kozono, Jennifer Donohue, Roger Preston Smith, Elizabeth Keen, Christopher Pilafian in "Mini-Quilt"
Top: Stuart Hodes in "Transit Gloria"

Manuel Alum in "East to Nijinsky"

**Sara Shelton, Jude Morgan
in "Daguerreotype"**

CHOREOGRAPHERS THEATRE
ChoreoConcerts Workshops

WASHINGTON SQUARE CHURCH
Director, Laura Foreman; Administrative Coordinators, Donna Moore, Jane D. Schwartz; Lighting Designer, Cheryl Thacker; Stage Manager, Rachel Lampert; Electrician, Nancy Offenhauser; Sound, Hank O'Neal; Production Coordinators, Martha Hudson, Gregory Parisek; Graphics, John Anthes, Gregory Parisek; Program Director, Phyllis Lamhut, with Frances Alenikoff, Laura Foreman, Donna Moore, Jane D. Schwartz

February 20–22, 1974
SERIES A: (all premieres) "Kindred" (Keith Jarrett, Erica Drew) danced by Erica Drew, Susan Schlessinger; "Fritz" (Treey Reilly) choreographed and danced by Kathleen Heath; "I Remain Silent" (Reader, Fred Courtney) choreographed and danced by Bruce Pacot; "He-She Duet" (Choreography, Vic Stornant) danced by Kathleen Gaskin, Vic Stornant; "Variations on a Walking Woman" (Jimmy Yancy) choreographed and danced by Karen Rimmer; "Cerberus///Another Face of God" (Xenakis, Henry Smith) danced by Harvey Konigsberg, Henry Smith

February 27–28, March 1, 1974
SERIES B: (all premieres) "2 into 1's" (Jacques Brel, Julie Maloney) danced by Joanne Edelmann, Julie Maloney; "Chronus" choreographed and danced by Vic Stornant; "Figuerines" (Poulenc, Bob Diaz) danced by Bob Diaz, Judy Yardley; "Part I: Thanks, I'm glad you brought up that point. Part II: 3 Passes" (Ruggiero, Diann Sichel) danced by Debbie Poulsen, Diann Sichel, Susan Thomasson; "Three Things That I Know of Her" (Alonso Barrios) choreographed and danced by Victoria Larrain; "Magnetic Rag" (Scott Joplin) choreographed and danced by Jerry Pearson, Sara Pearson

March 6–8, 1974
SERIES C: (all premieres) "Untitled Duet" (Tape, Barbara Berger) danced by Barbara Berger, Sue Barnes-Moore; "Cocoon" (Classical Chinese) choreographed and danced by Katherine Liepe; "Pair" (Paul Horn, Bob Diaz) danced by Felice Dalgin, Bob Diaz; "Listening to the Singing Insects" choreographed and danced by Megan Reisel; "Homosapiens: Two Halves" (Alice Coltrane-Weather Report, Thomas Pinnock; Costumes, Adufe) danced by Neol Hall, Shirley Rushing

Milton Oleaga Photos
Top Right: Sara and Jerry Pearson in "Magnetic Rag"
Below: Bob Diaz, Judy Yardley in "Figuerines"

Phyllis Lamhut in "Moment"

Joan Finkelstein, Theodora Yoshikami in "Rope Dance I"
Above: Douglas Dunn in "Nevada"

81

CLARK CENTER FOR THE PERFORMING ARTS
West Side YWCA

Director, Louise Roberts; Production Coordinator-Technical Director, Martin Henderson
October 20–22, 1973

THE FRED BENJAMIN DANCE COMPANY: Fred Benjamin, Terrin Miles, Karen Burke, Ralph Farrington, Marilyn Banks, Lindsay Crouse, Ben Harney, Henny Kammarman, Kerry Rolland, Keith Simmons, Jan Simons, Andy Torres (Guest Artist); Director-Choreographer, Fred Benjamin; Artistic Adviser, Winston DeWitt Hemsley; Costume Director, Olon Godare; Lighting, Owen Ryan
PROGRAM: "Ember" (Isaac Hayes, Winston DeWitt Hemsley; Costumes, Benjamin Wakefield), "Our Thing" (Hayes, Benjamin), "902 Albany Street" (Contemporary, Benjamin), and *premieres* of "Parallel Lines" (Herbert Laws-War, Benjamin), "Two Plus One" (Grover Washington, Benjamin; Costumes, Olon Godare), "Prey" (Alphonze Mouzon, Benjamin; Costumes, Godare), "Loneliness" (Benjamin), "Work in Progress" (Yusel Latief, Michele Murray)
October 27–28, 1973

NEW YORK MIME DUET (Rene Houtrides, Louis Gilbert) and THE LAUGHING CIRCLE MIME (Clare Long, Lynn Cataldo); Sound, Jayne Lieberson; Lighting, Judith Goodman
PROGRAM: "Juggling," "The Laughing Circle," "People and Animals," "There Was an Old Lady," "Balloon," "The Wall," "Where the Wild Things Are," "The Tightrope Walkers," "Shoes," "The Lion Tamer and the Lion," "The Fight"
Sunday, November 18, 1973

THE THEATRE DANCE COLLECTION: Maggie Gorrill, Michael Owens, Frank Pietri, Rodney Griffin, Lynne Taylor, Justin Ross, Jaclynn Villamil, Miriam Welch, Cynthia Roberts, Don Lopez, Laurie Kaplan; Stage Manager, Bill Conway; Sound, Michael Corbett
PROGRAM: "Harlequin" with choreography by the company; Music and Lyrics, Michael Corbett, Lynne Taylor; Costumes, Merrill Leighton; Lighting, Edward M. Greenberg; Set, Henry Millman; Director, Robert Lowe
December 1–3, 1973

ART BAUMAN MOVEMENT PROJECTS: Art Bauman, Connie Allentuck, Mickie Geller, Peggy Hackney, Lenore Latimer, Charles Madden, Myrna Packer, Kedzie Penfield, Ellen Robbins; Lighting Design, Edward I. Byers; Stage Manager, Tina Charney
PROGRAM: "Dances for Women," "Dialog" (Arranged and performed by Art Bauman; Film, Kirk Smallman; Sound Environment, Michael Czajkowski; Still Photography, Edward Effron)
December 15–16, 1973

NEW CHOREOGRAPHERS: "Inner Song" (Balinese) choreographed and danced by Katherine Leipe; "Bound Two" (Andrew Rudin) choreographed and danced by Jerome Sarnat and Lisa Nalven; "Decision" (Tape, Irene O'Brien) danced by Irene O'Brien, Jeanne Cox, Ruth Gould, Anet Ris, Daffi; "Pardon Me, But Haven't We . . . ." (Tape, Luise Wykell) danced by Luise Wykell, Richard Biles; "Can't Elope" choreographed and danced by Julia Hanlon; "Every Woman's Child—A Monument to Louise" (Hubert Laws-Vera Hall-Roberta Flack, Shawneequa Baker-Scott) danced by Shawneequa Baker-Scott and Diane Harvey; "Flung" choreographed and danced by Penelope Hill; "Reedsong" (Vaughn Williams-Arthur Benjamin, Daniel Maloney) danced by Elaine Anderson, Michael Bruce, Gwendolyn Bye, Patricia Thomas, Daniel Maloney; Lighting, Lauren Dong; Sound, Bernadine Jennings; Stage Manager, Ro Cunningham

Nathaniel Tileston Photos

Top Right: Fred Benjamin Company in "Parallel Lines"
Below: Rene Houtrides, Louis Gilbert (N. Y. Mime Duet)
Right Center: Theatre Dance Collection
in "Harlequin"

Art Bauman in "Dialog"

CLARK CENTER

January 12–20, 1974

A FESTIVAL WEEK OF SOLO WORKS: Lighting, John P. Dodd, Jon Andreadakis; Stage Manager, Marty Henderson; Sound, Bernadine Jennings. Jan. 12 & 20: Kei Takei with John Wilson, Frances Alenikoff, Maldwyn Pate, Lloyd Ritter, Joe Ritter performing "Talking Desert Blues" (Maldwyn Pate), and "Light Part VIII" (Lloyd Ritter). Jan 13 & 17: Barbara Gardner performing "Sophie's Hideaway," "Sails of Noah Zark" featuring "Sophie" and "Pearl." Jan. 14 & 18: Carolyn Lord performing "Song" (Richard Wagner). Jan. 16 & 19: Sally Bowden Dances.

February 2–4, 1974

CHARLES MOORE IN DANCES AND DRUMS OF AFRICA with Betty Barney, Audrey Mason Champion, Lavinia Hamilton, Adetunji Joda, Ella Thompson, and Ramona Candy, Robin-Laura Charres, Carolyn Clemons, Sylvia Ducksworth, Sandra Fernandez, Cassandra Ford, Franchesca Gilbert, Patricia Hipplewith, Yvonne Ogle, Sandra Pinkard, Albertine Rich, Susan Sandler, Ijalu Sweeny, Rosemarie Tirado, Laura Williams, James Budahazi, Antonio Carr Caruso, Roderick Tyler, Newt Winters; Lighting, Leonard Buggs, Jr.; Stage Manager, Karen DeFrancis.
PROGRAM: "Moon Dance," "Antelope Dance," "Oroye," "Sacred Forest Dance," "Sounds of Africa," "Fast Agbekor," "Awassa Astrige," "Tribal Society Dances," "Spear Dance," "Souvenir d'Haiti"

February 9–20, 1974

THE INCREDIBLE JOURNEY IN AMATERASU with Laura Simms, Karen Bernard, Allison Bradford, Rolando Vega, Maher Benham, Marjorie Katz, Fran Soector; Story Adapted and Directed by Laura Simms; Music, Chris Christodoulou, Dan Erkkila, Cherel Winett; Masks, Rolando Vega; Lighting, Keith Michael, Merrill Schwartz

February 23–25, 1974

THE THEATRE DANCE COLLECTION: Rodney Griffin, Bob Heath, Don Lopez, Frank Pietri, T. Michael Reed, Cynthia Roberts, Justin Ross, Lynn Simonson, Clay Taliaferro, Lynne Taylor, Jaclynn Villamil, Miriam Welch; Lighting, Edward M. Greenberg; Stage Manager, Robert Lowe; Sound, Michael Corbett
PROGRAM: "Kinetics" (Vivaldi-Rodrigo-Dowland, Lynne Taylor), and *premieres* of "A Point in Time" (Marvin Gaye, Lynn Simonson), "The Miraculous Mandarin" (Bela Bartok, Rodney Griffin; Scenario, Menyhert Lengyel; Costumes, Lee Mayman), "More Than Yesterday" (Harry Nilsson, Jaclynn Villamil; Costumes, Benjamin Wakefield), "Double Solitude" (Benjamin Britten-John Dowland, Lynne Taylor; Costumes, Colin McIntyre), "Misalliance" (Jacques Ibert, Rodney Griffin; Costumes, Holmes Easley)

March 2–3, 1974

JOAN MILLER AND THE CHAMBER ARTS/DANCE PLAYERS: Milton Bowser, Lee Connor, Joan Lombardi, Yon Martin, Joan Miller, Gail Reese, Chuck Davis (Guest Artist). Lighting, Gary Harris; Director-Choreographer, Joan Miller; Managing Director, Carol Indianer; Press, Margaret Hanks; Stage Manager, Carol Indianer; Sound, Bernadine Jennings
PROGRAM: "Mix" (David Coffee-Roebuck Staples-Billy Preston, Miller), "Pass Fe White" (Miller), "Blackout" (Chili Walker-Milton Bowser, Miller; Narrator, Chuck Davis), "Sponge" (Carole Weber, Miller), "Improvisation on a Theme" (Miller), "Soundscape" (Chili Walker-Gwendolyn Watson-Carole Weber), *N.Y. premiere* of "Thoroughfare" (J. Mayall-Watson Press, Miller)

Nathaniel Tileston Photos

**Top Right: The Theatre Dance Collection in "Misalliance"
Below: Kei Takei in "Light Part VIII"**

**Chamber Arts/Dance Players in "Thoroughfare"
Above: Charles Moore Dancers in "Souvenir d'Haiti"** 83

CLARK CENTER
March 9–11, 1974

THE CHUCK DAVIS DANCE COMPANY: Carol Awolowo, Marilyn Banks, Tara Barnard, Onika Bagemon, Milton Abdel Bowser, Victor Braxton, Sandra Burton, Jackie Coban, Chuck Davis, Linda Evans, William Fleet, Shirley Fogg, Earl Macks, Monifa Olajorin, Charles Wynn, Lynn Allen, Ayele Douglas, Theresa Freeman, Normadine Gibson, Gregory Hinton, Ben Jones, Jennifer Jones, Francine Quick, Juanita Tylor, John Young, Yomi Yomi Awolowo (Musical Director-Master Drummer)
PROGRAM: "Drum Invocation and Chant," "Ibedi-bedi and Fofo," "Drum Rhythms," "Embodiment of One," "A Simple Prayer," and *world premier* of "The Watcher (Religion X 5)" (Choreography and Costumes, Chuck Davis)
March 16–18, 1974

ELIZABETH KEEN DANCE COMPANY: Elizabeth Keen, Bill Cratty, Jennifer Donohue, Patty Kozono, Dalienne Majors, Christopher Pilafian, Roger Preston Smith, Michael Steele (Guest Artist); Director-Choreographer, Elizabeth Keen; Lighting, Edward Greenberg; Stage Manager, Robert Lowe; Sound, Marie Gaines; Management, Directional Concepts
PROGRAM: "The Unravish'd Bride" (Franz Schubert; Costumes, Dolores Bregan), "Dancing to Records" (Popular; Costumes, Whitney Balusen), "Poison Variations" (Gwendolyn Watson-Joel Press), and *premieres* of "Seasoning" (Marilyn Rosenberger; Costumes, Whitney Balusen), "Enclosure Acts" (Marilyn Rosenberger; Text, Authur Rimbaud; Reading, Bonnie Boxer)
March 23–25, 1974

MULTIGRAVITATIONAL EXPERIMENT GROUP: Stephanie Evansitsky, Robert Fiala, Suellen Epstein, Kay Gainer, Arthur-George Hurray, Donald Porteous, Barbara Salz, Bronya Wajnberg, Llewellyn Wheeler; Artistic Director-Choreographer, Stephanie Evanitsky; Assistant Artistic Director, Robert Fiala; Lighting, Charles Dexter; Resident Composers, Terance Thomas, Richard Hayman; Sound, Richard Hayman; Stage Manager, Charles Dexter
PROGRAM: "Splat" (Fiala, Evanitsky-Fiala), "Alien Connection" (Cream, Fiala), "Sure Was" (Thomas, Evanitsky), "Silver Scream Idols" (Joplin-Brown, Evanitsky)
April 6–8, 1974

PEPSI BETHEL AUTHENTIC JAZZ DANCE THEATRE: Pepsi Bethel, Linda Cleveland, Phillip Stamps, Otis Brockington, Monte Clarke, Alfred Gallman, Liz Morris, Amelie Oubre, Theresa Ross, Eddie Shellman, Sandra Thompson, Darlye Williams, and the Andrei Strobert Quartet; Director-Choreographer, Pepsi Bethel; Costumes, Pepsi Bethel, Phillip Stamps, Maria Contessa; Special Effects and Props, Linda Cleveland; Lighting, Marshall Williams; Stage Manager, Russell Burrowes; Sound, Lynn Bobbett; Assistant to the Director, Phillip Stamps; Manager, Zizi Richards
PROGRAM: "The Blues," "Carribean Rhythms," "New Orleans," "Jazz Suite," and *premier* of "Tabernacle"

Nathaniel Tileston Photos

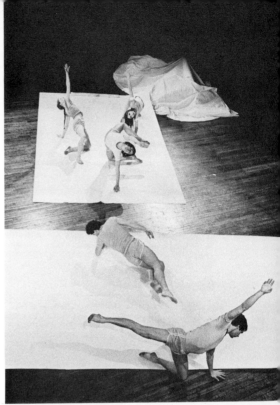

Top Right: Elizabeth Keen Dance Co. in "Enclosure Acts"

Chuck Davis Dance Company

Multigravitational Experiment Group in "Splat"

CLARK CENTER
April 20–22, 1974

BALLET HISPANICO OF NEW YORK: Sandra Rivera, Dolores
Garcia, Coco Pelaez, Nancy Ticotin, Rachel Ticotin, Alicia Roque,
Valerie Contreras, Lorenzo Maldonado, Ernesto Morales, Marcial
Gonzales, Antonio Iglesias, Roy Rodriguez; Artistic Director, Tina
Ramirez; Associate Director-Ballet Master, Ramon Segarra; Ad-
ministrator, Ron Christopher; Production Director, Robert Monk;
Press, Marush; Lighting, Chenault Spence; Stage Manager, Robbie
Monk; Sound, David Ticotin, Gilbert Figueroa
REPERTOIRE: "La Boda de Luis Alonso" (Gimenez, Paco Fer-
nandez; Costumes, Rupert and Puhma), "Deer Dance" (Yaqui In-
dian Music, Jose Coronado), "Quintet" (Laura Nyro, Alvin Ailey
restaged by Michele Murray; Costumes, Ruben Cruz), "Pi R2"
(Varese, Lois Bewley), *NY premieres* of "Echoes of Spain" (Albeniz
—The Temptations—Mandrill, Louis Johnson; Costumes, Diane
Fox), "Misa Criolla" (Ariel Ramirez, Ramon Segarra; Costumes,
Diane Fox), *World premieres* of "Fiesta en Vera Cruz" (J. Pablo
Moncayo, Jose Coronado; Costumes, Jose Coronado, Sara Sendra),
"Mira Todas Esas Bellas Rosas Rojas" (Santana, Talley Beatty;
Costumes, Edith Lutyens Bel Geddes, Julio Fernandez)

May 18–20, 1974

SOUNDS IN MOTION: Babafumi Akunyun, Issa Ayubu, Phillip
Bond, William Donald, Lonnetta Gaines, Bernadine Jennings,
Dianne McIntyre, Kenneth McPherson, Gwendolyn Nelson, Carol
Pennyfeather, Dorian Williams; Director-Choreographer, Dianne
McIntyre; General Manager, Amun Ankhra; Company Manager,
William Donald; Assistants, Mikki Ankhra, Alicia Adams; Press,
Howard Atlee, Clarence Allsopp; Stage Manager-Lighting, Sandra
Ross
REPERTOIRE: "Long Gones" (Memphis Jug Band-Bessie Smith-
Dixieland Jug Blowers, Dianne McIntyre; Costumes, Judy Dearing),
"Every Woman's Child—A Monument to Louise" (Hubert Laws-
Vera Hall-Roberta Flack, Shawneequa Baker-Scott; Costumes, Eleo
Pomare), "Lost Sun" (Gene Casey, McIntyre; Costumes, Willi
Smith), "Sounds from Inside," "Union" (Text, Langston Hughes,
Margaret Walker; Choreography, Dianne McIntyre; Voice Gwen-
dolyn Nelson), and *premieres* of "Dead Center" (Hank Johnson,
Dianne McIntyre; Set, Sue Irons, Charles Abramson), "Hymn"
(Traditional, Dianne McIntyre; Costumes, Gladys Gaines; Singer,
Gwendolyn Nelson) *Nathaniel Tileston Photos*

Sounds in Motion in "Union" Top Right: Ballet Hispanico of New York in "Missa Criolla"
Below: Pepsi Bethel Authentic Jazz Dance Theatre in "Tabernacle"

THE CUBICULO

Artistic Director, Philip Meister; Managing Director, Elaine Sulka; Program Director, Maurice Edwards; Production Manager, Quinton Raines; Resident Designer, Richard Tsukada

THE CUBICULO
June 4–5, 1973
    PEGGY CICIERSKA & SHEILA SOBEL
    with Maris Wolff, and Jay Friedman
PROGRAM: "Improvisation to Live Synthesizer" (Margette Watts, Cicierska), "Chairs Fit, Sometimes Tables" (Amy Sheffer, Sobel), "Harriet" (Humpback Whale) choreographed and danced by Peggy Cicierska, "Solo" (Collage, Cicierska), "Louie (Suite for Susan)" (Susan Ain) choreographed and danced by Peggy Cicierska
    Wednesday, June 6, 1973
KYRA LOBER with Jim Ferchen, Russ Hartenburger performing "Transformations," and evening of improvisations (Costume Designer, Ann Hall)
    June 11–12, 1973
THE LAURA PAWEL DANCE COMPANY: Laura Pawel, Pamela Finney, Raymond Healy, Kevin Mulligan (Director-Choreographer, Laura Pawel; Lighting, Nicholas Wolff Lyndon) performing "The Beast with Many Tales," "Sphinx" (Eleanor Hovda), "Close Quarters," "Snort Too," "In the Last Crunch"
    June 18–19, 1973
LIMB LITERAL. . . . OR LEG TECHNOLOGY VERSUS ARM TECHNOLOGY: Choreography, Gay Delanghe; Video Tapes, Tom Katosic; Juggling, Jay Green; Stage Manager, Susan Feldstein; with Alana Barter, Ellen Brown Bogart, John Cwiakala, Robert Handler, Alvin McDuffie, Sharon Lowen, Christine Mitchell, Carol Richard, Lynn Rosenfeld, Neil Shewmaker, Marilyn Zimmer
    June 25–26, 1973
PAUL KNOPF AND CLARE JOHNSON with April Berry, Garry Easterling; Choreography, Clare Johnson; Music and Poetry, Paul Knopf; in "A Defense of Scott Joplin," "Fantasies on a Summer Night," "The Gift," "The Sin of Avarice"
    July 9–10, 1973
JUDITH JANUS and Members of Theatre Encounter: Karen Campbell, Luanna Reid, Patrick Sarsfield, Beverly Tractenberg; Choreography, Judith Janus; Lighting, Cheryl Thacker; Technical Director, Richard Tsukadal Program: "Contrasts," "Encounter IV," "Bugs, or How to Smell with the Knees, Taste with the Feet, and Wear a Skeleton on the Outside"
    July 13–14, 1973
CUBICULO DANCE THEATRE V, PART I: "The I Do Not Know" (Debussy-Newman) choreographed and danced by Christopher Beck; "Close Quarters" (Choreographer, Laura Pawel) with Ed DiLello, Jim Finney, Pamela Finney, Raymond Healy; "Triptych" (Meredith Monk) choreographed and danced by Phoebe Neville; "Passage in Silence" (Choreography, Phoebe Neville) danced by Christopher Beck and Phoebe Neville; "Opening Dance" (Indonesian Folk Music) choreographed and danced by Sally Bowden; "Saeta" (Joaquim Homs, Jose Coronado) danced by Ilona Cooper, Robin Goldstein, Pamela Anthony, Esta Greenfield, Jose Coronado

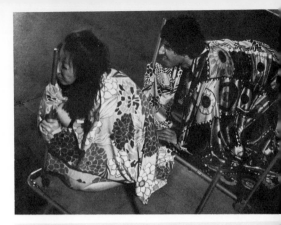

Multi-Movement Co. in "New Dance" Top Right: Sheila Sobel, Jay Friedman in "Chairs Fit, Sometimes Tables"

Laura Pawel, Pamela Finney in "Snort" Above: Kyra Lober

THE CUBICULO

July 16–17, 1973

CUBICULO DANCE THEATRE V, PART 2: "Smile, though Your Car Is Breaking" (Tape and Choreography, Valerie Hammer; Sculpture and Costumes, Phillip A. Haultcoeur) danced by Gary Cowan, Valerie Hammer, Debra Wanner, Robert Kahn, William Kleinsmith, Fern Zand; "Untitled" (Meredith Monk) choreographed and performed by Sincha Hong; "Duet" (Choreography, Sara Shelton) danced by Miss Shelton and Emery Hermans; "Taktiks" (Choreography, Jan Wodynski) danced by Kathy Eaton, Joanne Edelmann, David Monroe, Madeleine Perrone, Jan Wodynski, Mike Wodynski

July 23–24, 1973

CUBICULO DANCE THEATRE V, PART 3: "The Nose" performed by Jack Hill and Graciela Binaghi (The Mask and Mime Theatre); "Waltz" (Johann Strauss, Jr.) choreographed and danced by Jan Van Dyke; "Dinosaur Love II" choreographed and danced by Toby Armour; "The Creation of the World" and "Frog Lake" performed by Jack Hill and Graciela Binaghi; "Unfinished Drawing —Annunciation" (Choreography, Rolando Jorif) danced by Rolando Jorif and Clare Johnson; *Premiere* of "Heads" choreographed and danced by Toby Armour

September 24–25, 1973

SARA SHELTON, EMERY HERMANS, JEANETTE STONER in "Excerpts" (Choreography, Sara Shelton) danced by Emery Hermans and Sara Shelton; "Double Image #2" (Mimaroglu, Emery Hermans) danced by Emery Hermans, Jeanette Stoner; "Myth" (Ethiopean Music, Jeanette Stoner, Emery Hermans) danced by Jeff Eichenwald, Emery Hermans, Sara Shelton, Jeanette Stoner; "Double Image #1" (Ferrari, Emery Hermans) danced by Emery Hermans and Vic Stornant; "Crazy Dog Events" (Pink Floyd, Sara Shelton) danced by Jeff Eichenwald, Emery Hermans, Sara Shelton, Jeanette Stoner; Lighting, Will Owen

September 27–29, October 4–6, 1973

NEW YORK MIME FESTIVAL: "The Great Inflatable 42nd Street Angel" and "The Lighthouse Keeper" by Richard Clairmont; "Sonstage", "Carnival," "Greed" by Rebecca; "Invitation to the Voyage," "Lion Tamer," and "Images of Rain" by NY Mime Duet (Rene Houtrides, Louis P. Gilbert); "The Suicide," and "The Thief" by Robert Molnar; "Their First Dance," "Many Years Later," "Their Last Meeting" by Mimika (Jack and Harriet Scalici)

October 1–2, 1973

JOSE CORONADO & DANCERS: Pamela Anthony, Rick Hood, Jose Coronado, Ilona Copen, Robin Goldstein, Larry Samuel, Charlotte Honda, Fred McKitrick

PROGRAM: "Danse Sacree" (Debussy, Coronado), "Baile" (Revueltas, Sokolow), "The Rose Wound" (Olivas, Coronado), "Saeta" (Joms, Coronado), "Lento Desolato" (Berg, Sokolow), and *premieres* of "Dueto en Verde" (Bruno Maderna, Jose Coronado), "Three Pieces for Ellen" (John Harbison, Jose Coronado); Lighting, Louise Guthman

October 8–9, 1973

REKA AND THE MULTI MOVEMENT COMPANY: Susan Bibby, Gilda Gatti, Patricia Yenawine, Reka, Louise Weller (Choreography, Reka) performing "New Dance" (Collage), "Rally No. 2" (Luciano Berio), "Rainbow in Curved Air" (Terry Riley)

THOMAS HOLT AND DANCERS: Irene Belk, Laurie Kane, Denise Mitchell, Paulette Taylor, Aletha Winter, Stephanie Eley, Karen Sing, Thomas Holt, Cindy Gehrke, Peter Karow (Choreography, Thomas Holt; Lighting, Will Owen) performing "Broom Suite Opus I" (Bach), "The Conception of the Nativity" (Handel), and *premiere* of "Afterhours in Wonderland"

October 15–16, 1973

SATORU SHIMAZKI in a solo dance

TROPICAL FRUIT COMPANY: Deborah Chassler, Patricia Giovenco, Marvin Lamb performing "This Banana Is for You" (Choreography, Deborah Chassler)

October 26–27, 1973

BARBARA ROAN AND THE BLUE MOUNTAIN PAPER PARADE: Karin Chalom, Lenny Cowles, Charles Madden, Genny Kapuler, Joan Schwartz, Ruth Charney, Taffy Koenig, Ellen Robbins, Connie Allentuck, Anthony LaGiglia, Irene Feigenheimer, Ellen Jacob, Mary Benson, Art Bauman, John Moore, Jude Bartlett, Sue Barnes Moore, Jenny Donohue, Avi Davis, Barbara Roan, Amy Berkman, Laurie Uprichard, Dennis Florio, Nancy Scher, Bob Marinaccio, Holly Yoken, David Kramer, Jeff Duncan in "The October Parade" (Choreography, Barbara Roan; Lighting, Chip Largman; Production Coordinators, Lenny Cowles, John Moore, Anguss Moss; Sound Collage, Barbara Roan, Chip Largman; Recording, Gary Harris; Slide Photography, Vince Lalomia)

Top Right: Jose Coronado

Barbara Roan in "October Parade"

THE CUBICULO
October 28–29, 1973

REBECCA: A DANCE MIME CONCERT: "The Carousel" (Chopin), "The Lady" (Mymit), "Sleep" (Beethoven), "Onstage" (Mozart), "The Peasant" (Melancolica), "Belief" (Del Inca), "Deception" (Scarlatti), "Faith" (Lunarcito), "Expectation" (Sanz), "Carnival" (Mymit)
November 5–6, 1973

JAN WODYNSKI DANCE COMPANY: Kathy Eaton, Joanne Edelmann, Robert Kosinski, Julie Maloney, David Monroe, Madeleine Perrone, Paul Wilson, Jan Wodynski, Mike Wodynski (Choreography-Costumes, Jan Wodynski; Technical Director-Sound, Mike Wodynski) performing "Triad" (Mike Wodynski), "Five Minutes from Now," "Interspace" (Collin Walcott), "Taktiks" (Voice), premiere of "Pashun Zone: Sekter Five" (Khatchaturian)
November 12–14, 1973

TINA CROLL & COMPANY: Art Bauman, Mickie Geller, John Moore (Choreography-Props, Tina Croll; Lighting-Stage Manager, Edward I. Byers; Tape, John Moore) in "Short Stories": "In the Back of the Closet" (Scarlatti), "One Space, One Figure and Occasional Sounds" (Tape), "The Limestone Room" (Tape), "Solo with Two Ropes" (Cage-Neuhaus), and premieres of "Dance" (Satie) danced by Tina Croll, "Short Stories" (Randy Newman) danced by Mickie Geller, John Moore, Tina Croll
November 19–20, 1973

GOVINDA in "Court and Theatre Dances of South India" : "Alarippu," "Jatiswaram" (Ponniah Pillai), "Shabdam Venyuda" (Ponniah Pillai), "Venayaka Kavitvam" (Natyacharya V.P. Sarma), "Manduka Shabdam: (Melattur Kasinathayya)
October 30–31, 1973

THREE VERONICAS (a preview) choreographed by Jude Bartlett, and performed by Jude Bartlett, Nancy Scher, and Wendy Osserman; Lighting, Chip Largman, Will Owen; Sound, John Moore
Sunday, December 9, 1973

RITHA DEVI in Hindu Dances "Mahari Nritya" and "Kuchipudi"
December 10–11, 1973

KYRA LOBER with NEXUS KONSTANTINO and WENDY OSSERMAN No other details available.
December 17–19, 1973

FRANCES ALENIKOFF DANCE THEATER COMPANY: Frances Alenikoff, Carol-Rae Kraus, Myrna Packer, John DeMarco, Joan Schwartz, Ray Grist (Choreography, Frances Alenikoff; Lighting-Production Manager, Edward I. Byers) in "The One of No Way" (Charlie Morrow), "Terns in Place," "An Invitation to Nausicaa" (Collage, Frances Alenikoff; Poem, Joachim Neugroschel), "Belle" (Collage), "Pavana" (Scott Fields), and premiere of "Pomegranate" (Poem, set, set piece, film, slides, tape collage, Ray Grist) performed by Ray Grist and Frances Alenikoff
December 27–29, 1973

AILEEN PASSLOFF and the BARD THEATER OF DANCE AND DRAMA: Mario Donatelli, Seth Friedman, Judy Groffman, Walter Holland, Susan Jurick, Susan Seidler, Gale Strazza in "Entanglements" (Director, Aileen Passloff; Lighting Design, Eric Tishman; Stage Manager, Ann Bogart)
January 14–16, 1974

THE GREENHOUSE DANCE ENSEMBLE: Natalie Richman, Nada Reagan, Brian Webb (Guest Artist), Robert Yohn, Carol Conway, Beverly Brown, Lillo Way performing "Wind" (Bob Sambuca, Carol Conway; Set, James Pelletier) danced by Carol Conway; NY premiere of "Johnny's Dance" (Text, Witold Gomgrowicz) choreographed and danced by Brian Webb; "The Man They Say" (Text-Choreography, Robert Yohn; Narrator, Merrill Lemmon) danced by Robert Yohn, Carol Conway; "Windwing" choreographed and danced by Natalie Richman; "Summer Settings" (J. Miller, Nada Reagan; Costumes, Ruth Miller), and world premiere of "Cypher" (Gerard Schwarz) choreographed and danced by Lillo Way.
January 21–22, 1974

THE MANNING-FRIED DANCE COMPANY: Heidi Bunting, Terry Creach, Erica Drew, Dorothy Fried, Gary Kessinger, Manning Precht, Susan Schlessinger, Dania Stager, Ed Zawacki, Terry Bender (Guest Artist) (Director, Dorothy Fried; Artistic Director, Manning Precht; Lighting Design, John Kaplan) performing "Carmina Burana Part I" (Orff, Fried), "Heavy on the Mayonnaise" (Scott Joplin-Glen Miller-Garvarentz-Hirshhorn, Precht), "White Satin" (Barry White, Manning Precht), NY premiere of "Dance Drama on Woman" (Clarissa, Dried)

Top Right: Jan Wodynski Dance Co. in
"Pashun Zone::Sekter 5"(*Dave Monroe Photo*)

Below: Frances Alenikoff in "Pomegranate"
(*Don Manza Photo*)

88

Carol Conway, Robert Yohn of Greenhouse Dance
Ensemble in "The Man They Say"

THE CUBICULO

January 28–29, 1974

PAUL KNOPF & CLARE JOHNSON: with April Berry, Kyne Franks, Daniel Barton, in "The Gift" (Music and Poetry, Paul Knopf; Choreography, Clare Johnson), "Fantasies on a Summer Night," "The Cursing of the Fig Tree," "In the Streets," "In the Garden"

February 4–5, 1974

TINA CROLL & COMPANY: Mickie Geller, John Moore, Tina Croll (Choreography, Tina Croll) in "Short Stories" (Randy Newman), "One Space, One Figure and Occasional Sounds" (Tape, Tina Croll), premiere of "Dance #1 & #2" (Bach-Satie) danced by Tina Croll

PEGGY CICIERSKA in premieres of "Drifts" (Feldmen) choreographed and danced by Peggy Cicierska, "Vacuum" (Pink Floyd) danced by Peggy Cicierska, Erica Berland, John Moore

February 11–12, 1974

FRED MATHEWS AND DANCERS: Michael Bruce, Amanda Kreglow, Risa Steinberg, Mary Jo Buhl, Marjory Philpot, Fred Mathews, Gary Masters, Jan Peterson in "Rite" (Kodaly, Mathews), "Three Women" (Handel, Jose Coronado), "The Keepers" (Varese, Mathews), "Quietus" (Mathews), "Fugitive Vision" (Prokofiev, Jose Coronado), "Etude" (Brahms, Mathews; Lighting, Jene Youtt; Stage Manager, John R. Toland)

February 18–19, 1974

PHOEBE NEVILLE dancing "Triptych" (Meredith Monk), "Passage in Silence" danced by Phoebe Neville and Christopher Beck, and premiere of "Cartouche" (Purcell, Phoebe Neville) danced by Christopher Beck and Phoebe Neville

CHRISTOPHER BECK dancing NY premiere of "Heat Lightning" (Bach), and world premiere of "Dying Away" (Unaccompanied; Lighting, Nicholas Wolff Lyndon; Stage Manager, Nancy Offenhauser)

February 25–26, 1974

CONSORT DANCE ENSEMBLE: Selby Beebe, Myra Hushansky, Zina Moiseenko, Donna Mondanaro, Margaret O'Sullivan, Roxanne Pepe, Bobbie Silvera in "Onset" (Paul Spong, Myra Hushansky), "Pilgrim" (Varese, Hushansky), "Facets" (Choreography, Mondanaro), "Millennium" (Collage, Mondanaro); Lighting, Marion Schmidt; Costumes, Sylvia Woods; Stage Manager, Chuck Wilson

March 4–5, 1974

SANTORU SHIMAZAKI with Sybil Huskey dancing Mr. Shimazaki's "265–2138, so. . . ."

KATRINA & COMPANY: Nicholas Ay Ronalda, Michael Blue Aiken, J. Lang Kiernan, Kathy Ray, Gary Sorce, Jim Sorce, Emily Tincher, Katrina Velcich in "Breath of Fire," "Thou Art Thyself"

PATRICIA HRUBY with Patricia Miller, Wendy Osserman in "Your Play, My Move" (Vivaldi-Joplin, Hruby)

Monday, March 18, 1974

MAYA KULKARNI in "Bharata Natyam" dances of India: "Slokam," "Jathiswaram," "Varnam," "Padam," "Thillana" (Narration, Janak Khendry)

March 25–26, 1974

ROLANDO JORIF DANCE COMPANY: Joan Doberman, Ann Kennedy, Janis Roswick, Rolando Jorif, David Lee, Christina Hamm performing "Blue" (Schumann), "Movie" (Faure), "Required Reading" (Beethoven), "Glass" (Choreography, Rolando Jorif)

April 15–16, 1974

IRENE FEIGENHEIMER (Choreographer) with Barbara Roan, Jennifer Donohue, Annabelle Gamson, Ellen Robbins, Liz Thompson, Billy Siegenfeld performing "45 Seconds to Spring; 6 Minutes 15 Seconds to Summer" (Leon Russell and Hot Tuna) choreographed and danced by Irene Feigenheimer and Barbara Roan "Parts; Particles" (Partch) choreographed and danced by Irene Feigenheimer, "Especially" (Nickelodeon, Feigenheimer) danced by Billy Siegenfeld and Irene Feigenheimer, premieres of "Two Songs for Throwing Time" (Fairport Convention) choreographed and danced by Billy Siegenfeld, "Untitled Dance for Five Women" (John Smead, Feigenheimer)

Sunday, April 21, 1974

RITHA DEVI in "Sapta-Rashmi" (Seven Rays of the Sun): "Kathakali," "Mohiniattam," "Kuchipudi," "Bharatha Natyam," "Mahari Nritya," "Manipuri," "Satriya Nritya"

**Top Right: Erika Berland, John Moore
in "Vacuum"** (*Sue Barnes-Moore Photo*)

**Below: Phoebe Neville, Christopher Beck
in "Cartouche"**(*Philip Hipwell Photo*)

Right Center: Consort Dance Ensemble

Maya Kulkarni

THE CUBICULO
April 22–23, 1974

HANNAH KAHN, DALIENNE MAJORS AND DANCERS: Cameron Burke, Ann DeGange, Bill DeTurk, Jennifer Douglas, David Grossman, Carol Ann Hess, Kathryn Johnson, Steve Karlin, Frederick L. McKitrick, Cynthia R. Millman, Michael Rivera, Debra Zalkind performing "Money" (Stravinsky, Pamela Knisel), "The Rambler, The Grumbler, One Thistle, and a Rose" (Paul Hindes, Hannah Kahn), "Departures" (Popular, Jessica Fogel), "Intimate" (Schumann, Dalienne Majors), "Pulling Through" (Baden Powell, Hannah Kahn), "Simon Says" (Paul Simon, Dalienne Majors)

April 29–30, 1974

LAURA PAWEL DANCE COMPANY: Jim Finney, Pamela Finney, Raymond Healy, Laura Pawel dancing "Hoof and Mouth" (premiere), "The Sphinx Suite" (Eleanor Havda), "No Fur, No Hooves"; Choreography, Laura Pawel; Lighting Design, Joseph Maceda

May 6–7, 1974

CHOREOGRAPHY BY LUISE WYKELL danced by Gale Ormiston, Deborah Glase, Lisa Seiden, Abigail Waltz, Luise Wykell: "Pardon Me, But Haven't We . . ." (Collage), "Labyrinth" (Hyman), "Maillol, We Salute You!" (Purcell), "Anoles" (Aviary), "Tracking" (Schuller-T. Monk)

May 20–21, 1974

BHASKAR in "Dances of India" with Anjali: "Alaripu," "Thilana," "Natanam Adinar," "Thane Varamanam," "Tara," "Krishna Ni Baro," "Thala Nirtham," "Naga Nritham," "Surya Nritham"

May 23–24, 1974

MAGIC AND DANCE: "The Conjurer" designed and performed by Jeff Sheridan, "A Prayer to the Subway" (Michael Sahl, Anne Sahl) danced by Anne Sahl, Lee Connor; Lighting, Bryan Jayne

**Right: Renate Boue
Top: Bhaskar and Anjali**

Raymond Johnson in "Feathers"

THE CUBICULO
Saturday, May 25, 1974

THE NEW YORK IMPROVISATION ENSEMBLE: Martha Bowers, Nancy Mapother, Phillip Bond, Ann Woods, Colette Yglesias, directed by Doris Rudko; Lighting, Bryan Jayne; Founders and Musicians, Noah Creshevsky, Marianna Creshevsky; performing "Focus," "Wispen," "Rondo," "Duet" (Choreography, Nancy Mapother), "Rochester, New York, October 7, 1973" (Sound, Noah Creshevsky), "One Plus One," "Daisies Won't Tell"

May 28–29, 1974

RENATE BOUE DANCE COMPANY: Renate Boue, Suzanne Harris, Muriel Holub, Claire Macheret, Robert Mahon, Marcia Mungenast performing ("To Fly" Stanley Dominski, Boue), "When All Was New" (Hans Martin Linde, Boue), "Celebrating Sound Seasons"

May 30–31, June 1, 1974

FOOTWORK: "Talk's Cheap" (Aretha Franklin, Bill Kirkpatrick) danced by Bill Kirkpatrick, Bekka Eastman; "Intermotionally Woven" (John Fahey, Bekka Eastman) danced by Bekka Eastman, Gregorio Fassler, Mirran Von Essen; "Push and Collapse" (Bekka Eastman-Gregorio Fassler) choreographed and danced by Mirran Von Essen; "Dance to Dance" (Alan Stirell) choreographed and danced by Bekka Eastman; "Vestige" (Stravinsky) choreographed and danced by Bill Kirkpatrick; "Between Meals" (Assorted, Kirkpatrick) danced by Bekka Eastman, Bill Kirkpatrick, Eileen Desmond, John Sillings, Midge Tenney, Steve Walker

September 20–22, 1973

ZE'EVA COHEN AND RAYMOND JOHNSON in an evening of solo dances; "The One of No Way" (Scott-Yuize-Yamamoto, Frances Alenikoff), "Countdown" (Songs of the Auvergne, Rudy Perez), and "32 Variations in C Minor" (Beethoven, James Waring) danced by Ze'eva Cohen; "Black Dance" (Steve Reich, Raymond Johnson), "Tuesday's Tempered Terpsichore" (Count Basie, Johnson), and NY premiere of "Feathers" (Mozart, James Waring) danced by Raymond Johnson

DANCE THEATER WORKSHOP
June 1, 1973–May 31, 1974

Director, Jeff Duncan; Assistant Director, Art Bauman; Press, Judith Scott; School Director, Jan Wodynski; Administrative Assistant, Doris Ginsberg; Board of Directors, Art Bauman, Ze'eva Cohen, Jeff Duncan, Doris Ginsberg, Jack Moore, Cynthia Read, Judith Scott, Wendy Summit, John Wilson, Jan Wodynski.

CHOREOGRAPHERS: Frances Alenikoff, Juan Antonio, Karen Attix, Sue Barnes-Moore, Art Bauman, Mary Benson, Kathryn Bernson, Carol Boggs, Karen Lierley Bowman, Tina Croll, Ze'eva Cohen, Bob Diaz, Ben Dolphin, Jeff Duncan, Peggy Berg Gennis, Doris Ginsberg, Micki Goodman, Peggy Hackney, Julia Hanlon, Penelope Hill, Sybil Huskey, Deborah Jowitt, Elizabeth Keen, Hava Kohav, Judy Konopacki, Kathe Lee, Erin Martin, Irene Meltzer, Joan Miller, Jack Moore, Laura Pawel, Rudy Perez, Kathryn Posin, Megan Reisel, Barbara Roan, Nancy Scher, Judith Scott, Anna Sokolow, Gael Stepanek, Alice Teirstein, Laurie Uprichard, James Waring, Betsy Wetzig, John Wilson, Maida Withers, Jan Wodynski, Debra Zalkind, Randolyn Zinn

DANCERS: choreographers plus Connie Allentuck, Ariane Aruego, Mary Barnett, Freddie Berg, Art Berger, Bruce Block, Blue Mountain Paper Parade, Robert Bonfiglio, Francoise Brooks, Marsi Burns, Mary-Pat Carey, Suzanne Castelli, Ruth Charney, Fa Ching Chu, Julie Collins, Jane Comfort, Ilona Copen, Ellen Cornfield, Blondell Cummings, Dawn DaCosta, Rick de Fillips, John DeMarco, Suki Dewey, Matthew Diamond, Kathy Eaton, Joanne Edelmann, Mary Jane Eisenberg, Jim Finney, Pamela Finney, Mickie Geller, Jane Gillen, Deborah Glaser, Robin Goldstein, Mara Goodman, Maggie Gorrill, Raymond Healy, Karena Hoffman, Yukiko Iino, Genevieve Kapuler, John Kelly, Michael Kilgore, Kendall Klingbeil, Robert Kosinski, Carol-Rae Kraus, Paul Langland, Davidson Lloyd, Jeanne Lunin, Lorn MacDougal, David Malamut, Julie Maloney, Jim May, Lorry May, Molly Tucker McClure, Errol P. Merghart, David Monroe, John Moore, Stormy Mullis, Lee Olsen, Idelle Packer, Myrna Packer, Maldwyn Pate, Fred Patton, Carl Pellegrini, Gwen Pemberton, Kedzie Penfield, Madeleine Perrone, Pamela Pilkenton, Debbie Poulson, Valeria Pullman, Diane Quitko, Nadine Revene, Michael Richardson, Pam Robbins, Ron Rosselli, Ellen Sackoff, Nancy Salmon, Vicki Schick, Joan Schwartz, Lucie Signa, Robin Silver, Michelle Simon, Monica Solem, Linda Spikell, Yvonne Stadler, Kei Takei, Carol Thaler, Dale Townsend, Jeff Urban, David Van Tieghem, Missy Vineyard, Gwendolyn Watson, Peter Weinstock, Paul Wilson, Mahri Wilson, Mike Wodynski, Maris Wolff

COMPOSERS AND DESIGNERS: Bart Barlow, Richard Barnet, Ben Benson, Beth Burkhardt, Edward I. Byers, Walter Carlos, Kimberly Davis, Evelyn DeBoeck, John DeMarco, John P. Dodd, Gordon Emerson, Scott Fields, Mara Goodman, Ray Grist, Salvatore Guida, John Hagan, F. W. Hayman-Chaffey, Kenyon Hopkins, Eleanor Hovda, William Katz, John Kle, Desiree Koslin, Chip Largman, Fran Lipton, Peter Ludwig, Joseph Maceda, Ted Marks, Pierre Metral, Carl Michaelson, Charlie Morrow, Joseph Napodano, Lavinia Nielsen, Nora Nissenbaum, Kirk Nurock, Joel Press, Valerie Pullman, Mara Purl, Paul Rosal, Marilyn Rosenberger, Michael Rod, Donna Roz, Didi Shapiro, Cheryl Thacker, Terrence Thomas, Margaret Tobin, Rick Tsukada, David Van Tieghem, Gwendolyn Watson, Peter Weinstock, John Wilson, Mike Wodynski

THEATERS: American Theatre Laboratory, The Cubiculo, The Dance Gallery, Dance Theater Workshop, ERA (Geneva, Switz.), Exchange Teater, Kaufmann Concert Hall, Washington Square Methodist Church

Eric Reiner Photos

Top Right: Julia Hanlon in "A Bun in Her Oven"
Below: "By Tomorrow"

"Routes"

DANCE THEATRE WORKSHOP

REPERTOIRE

"Beginning" (Wetzig-Michaelson-Barnet), "Belle" (Holmes-Grist, Alenikoff), "Black Dance" (Led Zeppelin, Posin), "Bring Your Child" (Weitzig), "Butterfly" (Hovda, Goodman), "By Tomorrow" (Corelli, Stepanek), "Cathode" (Garbarek, Moore), "Changeover" (Wodynski, Wodynski), "Cloud Song" (Popular-Ludwig, Cohen), "Contours" (Winter, Wodynski), "Countdown" (Traditional, Perez), "A Dance" (Kohav), "Days" (Nurock, Posin), "Errands" (Collage, Bauman), "Escape" (Hopkins, Sokolow), "Farrago" (Wodynski, Improvisation), "Garden White" (Collage, Kohav), "Headquarters" (Barry, Bauman), "In the Back of the Closet" (Scarlatti, Croll), "Laser" (Harrison, Withers), "Lethe" (Rosal, Goodman), "The Limestone Room" (Collage, Croll), "Miami Beach 1959" (Michaelson, Hackney), "Mist" (Horn-Nielsen, Kohav), "Moments" (Collage, Kohav), "October Parade" (Largman, Roan), "One of No Way" (Morrow-Schwerner, Alenikoff), "Only Voice" (Michaelson, Hackney), "One Space, One Figure and Occasional Sounds" (Collage, Croll), "Palimpsest" (Henry, Jowitt), "Pass Fe White" (Watson, Miller), "Pavana" (Fields, Alenikoff), "Plastic Dance" (Rosal-Napodano, Goodman), "Poison Variations" (Press-Watson, Keen), "Port Authority" (Nurock, Posin), "Recipes" (Collage, Huskey), "Resonances" (Henry, Duncan), "Routes" (Collage, Teirstein), "Soaring" (Schumann, Humphrey), "Solo with Two Ropes" (Collage, Croll), "Soundscapes" (Improvisation, Wetzig-Rod), "Snapshots" (Martin), "Space Test" (Collage, Duncan), "Terns in Place" (DeMarco-Fields, Alenikoff), "32 Variations in C Minor" (Beethoven, Waring), "Timewarp" (Wodynski-Schwartz, Wodynski), "Tudo" (Partch, Wodynski), "Variations on a Theme of Rudy Perez" (Watson, Miller)

PREMIERES: "Acte sans Paroles" (Beckett, Wilson), "Anthem" (Beckett, Uprichard), "Architectural Landscape" (Takemitzu, Barnes-Moore), "Bauble" (Collage, Konopacki), "A Bun in the Oven" (Bach, Hanlon), "Carl Takes a Bow" (Bernson), "Cantiquede Cantiques" (Metral, Duncan), "Chusingura" (Lee), "Counterpart" (Goodman, Meltzer), "Crossings" (Coryell, Ginsberg), "Dance" (Satie-Davis, Croll), "Deca Dance" (Weinstock-Kle-Barlow, Scott), "Dejavu" (Syntonic, Diaz), "First Base" (Thomas-Katz, Antonio), "Flung" (Emerson, Hill), "Forecast" (Lipton-Marks, Teirstein), "Gingermania" (Konopacki), "Hello from Infinity" (Schuller, Wetzig), "Hoof and Mouth" (Pawel), "House Dances" (Bernson), "An Invitation to Nausicaa" (Neugroschel, Alenikoff), "Kentucky Women" (Traditional, Bowman-Gennis), "Kernel" (Dolphin & Zinn), "Koreotronics" (Wodynski, Wodynski), "Listening to the Singing Insects" (Reisel), "Moon Passage" (Traditional-Guida-Hayman-Chaffey, Kohav), "Nightshade" (DeBoeck, Moore), "Nightwork" (Nissenbaun-Pullman, Ginsberg), "No Fur, No Hooves" (Improvisation, Pawel), "Opium Starred Night" (Carpentier-Watson-Cocteau-Fuentes, Wilson), "Over Easy" (Muldaur, Martin), "Pashun Zone: Sekter Five" (Khatchaturian, Wodynski), "Period Piece" (Bartok, Scher), "Pieces in May" (Collage, Duncan), "Pomegranate" (Coursil-Grist, Alenikoff), "Present Piece" (Improvisation-Scott-Vantieghem), "Pulse-Off" (Benson), "Rags X's Two" (Improvisation-Bowman-Gennis), "Reveiller" (Bach, Attix), "Scene on the Sand" (Carlos-Roz, Zalkind), "Scenery" (Hagen, Bowman), "Seed" (Rosenberger-Burkhardt, Cohen), "Short Stories" (Newman, Croll), "Smallhouse (quietly changing)" (Purl-Benson, Martin), "The Sphinx Suite" (Hovda-Koslin, Pawel), "Sun Air Earth Trio for One" (Boggs), "13 Minutes on an Eggtimer" (Bowman-Gennis), "Thoroughfare" (Collage, Miller), "Toejam" (Popular, Attix), "Trix" (Russell, Attix), "Water Pieces (Women's Rite)" (Jowitt)

Top Right: Ze'eva Cohen in "Countdown"
Below: Peggy Hackney in "Sun, Air, Earth Trio for One"

"Laser"

DANCE UPTOWN

Director, Janet Soares; Lighting Designer, Jennifer Herrick Jebens, Dennis Parichy; Stage Managers, Jane V. Hays, Astrid Garcia, Steve Ungar; Technical Assistants, Peter Levitan, Ruth Roberts, Martin Soloway; Sound, Mark Seiden; Technical Director, Dennis Parichy

THIRTEENTH SERIES
January 24–26, 1974
THE DAN CETRONE GALAXY DANCE COMPANY: Janis Ansley, Karen Attix, Beth Blaskey, Eva Gholson, Jeannie Hutchins, Robert Kovich, Barbara Lias, David Lusby, Sandra Neels, Victoria Uris, Dan Cetrone (Manager), Suzanne Kinder (Administrator) performing the *premiere* of "Excerpts" (Charles Madden, Sandra Neels; Costumes, Cookie Terranova)
MULTIGRAVITATIONAL GROUP: Kay Gainer, Donald Porteous, Barbara Salz, Arthur-George Murray, Suellen Epstein performing "Sure Was" (Terence Thomas, Stephanie Evanitsky)
GAY DELANGHE AND DANCERS: Alana Barter, Ellen Brown Bogart, John Cwiakala, Gay Delanghe, Robert Handler, Alvin McDuffie, Tina Mitchell, Carol Richard, Lynn Rosenfeld, Neil Shewmaker, Tom Katosic (Tapes), Jim Nugent (Juggler) performing "Limbliteral or . . . leg technology versus arm technology" (Bach, Delanghe)
January 31, February 1–2, 1974
SANDRA GENTER AND DANCERS: Hannah Kahn, Sandra Genter, Carol Hess, Yumiko Kirai, Ilze Klavins, Dalienne Majors, Deborah Marks performing "Places" (Back, Genter)
LAURA FOREMAN DANCE COMPANY: Timothy Haynes, Sybil Huskey, Judi Pasarro, Nancy Salmon, Satoru Shimazaki, Graciela Torino dancing *premiere* of "City of Angels" (Choreography, Laura Foreman; Sound, John Watts; Lighting, Cheryl Thacker; Company Manager, Donna Moore; Manager, Jane Schwartz)
ELIZABETH KEEN DANCE COMPANY: Jennifer Donohue, Patty Kozono, Dalienne Majors, Christopher Pilafian, Roger Preston Smith, and Barnard Dancers Emily Andrews, Shaw Bronner, Ann Caplan, Jessica Chao, Michelle Chase, Catherine Cowdery, Elizabeth Evans, Elain Frezza, Yoho Otani, Ruth Susser, Kobie Shaker performing *premiere* of "Seasoning" (Popular-Marilyn Rosenberger, Elizabeth Keen; Costumes, Whitney Blausen; Management, Directional Concepts)

FOURTEENTH SERIES
March 7–16, 1974
All Premieres: "Bentwood Pieces" (Beethoven, Janet Soares) danced by Carol-Rae Kraus, Matthew Diamond; "Film" (Sound Track, Erin Martin, Davidson Lloyd; Erin Martin) performed by Kei Takei, Davidson Lloyd; "Auras" (Sound Collage) choreographed and danced by Sara Pearson, Jerry Pearson; "Toe/Ball/ Heel" (Radio King and his Court of Rhythm, Carol Richard) performed by Gay Delanghe, Carol Richard, John Cwiakala

(Milton Oleaga Photo)

**Top Right: John Cwiakala, Carol Richard
in "Limbliteral" Below: "city of angels"**

Elizabeth Keen Dance Co. in "Seasoning"

Carol-rae Kraus in "Bentwood Pieces"

MISCELLANEOUS NEW YORK CITY DANCE PROGRAMS
June 1, 1973–May 31, 1974

MUSEUM OF MODERN ART SCULPTURE GARDEN
June 1–2, 1973
The Museum of Modern Art Summergarden Series (Ed Bland, Program
Director; Ken Probst, Coordinator) presents:

LAURA FOREMAN DANCE COMPANY

and Composer John Watts; Director, Laura Foreman; Company
Manager, Donna Moore; Manager, Jane D. Schwartz; Lighting,
Cheryl Thacker; Sound, Hank O'Neal; Electricians, Nancy Offen-
hauser, Radford Polinsky

COMPANY

Timothy Haynes, Sybil Huskey, Jan Neuberger, Judi Pisarro, Satoru
Shimazaki, Denise Stampone, Graciela Torino, Christine Eccleston,
Martha Eddy, Heather McKelvey, Janis Pforsich, Jessica Sayre, Bill
Callum, Hank O'Neal, Sean Singer, Christian Singer, and guest
artist Catherine Rowe

PROGRAM

"Spaces" (John Watts-Hank O'Neal, Foreman), "Signals" (Watts,
Foreman; Costumes, Alice Schwebke), "Garden Piece (Watts),
"Elegy to Chimney: In Memoriam" (Watts)

AMERICAN THEATRE LAB
June 1–3, 1973
Choreographers Theatre Associated Productions presents:

CAROLYN LORD

Choreography, Carolyn Lord; Lighting, Charles Stanley; Music,
Van Zandt Ellis; Technicians, Jenny Ball, Ted Cosbey, Bob Taylor

PROGRAM

"Dances" (Premiere) performed by Carolyn Lord, Charles Stanley,
Van Zandt Ellis

FASHION INSTITUTE THEATER
Friday, June 8, 1973
The Fashion Institute presents:

ROMANTIC BALLET REPERTORY COMPANY

Artistic Director-Choreographer, Karoly Zsedenyi; Lighting,
Kenneth Weber; Sound, Lionel White; Stage Manager, Annelis
Meyer; Company Representative, Joanne Joseph; Costumes, Pa-
tricia Montalbano; Scenery, Karl Gengenbach

COMPANY

Susanna Organek, Mark Franko, Eric Sahadi, Harvy Rochman,
Genie Joseph, Peter Karow, Anthony Riolo, George Catravas, Ste-
phan Isaacson, Robert Chipok, Douglas Gourley, Joe Bascetta,
Daniel Dibdin, Angel Betancourt, Richard de Pasquale, Elizabeth
Kim, Judy Garfinkel, Sherri Wood, DeLinda Wood, Sylvia
Palumbo, Kay Johnson, Janet Kortright, Anthony Riolo, Barbara
Donahoe, Robert Chipok, Diane Allison, Nanette Bottinelli
PROGRAM: "Coppelia" (Leo Delibes, Karoly Zsedenyi)

**Top Right: Laura Foreman, Jan Neuberger, Christian
Singer, Sean Singer, Denise Stampone in "Signals"
Below: Carolyn Lord**
(Milton Oleaga Photos)

**Susanna Organek, Mark Franko (Romantic Ballet
Repertory Co.) in "Coppelia"** (*Terry Davidowitz Photo*)

AMERICAN THEATRE LAB
June 8–10, 1973
Dance Theater Workshop and American Theatre Laboratory present:

TINA CROLL & COMPANY
NANCY TOPF with JON GIBSON

PROGRAM: "Circle Solo since 1970 including the Body is Round and other Images" structured and danced by Nancy Topf to music composed and performed by Jon Gibson; "Collage 1973 (Farm and Other Stories)" choreographed and taped by Tina Croll; danced by Barbara Ellman, Mickie Geller, John Moore, Anne Sahl, Tina Croll Lighting Designer-Stage Manager, Nicholas Wolff Lyndon

WASHINGTON SQUARE CHURCH
June 9–10, 1973

SUSAN BRODY & BETSY POLATIN

with Alison Bradford, Ann Darby, Janet Frachtenberg, Ellen Saltonstall; Stage Managers-Lighting, Leora Amdur, Alexa Penzner

PROGRAM

"Susan's Dance, Your Choice" choreographed and danced by Susan Brody; "My Head Is My Only House unless It Rains" (Captain Beefheart and the Magic Band) choreographed and danced by Alison Bradford; "Trees Change" (Wolves-Dylan-Satie-Bromberglor, Betsy Polatin) danced by Betsy Polatin, Alison Bradford, Ellen Saltonstall; "Symbiont" (Thunderstorm, Susan Brody) danced by Ann Darby, Janet Frachtenberg; "Toyland" choreographed and danced by Betsy Polatin and Susan Brody

AMERICAN THEATRE LAB
June 14–17, 1973

THEATRE DANCE COLLECTION

David Anderson, Cynthia Roberts, Rodney Griffin, Lynne Taylor, Spencer Henderson, Jaclynn Villamil, Ira Ross Cohen, Miriam Welch, Don Bonnell, Frank Pietri

PROGRAM

"Reaching" (Isaac Hayes, Frank Pietri), "Not in Your Hands" (Arnold Schoenberg, Rodney Griffin), "My Father" (Judy Collins, Jaclynn Villamil), "Ends" (Rodney Griffin), "Puppets" (Jeffrey Kresky, Rodney Griffin), "Kinetics" (Vivaldi-Dowland-Rodrigo, Lynne Taylor), "Fly with Me" (Mike Corbett-Jay Hirish, Lynne Taylor), "Cave Paintings" (Lou Harrison, Rodney Griffin), "Sounion" (Lee Holdbridge, David Anderson), "Tintype" (Gabriel Faure, Griffin), "Ancestral Voices" (Moises Vivanco, Griffin), "Dream" Blood Sweat and Tears-Satie, David Anderson), "Flowers for Departed Children" (Corbett-Ives-Crosby-Stills-Nash-Young, Lynne Taylor)

Laura Veldhuis, Patrick Hayden in "Bull King"
Top Right: Mickie Geller, John Moore in
"Short Stories" (*Eric Reiner Photo*)

CONSTRUCTION COMPANY STUDIO
June 15–18, 1973
The Construction Company Dance Studio presents:

BARBARA GARDNER

in "Pirhouettes from the Pipe of Baba Shalom," Chapter III of "The Troublesome Fables of Achmed Flee"; by and with Barbara Gardner, Tom Gardner; Lighting, Barbara Gardner, Jenny Ball; Technical Assistants, Ted Cosby, Linnea Pearson; Music, The Eureka Brass Band

THEATRE OF THE RIVERSIDE CHURCH
June 20–24, 1973
The Theatre of the Riverside Church presents:

MARY ANTHONY DANCE THEATRE

Artistic Director-Choreographer, Mary Anthony; Associate Director, Ross Parkes; Company Manager, Ray Steehler

COMPANY

Ross Parkes, Yuriko Kimura, Daniel Maloney, Ulysses Dove, Patrick Suzeau, Gwendolyn Bye, Jacqui Carroll, Muriel Cohan, Chris Gillis

REPERTOIRE

"In the Beginning" (Sculthorpe, Anthony), "Rooms" (Hopkins, Sokolow), "Inside of Him" (Havens, Parkes), "Spoon River" (Ives-Diamond, Maloney), "Adagio from 1 2 3 4 5" (Barber, Parkes), "Blood Wedding" (Mary Anthony), "Trio" (Mary Anthony) PREMIERES: Wednesday, June 20, 1973 "Power" (Earth, Wind and Fire, Daniel Maloney); Thursday, June 21, 1973 "Tides" (Vaughan Williams, Ross Parkes); Saturday, June 23, 1973 "Chamber Piece" (Albioni, Muriel Cohan)

CENTRAL PARK MALL
Thursday, June 21, 1973
The New York City Department of Cultural Affairs of the Parks Administration presents:

LAURA VELDHUIS DANCE
COMPANY

Director-Choreographer, Laura Veldhuis; Technical Consultant-Designer, Joop Veldhuis; Sculpture, Salvatore Maida

COMPANY

Howard Anthony, Lionel Cruz, Brigitta Mueller, Cindy Owens, Laura Veldhuis

PROGRAM

"A Dance to the Bull King" (Sergei Prokofiev): Minoan Legend, Sumerian Legend, Persian Legend, Egyptian Legend

Tommy Hawkins (R) and Dance Co.

ELIZABETH KEEN DANCE COMPANY

Director-Choreographer, Elizabeth Keen

COMPANY

Jennifer Donahue, Pamela Knisel, Anthony LaGiglia, Roger Pre
ton Smith, Peter Sparling, Ted Striggles, Elizabeth Keen

PROGRAM

"Enclosure Acts," "Onyx," "The Unravish'd Bride," "Dancing
Records"

ACTORS PLAYHOUSE
July 12–15, 1973*

TOMMY HAWKINS & COMPANY
in
"Circus"

No other details submitted.

* August 10–12, 17–19, 1973 the company performed "Orgazm
August 24–25, 1973, "Plaztix"

METROPOLITAN MUSEUM OF ART
Tuesday, July 31, 1973
The Metropolitan Museum of Art presents:

ROD RODGERS DANCE COMPANY

Artistic Director-Choreographer, Rod Rodgers; Administrato
Helen Cash; Stage Manager, Vaughn Lowther; Technical Coordina
tor, Leonard Buggs; Costume Mistress, Pamela Rice; Assistant 1
the Choreographer, Thomas Pinnock; Coordinator, Rhena Pinnoc

COMPANY

Rod Rodgers, Shirley Rushing, Aramide Smci, Noel Hall, Ra
Lamb

PROGRAM

"Shout!", "To Say Goodbye," "Need No Help," "Inventions
"Mudbird" choreographed and danced by Rael Lamb, "Solo Worl
in-progress" (Noel Hall)

KATHARINE ENGEL CENTER
Thursday, August 2, 1973
The Katharine Engel Center Cultural Arts Programs presents:

FESTIVE ARTS BALLET

"Peasant Pas de Deux from Giselle" (Burgmuller, Correlli)
danced by Eleanore Kingsley and Dale Black
"Thillana," "Lotus Pond," "Raghu Pati Paghava" danced by Indra-
nila
"Austurias" (Albeniz) danced by Constanza
"Voices of Spring" (J. Strauss, R. Antic) danced by Eleanore Kingsley and Dale Black

NEW YORK CITY PARKS
Monday, August 13, 1973.*
New York City Department of Cultural Affairs, and the Mayor's Urban
Task Force present:

BALLET HISPANICO OF NEW YORK

Artistic Director, Tina Ramirez; Associate Director-Ballet Master, Ramon Segarra; President, Mrs. Norman Bel Geddes; Press,
Ron Christopher

COMPANY

Sandra Rivera, Dolores Garcia, Coco Pelaez, Nancy Ticotin, Rachel
Ticotin, Alicia Roque, Maria O'Neill, Marisa O'Neill, Valerie
Contreras, Lorenzo Maldonado, Ernesto Morales, Jose Suarez

REPERTOIRE

"Haitian Suite" (Traditional, Tina Ramirez-Charles Moore-Lee
Theodore), "La Novella" (Galt MacDermot, Julie Arenal), "Quintet" (Laura Nyro, Alvin Ailey-Michele Murray), "La Boda de Luis
Alonso" (Gimenez, Paco Fernandez), "Fiesta of the Skeleton" (Sil-
verio Revuelta, Arenal), "Verdiales" (Popular, Fernandez), "Tan-
quillo" (Popular, Antonio Santaella), "Tikiti" (Solano and Ochoa,
Ramirez), "Tango" (Matos Rodriques, Lee Theodore)

* Closed Aug. 26, 1973 after 10 performances. The company also
performed at Fordham University Plaza on Sunday, August 26,
1973.

Rod Rodgers in "Shout!"
(Bill Longcore Photo)

PHILIPPINE DANCE COMPANY OF NEW YORK

Artistic Director-Choreographer, Ronnie Alejandro; Assistant Director, Jamin Alcoriza; Dance Masters, Joseph de Guzman, Maiya Barredo; Founder-Executive Director, Bruna Seril; Costume Consultant, Gang Gomez; Technical Director, Chuck Golden; Props, Carl Hilario; Company Manager, Ramon de Luna; PAF Coordinator, Bob Rottenberg; President, Cynthia Evangelista

COMPANY

Melinda Acaac, Mandy Aquino, Jamin Alcoriza, Tessis Antonio, Gloria Sambat, Fely Rebanal, Eddie Mendoza, Nardz Peji, Eddie Sese, Danielle Shepherd, Tony Sol, Sonny Zapanta, Victoria Banung, Cora Canlas, Mistica Cantos, Benny Felix, Ching Valdes, Odie Tablit, Frida Padua, Vicky Tiangco, Jojo Valdes, Rosemarie Valdes, Michael Velayo, Cesar Villanueva, Manolita Advincula

PROGRAM

"Odeliana (Spanish Dances)," "Sarimanok (Muslim Dances)," "Salidom-Ay (Tribal Dances)," "Paru-Par-ong Bukid (Rural Dances)"
PREMIERES: "Polka Filipina" (Traditional-Kasilag, Alejandro-Alcoriza), "Idaw" (Traditional-Kasilag, Alejandro), "Dalagas ng Pasig" (Traditional, Alejandro-Alcoriza), "Putong" (Traditional-Kasilag, Alejandro)

This program was presented Oct. 14, 1973 at the Museum of Natural History, and Oct. 20, 1973 at Canarsie Beach Cultural and Civic Center. On Nov. 18, 1973 the company presented the following program at the Universalist Church for the West Side Artists Series: (all choreography by Alejandro unless noted) "Sunduan" (Gonzalez, Alejandro-Alcoriza), "Timawa" (Traditional), "Tolkabal" (Traditional-Kasilag, Alejandro after Aquino), "Paypay de Manila" (Traditional-Kasilag), "Jota Cavitena" (Traditional-Kasilag), "Aliping Namamahay" (Traditional), "Malong" (Traditional), "Tarjata" (Dadap, Alejandro after Goquingco), "Kalinga Wedding Dance" (Kasilag), "Apayao Maidens" (Traditional-Kasilag, Alejandro-Alcoriza), "Anihan" (Traditional, Alejandro-Alcoriza), "Binasuan" (Traditional), "Itik-Itik" (Traditional), "Dalagas ng Pasig" (Traditional, Alejandro-Alcoriza), "Banko" (traditional), "Pandanggo sa Ilaw" (Traditional), "Subli" (Traditional), "Tinikling" (Traditional), and *premiere* of "Pagdiriwang" (Traditional-Kaslag, Alejandro). This program was presented at Fifth Avenue Presbyterian Church on Feb. 23, 1974, and St Francis Xavier High School Auditorium on May 19, 1974.

MANJU PRASAD

in "Dances of India": "Alaripu, Varnam," "Krishna ni Begana Baro," "Kathak"

MULTIGRAVITATIONAL EXPERIMENT GROUP

Director, Stephanie Evanitsky; Assistant Director, Robert Fiala; Resident Composer, Terence Thomas; Lighting Designer, Charles Dexter; Costumes, Miharu Lane

COMPANY

Suellen Epstein, Kay Gainer, Arthur-George Hurray, Donald Porteous, Barbara Salz, Bronya Wajnberg, Llewellyn Wheeler

PROGRAM

"Alien Action" (Cream, Robert Fiala), "Silver Scream Idols" (Joplin-Brown-Tape, Evanitsky-Hurray), "Sure Was" (Thomas, Evanitsky), "Splat" (Robert Fiala, Evanitsky-Fiala)

* On May 31 and June 1, 1974 the group performed "Splat," "Alien Connection," "Sure Was," and "Silver Scream Idols"
Ken Probst Photo

Multigravitational Experiment Group

Top Right: Manju Prasad (*Ken Probst Photo*)
Below: Philippine Dance Company of New York

MUSEUM OF MODERN ART
September 21–23, 1973
Summergarden Museum of Modern Art presents:

ELAINE SUMMERS DANCE AND FILM COMPANY

Director-Choreographer, Elaine Summers; Technical Director, Albert Rossi; Lighting, Howard Nelsen; Technical Assistant, Joseph Giannone, Marva Nabili, Joan Petroff; Costumes, Tony Nunzio; Press, Joan Wallace

COMPANY

Elaine Summers, Tedrian Chizik, Roberta Escamilla, Antoinette Herring, Robert Kushner, Tony Nunziata, Alexandra Ogsbury, Yoland Roeburts, Ellen Saltonstall, Nannette Sievert, Michelle Sayegh, Marilyn Wood
PROGRAM: "Energy Changes" (Carman Moore-Philip Corner, Elaine Summers)

FELT FORUM
October 4–7, 1973
Madison Square Garden Productions and Columbia Artists Festivals Corporation presents:

BAYANIHAN PHILIPPINE DANCE COMPANY

Executive Director, Leticia Perez de Guzman; Choreographer, Lucrecia Reyes Urtula; Musical Director, Lucrecia R. Kasilag; Artistic Director, Jose Lardizabal; Costume Director, Isabel A. Santos; President, Helena Z. Benitez; Press, Bill Doll, Shannon & Co., Jim Torain; Production Manager, William Mullaney; Stage Manager, Robert Roces; Series Coordinator, Jean Dalrymple

COMPANY

Lolita Adea, Melanie Bernardez, Florina Capistrano, Mary Joan Fajardo, Mary Anne Garcia, Amy Rose Lim, Victoria Lim, Patricia Lim, Zenaida Lopez, Maria Theresa Mateo, Nerissa Montecillo, Sarah Santiago, Carmencita Santos, Orlando M. Bartolome, Romeo Go, Leonicio Grajo III, Earl M. Janairo, Edgardo Lualhati, Tomas Matias, Ely D. Rogado, Fernando Jose Sison III, Rodolfo Soriano, Dennis Y. Tan, Glicerio Tecson, Roberto Tongko, Jose M. Yelo, Purificacion Yuhico

PROGRAM

"Highland Tribal," "Ecos de la Ermita," "Mindanao Tapestry," "Halinhinan-Change and Interchange," "Bayanihan"

Bayanihan Philippine Dance Co.
(*Nath Gutierrez Photo*)

THEATRE AT SAINT CLEMENT'S
October 9, 23, 30, 1973
Theatre at Saint Clement's presents:

IMPULSES COMPANY

Direction-Dance, Margaret Beals; Stage Manager-Lighting, Edward Greenberg, Carol Indianer; Management, Meg Hunnewell, H Enterprises

COMPANY

Margaret Beals, Ira Newborn (guitar), Tulsi (voice, tamboura, bells Michael Rod (saxophone, flute), Gwendolyn Watson (cello), Glen Moore (bass), Collin Walsott (sitar, tablas), Lanny Harriso (monologuist), Janaki (voice)

PROGRAM

"Set I: Dancer—Instruments," "Interludes," "Words," "Were Yo There," "You Were," "Poems"

THEATRE OF THE RIVERSIDE CHURCH
October 11–14, 1973
The Alonso Castro Dance Theatre presents a tribute to Jose Limon with

THE ALONSO CASTRO DANCE COMPANY

Artistic Director-Choreographer, Alonso Castro; Business Manager, Ina Kahn; Lighting, Sally Small; Stage Manager, Kurt Say block

COMPANY

Alonso Castro, Helen Breasted, Rickey Edmondson, Diana Fond Clifton Jones, Shirley Hardie, Israel Valle, Alexa Brill, Janice Kasn Jonathan Green, Phyllis Briley, Lucile Amato, Beverly Teague Gregg Karel, Paul Kessman, Joseph DiLorenzo, Nicole Levinson

PROGRAM

"Concerto #5" (Bach, Castro), "Bolero Clasico" (Albeniz, Castro) "Journey" (Bloch, Castro), "Gospel 125th Street" (Hawkins, Castro), "Halleluja" (Handel, Castro), "Jota de Navarre" (Albeniz Castro), "Vignettes of Carmina Burana" (Orff, Castro), "Thresh old" (Baselon, Castro), "The Catch" (Granados-Drigo, Castro) "Psalm" (Handel, Castro)

Top: Elaine Summers Dance Co.(*Ken Probst Photo*)
Below: Margaret Beals

UTAH REPERTORY DANCE THEATRE
Salt Lake City, Utah

Production Manager-Lighting Designer, M. Kay Barrell; Technical Director-Stage Manager, Gary Justesen; Costumer-Designer, Ron Hodge; Press, Edie Harrison, Ellen Bayas; Company Manager, Sherryn C. Barrell

COMPANY

Richard Ammon, Kay Clark, Bill Evans, Martin Kravitz, Gregg Lizenberry, Kathleen McClintock, Ruth Jean Post, Ron Rubey, Manzell Senters, Linda C. Smith, Karen Steele, Lynne Wimmer

REPERTOIRE

"Tin-Tall" (Misra, Evans), "Tricycle" (Roldan-Harrison, Post), "The Brood" (Henry, Kuch), "Enchantment" (Traditional, Senters) NY PREMIERES: "Women Waiting" (Luigi Nono, Kay Clark), "Within Bounds" (Terry Riley, Bill Evans), "Opus Jazz Loves Bach" (Bach, Matt Mattoz), "Snack Pack" (Traditional, Linda C. Smith), "Footprint" (Morton Feldman, Kay Clark), "Spotlight" (John Cage, Ruth Jean Post), "Five Songs in August" (Stanley B. Sussman, Bill Evans), "Five in the Morning" (Choreography, Viola Farber), and *World Premiere* of "Stationary Flying" (George Crumb, Glen Tetley).

BALLET NACIONAL DE ECUADOR

Marcelo Ordonez, Founder-Director

COMPANY:
Names not submitted

PROGRAM:
"Aricuchos," "Pase del Nino Priostes," "Danzantes," "Rondaor," "Soledad," "Saraguros," "Plenitud," "Corazas," "Arpa Sanjuanes)," "Chargras"

TRANSFORMATIONS ON A SOHO STREET

Conceived and Coordinated by Ruth Heller Coron; Musical Accompaniment, Daniel Barrahanos; Production Assistants, Judith Rymer, Roberta Escamilla

DANCERS

Karin Bacon, Richard Burke, Tedrian Chizik, Roberta Escamilla, Nelson Howe, Elaine Krautman, Bob Kushner, Connie Collier Miller, Alex Moir, Tony Nunziata, Fran Page, Patricia Usakowska
An improvisational dance and audience involvement event using the industrial discards that the streets of Soho yield, and performed in those same streets.

RONDO DANCE THEATER

Artistic Director-Choreographer, Elizabeth Rockwell; Manager, Claire Miller; Tape Correlation, John Coleman

COMPANY

Joseph Holmes, Donald Griffith, Jerry Sarnat, Evyan Williams, Hannah Kahn, Marianne Polin, Iris Salomon, Patricia Strauss

PROGRAM

"Adventures in the Atmosphere of Space: Water, Earth, Air," "Inward Journey: Laughing, Quieting, Playing, Idling, Suffering, Rebelling, Grouping, Hiding, Escaping"

BARBARA GARDNER

in "Celebration" as told by Barbara Gardner; Chapter IV of "The Troublesome Fables of Achmed Flee"; Technical Assistants, Carolyn Lord, Nancy Golladay, Jenny Ball, Ted Cosbey.

Rondo Dance Theater Above: Barbara Gardner in "Sophie's Hideaway"(*Bruce Fields Photo*)

Top: Utah Repertory Dance Theatre in "Stationary Flying" Below: Ballet Nacional de Ecuador

GRAMERCY ARTS THEATRE
October 29–31, 1973
The Spanish Theatre Repertory Company (Gilberto Zaldivar, Producer), by arrangement with the Cultural Counsellor of Mexico in New York presents:

PILAR RIOJA

with Antonio de Cordoba (Singer), Simon Garcia (Guitarist), Poems of Antonio Machado read by Luis Ruis and Isabel Segovia; Lighting, Leonard Simoncek; Production Assistant, Harlan Villegas; Rene Buch, Artistic Director; Associate Producer, Robert Federico

PROGRAM

"Allegro assai" (Bach), "Folia" (Corelli), "Moto Perpeuto" (Paganini), "Grave Assai y Fandango" (Boccherini), "El Cafe de Chinitas" (Garcia Lorca), "El Vito" (Nin), "Sevillanas del siglo XVIII" (Garcia Lorca), "Lorquiana," "Anda jaleo" (Garcia Lorca), "Tangos del Piyayo" (Anonimo), "Baladilla de los Tres Rios," "Farruca" (Anonimo), "Siguiriya" (Anonimo)

FELT FORUM
October 30–November 11, 1973
Madison Square Garden Productions and Mel Howard Productions present:

YUGOSLAVIAN NATIONAL FOLK ENSEMBLE
Ivo Lola Ribar

Artistic Director-Choreographer, Vladeta Vlahovic; Managing Director, Milenko Vujovic; Artistic Director for this production, Konstantin Simonovitch; Choreographer for this production, Bratislav Grbic; Composer, Sndjan Baric; Administrator, Djondje Kastel; Conductor, Milutin Popovic; American Production Manager, Peter Schneider; Lighting Supervisor, William Mintzer; Series Coordinator, Jean Dalrymple

PROGRAM

FRESKA VIVA: "Skromasi," "Vrlicko Kolo," "Zenska Makedonska Igra," "Rusalije," "Dodole," "Oro," "Koleda," "Povrateskoto," "Eeskoto," and "Serbian Dances," "Albanian Dances," "Komita Dances," "Dances from Slavonia," "Dances from Vranje," "Vlaske Igre," "Sopske Igre," "Vrlicka Igra," "Osogovka"

Company Manager: Virginia Snow
Press: Jim Torain, Thomas Rodgers

PLAYERS WORKSHOP
November 5–6, 1973

ROLANDO JORIF DANCE COMPANY

Artistic Director-Choreographer, Rolando Jorif

COMPANY

Rolando Jorif, David Lee, Janis Roswick, Joan Doberman, Clar Johnson

PROGRAM

"Hanging Gardens," "Blue," "Glass"

DONNELL LIBRARY CENTER AUDITORIUM
November 7 & 10, 1973
The Donnell Library Center presents:

LEONARD FOWLER TRIO

Artistic Director-Choreographer, Leonard W. Fowler

Kevin Alen
Gail Judith Allen
Irene Buchinskas

PROGRAM: "Jazz Poem" (Coltrane), "Poupees" (Francaix), "KI (Avshalomov), "The Dream" (Rachmaninoff), "Canciones (Halffter), "Easy Does It" (Slade)

LOEB STUDENT CENTER
Friday, November 9, 1973
The Daniel Nagrin Theatre and Film Dance Foundation present:

THE WORKGROUP

Director-Choreographer, Daniel Nagrin; Lighting, Gary Harris Press, Leora Amdur

COMPANY

Lee Connor, Ara Fitzgerald, Alain Lerazer, Lorn Macdougal, Daniel Nagrin, Mary Anne Smith

PROGRAM

Premiere of "Hello Farewell Hello" (C. S. Hayward-Martha Siegel Daniel Nagrin; Lighting, Gary Harris)

Gail Judith Allen, Kevin Alen, Irene Buchinskas in "KI"
(*Leonard Fowler Photo*)
Top Right: Pilar Rioja

November 9–11, 1973
Dance Theater Workshop presents:

DECA DANCE

Concept and Direction, Judith Scott; Production, John Kle, Bart Barlow; Art Director, Suki Dewey; Costumes, Fa Ching Chu, Judith Scott, Suki Dewey; Lighting, John Kle, Bart Barlow; Musical Directors, Peter Weinstock, Phil Lowe

COMPANY

Judith Scott
Fa Ching Chu
Fred Patton

AMERICAN THEATRE LAB
November 9–11, 1973
The Black Cat presents:

THOMAS HOLT DANCERS

Lighting, Joanna Schielke; Sound, Kim Ptak; Stage Managers, Debbie Lepaye, Rhonda Zhawm

COMPANY

Thomas Holt, Irene Belk, Laurie Kane, Denise Mitchell, Paulette Taylor, Aletha Winter, Stephanie Eley, Karen Sing, Phillip Tietz, Gary McKay, Cindy Gehrke, June Panagakos, Peter Karrow, Evelyn Shepard

REPERTOIRE

"Broom Suite Opus I" (Bach, Holt), "Goblins on Parade" (Selected, Holt), ". . . . and in the Night" (Bartok, Elizabeth Brotman), "The Last Supper" (Selected, Holt; Tap, Cindy Gehrke), "The Conception of the Nativity" (Handel, Holt), "Children's Corner" (Debussy, Stephanie Eley), "Arienata" (Vivaldi, Holt), "Afterhours in Wonderland" (Jefferson Airplane-Pfeiffer-Hiller, Holt), "Este a Szekeyeknel" (Bartok, Joenine Roberts), "Duet for Summer" (Holdridge, Holt)

Thomas Holt Dancers (Betsy Baron, Thomas Holt, Lucinda Gehrke) in "Afterhours in Wonderland"

THE SPACE
November 10–11, 1973
Louis-Nikolais Dance Theatre Lab presents:

BRUCE KING DANCE CONCERT

with
Emily Wadhams
Barbara Kravitz
Dale Townsend

Director-Choreographer, Bruce King; Stage Manager, William Marshall; Lighting Technician, Gen Barry Casey; Management, Keynote Lecture Bureau; Production Coordinator, Ruth Grauert; Costumes, Alfred Pounders

PROGRAM

"Omens and Departures" (Edgar Varese), "Rondo toward Death" (Pierre Boulez), "Themes" (Edgar Varese), "Ghosts" (Anton Webern), "Bamboo" (Lou Harrison), "Echoes" (Pierre Boulez), "Walk in Splendor" (Alan Hovhaness), "Vigil" (Charles Ives), "After Guernica" (Morris Knight)

EXCHANGE THEATRE
November 13–14, 1973
Circum-Arts Foundation presents:

GALE ORMISTON DANCE COMPANY

Director-Choreographer-Costume Designer, Gale Ormiston; Lighting Designer, Jon Garness; Stage Managers, Jon Garness, William Campbell; Technical Assistant, Frank Salmonese

COMPANY

Richard Biles, Amy Ernlund, Susan Lundberg, Jeffrey Maer, Janet Markovitz, Joanna Mendl Shaw, Irene Soler, Sturge Warner, Luise Wykell

PROGRAM

"Acescents," "Convergence" (Xenakis), "RePlay" (Roldan-Cowell), "Take 3" (New Vaudeville Band-Slugger Ryan), "ODDyssey" (Collage)

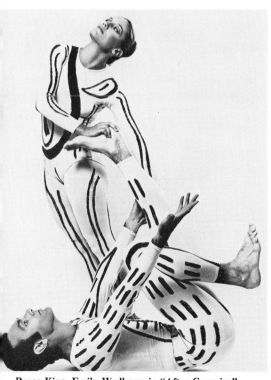

Bruce King, Emily Wadhams in "After Guernica"
(*Jack Mitchell Photo*)

CARNEGIE HALL
November 21–22, 1973

The Carnegie Hall Coporation by arrangement with the New York Department of Cultural Affairs presents:

KATHAKALI: KERALA KALAMANDALAM COMPANY OF INDIA

Troup Leader, Induchudan; Business Manager, Gopalan; Company Manager, Graeme Vanderstoel; Management, Kazuko Hillyer International

COMPANY

Vasudevan Nair, Vasunni, Vijayan, Ramachandran, Haridasan, Rajasekharan, Padmanabhan Nair, Unnithan, Parameswaran, Ramankutty Nair, Gopi

PROGRAM: "Mahabharata," "Ramayana"

FASHION INSTITUTE OF TECHNOLOGY
November 23–25, 1973

The Fashion Institute of Technology presents:

ROD RODGERS DANCE COMPANY

Artistic Director-Choreographer, Rod Rodgers; Administrator, Helen Cash; Press, Anita Saewitz; Lighting, Shirley Prendergast; Stage Manager, Vaughn Lowther; Technical Coordinator, Leonard Buggs; Costume Mistress, Pamela Rice; Assistant to the Choreographer, Thomas Pinnock; School Coordinator, Rhema Pinnock

COMPANY

Rod Rodgers, Ellen Robbins, Barbara Roan, Shirley Rushing, Thomas Pinnock, Lillie Andrews, Aramide Smci, Noel Hall, Rael Lamb, Bonita Jackson, Ronald Pratt

REPERTOIRE

"Dances in Projected Space" (Gwendolyn Watson), "Sweet Blues" (Aretha Franklin, Noel Hall), "Tangents:" (L. Harrison-H. Cowell), "Box" (Sydney Smart), "Rhythm Ritual" (Percussion), "Inventions," "Mudbird" (Gursten Kingsley, Rael Lamb), "Percussion Suite," and *World Premiere* of "Vuca" (Woody B. Vasulka, Rod Rodgers; Costumes, Pamela Rice; Set, B. Fuller, Anguss Moss)

Rod Rodgers Dance Company in "Box"
(*Bill Hilton Photo*)

WASHINGTON SQUARE METHODIST CHURCH
November 28–30, December 1–2, 1973

The Washington Square Methodist Church presents:

ROBERT STREICHER DANCE COMPANY

Artistic Director-Choreographer, Robert Streicher; Music Director, Rhys Chatham; Lighting, Angus Moss; Sound, David Andrews; Production Assistant, Joanne Joseph; Press, Michael Groob

PROGRAM

"The Ecstasy of Saint Theresa" conceived and choreographed by Robert Streicher; Suggested by Bernini's sculpture; Music, Rhys Chatham, Monteverdi, Chopin, Lully, Mouret, Stravinsky, Couperin; with David Kolatch, Carolyn Lord, Robert Streicher, Andrea Cottrell, Larry Browne, Sally Bowden, Michael Arian, Scott Caywood, Joe Bascetta, P. J. Tome, Deva Kabat

PUBLIC SCHOOL 41
Thursday, November 29, 1973*

The Board of Education of the City of New York, Office of Continuing Education presents:

LAURA VELDHUIS DANCE COMPANY

Artistic Director-Choreographer, Laura Veldhuis; Technical Director-Designer, Joop Veldhuis; Lighting Designer, Harry Wildfeuer

COMPANY

Ellen Ashcraft, Patrick Hayden, Brigitta Mueller, Cindy Owens, Henry Smith, Laura Veldhuis

PROGRAM

"Bull King" (Prokofiev, Veldhuis), "Walk Softly" (Kenton), "Untitled" (Britten), "Earth, Fire, Water" (Akira Miyoshi)

* Program was presented again on Feb. 6, 1974 with the addition of a premiere "The Story of Daniel" (Twentieth Century, Veldhuis; Poetry, W. H. Auden)

Robert Streicher Dance Co. in "The Ecstasy of St. Theresa"
(*Allen Liffman Photo*)

THERESA L. KAUFMANN CONCERT HALL
Thursday, November 29, 1973

BALLET OF CONTEMPORARY ART

Director, Keith Lee; Artistic Director, Donald Saddler; Rehearsal Assistant, Juan Antonio; Choreographers, Keith Lee, Buddy Balough; Guest Choreographers, Bill Carter, Steven-Jan Hoff, Lar Lubovitch; Lighting, Robert Holland; Music, Charles Cecil; Dance Notation, Joan Ingalls; Stage Production, Truman Kelley; Press, Charles France; General Administrator, Charles G. Cecil; General Manager, Joan Ingalls

COMPANY

Buddy Balough, Emmanuelle Davis, Glen Ferrugiari, Ingrid Fraley, Kenneth Hughes, Lisa Johnson, Elaine Kudo, Keith Lee, Dennis Marshall, Jacquelin Marshall, Steven Mones, Robin Priess, Cathryn Rhodes, Jacqueline Smith, Pat Wesche
GUEST ARTISTS: Gary Chryst, Alaine Haubert, Bonnie Mathis

PROGRAM

"The Moor's Pavane" (Henry Purcell, Jose Limon; Costumes, Pauline Lawrence, Charles Tomlinson; Lighting, Jean Rosenthal), "Us" (Gustav Mahler, Keith Lee; Costumes, Marcos Paredes; Lighting, Stephan Hoff), "Times Past" (Cole Porter-Scott Joplin, Keith Lee; Costumes, Marcos Paredes; Lighting, Stephan Hoff), *World Premiere* of "Our Saving Grace" (Stockhausen-Yuize-Sounds, Keith Lee; Costumes, Marcos Paredes; Lighting, Stephan Hoff)

INTERNATIONAL HOUSE
Friday, November 30, 1973
Volunteers in Service for Education in India presents:

SUDHA RAMESH

performing classical dances in Bharatha Natyam, Kuchipudi, and Odissi styles.

HUNTER COLLEGE PLAYHOUSE
Saturday, December 1, 1973
Trimurti presents:

MAYA KULKARNI
JANAK KHENDRY

in a Bharata Natyam recital; Choreography, Janak Khendry, Maya Kulkarni; Music, Suresh Shukla; Adviser, R. S. Perinbanayagam; Vocals, Madau Bhatki; Musicians, Suresh Shukla, Gumati Sunderam, Kathleen, Ramand Raghauan

PROGRAM

"Allaripu," "Padam: Krishna Nee Begne Baro, Mata Kali Kali, and Ramonan," "Jathiswaram." "Varnam," "Tillana," and "The Dance of Siva"

HUNTER COLLEGE PLAYHOUSE
December 1–2, 1973
The Department of Theatre and Cinema of Hunter College presents:

GOVINDA & RATILEKHA
in
Sacred Dances of India

with Guest Artist Vishakha; Narrator, Swati Desai; Lighting Director, Leonard Suib; Sound, Beth Heller; Press, Anita Volland

PROGRAM

"Mangalam Charan," "Batu Nritya," "Alarippu," "Jatisvaram," "Shabdam: Sarasijakshulu," "Kalyan Pallavi," "Abhinaya," "Dasavatar," "Kirtanam: Natanam Adinar, Bhukhana Bhujanga," "Javali: Tarumaru," "Tillana"

CARNEGIE HALL
Monday, December 3, 1973
The Performing Arts Program of the Asia Society in association with Carnegie Hall Corporation and NYC Department of Cultural Affairs presents:

SUZUSHI HANAYAGI

dancing "Yuki (Snow)," "Kyo no Shiki," "Urashima," "Manzai"

Govinda and Ratilekha
Top Right: Ballet of Contemporary Art
(*Bil Leidersdorf Photo*)

INDRA-NILA DANCES

"Shiva Slokam," "Ananda Natanam," "Allarrippu," "Natanam Adinar," "Juggat Janani," "Lasya Nritta," "Suddha Paityakaran," "Gowri Kalyanam," "Maha Ganapati," "Kartikeya," "Kurathy," "Thillana," "Lotus Pond," "Mayura," "Raghu Pati Raghava"

* Program was presented Saturday, Feb. 16, 1974 at Wagner College.

FELT FORUM
December 4–9, 1973
Madison Square Garden Productions and Mel Howard Productions present:

NATIONAL FOLK ENSEMBLE OF PAKISTAN

Director, Zia Mohyeddin; Resident Composer, Sohail Rana; Choreographers, Raffi Anwar, Nazir Ahmed, Ghulam Shabbir, Khursheed Haleem; Costume Director, Shamin Abdulsattar; Production Manager, Ahmed Hussain; Stage Director, Wagar Ullah Qureshi; Press, Thomas Rodgers, Jim Torain; American Company Manager, Virginia Snow; Tour Coordinator, Don Harrington

COMPANY

Naheed Siddiqui, Amin Qasim, Raffi Anwar, Sahira Shahjehan, Saelha Begum Shelly, Nargis Akhtar, Suraiya Moosa, Sehr Siddiqui, Rehana Hakim, Pervaiz Kamal, Zarka Chaudhury, Salma Fareena, Mariam Hussain, Shireen Hussain, Rukhsana Ahmed, Nazir Ahmed, Pervaiz Butt, Mohammed Jamal, Ali Ahmed, Hasan Qaiser, Mohammed Shams, Ghulam Shabbir, Dilawar Hussian, folk singer Faiz Mohammed Balooch, and 12 musicians

PROGRAM

"Sindhi Jhoomer" (Sheela, Anwar), "The Fisherman" (Sheela, Anwar), "Leva" (Rana, Ahmed), "Jaltrango Solo," "The Cotton Pickers" (Sheela, Ahmed), "The Peddler" (Joseph-Zafer, Ahmed), "Folk Songs," "Bhangra" (Khan, Anwar), "Khattak" (Rana, Ahmed), "Sitar Solo," "The Harvest" (Khan, Anwar), "Flute Solo," "Kafiristan" (Khan, Anwar), "Kathak" (Sheela, Ahmed), Finale (Rana, Anwar)

Indra-nila

CONSTRUCTION COMPANY STUDIO
December 7–8, 1973
The Construction Company Dance Studio presents:

JUST A GLIMPSE

Choreographed by Barbara Clay; Segments, Lucina Kathmann Cathy Heinrich; Lighting, Ted Wolffe; Music, Daniel Carter

COMPANY

Tom Holt, Barbara Clay, Melissa Matterson, Lucina Kathmann Cathy Heinrich, Martha Murphy, Bob Taylor

HUDSON GUILD THEATRE
December 7–8, 1973
The Hudson Guild Theatre presents:

EUGENE JAMES DANCE COMPANY

Director-Choreographer, Eugene James; Assistant Choreographer, Larl Becham; Lighting, Leonid Levine; Costumes, Peterson/ Gilbert

COMPANY

Eugene James, Lucinda Ransom, Johnn Harris, Loretta Durham, June Segal, Philip Stamps, Lois Hayes, Esther Pullian, Marcia Dixon, Andre Robinson, and Guest Artists: Larl Becham, Kalua Dundde, Scat Wilson Musicians

PROGRAM

"Lagniappe" (Hayes-Legrand-White-Garner), "The Faces of Jazz" (Barker, Liz Williamson), "Drums at Dawn" (Folk), "Blues, Saturday Night" (Hawkins), "Color of Tears" (Ortolani), "Carnival Sketches" (Folk-Jobin)

Eugene James, Lucinda Ransom
in "Carnival Sketches"
(Jack Mitchell Photo)

EISNER-LUBIN AUDITORIUM
December 8 & 14, 1973*
The Loeb Student Center presents:

LAURA DEAN AND DANCE COMPANY

Director-Choreographer, Laura Dean

COMPANY

Janis Beaver, Barbara Chenven, Beverly Crook, Laura Dean, Marcos Dinnerstein, Andrew Floud, Dakota Jackson, Diane Johnson, Pamela Kekich, Pedro Lujan, Edward Marsan, Lee Wasserwald, Kathleen Weir, Linda Werner, Tim Ferchen

PROGRAM

"Stamping Dance," "Circle Dance," "Jumping Dance," "Changing Pattern Steady Pulse"

* on April 12 & 13, 1974 Miss Dean and company presented two new works: "Spinning Dance," and "Response Dance"

EXCHANGE THEATRE
December 13–14, 1973

JAN WODYNSKI DANCE COMPANY

Choreography and Costumes, Jan Wodynski; Technical Director-Sound, Mike Wodynski; Technician, Rich Tsukada

COMPANY

Kathy Eaton, Joanne Edelmann, Robert Kosinski, Julie Maloney, David Monroe, Madaleine Perrone, Dale Townsend, Paul Wilson, Jan Wodynski, Mike Wodynski

PROGRAM

"Pashun Zone: Sekter Five" (Khatchaturian), "Tudo (for Charles)" (Partch), "Farrago (Structured improvisation)." "Koreotroniks" (Sound Tubes)

**Top Right: Laura Dean Dance Company
in "Changing Pattern Steady Pulse"** (*Phillip Jones Photo*)
**Below: Jan Wodynski Dance Company
in "Farrago"**(*Mike Wodynski Photo*)

NYU BOBST LIBRARY
Friday, December 14, 1973
NYU School of Education presents:

GUS SOLOMONS JR./DANCE
and
STEVE SUNSHINE

(No other details available)

ST. PAUL THE APOSTLE CHURCH
December 14–16, 1973
The Dance Department of Fordham University presents:

THE UNICORN, THE GORGON AND THE MANTICORE

Music by Gian-Carlo Menotti; Staged by Marian Horosko; Danced by Marian Horosko, Eric Concklin, and students of Fordham Dance Department

330 BROOME STREET
December 14–16, 28–30, 1973*

CLIFF KEUTER DANCE COMPANY

Artistic Director-Choreographer, Cliff Keuter; Musical Director, John Herbert McDowell; Lighting Designer, Nicholas Wolff Lyndon; Costumes, Karla Wolfangle, John Dagger; Manager, Allan Kifferstein; Management, Directional Concepts

COMPANY

Joan Finkelstein, Ellen Jacob, Ellen Kogan, Elina Mooney, Karla Wolfangle, Christopher Beck, Bill DeYoung, Toby Towson, Cliff Keuter

PROGRAM

Premieres of: "Musique de Taverni" (Couperin), "Unusual in Our Time" (McDowell-Woody), "Visit" (Hellerman), "Plaisirs d'Amour" (Smoliar)
* Program repeated Feb. 20, 1974 at Hunter College Playhouse.

**Cliff Keuter, Karla Wolfangle
in "Plaisirs d'Amour"**

MARYMOUNT MANHATTAN COLLEGE
December 16–18, 1973
Marymount Manhattan College presents:

RUDY PEREZ DANCE
THEATRE/DANCE POOL

Director-Choreographer-Sound, Rudy Perez; Stage Manager-Lighting Design, Chip Largman; Assistant to Mr. Perez, David Varney; Technical Assistants, Warren Backer, Jerome Johnson, Guy Woertendyki; Audio Construction, John Moore

COMPANY

David Varney, Diann Sichel, Laurie McKirahan, Ruedi Brack, Steve Witt, Rudy Perez

PROGRAM

"Excerpts from Quadrangle," *NY premiere* of "Asparagus Beach," *world premiere* of "Running Board for a Narrative," *NY premiere* of "Walla Walla" (an addition to Quadrangle)
April 12–14, 1971 "Movement Experience Workshop," and *premieres* of "Quadrangle," and "District One" with dancers John Moore, Ann Sahl, Diann Sichel, David Varney

CONSTRUCTION COMPANY STUDIO
December 22–24, 29–30, 1973
Choreographers Theatre Associate Productions presents:

SALLY BOWDEN

Choreography, Sally Bowden; Lighting, Jenny Ball; Sound, Linnea Peasson; Technical Assistants, Carolyn Lord, Ted Cosberg; Coordinator, Jane D. Schwartz

PROGRAM

"The Ice Palace" (Tchaikovsky, Bowden) performed by Sally Bowden with Linda Eskenas as story teller

CHURCH OF ST. PAUL THE APOSTLE
Monday, December 24, 1973
The Broadway United Church of Christ presents:

MARY ANTHONY DANCE THEATRE

Artistic Director-Choreographer, Mary Anthony; Associate Director, Ross Parkes; Lighting, Thomas Munn; Costumes, Leor C. Warner; Stage Manager, Barbara Rosoff; Company Manager, Ray Steehler

COMPANY

Michael Bruce, Gwendolyn Bye, David Chase, Muriel Cohan, Linda Hayes, Yuriko Kimura, Daniel Maloney, Mary Price, Pat Thomas, Esteban Toscano, with the Broadway United Church of Christ Choir (Walter Klauss, Conductor), and Susan Jolles (Harpist)

PROGRAM

"A Ceremony of Carols" (Benjamin Britten, Mary Anthony)

THE SPACE
January 11–13, 1974
Louis-Nikolais Dance Theatre Lab of Chimera Foundation for Dance presents:

DON REDLICH DANCE COMPANY

Artistic Director-Choreographer, Don Redlich; Costumes, Margaret Tobin, Sally Ann Parsons; Masks, Ralph Lee; Lighting, Jennifer Tipton, Nicholas Wolff Lyndon; Stage Manager, Nicholas Wolff Lyndon; Technical Assistants, Joan Finkelstein, Nancy Offenhauser, Jean Iglesias; Production Coordinator, Ruth Grauert; Management, Sheldon Soffer

COMPANY

Don Redlich, Irene Feigenheimer, Wanda Pruska, Barbara Roan, Billy Siegenfeld

PROGRAM

"Earthling" (Debussy), "Estrange," "Harold" (Arranged), "Opero" (John Herbert McDowell), and *premieres* of "Patina" (Besard-Caroso-Galilei-Gianoncelli), "Three Bagatelles" (Lukas Foss)

Rudy Perez in "Running Board for a Narrative"
(Robert Alexander Photo)

**Mary Anthony Dance Theatre in
"A Ceremony of Carols"**(*Ellen Tittler Photo*)

Don Redlich Dance Company in "Patina"

AMERICAN THEATRE LAB
January 18–19, 1974*

MUTUAL RESPECT
DANCES BY BEN DOLPIN

Choreography, Ben Dolphin; Lighting, Ruis Woertendyke, Bill Megalos; Stage Manager, Debra M. Naeme; Pianists, Julie Dolphin, Terry Dolphin; Vocalist, Nora Guthrie; Drums, Manuel Gerena; Song "Shall I," Art, Sculpture, Jewelry by Josephy Dolphin

COMPANY

Julie Dolphin, Ben Dolphin, Nora Guthrie, Saudia Young, Ted Rotante, Rael Lamb, Ruedi Brack, Terry Dolpin, Joseph Dolphin, Christel Wallin, March Keelen, Manuel Gerena

PROGRAM: "Right Arm" (Collage, Ben Dolphin), "I Got Plenty of Nuttin" (George Gershwin, Ben Dolphin)

* Repeated on Saturday, Feb. 2, 1974 at Ornette Coleman's Artist's House.

Ben Dolphin and Company in "I Got Plenty of Nuttin' "
(*Johan Elbers Photo*)

WASHINGTON SQUARE CHURCH
January 25–26, 1974

SUSAN BRODY & FRIENDS

Lighting, Steve Zalph; Costumes, Ann Darby, Ellen Saltonstall; Coaching, Francis Cott; Technical Assistant, Jim Moss; Percussion, Eleanor Gilbert; Harmonica, Ed Silberman

COMPANY

Susan Brody, Alison Bradford, Pat Catterson, Ann Darby, Janet Frachtenberg, Ellen Likwornik, Ellen Saltonstall

PROGRAM: "Dances for You"

CUNNINGHAM STUDIO AT WESTBETH
February 9–10, 1974

MERCE CUNNINGHAM & DANCE
COMPANY

Director-Choreographer, Merce Cunningham; Lighting, Nancy Golladay; Music Coordinator, David Behrman; Administration, Erika Bro, Scott Hatley, Martha Lohmeyer, Gail Notarmuzi, Jean Rigg; Stage Managers, Charles Atlas, Nancy Golladay

PROGRAM

"Events Number 83 and 84" (sections from Mr. Cunningham's "TV Rerun," "Changing Steps," and "Loops"; Music, "Clockwork Video" by Yasunao Tone) performed without intermission

Merce Cunningham Dance Company in "Event #84"

WAGNER COLLEGE
Wednesday, February 13, 1974
The Board of Social and Cultural Affairs presents:

ELIZABETH KEEN DANCE COMPANY

Director-Choreographer, Elizabeth Keen; Lighting Design, Edward M. Greenberg; Management, Directional Concepts

COMPANY

Elizabeth Keen, Bill Cratty, Jennifer Donohue, Patty Kozono, Dadienne Majors, Christopher Pilafian, Roger Preston Smith, Michael Steele

PROGRAM

"Seasoning" (Marilyn Rosenberger), "Enclosure Acts" (Marilyn Rosenberger), "The Unravish'd Bride" (Schubert), "Poison Variations" (Gwendolyn Watson-Joel Press)

**Elizabeth Keen Dance Company
in "Poison Variations"**

RUDY PEREZ DANCE THEATER

Director-Choreographer-Sound Collage, Rudy Perez; Technical Supervisor, Al Wagner; Coordinator, Jane E. Gardner; Management, Directional Concepts

COMPANY

Laurie McKirahan, David Varney, Steve Witt, Rudy Perez, and the Dance Pool: Lauren Dong, Jane Sue Hoffner, David Koch, Carolyn Rosenfeld, George Titus

PROGRAM

"Asparagus Beach," "Quadrangle," "Running Board for a Narrative," "Movement Experience for the Audience"

Rudy Perez Dance Theater in "Quandrangle"
(*Robert Alexander Photo*)

JOAN MILLER AND THE CHAMBER ARTS/DANCE PLAYERS

Artistic Director-Choreographer, Joan Miller; Lighting Designer, Robert Engstrom; Executive Director, Carol Indianer; Managing Director, Naomi Rhoads; Press, Olive Johns; Resident Composer, Gwendolyn Watson

COMPANY

Milton Bowser, Joan Miller, William R. Munroe, Wanda Ward, Peter Woodin, Sawako Yoshida, and musicians Gwendolyn Watson, Carole Weber, William R. Munroe
GUEST ARTISTS: Chuck Davis, Jackie Earley

PROGRAM

"Improvisations on a Theme by Rudy Perez," "Blackout," "PLUS or minus" (Watson), "Pass Fe White" (Watson), "Soundscape," "Mix" (Staples-Coffee-Preston)

**Joan Miller Chamber Arts/Dance Players
in "Improvisation on a Theme by Rudy Perez"**

BALLET OF THE XX CENTURY

Artistic Director-Choreographer, Maurice Bejart; Administrator, Anne Lotsy; Assistant Artistic Director, Jorg Lanner; Ballet Masters, Pierre Dobrievich, Jorg Lanner; Stage Managers, Marie Deville, Guy Brasseur; Lighting, John Vanderheyden; Sound, Mesias Maiguasha, Alain Cantillana; Wardrobe Mistress, Michele Noel; Stage Director-Tour Coordinator, John Capp; U.S. Management, Mel Howard Productions

COMPANY

Hitomi Asakawa, Jorge Donn, Niklas Ek, Dyane Gray-Cullert, Jorg Lanner, Jean-Marie Limon, Daniel Lommel, Dwight Hughes, Bertrand Pie, Monet Robier, Catherine Verneuil, Angele Albrecht, Andrzej Ziemski, and the Collegium Vocale Cologne (Wolfgang Fromme, Director)

PROGRAM

"Stimmung" with Music by Karlheinz Stockhausen; Choreography, Maurice Bejart; Scenic Design, Roger Bernard; Costumes, Joelle Roustan

**Ballet of the XXth Century
in "Stimmung"**

THERESA L. KAUFMANN CONCERT HALL
Saturday, February 16, 1974

HAVA KOHAV AND DANCE COMPANY

Director-Choreographer, Hava Kohan; Costumes, Hava Kohav, Joan Sellers, Lavinia Nielsen, Salvatore Guida, F. W. Chaffey; Stage and Lighting Design, F. W. Hayman-Chaffey; Technical Assistants, Diane Smith, Bruce Monroe, Bruce Martin

COMPANY

Hava Kohav, Diane Quitko, Bruce Block, Ilona Copen, Errol P. Merghart, Lucie Signa, Maggy Gorrill, Nadine Revene

REPERTOIRE

"A Dance" (Scarlatt-Purcell), "Mist" (Horn), "Moments" (Alpert-Standen), "Garden White" (Watson-Reich-Alpert), and *premiere* of "Moon Passage" (15th Century and later)

Hava Kohav and Dance Company
in "Moon Passage"
(*Johan Elbers Photo*)

EISNER-LUBIN AUDITORIUM
March 11–13, 1974
The Loeb Program Office presents:

KATHRYN POSIN DANCE COMPANY

Artistic Director-Choreographer, Kathryn Posin; Musical Director, Kirk Nurock; Lighting Design, Edward I. Byers; Stage Manager, Ro Cunningham; Management, Directional Concepts; Sound, Gary Harris, Technical Assistant, Rick Munroe

COMPANY

Karen Attix, John Cwiakala, Jennifer Douglas, Jim May, Rosalind Newman, Kathryn Posin, Lance Westergard

PROGRAM

"Days" (Kirk Nurock, Posin), "Bach Pieces" (Bach, Posin), and *premieres* of "Nuclear Energy" (Kirk Nurock, Posin), and "Children of the Atomic Age" (John McLaughlin and the Mahavishnu Orchestra, Kathryn Posin)

Right: John Cwikala, Kathryn Posin,
Lance Westergard in "Nuclear Energy"
(*Johan Elbers Photo*)

THEATRE OF THE RIVERSIDE CHURCH
March 14–17, 1974
The Theatre of the Riverside Church presents:

RONDO DANCE THEATRE

Artistic Director-Choreographer, Elizabeth Rockwell; Chairman, Donald H. Miller, Jr.; Lighting, Dick Abrams, Beth Zakar, Lee Goldman; Sound, Ralph Salomon; Manager, Claire Miller

COMPANY

Donald Griffith, Joseph Holmes, Kathryn Johnson, Hannah Kahn, Henry Kamerman, Milton Myers, Iris Salomon, Patrician Strauss, Catherine Sullivan

PROGRAM

"The Last Unicorn" (Jolivet, Elizabeth Rockwell), "Solo from Lyric Suite" (Berg, Anna Sokolow), "Holy Moses" (Milton Myers), "Take Five" (Desmond, Rockwell), "Palomas" (Oliveros, Manuel Alum), "The Interloper" (Hancock, Fred Benjamin), "Ode?" (Collage, Donald Griffith), "Afro Improvisation" (Joseph Holmes), "Apache" (Jones, LeVon Campbell)

Rondo Dance Theatre
in "Palomas"

GRAMERCY ARTS THEATRE

Monday, March 18, 1974*

The Spanish Theatre Repertory Company (Gilberto Zaldivar, Producer) presents:

ARGENTINE FOLK DANCE COMPANY

Directors, Alejandro Dondines, Luis Leal; Costumes, Juana Sandoval; Lighting, Russell Krum

COMPANY

Alejandra Dondines, Luis Leal, Oscar Benvenuto, Jr., Carmen Carrillo, Claudio Carvajal, Mercedes Carvajal, Esmeralda Hidalgo, Odilia Parodi, Guzman Parodi, June Philips, Ricardo Rodriguez, and guitarists Oscar Benvenuto, Eduardo Echeverria, drummer Oscar Benvenuto, Jr.

PROGRAM

"Procesion y Ofrenda," "Sombrerito," "Bailecito," "Cuequita," "Carnavalito," "Gato," "Zamba," "Sereno," "Tunante," "Arunguita," "Malambo," "El Casamiento"

* Repeated Mar. 25, Apr. 4, 15, 18, 1974 (5 performances)

Alejandra Dondines

NYU SCHOOL OF EDUCATION AUDITORIUM

Thursday, March 21, 1974*

Dance Programs of the division of creative arts of NYU's School of Education presents:

MARY ANTHONY DANCE THEATRE

Artistic Director-Choreographer, Mary Anthony; Associate Director, Ross Parkes; Lighting, Thomas Munn; Costumes, Leor C Warner; Stage Manager, Barbara Rosoff; Company Manager, Ra Steehler

COMPANY

Ross Parkes, Yuriko Kimura, Daniel Maloney, Linda Hayes, Gwendolyn Bye, Pat Thomas, Elaine Anderson, Michael Bruce, Davi Chase, Muriel Cohan, Patrick Suzeali

PROGRAM

"Adam from 'In the Beginning'" (Sculthorpe, Anthony), "Songs (Debussy, Anthony), "Power" (Earth, Wind and Fire, Maloney) "Rooms" (Hopkins, Sokolow)

* On May 7, 1974 Ross Parkes and Yuriko Kimura performed "I the Beginning" at Theresa Kaufmann Concert Hall.

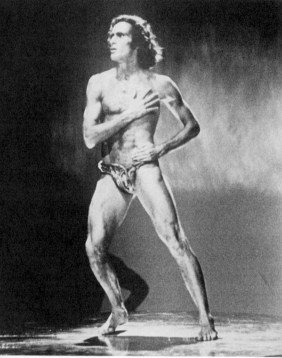

Ross Parkes in "Adam"

CARNEGIE HALL

Thursday, March 28, 1974

The Performing Arts Porgram of the Asia Society in association with the Carnegie Hall Corporation and the Department of Cultural Affairs of the City of New York presents:

BIRJU MAHARAJ
and Company

performing "Kathak," the classical dance of North India, with leading female dancers Kumudini Lakhai, Saswati Sen, and Indian musicians.

Birju Maharaj

INTERNATIONAL CENTER
Saturday, March 30, 1974

TONY WHITE

in a one-man show "Artistry Is Here to Stay": A Dance Suite in Four Parts; choreographed and performed by Tony White with innovations in modern jazz tap dancing.

Right: Tony White

TEARS REALTY
March 30–31, 1974

DANCE CONCERT

"Orange Pieces" (Faure, Rosalind Newman; Lighting, Suzanne Joelson) danced by Naomi Dworkin, Lori Giannini, Susan Goldstein, Gretchen Henry, Stormy Mullis, Rosalind Newman, Candy Prior, "Thus Spake Sarabelka" (Chinese Traditional; Costume, Eleanor de Vito) choreographed and performed by Irving Burton, "Arrangement—Part of a Series (Dedicated to John Wilson)" (Marcello-Sound Effects-African, Deborah Jowitt) danced by Lee Olsen, Maris Wolff, "Short" (Tape Collage) choreographed and danced by Candy Prior, "San Diego Zoo" (Choreography, Stormy Mullis; Lighting, Suzanne Joelson) danced by Stormy Mullis, and Kathy Bernson

AMERICAN THEATRE LAB
April 4–6, 1974*
Associated Productions of Dance Theater Workship presents:

JAN WODYNSKI DANCE COMPANY

Choreography and Costumes, Jan Wodynski; Technical Director-Sound, Mike Wodynski; Technicians, Jim Hunter, Jodi Strano

COMPANY

Kathy Eaton, Joanne Edelmann, John Kelly, Robert Kosinski, Julie Maloney, Madeleine Perrone, Kik Urban, Paul Wilson, Jan Wodynski, Mike Wodynski

PROGRAM

"Koreotroniks" (Sound-tubes), "Changeover" (Mike Wodynski), "Timewarp" (Schwartz, M. Wodynski), "Contours" (Paul Winter Consort)

* On May 5–6, 1974 at Theatre in Space, the company performed "Optik" (Partch), "Interspace" (Walcott), "A Work in Progress" (Environmental Sounds), and "Pashun Zone: Sekter Five" (Khatchaturian)

THE SPACE
April 5–7, 1974
Louis-Nikolais Dance Theatre Lab presents:

PHYLLIS LAMHUT DANCE COMPANY

Director-Choreographer, Phyllis Lamhut; Production Coordinator-Lighting Design, Ruth Grauert

COMPANY

Phyllis Lamhut, Donald Blumenfeld, Diane Boardman, Jeffrey Eichenwald, Diane Elliot, Patrice Evans, Joan Gedney, Kathleen Gaskin, Natasha Simon, Vic Stornant

PROGRAM

"Z Twiddle," "Terra Angelica," and *premiere* of "New Work" (Thomas Mark Edlun, Phyllis Lamhut; Costumes, Frank Garcia, Gedney-Cady; Lighting, Ruth Grauert)

Jan Wodynski Dance Company in "Koreotroniks"

EXCHANGE THEATER
April 5–11, 1974
The Exchange Theater presents:

MIMI GARRARD DANCE COMPANY

Artistic Director-Choreographer, Mimi Garrard; Lighting, Jon Garness, Bill Campbell; Stage Manager, Bill Campbell; Special Effects, James Seawright; Assistant Stage Manager, Ed Marsan; Technical Director, Keith Harewood; Costumes, Frank Garcia; Press, George Cochran

COMPANY

Mimi Garrard, Gary Davis, Karen Levin, Gloria McLean, Gale Ormiston, Lynn Ruthenberg, Irene Soler, Janet Towner, Bil Setters

REPERTOIRE

CONCERT I: "Spaces" (Bayle), "A Minor Intermezzo (work in progress)" (Brahms), "Six, and 7" (Arel), "Game (a child's view)" (Mozart), "Video Variations" (Schonberg), "Alla Marcia" (Popular), "Phosphones" (Ghent)
CONCERT II: "Dualities" (Ghent), "Transaction" (Ghent), "Flux" (Arel), "Dreamspace" (Trimble), "Phosphones" (Ghent)

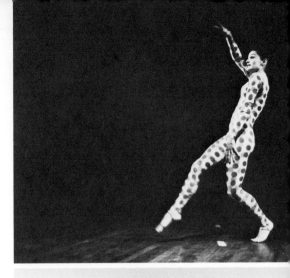

FORTUNE THEATRE
April 8–14, 1974
The New York Theatre Ensemble presents:

BALLET PLAYERS

Director-Choreographer, Anthony Bassae

COMPANY

Anthony Bassae, Ani Blackburn, David Gleaton, Brigitta Mueller, Marvin Gordon, Gordon Taylor, Beth Kurtz, Eric Concklin, Marian Horosko

REPERTOIRE

"Gemini Suite" (Lord, Bassae), "Fantasia" (Williams, Charles Neal), "Capriol Suite" (Warlock, Bassae), "Liebeslieder Walzer" (Brahms, Bassae), "Delibiana"
PREMIERES: "Hearts and Flowers" (Richard Strauss, Anthony Bassae), "The Devil's Salesman" (Brahms-Dvorak, Bassae), "Present Tense" (Grieg, Charles Neal), "Transients" (Rod Levitt, Marvin Gordon), "Silent Movies" (Movie Tracks-Sounds-Samuel Barber, Marian Horosko)

WASHINGTON SQUARE CHURCH
April 16–17, 1974
Foundation for the Advance of Dance presents:

EDITH STEPHEN DANCE COMPANY

Artistic Director-Choreographer, Edith Stephen; Production Manager, David H. B. Drake; Production Assistant, Christina Winsey

COMPANY

Edith Stephen, Frederick Courtney, Annabella Gonzalez, Patricia Hruby, Arthur Jamison, Ralph M. Thomas, Paula Schapiro, Anthony Berlech, Meredith Evans

PROGRAM

PREMIERES of "This Side of Paradise" (O. K. Joshee), "Whizpizbamwam Powwow" (Hot Butter), "The Dream of the Wild Horse" Jaque Lasri; Film, D.C. DeDaunant), and "Love in Different Colors" (Michael Dreyfuss; Film, Rosalind Schneider)

JAPAN HOUSE
Wednesday, April 17, 1974
The Japan Society Inc. presents:

SACHIYO ITA

with koto player Fusako Yoshida; Choreography, Sachiyo Ito; Lighting Designer, Bob Phillip; Stage Manager, E. St. John

PROGRAM

"Fuji Ondo (Wisteria Melody)," "Midare (Disorder)," "Urashima (Kabuki)," "Mitsu No Asobi (Three Children's Games)," "Shinsencho Bukyoku (Country Suite Dance)," "Sagi Musume (White Heron Maiden)"

Sachiyo Ito Above: Edith Stephen Dance Co.
Top: Mimi Garrard in "Game"(*Peter Moore Photo*)

HARLEM CULTURAL CENTER
April 19–21, 1974
The Harlem Cultural Council and the Foundation for the Vital Arts present:

ELEO POMARE DANCE COMPANY

Artistic Director-Choreographer, Eleo Pomare; Managing Director, Michael E. Levy; Company Manager, Virgil D. Akins; Lighting, David H. B. Drake; Management, Kazuko Hillyer

COMPANY

Jennifer Barry, Charles Grant, Strody Meekins, Carl Paris, Martial Roumain, Carole Simpson, Rosalie Tracey, Henry Yu Hao Yen, Mina Yoo, Vandetta Mathea

PROGRAM

"Climb" (Kelemen), "Serendipity" (Handel), "Nother Shade of Blue" (Traditional-Flack-Collins-Nyro), "Narcissus Rising" (Collage), "Passage" (Fellegara), "Blues for the Jungle" (Traditional)

AMERICAN THEATRE LAB
April 19–21, 1974
Dance Theatre Workshop presents:

PEGGY CICIERSKA
LAURA PAWEL

PROGRAM

"Drifts" (Feldman) choreographed and danced by Peggy Cicierska; "The Beast with Many Tales" (Laura Pawel) danced by Jim Finney, Pamela Finney, Raymond Healy, Laura Pawel; "Harriet" (Songs of the Humpback Whale) choreographed and danced by Peggy Cicierska; "Vacuum" (Pink Floyd-Salvatore Martirano, Peggy Cicierska) danced by Erica Berland, John Moore, Peggy Cicierska; and *premiere* of "Going Going Gone" (Bob Dylan, Peggy Cicierska) danced by Erica Berland, John Moore

CARNEGIE HALL
Saturday, April 20, 1974
Arthur Shafman International Ltd. presents:

JOSE MOLINA BAILES ESPANOLES

Director-Choreographer, Jose Molina; Choreographers, Luis Montero, Jose Granero, Thomas de Madrid; Production Manager, Lewis Rosen; Production Associate, Susan Shafman

COMPANY

Jose Molina, Luis Montero, Elena Santana, Luis Porcel, Pablo Rodarte, Maria Miranda, Esther, Maria Antonia, Beltran Espinosa (Solo Guitarist), Antonio Villaneuva (Flamenco Singer), Jesus de Araceli (Guitarist), Zeneida Manfugaz (Pianist)

PROGRAM

"Del Siglo XVIII" (Albeniz), "Maria de La O" (Popular), "La Noche," "Albaicin" (Albeniz), "Pensamiento," "Romeras" (Popular), "Jota Espana" (Chabrier), "Zapateado" (Breton), "Soleares" (Popular), "Cuadro Flamenco"

WHITNEY MUSEUM
Tuesday, April 23, 1974

JOSE CORONADO & DANCERS

Director-Choreographer, Jose Coronado

COMPANY

Lisa Brosky, Ilona Coper, Jose Coronado, Judy Epstein, Robin Goldstein, Seth Goldstein, Esta Greenfield, Peter Lawrence, Nancy Mikota

PROGRAM

Rites of Spring: "Saeta" (Joaquim Homs, Jose Coronado), "Mujeres, Parts I and II" (Handel, Coronado), "Vigil" (Penderecki, Coronado)

Jose Molina (R) in "Cuadro Flamenco" Above: Peggy Cicierska in "Harriet" Top: Eleo Pomare Dance Co. in "Serendipity"(*Jonathan Atkin Photo*) **113**

ANNABELLE GAMSON

In an evening of solo dances; Pianist, James Gemmell; Lighting Designer, Snowdon Parlette

PROGRAM

"Dances by Isadora Duncan: Water Study (Schubert), Five Waltzes (Brahms), Dance of the Furies (Gluck), Etude (Scriabin)," and *Premieres* of "Three Quarter Tone Pieces" (Charles Ives, Anna Sokolow), "First Movement" (Mozart, Gamson), "Portrait of Rose" (Scriabin, Gamson)

Left: Annabelle Gamson

THE SPACE
April 26–28, 1974
Louis-Nikolais Dance Theatre Lab presents:

BEVERLY SCHMIDT-BLOSSOM
featuring Somedancers, Inc.

Choreography, Beverly Schmidt-Blossom, except where noted; Production Coordinator-Lighting Designer, Ruth Grauert; Technical Assistants, Kathy Heath, Bill Campbell; Stage Managers, Elven Riley, Ron Laszewski; Music, Phil Musser, J. Gordon Wilson

COMPANY

Beverly Schmidt-Blossom, and Somedancers: Jenny Anderson, Marilyn Brda, Anita Feldman, Debra Loewen, Deborah Riley, Margo Sancken, Laurel Simerl, Ana Sussman, Barbara Berger, Kathryn Buchanan, Pam Budner, Gabrielle Gottlieb, Lynn Lipke, Betsy O'Neill, Betty Schneider

PROGRAM

"I Look Back, I . . ." (Bach), "Blue" (Gluck), "Black Traveler" (Cartoon Sounds) all performed by Beverly Schmidt-Blossom, "Flashback" (Drums-Bach-Tarrega), "Assembly" (Philip Musser), "Moonlight Sonata" (Beethoven-J. Gordon Wilson), "Movement Loops with Bumbershoots" (Jug Bands), "Somedancers Solos" (Philip Musser, choreography by each soloist) all performed by Somedancers, and "Poem for the Theatre #6" (Villa-Lobos, Blossom-Schmidt-Tropp) performed by Marilyn Brda

Beverly Schmidt-Blossom in "I Look Back.."

FORTUNE THEATRE
April 26–May 12, 1974

EKATHRINA SOBECHANSKAYA
with the
TROCKADERO GLOXINIA BALLET

Director, Larry Ree; Stage Manager, George Ritter; Ballet Master, C. Kulczki; Press, Frank Schmitt; Lighting, Earl Eidman; Sound Jim Brown; Wardrobe Mistress, Zenubia Gaborgias; General Manager, Ozzie Daljord; Artistic Director, Nancy Tallayco; Technical Director, David Andrew

COMPANY

Ekathrina Sobechanskaya, Olga Plushinskaya, Golenka, Edith Tresahar, Grace Maximova, Phyhena Lipuart, Tatiana Yusophova, Natalia Veceslova, Rosaria Buchinska

PROGRAM

"Russian Snowflakes" (Tchaikovsky, Pavlova; Costumes, Lohr Wilson), "Red" (Rimsky-Korsakov), "The Tragic Heart of Gloom and Despair" (Gould, Olga Plushinskaya), "Dragonfly" (Kreisler, Pavlova), "Surprise!," "Raymonda Act III" (Glazounov, Larry Ree; Costumes, Lohr Wilson)

Ekathrina Sobechanskaya (C) and Trockadero Gloxinia Ballet in "Raymonda" (*Roy Blakey Photo*)

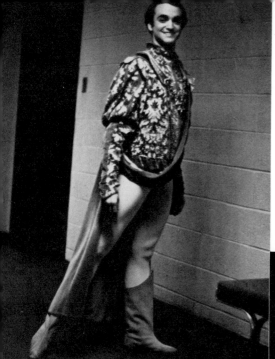

GREENWICH MEWS THEATRE
April 28–30, 1974
The Greenwich Mews Theatre presents:

J. DEVON DANCE ENSEMBLE

Director-Choreographer, Peter J. Humphrey

COMPANY

Larry Leritz, Kristine Lewis, Barbara McKinley, Linda Novick, Natan Oken, Joel Rosina, Donna-Marie Rossini, Suzanne Sponsler, Ron Zarr

PROGRAM

"Santa Maria," "Rhapsody in White/Funky Stuff," "Pine Apple Rag," "Fantasy," "String of Pearls," "Sometimes," "New Year's Eve," "Peoples," "Satin Doll," "Variation," "Everywhere I Go"

Left: Larry Leritz in "Variation"

AMERICAN THEATRE LAB
May 3–5, 1974

BRUCE KING DANCE CONCERT

with
Emily Wadhams
Dale Townsend
Harry Streep III

Director-Choreographer, Bruce King; Lighting Designer, John Dodd; Sound and Lights, Charles Stanley; Stage Manager, Bettina Dearborn

PROGRAM

"Walk in Splendor" (Alan Hovhaness), "Rondo toward Death" (Pierre Boulez), "Bamboo" (Lou Harrison), "After Guernica" (Morris Knight; Costumes, Alfred Pounders), "Vigil" (Charles Ives) PREMIERES: "Leaves" (William Penn), "Parable" (Harry Partch), "Swarm" (Antonio Soler)

Bruce King
(Jack Mitchell Photo)

CENTRAL PARK-LINCOLN CENTER
Saturday, May 4, 1974

A/P IMPROV GROUP

Artistic Director, Judith Scott; Business Manager, Juan Aruego

COMPANY

Ariane Aruego, Suki Dewey, Fred Patton, Judith Scott, David Van Tieghem, Peter Weinstock

PROGRAM

Improvisations

A/P Improv Group

May 4–5, 1974
The Theatre of the Riverside Church presents:

JOAN MILLER AND THE CHAMBER ARTS/DANCE PLAYERS

Artistic Director-Choreographer, Joan Miller; Artistic Adviser-Rehearsal Director, Leon Danielian; Musical Director-Resident Composer, Gwendolyn Watson; Managing Director, Carol Indianer; Promotional Coordinator, Margaret Hanks; Lighting Designer, Diana Banks

COMPANY

Milton Bowser, Lee Connor, Chuck Davis, Joan Lombardi, Yon Martin, Joan Miller, Gail Reese, musicians Gwendolyn Watson, Carole Weber, apprentices Sandie Ferranti, Sylvia Rincon, and special guests Nikki Giovanni, Keith Lee, Buddy Balough, Kevin Haigen, and the Gramercy String Quartet

PROGRAM

"Finale from Times Past: The Passing Parade" (Scott Joplin-Cole Porter, Keith Lee) a *premiere*, "Pass Fe White," preview of a work in progress: "Sponge" (Carole Weber, Joan Miller), "Soulscape" (Poet Narrator, Nikki Giovanni), "Thoroughfare" (J. Mayall-Watson Press, Joan Miller), "Times Past" (Joplin-Porter, Lee), *world premiere* of "Escapades" (Gwendolyn Watson, Joan Miller; Costumes-Decor, Pat Coppedge)

Top Left: Joan Miller in "Pass fe White"

THE SPACE
May 10–11, 1974
Louis-Nikolais Dance Theatre Lab of Chimera Foundation for Dance, Inc. presents:

SARA AND JERRY PEARSON

Production Coordinator-Lighting Design, Ruth Grauert; Stage Manager, Bill Campbell; Technicians, Edward Marsan, Diane Markham, Julie Bryan, Deborah Glaser; Technical Tape Assistant, Mitchell Rose

COMPANY

Sara Pearson, Jerry Pearson, Kent Baker, Rick Davis, Mark Esposito, Deborah Glaser, Gary McKay, Patrick Ragland, Mitchell Rose, Luise Wykell

PROGRAM

"Vis a Vis" (Vivaldi, Gladys Bailin), "Auras" (Jerry Pearson-Dean Granrose, Sarah and Jerry Pearson), "Magnetic Rag" (Scott Joplin, Sara and Jerry Pearson), and *premieres* of "Amnesia" (Takemitsu-Vivaldi, Sara Pearson), and "A Mild Mannered Reporter" (Big Brother and the Holding Company, Jerry Pearson)

Left Center: Sara and Jerry Pearson in "Auras"
(*Caravaglia Photo*)

CUNNINGHAM DANCE STUDIO
May 10–11, 1974
The Cunningham Dance Foundation presents:

ITHACA DANCEMAKERS

Production and Publicity Managers, Saga Ambegaokar, Stephen Buck; Lighting Design, Willy Pierce; Technical Supervisor, Nancy Golladay; Sound, David Stringham

COMPANY

Helen Alexander, Saga Ambegaokar, Stephen Buck, Janice Kovar, Leslie Wilson-Wirtz, Peggy Lawler, Maureen Cosgrove, Sue Penney, Debby Samelson, Chas Bruner, Barbara Dickinson, Jill Lerner, Carl Thomsen, and members of the Cornell football team: Jack Corrigan, Sam Costa, Don Lombardo, Joe Meaney, Jim Popielinski, Jon Yonkondy

PROGRAM

"No. 12 (Solo for 1, 2, 3, or 4)" (David Stringham, Helen Alexander), "Interabang" (David Stringham, Leslie Wilson-Wirtz), "Venus in Capricorn" (Tony Scott-Shinichi Yuize-Hozan Yamamoto, Janice Kovar), "Slow Dash" (Choreographer, Stephen Buck), "Cornell Suite" (David Borden, Saga Ambegaokar)

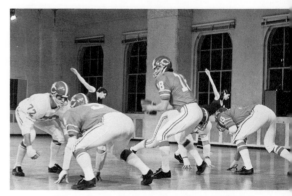

Ithaca Dancemakers and members of Cornell football team in "Cornell Suite" (*Jean Rigg Photo*)

BRUCE PACOT AND DANCERS

Director-Choreographer, Bruce Pacot

PROGRAM

"Sections +" (Varese-Braunstien) danced by Bill Cratty, Hermine von Essen, Nancy Mapother, Bruce Pacot, Maria Valdes; "Wheatfields" danced by Ellen Ducker, Penny Hutchinson, Bruce Pacot, Dana Roth, Colette Yglesias (No photos available)

PACE UNIVERSITY SCHIMMEL CENTER
May 14–17, 1974
Schimmel Center for the Arts presents:

KAZUKO HIRABAYASHI DANCE THEATRE

Director-Choreographer, Kazuko Hirabayashi; Production Supervisor, Technical Assistance Group; Stage Manager, Maxine Glorsky; Management, Castalia Enterprises; Lighting, Jennifer Tipton

COMPANY

Hugh Appet, Thomas Bain, David Chase, Frank Colardo, Tony Constantine, Ralph Farrington, Anthony Ferro, Sharon Filone, Chris Gillis, Dianne Hulbert, Katherine Liepe, Jim May, Felicia Norton, Susan Osberg, Christopher Pilafian, Rebecca Slifkin, Robert Swinston, Eve Walstrum, Shelley Washington, Teri Weksler, Lance Westergard

PROGRAM

"Triste" (Royhei Hirose), "Black Angels" (George Crumb), "In a Dark Grove" (Lawrence Rosenthal), "The Stone Garden" (Royhei Hirose), *company premiere* of "Night of the Four Moons with Lone Shadow" (George Crumb), and *world premiere* of "The Crimson Lotus" (Ryohei Hirose, Kazuko Hirabayashi; Lighting, Jennifer Tipton) No photos available.

HUNTER COLLEGE PLAYHOUSE
May 17–19, 1974
The Hunter College Concert Bureau presents:

BELLA LEWITZKY DANCE COMPANY

Artistic Director-Choreographer, Bella Lewitzky; Music Director, Cara Bradbury Rhodes: Costume and Lighting Designer, Darlene Neel; Scenic Director, Cliff Nelson; Technical Director, Bill Davenport

COMPANY

Names not submitted

PROGRAM

"Bella and Brindle" (Reginald Smith-Brindle, Bella Lewitzky), "On the Brink of Time" (Morton Subotnick, Lewitzky), "Ceremony for Three" (Cara Bradbury Rhodes, Lewitzky), "Spaces Between" Electronic Score, Lewitzky; Decor, Newell Taylor Reynolds), "Scintilla"

Cliff Nelson Photos

Bella Lewitzky in "On the Brink of Time"
Top: Bella Lewitzky Dance Company

Black Heritage Dancers in "Toute Bagai"
(*Art Phipps Photo*)

AMERICAN THEATRE LAB
May 17–19, 1974
The Blue Mountain Paper Parade and Dance Works Inc. present:

TRUE SPIRITS PLUS NEW WORKS

Artistic Directors, Barbara Roan, Irene Feigenheimer; Administrative Director, Robert Marinaccio; Lighting Designer-Stage Manager, Chip Largman; Sound, John Moore; Banners, Gerard Murrell; Technical Assistants, Steve Lewis, Ruis Woertendyke, Jig Gillespie

PROGRAM

"Range" (Lloyd McNeill, Barbara Roan) danced by Betty Salamun, Avi Davis, John Moore, Hollyce Yoken, Karen Chalom, Laurie Uprichard, Sue Barnes Moore, Tim Haynes, Amy Berkman, Jude Bartlett; "Dedicated" (Traditional) choreographed and performed by Jude Bartlett; "Stages" (Charles Madden, Irene Feigenheimer) performed by Hollyce Yoken, Dennis Florio, Jude Bartlett, Genevieve Kapuler, Laurie Gittelman, Sue Barnes Moore, Laurie Uprichard, Mary Benson, Ruth Charney, Charles Madden, Avi Davis, John Moore, Ruis Woertendyke; "True Spirits" conceived by Barbara Roan; Choreographed and directed by Irene Feigenheimer, Barbara Roan, Anthony LaGiglia; Additional Choreography, Annabelle Gamson, Jude Bartlett, and members of the company; Tape Collage, Barbara Roan; danced by Amy Berkman, Sue Barnes Moore, Laurie Uprichard, Dennis Florio, Laurie Gittelman, Irene Feigenheimer, Jude Bartlett, Nancy Scher, Avi Davis, Barbara Roan, Ellen Robbins, Robert Marinaccio, Hollyce Yoken, Genevieve Kapuler, Charles Madden, Betty Salamun, Ruth Charney, Jennifer Donahue, Annabelle Gamson, Mary Benson, Ellen Jacob, John Moore, Karen Chalom

Chuck Davis
Right Center: "True Spirits"

BILLIE HOLIDAY THEATRE
Friday, May 17, 1974
Michela DeSandies and Barbara Lewis Johnson present:

BLACK HERITAGE DANCERS

Director-Choreographer, Kenneth McPherson; Artistic Consultant, George Faison; Costumes, Kenneth McPherson; Business Manager, Gina Burns Tabourn; Make-up, Stacy Pharr; Program Coordinator, Toni Brabham; Technical Director, Raymond Daniels; Lighting, Prince Thomas; Stage Manager, Ezrick Spooner

COMPANY

Kenneth McPherson, Judith DeJean, Geneva Best, Marcella DeSandies, Stanley Sears, Carole Reveillac, Hilda Moore, and Special Guest Artist: LeVon Campbell

PROGRAM

"Primitives," "Sachee," "Bacchanal," "Jubillo," "Calypso Samba," "Drumology," "Taute Bagai"

BRONX COMMUNITY COLLEGE
Saturday, May 18, 1974
Bronx Community College Center for Continuing Education and Community Services presents:

BALLET HISPANICO OF NEW YORK
CHUCK DAVIS DANCE COMPANY

BALLET HISPANICO; Artistic Director-Choreographer, Tina Ramirez; Associate Director-Ballet Master, Ramon Segarra; Administrator, Ron Christopher; Technical Director, Ron Bunt; Production Director, Ron Monk; Sound, David Ticotin, Gilbert Figueroa; Stage Manager, Robbie Monk; Press, Marush; Wardrobe Mistress, Penelope Pankhurst

COMPANY

Sandra Rivera, Delores Garcia, Coco Pelaez, Nancy Ticotin, Rachel Ticotin, Alicia Roque, Valerie Contreras, Lorenzo Maldonado, Ernesto Morales, Marcial Gonzales, Antonio Iglesias, Roy Rodriquez

PROGRAM

"Mira Todas Esas Bellas Rosas Rojas" (Santana, Talley Beatty; Costumes, Edith Lutyens Bel Geddes, Julio Fernandez), "Fiesta en Vera Cruz" (J. Pablo Moncayo, Jose Coronado; Costumes, Jose Coronado, Sara Sendra), "Echoes of Spain" (Albeniz, Louis Johnson; Costumes, Diane Fox)
CHUCK DAVIS DANCE COMPANY: Artistic Director-Choreographer, Chuck Davis; Musical Director, Yomi Awolowo; Lighting and Technical Consultant, Gerald Smith; Stage Manager, Rashon

COMPANY

Carol Awolowo, Marilyn Banks, Tara Barnard, Onika Bagemon, Milton Bowser, Victor Braxton, Sandra Burton, Jackie Coban, Chuck Davis, Linda Evans, William Fleet, Monifa Olajorin, Tommy Manigault, Gregory Hinton, Larry Sanders, Ben Jones, John Young

PROGRAM

"Simple Prayer" (Miriam Makeba-Staple Singer, Chuck Davis), "Drums," "Kakilembe" (Choreography, Italo Zambo; Costumes, Italo Zambo, Gila Troure, Carol Awolowo; Masks, Yomi Awolowo, Charles Abramson), "West African Salute" (Chuck Davis; Costumes, Chuck Davis, Tina Ramirez)

Theatre Dance Collection
in "Misalliance"

THEATRE OF THE RIVERSIDE CHURCH
May 23–25, 1974
The Theatre of the Riverside Church presents:

THEATRE DANCE COLLECTION

David Anderson, Cynthia Roberts, Rodney Griffin, Lynne Taylor, Jaclynn Villamil, Ira Ross Cohen, Bill Cratty, Lynne Simonson, Justin Ross

PROGRAM

"Misalliance" (Rodney Griffin), "Flowers for Departed Children" (Selected, Lynne Taylor), "Cave Paintings" (Lou Harrison, Rodney Griffin), "Courtley Dances" (Rodney Griffin)

Larry Richardson and Company
in "Kin"

THERESA L. KAUFMANN CONCERT HALL
Sunday, May 19, 1974
The 92nd Street YM-YWHA (Fred Berk, Producer) presents:

DANCE CONCERT ON JEWISH THEMES

"Women" (Traditional Yemenite, Karen Kaufman) danced by Kathleen Balsamo, Lisa Goldberg, Sharon Lieberman (Brooklyn College Dance Theatre) "Rite" (Aldema) choreographed and danced by Hava Kohav; "When I Consider" (Merve & Merla Watson) choreographed and danced by Gregory Mitchell, "A Point of Doctrine" (Tucker, Sophie Maslow) danced by Nedra Marlim, Stanley Berke, "In the Arabic-Israeli Idiom" (Amiron-Halevi-Zamir) choreographed and danced by Hadassah Badoch-Kruger, "Chad Dagya" (Traditional, Bruce Block; Masks, Rolanda Vega) danced by Jane Davidson, Debbie Eichler, Carolyn Fried, Irene Goldberg, Deedee Gross, Leslie Gruss, Diane Kopecky, Eve Leeman, Dina Markson, Malky Merling, Beth Motzkin, Elizabeth Rothman, Georgette Thaler; "Mist" (Horn, Hava Kohav; Costumes, Lavinia Nielsen) danced by Diana Quitko, Bruce Block , "Kadish" (Ravel, Anna Sololow) danced by Hadassah Badoch-Kruger, "Two Landscapes" (Hovhaness-Cage, Ze'eva Cohen) danced by Myrna Packer; "Holiday in Israel" (Arranged by Paul Spong, re-constructed by Karen Barracuda, Betsy Carden) danced by Bruce Block, Anna Dancyger, Lisa Goldberg, Vicki Grubman, Arlene Karash, Karen Kaufman, Sharon Lieberman, Lynn Rothman, Lorraine Saraceno, Carolyn Vance, Steve Zalph (Brooklyn College Dance Theatre)

Diane Quitko, Bruce Block in "Mist"
(*M. Goodman Photo*)

DANCE GALLERY
May 23–June 9, 1974
The Larry Richardson Dance Foundation presents:

LARRY RICHARDSON & DANCE COMPANY

Director-Choreographer, Larry Richardson; General Administrator, J. Antony Siciliano; Assistant Administrator, Myrtle Lada; Counsel, John Afton; Costumes, DeBenedetti; Masks, Salvatore Guida; Lighting, Jon Knudsen; Technical Director, Antony Sklarew

COMPANY

Bebbie Belote, Douglas Boulivare, Mary Jo Buhl, Ricky Davenport, Alex Dolcemascolo, Doris Pasteleur, Valerie Raieff, Larry Richardson, Sandra Small, Wendy Stein, and guest artist Janet Blake

PROGRAM

Premiere of "Kin" in three acts (Bach-Shutz-Xenakis-Buxtehude, Larry Richardson; Costumes, DeBenedetti; Masks, Salvatore Guida; Lighting, Jon Knudsen)

CHURCH OF THE BELOVED DISCIPLE
Saturday, May 25, 1974
The Black Cat presents:

THOMAS HOLT DANCE ENSEMBLE

Betsey Baron, Cynthia Dumsha, Lucinda Gehrke, John Killacky, Thomas Holt, Allan Seward, Paulette Taylor, Phillip Tietz, Karen Sing, Gary McKay, Laurie Kane

PROGRAM

"The Last Supper" (Hassler-Moderne-Demantius-Gervaise-Phalese, Thomas Holt;) "Westward" (Rodrigo, Holt-Taylor), "Phillip and John" (John Killacky-Phillip Tietz), "Arienata" (Vivaldi, Holt), "Duet for Summer" (Holdridge, Holt), "Afterhours in Wonderland" (Holzman-Jefferson Airplane-Pfeiffer-Hiller-Exuma, Holt)

THEATRE AT ST. CLEMENT'S
Saturday & Sunday, May 25, 26, 1974
New Dance Group Studio presents:

SPRING CONCERTS

LITTLE FELONIES (Mozart, Margot Colbert; Lighting, Patricia Stern; Costumes, Louise Krozek, Mari DiLena; Stage Manager, Jason Buzas) danced by E. J. Chaves, Mari DiLena, Joanna A. Mauer, Margot Colbert, Joseph John, Marina Valanti, Joanne Legano, Lynn Perrott, Beth Schlansky, Margie Sloven, Carol Alaskewicz, Carolyn Claunch, Tracy Davie, Phyllis Finkelstein, Karen Gorney, Christine Sullivan, Suzanne Vega, Lindy Wankoff
A DANCE MASS (John D. Parkinson, Ana Marie Forsythe; Lighting, Charles Frost; Sound, Greg Squires; Rehearsal Assistant, Joanne Legano) danced by Anna Marie Forsythe, James Bontempo, Mary Farrell, Richard Martin, Hannah Schwarzschild, Radha Sukhu, Donna Ward

**Brenda Schneider, Jean Erdman, Andrea Stark
in "Haitian Suite '74"**(*Delilah McKavish Photo*)

EXCHANGE THEATRE
May 28–June 3, 1974
The Open Eye presents:

SOLO DANCES & HAITIAN SUITE'74

Artistic Director, Jean Erdman, Administrative Director, Louise Westergaard; Secretary-Treasurer, Marcia Sherman; Lighting, George Gracey; Costumes, Vanya Franck, Kay Stuntz, Cherel Winett; Stage Manager, Tony Davis

PROGRAM

"Cantaloupe Island" (Herbie Hancock) choreographed and danced by Edward Henkel; "Motifs" (Bach) choreographed and danced by Andrea Stark; "Marianne" (Poems and Songs, Yvette Guilbert) choreographed and danced by Elizabeth Lage; Directed by John FitzGibbon; "Frieze" (Dan Erkkila-Genji Ito-Teiji Ito) choreographed and danced by Andrea Stark; "Haitian Suite '74" (Teiji Ito) with Jean Erdman, Andrea Stark, Elizabeth Lage, Esther Chaves, John Genke, Edward Henkel, John FitzGibbon
MUSICIANS AND CHORUS: Esther Chaves, Johnnie Dinstuhl, Jean Erdman, Wendy Erdman, Dan Erkkila, John FitzGibbon, John Genke, Genji Ito, Teiji Ito, Elizabeth Lage, Brenda Schneider, Andrea Stark, Cherel Winett

MERCE CUNNINGHAM STUDIO
May 29, 30, 1974

DANCE THEATRE

Choreography by Claire Henry; Costumes, Jennifer Von Mayrhauser; Stage Manager, David Markay; Props, Tom Vallone, Margo Nielsen; Lighting, Margo Nielsen

COMPANY

Carlotta Willis, Raymond Healy, Kas Self, Frances Cott, Harriet Zucker, Kathy Gordon, Ben Gotlieb, Mary Joiner, Christy Wilson, Harriet Zucker, Margo Kaminsky

PROGRAM

"Words to Remove the Charm That Eats Away the Toes" (Text, Susan Miller), "Billie's Blues" (Billie Holiday), "He's Funny That Way" (Billie Holiday), "Yesterdays" (Billie Holiday), "Knots" (Text, R. D. Laing), "Let's Get Settled" (Edwin Roberts; Costumes, Jennifer Von Mayrhauser)
KAY WYLIE and HER BIG APPLE DANCE THEATRE with Luba Ash, Maggie Bohrer, Christine Campbell, Marilyn Klaus, Christy Wilson, Kay Wylie; Musician, Ken Sullivan; Lighting, Norman Jacob; Sound, Tim Simmons; Costumes, Diana Murphy; Choreography, Kay Wylie; "Ragtime" (Pee Wee Hunt-Cliff Jackson-Santo Pecora-Crazy Otto), "Wonder" (Stevie Wonder), "Night in the City" (Ray Charles-Joni Mitchell-Ken Sullivan; Poem written and read by Christine Campbell)

**Marilyn Klaus, Christy Wilson, Maggie Bohrer,
Kay Wylie (Big Apple Dance Theatre)
Above: Ben Gotlieb in "Knots"**

PUBLIC/NEWMAN THEATER
Opened Thursday, May 30, 1974*
Original Ballets Foundation and the New York Shakespeare Festival Public Theatre (Joseph Papp, Producer) present:

ELIOT FELD BALLET

Director-Choreographer, Eliot Feld; Lighting, Jennifer Tipton; Administrator, Cora Cahan

COMPANY

Helen Douglas, Diane Duffy, Suzanne Erlon, Valerie Feit, Eliot Feld, Paul Gifford, Richard Gilmore, Laurie Ichino, Jonathan Kelly, Victoria Keonig, Elizabeth Lee, Remus Marcu, George Montalbano, Lawrence Rhodes, Lawrence Rosenberg, Christine Sarry, Naomi Sorkin, John Sowinski

REPERTOIRE

"Theatre" (Richard Strauss), "The Gods Amused" (Debussy), "Intermezzo" (Brahms), "At Midnight" (Mahler), "Cortege Parisienne" (Chabrier)
WORLD PREMIERES: "Sephardic Song" Thursday, May 30, 1974 (Traditional arranged by Manuel Valls, Eliot Feld; Setting and Costumes, Santo Loquasto), "The Tzaddik" Sunday, June 2, 1974 (Aaron Copland, Eliot Feld; Setting and Costumes, Boris Aronson; Lighting, Jennifer Tipton, Gladys Celeste Mercader)
Press: Merle Debuskey, Susan L. Schulman

* Closed July 7, 1974 after 34 performances.

Tom Victor Photos

Christine Sarry, John Sowinski in "At Midnight"
Top Right: Sowinski, Eliot Feld, Richard Gilmore in "Tzaddik"

Lawrence Rhodes in "At Midnight"
Above: "The Gods Amused"

THERESA L. KAUFMANN CONCERT HALL
Thursday, May 30, 1974
The Dance Center of the 92nd Street YM-YWHA presents:

A STAFF DANCE CONCERT

Chairman Dance Department, Lucile Nathanson; Education Director, Omus Hirshbein; Secretary Dance Department, Gale King; Stage and Lighting Design, Frederick Hayman-Chaffey; Technical Director, Diane Smith

PROGRAM

"Illusion" (Hindemith-Bach, Marilyn Baker) danced by Marilyn Baker and Dale Townsend; "Snapshots" (The Ronettes) choreographed and danced by Susan Schickele, "CAR/Rance" (Madden, Bruce Block) danced by Sherry Sable and Bruce Block, "Road" (Consort, Sara Sugihara) danced by Sara Sugihara and Carrie Klein, "Moments" (Alpert-Standen) choreographed and danced by Hava Kohav, "Bamboo" (Harrison, Bruce King) danced by Bruce King and Dale Townsend, "Curved Air" (Terry Riley, Susan Schickele) danced by Sarah Byrne, Kelly Hogan, Sara Sugihara

Left: Hava Kohav in "Moments"
(Jack Mitchell Photo)

HUNTER COLLEGE PLAYHOUSE
May 30–31, June 1, 1974
Kazuko Hillyer and Hunter College Concert Bureau in cooperation with the Foundation for the Vital Arts present:

ELEO POMARE DANCE COMPANY

Artistic Director-Choreographer, Eleo Pomare; Managing Director, Michael E. Levy; Company Manager, Virgil D. Akins; Lighting, Gary Harris; Stage Manager, David H. B. Drake

COMPANY

Frank Ashley, Jennifer Barry, Charles Grant, Dyane Harvey, Vendetta Mathea, Strody Meekins, Carl Paris, Roberta Pikser, Martial Roumain, Carole Simpson, Rosalie Tracey, Mina Yoo, Henry Hao Yen Yu, Alistair Butler, Lonnetta Gaines, Earl Mack, Rick Stotts

PROGRAM

"Climb" (Kelemen), "Serendipity" (Handel; Costumes, Eleo Pomare), and *World Premieres* of "Descent and Portals" (I. Yun, Eleo Pomare; Costume, Judi Dearing), and "Hushed Voices" (Ornette Coleman-Charles Mingus-Leon Thomas-Don Cherry-Chicago Art Ensemble, Eleo Pomare; Costumes, Judi Dearing; Props, Michael Melitanov)

Left: Carl Paris, Strody Meekins in "Hushed Voices"*(Jonathan B. Atkin Photo)*

MERCE CUNNINGHAM STUDIO
May 31, June 1, 2, 6–9, 1974

VIOLA FARBER DANCE COMPANY

Artistic Director-Choreographer-Designer, Viola Farber; Musical Director, Alvin Lucier; Stage Manager, Jim Harrison; Company Manager, Margaret Wood; Administration, Performing Artservices

COMPANY

Viola Farber, Larry Clark, Willi Feuer, June Finch, Anne Koren, Susan Matheke, Ande Peck, Jeff Slayton, John Condon, Viola Slayton

REPERTOIRE

"Dune" (Lucier), "Willi I" (Lucier), "Three Duets: Excerpt, Area Code, Tendency," "No Super, No Boiler" (Lucier-Richter), "Dinosaur Parts" (David Tudor)

Ande Peck, Anne Koren, Viola Farber, Jeff Slayton in "Poor Eddie"*(Mary Lucier Photo)*

DANCE COMPANIES AT BROOKLYN ACADEMY OF MUSIC
Harvey Lichtenstein, Executive Director

BROOKLYN ACADEMY OF MUSIC
November 15–18, 1973*
The Brooklyn Academy of Music in association with the Pennsylvania Ballet Association presents the:

PENNSYLVANIA BALLET

Artistic Director, Barbara Weisberger; Associate Artistic Directors, Benjamin Harkarvy, Robert Rodham; Music Director, Maurice Kaplow; Ballet Mistress, Fiona Fuerstner; Lighting Designer, Nicholas Cernovitch; President-General Manager, Richard E. LeBlond, Jr.; Associate General Manager, Timothy Duncan; Press, Craig Palmer, Elizabeth Clure; Stage Managers, Jane Clegg, David K. H. Elliott; Costume Supervisor, E. Huntington Parker; Wardrobe Mistress, Lilliam Avery; Production Assistant, Peter Dudley; Assistant Conductor, Daniel Forlano

COMPANY

PRINCIPALS: Alba Calzada, Joanne Danto, Fiona Fuerstner, David Kloss, Michelle Lucci, Keith Martin, Lawrence Rhodes, Barbara Sandonato
SOLOISTS: Marcia Darhower, Dane La Fontsee, Laurence Matthews, Gretchen Warren
CORPS: Sandra Applebaum, Dana Arey, Christina Bernal, Enid Britten, Karen Brown, Kimberly Dye, David Jordan, Barry Leon, Remus Marcu, Barbarajean Martin, Anya Patton, Reva Pincusoff, Richard Rein, Ramon Rivera, Constance Ross, Janek Schergen, Missy Yancey, Linda Zettle

REPERTOIRE

"Madrigalesco" (Vivaldi, Harkarvy), "After Eden" (Hoiby, Butler), "Raymonda Variations" (Glazounov, Balanchine), "Scotch Symphony" (Mendelssohn, Balanchine)
NY PREMIERES: Thursday, Nov. 15, 1973 "Quartet" (Toru Takemitsu, Benjamim Harkarvy; Set and Lighting, David K. H. Elliott) danced by Enid Britten, Dane LaFontsee, Gretchen Warren, Janek Schergen; Friday, Nov. 16, 1973 "In Retrospect" (Benjamin Britten, Robert Rodham; Costumes, Frank Thompson; Set, Robert Mitchell; Lighting, Nicholas Cernovitch), and "Recital for Cello and Eight Dancers" (Bach, Benjamin Harkarvy)

* The company returned May 2–5, 1974 performing "The Four Temperaments" (Hindemith, Balanchine), "Concerto Barocco" (Bach, Balanchine), "Carmina Burana" (Orff, Butler), and NY premieres of "Black Angel" (George Crumb, John Butler; Set and Costumes, Rouben Ter-Arutunian), and "Time Passed Summer" (Tchaikovsky, Harkarvy; Costumes, Neil Bierbower) on May 2, 1974; "Opus Lemaitre" (Bach, Hans Van Manen; Set and Costumes, Jean Paul Vroom) on May 3, 1974.

"Raymonda Variations" Top Right: "Quartet"
(*Jack Mitchell Photo*) **Below: "Scotch Symphony"**

Joanne Danto, David Kloss in
"Concerto Barocco"(*Michael Friedlander Photo*)

BROOKLYN ACADEMY OF MUSIC
November 23–25, 1973
The Brooklyn Academy of Music (Harvey Lichtenstein, Executive Director) presents:

INNER CITY REPERTORY DANCE COMPANY

Administrative Director, Gloria Calomee; Production Manager, Annete Ensley; Stage Manager, Lloyde Hardy; Costume Supervisor, Darlene Naylor; Rehearsal Director, Carolyn Dyer; Lighting, Doris Einstein Siegel, William Grant III

COMPANY

Regina Bell, Gail Benedict, Ron Bush, Barry D'Angelo, Clif de Raita, Jaqueline DeRouen, Anita Littleman, Ruby Millsap, Delilah Moseley, Cleveland Pennington, Stanley Perryman, Marvin Tunney, Anthony White, Linda Young, Wanda Evans

PROGRAM

"Songs of the Disinherited" (Voices from the Black Diaspora, Donald McKayle; Costumes, Terence Tam Soon), "Rainbow 'Round My Shoulder" (Collection of John and Alan Lomax, Donald McKayle; Conductor, Howard Roberts; Soloist, George Tipton), *NY premiere* of "Caravansarai" (Santana, Talley Beatty; Costumes, Cleveland Pennington)

Lyn Smith Photos

Right: Cast of "Games"
(*Martha Swope Photo*)

"Rainbow 'Round My Shoulder"
(also above and right)

124
INNER CITY REPERTORY DANCE CO.

BROOKLYN ACADEMY OF MUSIC
November 29–30, December 1–2, 1973
The Brooklyn Academy of Music presents:

MANUEL ALUM DANCE COMPANY

Artistic Director-Choreographer, Manuel Alum; Lighting Design, Gary Harris; Stage Manager, Judy Kayser; Set Designs, J. W. Jason Strawn; Costumes, Manuel Alum; Administrator, John Hebel; Rehearsal Assistants, Gerri Houlihan, Yon Martin, Willa Kahn

COMPANY

Brunilda Ruiz, Malou Airaudo, Sandra Neels, Gerri Houlihan, Felicia Norton, Joan Lombardi, Kathleen Carlin, Yon Martin, Lance Westergard, Chris Komar, Manuel Alum

REPERTOIRE

"Palomas" (Oliveros), "East—to Nijinsky" (J. Tal), "W.O.M.B.—Pray for Us" (Verdi), "Era" (Penderecki), *New York premiere* of "Deadlines" (Bach), *World Premiere* Nov. 29, 1973 of "Steps—A Construction" (Alexander Calder, Manuel Alum; Set, J. W. Jason Strawn). No photos available.

BROOKLYN ACADEMY OF MUSIC
January 3–5, 1974
The Brooklyn Academy of Music presents:

ERICK HAWKINS DANCE COMPANY

Director-Choreographer, Erick Hawkins; Composer, Lucia Dlugoszewski; Lighting Designer, Robert Engstrom; Manager, Mark Z. Alpert; Production Manager, Paul Butler; Management, Sheldon Soffer

COMPANY

Erick Hawkins, Beverly Brown, Carol Conway, Nada Reagan, Natalie Richman, Cathy Ward, Robert Yohn, and the American Symphony Orchestra (Joel Thome, Conductor)

PROGRAM

"Angels of the Inmost Heaven" (Dlugoszewski; Set, Robert Engstrom), "Naked Leopard" (Zoltan Kodaly; Set, Ralph Dorazio), "Geography of Noon" (Dlugoszewski; Designs, Ralph Dorazio), "Dawn Dazzled Door" (Toru Takemitsu; Sculptures, Ralph Dorazio), "Classic Kite Tails" (David Diamond; Sculptures, Stanley Boxer)

Kenn Duncan Photos

Right: Lucia Dlugoszewski, Erick Hawkins in "Geography of Noon" (*Michael Avedon Photo*)

**Robert Yohn
in "Classic Kite Tails"**

**"Angels of the Inmost Heaven"
Above: "Classic Kite Tails"**

BROOKLYN ACADEMY OF MUSIC
March 1–2, 1974
The Brooklyn Academy of Music presents:

MERCE CUNNINGHAM & DANCE COMPANY

Director-Choreographer, Merce Cunningham; Lighting Designer, Richard Nelson; Artistic Adviser, Jasper Johns; Stage Managers, Richard Nelson, Charles Atlas

COMPANY

Ellen Cornfield, Merce Cunningham, Meg Harper, Susana Hayman-Chaffey, Cathy Kerr, Chris Komar, Robert Kovich, Brynar Mehl, Charles Moulton, Julie Roess-Smith, Valda Setterfield, and musicians David Behrman, Jacques Bekaert, John Cage, Gordon Mumma

PROGRAM

"Events Number 89 and 90" (Sections from Mr. Cunningham's "TV Rerun," "Changing Steps," and "Loops") performed without intermission

Right: Merce Cunningham
(*Jack Mitchell Photo*)

"TV Rerun"

"TV Rerun"
(*James Klosty Photos*)

PAUL TAYLOR DANCE COMPANY

Director-Choreographer, Paul Taylor; Costumes, George Tacit; Lighting, Jennifer Tipton; General Manager, Judith E. Daykin; Administrator, Neil S. Fleckman; Musical Director, John Herbert McDowell; Production Manager, Penelope Curry; Tour Coordinator, Jack Damlos; Stage Manager, Alan Gerberg; Wardrobe Supervisor, Kathi Horne; Rehearsal Mistress, Bettie deJong; General Understudy, Raymond Kurshals

COMPANY

Paul Taylor, Carolyn Adams, Bettie deJong, Eileen Cropley, Ruby Shang, Nicholas Gunn, Monica Morris, Eilie Chaib, Lila York, Greg Reynolds

PROGRAM

AMERICAN GENESIS (Choreography, Paul Taylor; Costumes, George Tacit; Lighting, Jennifer Tipton) in three acts and five sections: "The Creation" (Bach), "Before Eden (Josef Haydn), "So Long Eden" (John Fahey), "West of Eden" (Bohuslav Martinu), "The Flood" (Louis Moreau Gottschalk)

Zachary Freyman Photos

Carolyn Adams and company
in "American Genesis"

Daniel Williams, Ruby Shang, Nicholas Gunn
Above: (R) Bettie deJong, Paul Taylor 127

JAMAICA NATIONAL DANCE THEATRE COMPANY

Artistic Director-Choreographer, Rex Nettleford; Musical Director, Marjorie Whylie; Lighting, George Carter; Sound, Baldwin Lennon; Stage Manager, Freddie Hickling; Wardrobe Mistress, Barbara Kaufman

COMPANY

Rex Nettleford, Andrea Anderson, Sheila Barnett, Audley Vutler, Jean Binns, Joyce Campbell, Bridget Casserly, Noelle Chutkan, Dorothy Fraser, Jackie Guy, Pansy Hassan, Monica McGowan, Barry Moncrieffe, Patricia Ricketts, Barbara Requa, Bert Rose, Tony Wilson, Melanie Cook, Eleanor Ferguson, Yvonne Ffrench, Fitzroy Hunt, Sandra Monroe, Judith Pennant, Marylin Sanguinetti, Neil Summers, with singers, drummers, and musicians

PROGRAM

"Myal—Revelry" (Traditional, Nettleford), "Interlude of Songs," "Thursday's Child" (Whylie, Bert Rose), "Homage" (Various, Nettleford), "Street People" (Reggae Tunes, Nettleford), "Windsongs" (Jones, John Jones), "Kumina" (Traditional, Nettleford), "Celebrations" (Traditional, Nettleford), "Mountain Women" (Whylie, Sheila Barnett), "African Scenario" (Traditional, Nettleford), "Dialogue for Three" (Nettleford)

Joyce Campbell, Pansy Hassan, Barbara Requa, Sheila Barnett in "Scarf Dance"
Top Right: Audley Butler, Patsy Ricketts in "Windsongs"(*Maria La Yacona Photos*)

BROOKLYN ACADEMY OF MUSIC
May 18–19, 23–24, 1974
Modern Dance Artists Inc. presents:

SANASARDO DANCE COMPANY

Artistic Director-Choreographer, Paul Sanasardo; Associate Director, Diane Germaine; Lighting, Owen Ryan; Production Manager, Judy Kayser; Executive Director, William Weaver; Management, HI Enterprises

COMPANY

Diane Germain, Willa Kahn, Jacques Patarozzi, Dominique Petit, Michele Rebeaud, Christine Varjan, Joan Lombardi, Gerri Houlihan, Judith Mercer, Paul Sanasardo
GUEST ARTISTS: Miguel Godreau, Bonnie Mathis, Dennis Wayne

REPERTOIRE

"Metallics" (Cowell-Badings), "Shadows" (Satie-Scarlatti-Bach), "Footnotes" (Lester), "The Path" (Drews), and *PREMIERES* of "Ecuatorial" (Edgar Varese, Anna Sokolow; Costumes, Alan Madsen" on Saturday, May 18, 1974; "The Platform" (Bach, Paul Sanasardo; Decor, Robert Natkin; Costumes, Alan Madsen) on Thursday, May 23, 1974

**Right: Michele Rebeaud, Paul Sanasardo
in "The Path" Below: "Ecuatorial"**

**Diane Germaine, Michele Rebeaud, Sara Singleton,
Paul Sanasardo in "Shadows" Above: Willa Kahn,
Christine Varjan, Dominique Petit in "Metallics"**

**Paul Sanasardo
in "The Platform"**

129

ANNUAL DANCE FESTIVALS IN 1973
CONNECTICUT COLLEGE AMERICAN DANCE FESTIVAL

New London, Connecticut
June 28–August 4, 1973
Twenty-sixth Year

"Dedicated to the genius of Jose Limon"; Director, Charles Reinhart; President, Charles E. Shain; Dean, Martha Myers; Administrator, Kay McGrath; Press, Jane Hughes; Assistant to the Director, Lisa Booth; Administrative Assistants, Deborah Lin Smith, Celia Halstead; Press Assistant, Kitty Bowe Hearty; Technical Directors, Fred Grimsey, Mark Litvin, Lindsey Miller; Sound and Video, Ben Howe, Eric Kaufman; Lighting, Wendy Coleman, Sara Schrager
Friday, June 29, 1973

NIKOLAIS DANCE THEATRE with choreography, sound score, costumes, and lighting designs by Alwin Nikolais; Manager, Peter Obletz; Technical Director, Duane Mazey; Stage Manager, George Gracey; Technician, Mark Goodman; with Lisbeth Bagnold, Rob Esposito, Steven Iannacone, Lynn Levine, Suzanne McDermaid, Gerald Otte, Anne Marie Ridgway, Gladys Roman, James Teeters, Fred Timm, performing "Somniloquy," "Foreplay," "Tower"
Saturday, June 30, 1973

NIKOLAIS DANCE THEATRE performing "Foreplay," "Scenario," "Tent"
Friday, July 6, 1973

ERICK HAWKINS DANCE COMPANY; Director-Choreographer, Erick Hawkins; Conductor, Joel Thome; Music, Lucia Dlugoszewski; Designs, Ralph Dorazio; Manager, Mark Z. Alpert; Lighting, Frank Davis; Stage Manager, Ken Longert; with Erick Hawkins, Beverly Brown, Robert Yohn, Carol Conway, Natalie Richman, Cathy Ward, Nada Reagan performing "Angels of the Inmost Heaven," "Black Lake," *Premiere* of "Choros of the Daughters of Okeanos" from "Greek Dreams with Flute," "Cantilever"
Saturday, July 7, 1973

ERICK HAWKINS DANCE COMPANY performing "Early Floating," "Angels of the Inmost Heaven," "Geography of Noon," "Choros of the Daughters of Okeanos," "Cantilever"
Friday, July 13, 1973

JOSE LIMON DANCE COMPANY; Artistic Director, Ruth Currier; Choreography, Jose Limon; Production Manager, John Toland; Sets and Costumes, Charles D. Tomlinson, Pauline Lawrence; Lighting, Jennifer Tipton; with Carla Maxwell, Laura Glenn, Edward DeSoto, Jennifer Scanlon, Louis Solino, Ann Vachon, Aaron Osborne, Peter Sparling, Risa Steinberg, Nina Watt, Marc Stevens, Robyn Cutler, Clay Taliaferro, Gary Masters, Ryland Jordan, Marjory Philpott, performing "A Suite of Psalms" (Choreographed in memory of Jose Limon by Carla Maxwell; Music, John W. Getman), "Dances for Isadora" (Chopin, Limon), "The Emperor Jones" (Villa-Lobos, Limon), "Choreographic Offering" (Bach, Limon), "Orfeo" (Beethoven, Limon)
Saturday, July 14, 1973

JOSE LIMON DANCE COMPANY performing "Choreographic Offering," "Carlota" (Limon), "La Malinche" (Lloyd, Limon), "The Moor's Pavane" (Purcell, Limon)
Friday, July 20, 1973

DANCE THEATRE OF HARLEM; Directors, Arthur Mitchell, Karel Shook; Company Manager, Richard A. Gonsalves; Press, Ruth Wills; Musical Director-Conductor, Tania Viera Leon; Costumes, Zelda Wynn; Ballet Master, William Scott; Stage Manager, Gary Fails; Sets and Lighting, Fred Barry; with Lydia Abarca, Virginia Johnson, Roslyn Sampson, Laura Brown, Gayle McKinney, Brenda Garrett, Yvonne Hall, Susan Lovelle, Melva Murray-White, Sheila Rohan, Ronda Sampson, Miriam Bacot, Walter Raines, Paul Russell, Gerald Banks, William Scott, Joseph Wyatt, Edward Moore, Derek Williams, Ronald Perry, Homer Bryant, Samuel Smalls, Roman Brooks, Lindsey Jones, performing "Tones" (Tania Viera Leon, Arthur Mitchell), *Premiere* of "Haiku" (Leon, Walter Raines; Costumes, Walter Raines; Lighting and Projections, Gary Fails), "Ancient Voices of Children" (George Crumb, Milko Sparemblek), "Rhythmetron" (Marlos Nobre, Mitchell)

Top Right: Erick Hawkins (R) and company
in "Black Lake" Below: Dance Theatre
of Harlem in "Agon"(*Martha Swope Photo*)

Pilobolus Dance Theatre in "Spyrogyra"
(*Tim Matson Photo*)

ANCE THEATRE OF HARLEM performing "Haiku," "Ancient Voices of Children," "Agon" (Stravinsky, Balanchine), "Forces of Rhythm" (Traditional, Louis Johnson)

Thursday, July 26, 1973

RUDY PEREZ DANCE THEATER; Choreography and Sound Collage, Rudy Perez; Assistants, John Moore, David Varney; Lighting, Fred Grimsey; Stage Manager, Chip Largman; with John Moore, David Varney, Susan Ishino, Timothy Haynes, Rudy Perez, and students Bill DeYoung, Eileen Herman, Cynthia May, Carol Lynne Moore, Donna Kay Moore, Dagmar Nissen, Heather Shepley, Roger Tolle, performing "Quadrangle," "Countdown," and *Premiere* of "Walla Walla"

Friday, July 27, 1973

MARJORIE GAMSO'S DANCE CONCOCTIONS; Choreography, Marjorie Gamso; with Marjorie Gamso, Elizabeth Fain, Jonathan Hollander, Janaki Patrik, Daniel Press, Dana Reitz, Karen Robbins, Nancy Topf, performing "Floatsam and Jetsam," "The Recurring Duet," *Premiere* of "Delicate Negotiations"

PILOBOLUS DANCE THEATRE; Scores by Jon Appleton, Ken Jacobs, Robb Pendleton, Jonathan Wolken, Charles L. Roberts, Lou Carter; Stage Manager, Chris Ashe; Technical Director, George Gracey; with Robby Barnett, Alison Becker Chase, Lee Harris, Robb Pendleton, Martha Clarke, Jonathan Wolken, performing "Pilobolus," "Geode," "Two Bits," "Walklyndon," "Untitled Work in Progress," "Syzygy," "Aubade," "Anaendrom," "Ocellus," "Cameo," "Spyrogyra"

JANE KOSMINSKY and BRUCE BECKER'S 5 by 2 DANCE COMPANY; Manager, Richard Dean; Stage Manager, Rick Thorelson; with Jane Kosminsky and Bruce Becker

Saturday, July 28, 1973

MARJORIE GAMSO'S DANCE CONCOCTIONS performing "Two Weeks," "Decination," "Chinese Notebook," "Circle Solos" 5 BY 2 DANCE COMPANY (Jane Kosminsky, Bruce Becker) performing "There Is a Time" (Dello-Joio, Limon), "Sola" (Pennldham, Mario Delamo), "Meditations of Orpheus" (Hovhannes, Norman Walker), "Negro Spirituals" (Traditional, Helen Tamiris), "A Cold Sunday Afternoon, A Little Later" (Donald Erb, Cliff Keuter)

RUDY PEREZ DANCE THEATER in *Premiere* of "Americana Plaid"

Sunday, July 29, 1973

MARJORIE GAMSO'S DANCE CONCOCTIONS in "Rough Draft," "Rotogravure/Third Edition," "Epilogue" NORA GUTHRIE and TED ROTANTE performing "Frank" (Kenny Rankin—Arlo Guthrie—Woody Guthrie, Nora Guthrie), "Faith" (Collage, Guthrie), "Undercurrents" (Ted Rotante), "Break" (Meredith Monk), *Premiere* of "Corporate Images" (John McLaughlin Mahavishnu Orchestra, Ted Rotante)

Friday, Saturday, August 3, 4, 1973

INNER CITY REPERTORY DANCE COMPANY; Executive Director, C. Bernard Jackson; Administrative Director, Gloria Camee; Lighting, William Grant; Production Manager, Annette Ensy; Stage Manager, Lloyd Hardy; Costume Supervisor, Anthony White; with Gail Benedict, Ed Brown, Ron Bush, Barry D'Angelo, Alif de Raita, Jaqueline DeRouen, Wanda Evans, Anita Littleman, Ruby Millsap, Stanley Perryman, Marvin Tunney, Leslie Watanabe, Linda Young, performing "Songs of the Disinherited" (Donald McKayle), "Sojourn" (Jolivet, McKayle), "Rainbow 'Round My Shoulder" (Collection of John and Alan Lomax, McKayle), and *Premiere* of "Caravanserai" (Santana, Talley Beatty)

Top Right: 5 by 2 Dance Company (Bruce Becker, Jane Kosminsky) in "There Is a Time"

Leslie Watanabe (Inner City Co.) in "Sojourn"
(*Martha Swope Photo*)

JACOB'S PILLOW DANCE FESTIVAL

Lee, Massachusetts
July 3—September 1, 1973

Founder, Ted Shawn (1881–1972); Acting Director, Walter
Terry; General Manager, Tom Kerrigan; Administrator, Grace
Badorek; Press, Nancy S. Mason
July 3–7, 1973
MARGOT FONTEYN dancing premiere of "In Nightly Revels"
(Bach, Peter Darrell; Harpsichordist, Jess Meeker) assisted by stu-
dents of the Jacob's Pillow School
ROSARIO GALAN BALLET ESPANOL: Esperanza Galan,
Graciela Galvez, Gloria Catala, Nydia Valez, Sandra Mesina, An-
tonia Lorca, Juan Tapia, Salvador Vivez (Choreography, Rosario
Galan; Lighting and Costumes, Manolo Galan; Guitarists, Beltran
Espinosa, Santiago; Pianists, Silvio Masciarelli, Nino Garcia) per-
forming "Sevilla" (Albeniz), "Seguiriya," "Aragoneza," "Tan-
guillo," "El Amor Brujo" (de Falla), "Leyenda" (Albeniz),
"Verdiales" (Traditional), "Cuadro Flamenco"
July 10–14, 1973
HARTFORD BALLET COMPANY: MICHAEL UTHOFF,
LISA BRADLEY, Jack Anderson, Kevin Aydelotte, Leslie Craig,
Charlotte Dickerson, Judith Gosnell, John Perpner, Sandra Ray,
John Simone, Jeanne Tears, Brian Adams, Catherine Chagnon,
Robin Wagge, Deborah Whitehead (Artistic Director, Michael
Uthoff; Executive Director, Enid Lynn; Technical Director, Fred
Thompson) performing "Danza a Quattro" (Donizetti, Uthoff),
"Dusk" (Satie, Uthoff), "La Malinche" (Lloyd, Limon), "Day on
Earth" (Copland, Humphrey), "Windsong" (Elgar, Uthoff), "Con-
certo Grosso" (Vivaldi, Uthoff), *premiere* of "Ten Seconds and
Counting" (Uthoff), "Grandstand" (Compiled, Lynn), "Peter and
the Wolf" (Prokofiev, Uthoff), *premiere* of "Variation for Tape and
Choreography" (Josef Tal, Enid Lynn)
July 17–21, 1973
BALLET BRIO: Sandra Balestracci, Candace Itow, Georgette Mar-
cel, Linda Kuchera, Christopher Corry, William Forsythe, John
Fogarty, Samuel McManus (Producer-Director, Thomas Andrew)
performing "Excerpts from the Red Poppy" (Gliere, Thomas An-
drew), "Don Quixote Pas de Deux" (Minkus, Petipa), "Persecond"
(Electronic, Andrew), "Battered Bacchanal" (Ponchielli, Andrew)
TWYLA THARP with Sara Rudner, Rose Marie Wright, Isabel
Garcia-Lorca, Kenneth Rinker, Nina Wiener, Cam Lorendo, Tom
Rawe, performing "The Bix Pieces" (Bix Beiderbecke, Tharp), "The
Raggedy Dances" (Rags Condensed by David Horowitz, Twyla
Tharp)

Top Right: Margot Fonteyn

Rosario Galan

Michael Uthoff, Lisa Bradley

JACOB'S PILLOW

July 24–28, 1973

NATIONAL BALLET: Christine Knoblauch, Michelle Lees, Carmen Mathe, Kirk Peterson, Dennis Poole, Stuart Sebastian, Fredric Strobel, Diane Duffy, Susan Frazer, Hiller Huhn, Andrea Price, Judith Rhodes, Leslie Andres, Sergio Cal, Ronald Darden, Nancy Davis, Charlene Gehm, Deidre Grohgan, Jennifer Holmes, Linda Lintz, Edmund LaFosse, Eve Leyman, Suzanne Longley, Alfredo Martin, Kevin McKenzie, Rosemary Miles, Dorio Perez, Robert Petersen, Guy Pontecorvo, Abigail Rigby, Lauren Rouse, Susan Smith, Christine Spizzo, Elizabeth Wade (Directors, Frederic Franklin, Ben Stevenson) performing "The Story of Cinderella" (Prokofiev, Stevenson; Scenery, Edward Haynes; Costumes, Norman McDowell)

July 31–August 4, 1973

Pas de Deux Program:

BRUCE BECKER & JANE KOSMINSKY dancing "Meditations of Orpheus" (Hovhannes, Walker), and "Negro Spirituals" (Arranged, Tamiris) danced by Mr. Becker

RONI MAHLER & PAUL RUSSEL dancing "Paquita Pas de Deux" (Minkus, Mme. Gabi Taub-Darvash) The American debut of Paris Opera Ballet stars JACQUELINE RAYET & JEAN-PIERRE FRANCHETTI dancing "Webern Opus 5" (Webern, Bert), and "Pas de Deux d'Auber" (Auber, Gsovsky)

MELISSA HAYDEN & PETER MARTINS dancing the *world premiere* of "Aves Mirabiles" (Lukas Foss, Michael Uthoff)

August 7–11, 1973

CARMEN DE LAVALLADE dancing "The Incense and the Yogi" (Loomis—Alexay, St. Denis), "Songs of the Auvergne" (Canaloupe, Holder), premiere of "The Vagabond" (Writings from Colette), "The Creation" (Holst, Holder)

Members of the DANCE THEATRE OF HARLEM: Lydia Abarca, Homer Bryant, Virginia Johnson, Susan Lovelle, Melva Murray-White, Ronald Perry, Paul Russell (Co-Directors, Arthur Mitchell, Karel Shook) performing "Design for Strings" (Tchaikovsky, Taras), "Pas de Trois from Holberg Suite" (Grieg, Mitchell), "Pas de Trois from Agon" and "Pas de Deux from Agon" (Stravinsky, Balanchine)

Twyla Tharp
Top Right: Roni Mahler

Carmen de Lavallade

133

JACOB'S PILLOW
August 14–18, 1973

MARCIA HAYDEE & RICHARD CRAGUN dancing "Pas de Deux from Romeo and Juliet" (Prokofiev, Cranko), and "Pas de Deux from "The Taming of the Shrew" (Kurt-Heinz Stolze after Domenico Scarlatti, Cranko)

CINCINNATI BALLET COMPANY (names not available) dancing three Lester Horton works: "Dedication to Jose Clemente Orozco," "The Beloved," "Face of Violence (Salome)," and Artistic Director David McLain's "12 × 11 in 6"
August 21–28, 1973

CYNTHIA GREGORY & TERRY ORR with other dancers of AMERICAN BALLET THEATRE: Fernando Bujones, Marianna Tcherkassky, Hilda Morales, Janet Shibata, Zhandra Rodriguez, Clark Tippet (Producer, Terry Orr) performing "Divertissement D'Auber" (Auber, Lew Christensen), premiere of "Three Bach Dances" (Bach, Bill Evans), "La Bayadere Pas de Deux" (Minkus, Petipa), "Dying Swan" (Saint-Saens, Maria Swoboda after Pavlova) danced by Cynthia Gregory, "Divertissement from Napoli" (Helsted, Bournonville).
August 28—September 1, 1973

ELEANOR D'ANTUONO & IVAN NAGY dancing "Coppelia Pas de Deux" (Delibes, Saint-Leon)

HARKNESS BALLET (Artistic Director, Rebekah Harkness) performing "Night Song" (Hovhaness, Walker), "Three Preludes" (Rachmaninoff, Stevenson), "Gemini," (Mahler, Nebrada), and "Time out of Mind" (Delibes, Saint-Leon)

Top Right: Marcia Haydee, Richard Cragun
Below: Cincinnati Ballet in "Face of Violence"
(Sandy Underwood Photo)

Cynthia Gregory

Harkness Ballet in
"Time Out of Mind"

SUMMER FESTIVAL OF ETHNIC DANCE

Barnstable, Massachusetts
July 12–August 24, 1973
Fourth Season

Presented by Ethnic Dance Arts, Inc.; Artistic Director, La Meri; Administrator-Technical Director, A. L. Wendel; Stage Manager, Jean Condit; Lighting, Jack Vetorino; Press, Evelyn Lawson
July 12–13, 1973
GOVINDA & RATILEKHA performing "Mangalam Charan," "Batu Nrutya," "Alarippu," "Natanam Adinar," "Krishnani Begane Baro," "Tillana," "Raga Shankaravaran," "Abhinaya," "Dasavatar," "Venayaka Stuti," "Manduka Shabdam"
July 20, 1973
SAHOMI TACHIBANA performing "Dojoji," "Ocho," "Osono," "Urashima," "Byakko Tai," "Anja Bushi"
July 26–27, 1973
LA MERI'S ETHNIC DANCE GROUP: Cynthia Maddux, Jean Mellichamp, Patricia Phillips, Amelie Hunter, Jadine Lee, Barry Edson, performing "Drinshyakava" (Vivaldi, La Meri), "Fifty Years of Spanish Dance:" "Fandanguillo (Sepeno, Otero), "Gitanerias" (Lecuona, Eugenie), "Serenata" (Malats, La Meri), "Las Morenas" (Popular, La Meri), "Zambra" (Gomez, La Meri), "Caracoles" (Puertas, Roman), "Farruca" (Falla, Parra), "Luciamiento del Monton" (Falla, La Meri)
August 3, 1973
LUIS OLIVARES with Malena Vargas and Alessandra Greco in lecture-demonstration
August 9–10, 1973
SUNG HAE OH & ALAN CHOW performing "The Crown Dance," "Sacred Lantern Dance," "Huwang Chin I," "Riding a Horse," "Monk's Dance," "Nobel Man's Dance," "Mask Dance," "Chinese Spear Dance," "Korean Fan Dance," "Waiting for My Lover," "Korean Drum Dance"
August 17, 1973
MANJUSRI CHAKI-SIRCAR performing "Ras Nritya," "Gastha Parang," "Lai-Haroba," "Alarippy," "Tillana," "Navarasa," "Gaity," "Loud Beats the Drum"
August 23–24, 1973
LUIS RIVERA SPANISH DANCE COMPANY with Gisela Noriega (Guest Artist), Luis Vargas (Singer), Barbara Picardo, Emilio Prades (Guitarists) performing "Fandango" (Vives), "Alegrias" "Canto Flamenco," "Intermezzo" (from "Goyescas," Granados), "Danza No. 1" (from "Vida Breve," Falla), "Viva la Jota" (Montorio-Olmeda), "En el Palacio Real" (Milan-Narvaez), "Asturias" (Albeniz), "Encuentra en la Noche," "Caracoles," "Soleares"

Sahomi Tachibana
Top Right: Manjusri Chaki-Sircar

Sung Hae Oh

REGIONAL AND PROFESSIONAL DANCE COMPANIES
(Failure to meet deadline necessitated omission of several companies)

ALBERTA CONTEMPORARY DANCE THEATRE
Edmonton, Alberta, Canada

Co-Directors, Jacqueline Ogg, Charleen Tarver; Choreographers, Jacqueline Ogg, Charleen Tarver, Morgan Dale, Keith Burgess; Designers, Bruce Bentz, Sheryl Walton; Projectionists, David Lovett, Bryce Missal; Costumes, Wendy Albrecht, Diane Ulrich; Secretary-Treasurer, David Liles; Management, Upstage Enterprises.

COMPANY

Martha Clee, Morgan Dale, Gayle Fekete, Robert Fleming, Catherine Geddes, Maureen Hermon, Ron Holgerson, Joanne Johnstone, Mary Kooy, Darryl Mickleborough, Mary Concrieff, Sherry Ogg, Oscar Riley, Kelly Rude, Sam Walton

REPERTOIRE

"Alberta Suite" (Walter Carlos-Lalo Schifrin-Aaron Copeland, Charleen Tarver), "Circles of Silence" (Violet Archer-Malcolm Forsyth, Jacqueline Ogg), "Crystals" (Prokofiev, Tarver), "Feeling versus Time" (Enesco-Shankar-Sibelius, Keith Burgess), "Four Inventions (Patent Pending)" (Bach, Morgan Dale), "Haute Mer" (Ravel, Ogg; Poem, Jules Supeivielle), "In Just Spring" (Walter Toleson, Ogg; Poem, e. e. cummings), "On the Road" (Jerry Jeff Walker—Kristen Glade—Allan Bell, Charleen Tarver), "Parmi les Reves" (Lasry—Ouzounoff—Bashet, Ogg), "Saraband" (Visee, Ogg; Poem, Eugenio Montale), "Stones" (Harry Partch, Morgan Dale), "Three Wealthy Sisters" Lloyd Nicholson, Jacqueline Ogg; Poem, e. e. cummings), "Truncated Icosadodecahedron" (Harry Partch, Ogg)

Forrest Bard Photos

"Truncated Icosadodechedron"
Above: "Parmi les Reves"
Alberta Contemporary Dance Theatre

AMERICAN MIME THEATRE
New York, N.Y.
Twenty-second Year

Director, Paul J. Curtis; Assistant to the Director, Rick Wessler Press, Jean Barbour; Stage Managers, Charles Barney, Joel S Charleston

COMPANY

Jean Barbour	Marc Maislen
Charles Barney	Nina Petrucelli
Paul Curtis	Rick Wessler
Kender Jones	Arthur Yorinks
Marion Knox	Mr. Bones

REPERTOIRE

"The Lovers," "The Scarecrow," "Dreams," "Hurlyburly," "Evolution"

Jim Moore Photos

Rick Wessler, Paul J. Curtis, Charles Barney
in "Hurlyburly"

ANDAHAZY BALLET BOREALIS
Minneapolis/St. Paul, Minnesota

Directors-Choreographers, Lorand and Anna Adrianova Andahazy, Marius Andahazy; Conductor, Isaiah Jackson; Designers, Lorand, Anna, and Marius Andahazy, Cornelius A. Bartels, Helen Beaverson, Victor Hubal, Floyd Romslo; Press: Staff of Project Discovery, Ken Miller

COMPANY

PRINCIPALS: Anna Adrianova Andahazy, Lorand Andahazy, Marius Andahazy, Linda Finholt
SOLOISTS: Celeste Anderson, Wilor Bluege, Martha Connerton, Laurie Edwards, Jane Keyes, Kathleen Marcy, Sarah Mooney, Kay Page, Janet Smith
CORPS DE BALLET: Leah Abdella, Adele Arthur, Rachel Baker, Regan Barke, Anita Bartolatta, Diana Brainard, Gilbert Bauman, Deborah Clarke, Ellen Coleman, Roger de Lange, Michael Denber, Susan Dooley, Stephen Elliott, Pamela Fitzgerald, Linda Gaylord, Roger Gray, Ann Hill, Helen Hodgins, Brian Jacobsen, Cherie Kaspar, Julie Lemon, Sandra Lochen, William Lochen, Kamala Madhu, Laura McLellan, Caroline Meldahl, Sandra Mussig, Brigita Nagobads, Andrea Oien, Karen Paulson, Mary Peloquin, Linda Purdy, Karen Rasmussen, Joanne Raymond, Michael Roberts, Julie Stanzak, Marcy Sund, Robert Sund, Karen Ventura, Blythe Williams, Andre Zawitkowski, Michael Ziegahn
GUEST ARTISTS: Eleanor D'Antuono, Fernando Bujones, Diana Lewis

REPERTOIRE

"Les Sylphides" (Chopin, Fokine), "Scheherazade" (Korsakov, Fokine), "Don Quixote Grand Pas de Deux" (Minkus, Petipa), "Vivaldi Concerto" (Vivaldi, Marius Andahazy), "Black Swan Pas de Deux" (Tchaikovsky, Petipa-Ivanov), "Los Seises" (Rodrigo-Albeniz, Adrianova)
Daniels Studio Photos

Anna Adrianova Andahazy, Lorand Andahazy and Andahazy Ballet Borealis in "Scheherazade" Left Center: Arizona Civic Ballet in "Sleeping Beauty"

ARIZONA CIVIC BALLET
Scottsdale, Arizona

Founder-Artistic Director-Choreographer, Ruth Sussman; Assistant Director, Norman Macdonald; Costumes, Mrs. Duncan Jennings, Mrs. Terry Nelson, Mrs. Oscar Spangler, Mrs. Lincoln Westman, Mrs. Haruto Yamanouchi; Make-up and Special Effects, Renee Parr; Stage Manager, Lighting Technician, Michael Slagle; Press, Marilyn Carberry

COMPANY

SOLOISTS: Lori Caliendo, Ann Nelson, Kim Yamanouchi
CORPS: Jennie Chavez, Mary English, Laura Marshall, Dan Nissen, Tim Stember, Patty Tang, Tara Westman, Nancy Williamson, Shelli Yares, Jean Zimmerman
JUNIORS: Beth Alt, Anne Conlin, Jeanne Heileman, Roseann Miller, Becky Ocheltree, Lori Spangler, Rosemarie Tan
GUEST ARTISTS: Sharon Bowdich and Kevin Brown of Dallas Civic Ballet

REPERTOIRE

"Ballet Class," "Sleeping Beauty Act III" (Tchaikovsky, Sussman after Petipa)

ARLINGTON DANCE THEATRE
Arlington, Virginia

Formerly Arlington-St. Mark's Dance Company; Director, Mary Craighill; Ballet Mistress M'Liss Gary; Choreographers, Mary Craighill, M'Liss Gary, Michael Kilgore, Kathryn Stephenson; Managers, Pat Gebhard, Michele Gressman; Designers, Carmen Schein, Marge Coffin; Lighting, Harry Morse, Reese Jones

COMPANY

Charlotte Belcher, Rosetta Brooks, Mary Craighill, M'Liss Gary, Michael Kilgore, Kathryn Stephenson, Michael Stephenson
GUEST ARTISTS: Michele Gressman, Joan Kelley, Caitlin Kelley, Samuel Maddy

REPERTOIRE

"Peter and the Wolf" (Prokofieff, Craighill), "Romping" (Prokofieff, Craighill), "Treffin I & II" (Kalvert Nelson, Michael Kilgore), "Folk Dance Suite" (Traditional, Craighill)
PREMIERES: "Wild Things" (Moussorgsky-Ravel, Craighill), "Suite from the Magnificat" (Bach, Craighill), "Scarlatti Suite" (Craighill), "Insect Comedy" (Brahms, M'Liss Gary), "Michka Pas de Trois" (Glazounov, Gary), "Cruel Sea" (Rodrigo, Gary), "Ah, Trivia" (Collage, Kathryn Stephenson)
Bob Fonda Photo

Kathryn Stephenson, M'Liss Gary, Michael Stephenson in "Michka Pas de Trois" (Arlington Dance Theatre)

137

ATLANTA BALLET
Atlanta, Georgia

Director-Choreographer, Robert Barnett; Founder-Consultant, Dorothy Alexander; Associate Directors, Virginia Barnett, Carl Ratcliff, Merrilee Smith; General Manager-Production Stage Manager, Charles Fischl; Administrative Assistant, Linda C. Fischl; Stage Managers, Lee Betts, Phil Hutcheson; Choreographers, Norbert Vesak, Carl Ratcliff, Ginger Prince Hall; Costumes, Tom Pazik; Conductor, John Head; Lighting, Charles Fischl

COMPANY

SOLOISTS: Rose Barile, Anne Burton, Merry Clark, Amy Danis, Susan Hall, Melinda Jordon, Kathryn McBeth, Ben Hazard, Ronald Jones, Robert Archard, Tom Pazik
CORPS DE BALLET: Candy Allen, Andrea Berta, Wendy Crawford, Marilyn Gaston, Kathleen Frey, Jaimie Kirk, Michele Laboureur, Jennifer Manning, Sandy May, Joanne McKenney, Jennifer Potts, Ellen Richard, Mary Ann Schladenhauffen, Ellen Taylor, Barbara Whipple, Chuck Benoit, David Hackney, James Lee

REPERTOIRE

"Abyss" (Copland, Ratcliff), "Carmina Burana" (Orff, Ratcliff), "Fifth Symphony" (Schubert, Barnett), "Giselle" (Adam, Blair), "The Nutcracker" (Tchaikovsky, Balanchine), "Serenade" (Tchaikovsky, Balanchine), "Sleeping Beauty" (Tchaikovsky, Blair), "Raymonda Variations" (Glazounov, Balanchine)
PREMIERES: "Gift to Be Simple" (Marjorie LeStrenge—Betty Phillips—Ross Laidley-David Gryn-Jones, Norbert Vesak), "The Good-Morrow" (Gustav Mahler, Norbert Vesak), "Lifeline" (Karel Husa, Ginger Prince Hall), "Valse" (Josef Strauss-Josef Gungl, Robert Barnett), "Concerto de Aranjuez" (Joaquin Rodrigo, Robert Barnett)

Top Right: Anne Burton, Robert Barnett in
"Fifth Symphony" (*King Douglas Photo*)
Below: "Serenade" (DeCasseres Photo)

Melinda Jordon, Ronald Jones in
"Concierto de Aranjuez"

Rose Barile, Tom Pazik, Ronald Jones
in "Lifeline" (*Paul Buckholdt Photo*)

AUGUSTA BALLET COMPANY
Augusta, Georgia

Artistic Director-Choreographer, Ron Colton; Assistant to the Director, Zanne Beaufort; Production Manager-Lighting Designer, Jim Thomas; Costumes Designers, Tom Pazik, Betty Williams, Michael Hotopp

COMPANY

Zanne Beaufort, Kelly Bowers, Karen Carter, Lil Easterlin, Brenda Elliott, Cammy Fisher, Laurie Hardman, Karen Harpe, Peggy Hardman, Julie Jacobs, Crystal Rangos, Pam Willingham
GUEST ARTISTS: Anne Burton, Robert Barnett, Ronald Jones, Tom Pazik

REPERTOIRE

"Pas de Trois" (Minkus, Balanchine), "Trio" (Mozart, Stanley Zompakos), "Love Song" (Suk, Duncan Noble), "Mystere" (Albinoni, Noble), "Design" (Varese, Colton), "Dans le Bois" (Ibert, Zompakos), "Peter and the Wolf" (Prokofiev, Colton), "Symphony in D" (Mozart, Zompakos), "Symphony 13" (Haydn, Noble), "Reflections with Voice" (Stockhausen Colton), "Gas" (Mason Williams, Colton-Smotrel), "Poems" (Ravel, Colton; Poems, John Van Brakle)
PREMIERES: "A Brandenburg Movement" (Bach, Zompakos), "The Rookery" (Iannis Xenakis-Karel Husa, Ginger Prince Hall)

Fitz-Symms Photo

Augusta Ballet Company

Austin Ballet Theatre

AUSTIN BALLET THEATRE
Austin, Texas

Artistic Adviser-Choreographer, Stanley Hall; Company Director, Judy Thompson; School Director, Renata Sanford; Sets and Costumes, Kathleen H. Gee, Marguerite Wright, Elizabeth Cameron; Sound, Lee Thompson; Press, Jane Koock, Katy Bergquist

COMPANY

PRINCIPALS AND SOLOISTS: Joni Bergquist, Oscar Elizondo, Andrea Gorrell, Byron Johnson, Susan Miller, Ken Owen, Renata Sanford, Shelley Schleier, Judy Thompson, Buddy Trevino, Terri Lynn Wright
CORYPHEE AND CORPS DE BALLET: Gina Adams, Gemee Alexander, Bonnie Bratton, Gail Brown, Cindy Burnette, Nora Byrd, Lisa Frantz, Debbie Glick, Arletta Howard, Lea Johnson, Eve Larson, Rosemary Thomas, Lucia Uhl, Anna Kay Ward, Mary Claire Ziegler, Lynda Lindsay, Steve Brule, Anthony Chiu, Victor Culver, Dave Larson, George Stallings.

REPERTOIRE

"Cinderella" (Prokofiev), "The Nutcracker" (Tchaikovsky), "The Rites of Joseph Byrd" (Byrd), "Dante" (Berio-Hindemith), "Patineurs" (Meyerbeer), "Rosenkavalier" (Strauss), "Le Corsaire" (Drigo)
PREMIERES: (All choreographed by Stanley Hall) "Flickers" (American Ethnic Dances), "Concerto" (Tchaikovsky), "La Peri" (Bugmuller), "Birthday Waltz" (Tchaikovsky), "Le Combat" (Khatchaturian), "Pas de Six" (Tchaikovsky), "Ballet Class" (Glazounov), "Tregonell" (Goldsmith-Ussachevsky), "Pas Classique" (Glazounov), "Gemini" (Massenet)

Bill Records Photos

"Snow Queen" (Ballet des Jeunes)

BALLET DES JEUNES
Philadelphia, Pennsylvania
Pennsauken, New Jersey

Artistic Director-Choreographer, Ursula Melita; Choreographers, Carmecita Lopez, Ruth Skaller; Assistant Ballet Mistress, Nancy Sterling; Technical Director, Joe Gasperic; Lighting, Sherry Bazell; Stage Manager, Janet Feldenkreis; Production Manager, David Jenkins; Musical Director, Irene Andrews; Press, Fay Smelkinson

COMPANY

Cindy Alberts, Theresa Baxter, Myra Bazell, Doris Bencic, Susan Berger, Ann Marie Bright, Karen Cebular, Janet Celi, Maria DeRosa, Amelia DeRosa, Joy Edelman, Eve Edelman, Claudia Fieo, Carolyn Franzen, Marina Iossifides, Sally Jackson, Jennifer Jenkins, Sarah Jones, Barbara Kates, Janice Kates, Jennifer Lockwood, Michele Murray, Carol Maloney, Amy Orloff, T. T. Pearlman, Lisa Rosenfeld, Holly Ruckdeschel, Jenny Ruckdeschel, Helen Sadler, Mary Ann Sherman, Donna Tambussi, Marianne Sinnott, Michele Triolo, Renee Vekkos, Chris Vlaskamp, Douglas Vlaskamp, Michele Wood, Barbara Yeager, Evelyn Wang, Caren Schussler, Sheila Jones, Kathy Miller, Diane Landers, Jackie Reisman, Dina Terry, Debbie O'Hara, Debbie Lang, Jill Marchione, Linda Marchione, Caroline Krakower, Marylyn Morris, Theresa Scott, Elizabeth Moshes, Sandy Bender

REPERTOIRE

"The Three-Cornered Hat" (DeFalla), "Slavonic Suite" (Dvorak), "Spanish Suite" (Popular), "Pas de Quatre" (Pugni), "Paintings by Degas" (Pugni, Ruth Skaller)
PREMIERES: "Snow Queen" (William Mayer, Ursula Melita), "Hello World" (Mayer, Melita), "Pot Pourri" (Chopin, Melita), "Serenade" (Mozart, Melita), "Search for Spring" (Shostakovich, Melita), "Sorcerer's Apprentice" (Dukas, Melita)

BALLET PACIFICA
Laguna Beach, California

Formerly Laguna Beach Civic Ballet; Founder-Artistic Director-Choreographer, Lila Zali; General Director, Douglas Reeve; Ballet Mistress, Kathy Jo Kahn; Technical Director, Carl Callaway; Press, Sally Reeve; Wardrobe Mistress, Myrth Malaby; Choreographers, Jeannette Cozzone, Kathy Jo Kahn, Carrie Kneubuhl, Victor Moreno, Benjamin Sperber; Lights and Crew, Zachary Malaby, Buddy Baker, Mike Modiano, Mark Vuille; Costumes, Tania Barton, Hildur Mahl, Lila Zali; Set Designer, Tania Barton

COMPANY

PRINCIPALS: Charles Colgan, Louise Frazer, Joan Ross Gair, Mary Hanf, Caroll Stasney
CORPS: Randy Barnett, Julie Bradley, Barbara Byrnes, Adele Canetti, Louis Carver, Louisa Davis, Jennifer Engle, Roger Faubel, James Jones, Kathy Jo Kahn, Chris Kirby, Carrie Kneubuhl, Jayne Lynch, Molly Lynch, Kathy Mason, Robert Petel, Billie Pulliam, Lisa Robertson, Mary Sayers, Dee Dee Schlarb, Belinda Smith, Elizabeth Snyder, Benjamin Sperber, Peggy Stamper, Kristi Stephens, Barbara Stuart, Nancy Sutton, Cynthia Tosh, Arabella Wibberley
ARTISTS IN RESIDENCE: Paul Maure, Victor Moreno

REPERTOIRE

"Ballet Portraits 18th Century" (Corelli, Zali), "Carnival of the Animals" (Various, Kahn), "Carnival Tutu" (Milhaud, Ford), "Delibiana" (Delibes, Zali), "Golden Moments of Ballet" (Various, Norman), "Le Pas de Quatre" (Pugni, Zali), "Moldavian Dances" (Traditional, Moreno), "Nutcracker" (Tchaikovsky, Zali after Petipa), "Peter and the Wolf" (Prokofiev, Zali), "Sleeping Beauty" (Tchaikovsky, Zali after Petipa), "Snow White and the Seven Dwarfs" (Various, Kneubuhl), "Swan Lake Act II" (Tchaikovsky, Zali after Ivanov), "Enchanted Toyshop" (Bayer, Zali), "Tubby the Tuba" (Kleinsinger, Zali), "Black Swan Pas de Deux" (Tchaikovsky, Zali after Ivanov), "Don Quixote Pas de Deux" (Minkus, Zali after Celli)
PREMIERES: "Concierto de Aranjuez, First Movement" (Rodrigo, Cozzone), "Graduation Ball" (Strauss, Lichine), "Illusion" (Ravel, Kahn), "In A-Chord" (Bach, Smith), "Polovetsian Dances from Prince Igor" (Borodin, Moreno), "Sketches in Blue" (Davis, Sperber), "The Owl and the Pussycat" (Stravinsky, Kahn)

Sally Reeve Photo

Belinda Smith, Roger Faubel, Lisa Robertson in "Sleeping Beauty" (Ballet Pacifica)

BALLET REPERTORY COMPANY
New York, N.Y.

Director-Choreographer, Richard Englund; Assistant to the Director, Henley Haslam; Company Manager, Robert Yesselman; Ballet Mistress, Joysanne Sidimus; Rehearsal Coach, Gage Bush; Wardrobe Mistress, Harriet Wallerstein; Stage Manager, Paul Murgatroyd; Presented by American Ballet Theatre and Ballet Theatre Foundation.

COMPANY

Lynne Charles, Fanchon Cordell, Laura Crain, Ellen English, Miguel Garcia, Cynthia Gast, Aurea Hammerli, Enrico Labayan, Jan Lathrop, Linda Marx, Pamela Mitchell, Michael Owen, Gernot Petzold, Leigh Provancha, Stephen Rockford, Raymond Serrano

REPERTOIRE

"Bournonville Divertissement" (Helsted-Paulli, Bournonville), "Crazy Quilt" (Copland, Englund), "Jigs 'n' Reels" (Arnold, Englund), "Icarus" (Matsushita, Hoving), "La Malinche" (Lloyd, Limon), "Impressions" (Schuller, Sanders), "Trio" (Copland, Higginbotham), "Don Quixote Pas de Deux" (Minkus, after Petipa), "Le Corsaire Pas de Deux" (Minkus, after Petipa), "Annual" (Collage, Perez)
PREMIERES: "Albinoni" (Albinoni, Jacobsen), "Mosaics" (Ginastera, Englund), "Sans Amour" (Berlioz, Englund), "Variations Capriccioso" (Mendelssohn, Higginbotham)

Jack Mitchell Photo

Laura Crain, Michael Owen in "Le Corsaire"
(Ballet Repertory Company)

BALLET ROYAL
Winter Park, Florida

Artistic Director-Choreographer, Edith Royal; Technical Director-Business Manager, Bill Royal; Costume Design-Wardrobe Mistress, Phyllis Watson

COMPANY

SOLOISTS: Sally Gage, Carol Willson, Murphy James
CORPS DE BALLET: Laurie Anderson, Dawn Barker, Janet Bennett, Jane Bliven, Angela Berry, Cindy Bryant, William Bartlett, Gary Coburn, Angel Casteleiro, Benita Cherry, Denise Carlson, Mimo Clausen, Christy Donohoe, Pam Duda, DeeDee Dykes, Patti Erlacher, Jeanette Gurinskas, Tracy Goodson, Ann Greenman, Stephanie Heafner, Lori Hendry, Terri Hall, Michael Hall, Welty Davies, Pamela Jenkins, Jill Jaeb, Jamie Heileman, Jan Koshar, Punky Leonard, LuAnne Leonard, Teegie Lehmann, Lisa Lewenthal, Elizabeth Mengel, Kim Maxwell, Cindy Maxwell, Cindy Mason, Robin Maples, Jeannie McMullen, Deede Murrell, Kathy Nolle, Susan Polaski, Suzanne Rogers, Cindy Ratcliffe, Lynn Rade, Kim Suellau, Rhonda Sward, Shelly Segrest, Lisa Siegfried, Livia Sherman, Jeanne Thiele, Debbie Young, Karen Yates, Sharon Will
GUEST ARTISTS: Denise Jackson, Russell Sultzbach

REPERTOIRE

"Nutcracker" (Tchaikovsky, Royal), "Soiree Musicale" (Britten-Rossini, Tudor), "The Devil Is a Clown" (Prokofiev, Royal), "La Vie" (Offenbach, Royal), "Pas de Cinq" (Traditional, Royal), "Mother and Child" (Saush, Carol Willson), "La Valse" (Minkus, Sally Gage), "The Law of the Land" (Unknown, Carol Willson), "The Comedians" (Smetana, Royal)

Kim Suellau, Susan Polaski, Kim Maxwell
in "Soiree Musicale" (Ballet Royal)

141

BALLET SPECTACULAR
Miami, Florida

Conceived, Created, and Directed by Francis Mayville; Associate Director, A. Robert Owens; Assistant to the Director, Richard Gobeille; Conductors, Walter Hagen, Kenneth Schermerhorn, Ottavio de Rosa, Simon Sadoff, Richard Dunn, Dean Ryan; Stage Managers, Eugene Lowery, Demetrio, Maria Zeida

ARTISTS

Margot Fonteyn, Karl Musil, Heinz Bosl, Atillio Labis, Nina Novak, Fernando Bujones, Lydia Diaz Cruz, Kathleen Smith, Radu Ciuca, Leo Ahonen, Soili Arvola, Luis Fuente, Annette av Paul, Nina Bzorad, Juliu Horvath, Douglas Hevenor, Jacques d'Amboise, Melissa Hayden, Lupe Serrano, Scott Douglas, Lois Smith, Earl Kraul, Dean Crane, Robert Seevers, Zane Wilson, Linda di Bona, Tanju Tuzer, Clara Cravey, Richard Devaux, Earle Sieveling, Marina Svetlova, Grace Doty, David Anderson, Thatcher Clarke, Estrelita and Raul, Allegra Kent, Mimi Paul, Patricia Neary, Ramon Segarra, Rochelle Zide, Fiona Fuerstner, Lawrence Rhodes, Sonia Arova, Frank Ohman, Judith Reece, Karen Batizi, Christine Henessey, Oleg Briansky, George Zoritch, Irina Kovalska, Edmund Novak, Gustavo Portillo, Rafael Portillo, Celeste Velasquez, Robert Gladstein, Claudia Cravey, Richard Dodd, Leslie Gearhart, Mariano Parra, Robert Davis, First Chamber Dance Company, Helgi Tomasson, Royes Fernandez, John Clifford, Jean-Paul Comelin, John Prinz, Marnee Morris, Karel Shimoff, Renee Estopinal, Christine Redpath, James Bogan, Marjorie Spohn, Thor Sutowski, Kathi Durant, Kurt Putzig, William Pizzuto, Gladys Garcia, Milenko Banovitch

REPERTOIRE

"La Favorita," "Flower Festival," "Paradox," "Swan Lake Act II," "Les Sylphides," "Fandango," "Meditation from Thais," "Spring Waters," "Dying Swan," "Le Corsaire," "Ribbon Dance," "Raymonda Variations," "Afternoon of a Faun," "Pas de Trois '20's," "Night Shadow," "Le Combat," "Irish Fantasy," "Opus II," "Hungarica," "Les Deux," "Paganini Solo," "You Are Love," "Apollo," "Still Point," "Valse Fantaisie," "Bergamasca," and Pas de Deux from: "Giselle," "Don Quixote," "Black Swan," "Blue Bird," "Stars and Stripes," "Mendelssohn," "Sleeping Beauty," "Nutcracker," "Sylvia," "Tchaikovsky," "Coppelia," "Glazounov," "Pas de Dix," "La Fille Mal Gardee," "Stravinsky," "Slavonic Dancers," "Nutcracker Snow Scene," "Romeo and Juliet," "Paquita," "Bayadere," "Raymonda," "AC–615," "Faust"
PREMIERES: "Stimmung" (Wagner, Sutowski), "Concierto de Aranjuez" (Rodrigo, Lefevre), "Les Millions d'Arlequin" (Drigo, Novak)

Lydia Diaz Cruz

BALLET TACOMA
Tacoma, Washington

Director-Choreographer, Jan Collum; Costumer, Judy Loiland; Press, Lois Hampson

COMPANY

Beverly Brennan, Nannette Bales, Candi Crocker, Jolene Chaney, Immaculada Dodd, Joan Everson, Deidre Gimlett, Judy Harter, Hunter Hale, Valli Hale, Leslie Jane, David Hitchcock, Leslie Hull, Candy Joachim, Gonya Klein, Michael Kane, Janet Kinsman, Cheri Loiland, Blake Little, Teresa Newton, Dale Petersen, Monica Tarpenning, Adelaide Talamantes, Charles Talamantes, Panchito Talamantes, Irene Tomaris, Erin Walk, Lorna Newton, Patty Shippy, Jan Wolf

REPERTOIRE

"All in a Garden Green" (Traditional, Collum), "Relievo" (Marcello-Cimarosa, Collum), "Evanescence" (Bartok, Norbert Vesak), "You Can't Be in Two Places at One Time, Unless You're Syndicated" (William Russo, Michael Kane), "Roanoke River" (Buffy Sainte-Marie-Traditional, Charles Bennett), "Cycle" (Stravinsky, Leslie Jane)

"Evanescence" (Ballet Tacoma)
(*Walters of Tacoma Photo*)

BALLET WEST
Salt Lake City, Utah

Artistic Director-Choreographer, William F. Christensen; Ballet Mistress, Bene Arnold; Assistant Ballet Mistress, Sondra Sugai; Costume Mistress, Sarah B. Price; Assistant Costume Mistress, Veronica Willis; Wardrobe Mistress, Elora Carlin; Assistant Wardrobe Mistress, Klea Ernst; Associate Production Manager-Stage Manager, David Kent Barber; Associate Production Manager-Lighting, Greg Geilmann; Assistant Lighting Designer, John S. Stasco; Technical Assistant, Craig Gerber; Pianists, Marie Williams, Marge Carleson; Special Adviser, Mattlyn Gavers; Executive Vice President-General Manager, Robert V. Brickell; Company Manager, Steven H. Horton; Press, Connie Christensen, Patricia Dasko.

COMPANY

PRINCIPALS: Janice James, Tomm Ruud, Victoria Morgan, John Hiatt, Patricia Rozow, Bruce Caldwell, Sabine Salle, Thierry Dorado

SOLOISTS: Vivien Cockburn, Kristine Miller, Catherine Scott, Cary Tidyman, Cynthia Young, Christopher Fair, Charles Fuller, Philip Fuller, Jay Jolley, John Nelson, Michael Onstad, Rocky Spoelstra

CORPS DE BALLET: Mary Bird, Sharee Lane, Tenley Taylor, Frank Hay, Michael Rozow, Martine Dorado, Cheryl Fitts, Edward Staver, Shirley Acheson, Connie Burton, Rebecca Drenick, Francine Kessler, Leonore Maez, Drusilla Milam, Elizabeth Nesi, Natalie Niemi, Carole Ann Ramme, Eugenie Wingate, Corey Farris, Derryl Yeager

GUEST ARTISTS: John Butler, Victoria Simon, Yurek Lazowski, Milorad Miskovitch

REPERTOIRE

"Black Swan Pas de Deux" (Tchaikovsky, Petipa), "Blue Tournament" (Handel, Christensen), "Bluebird Pas de Deux" (Tchaikovsky, Petipa), "Bravura" (Chabrier, Christensen), "Chaos" (Karl-Birger Blomdahl, Richard Kuch), "Cinderella" (Prokofiev, Christensen), "Con Amore" (Rossini, Lew Christensen), "Concerto Barocco" (Bach, Balanchine), "Coppelia" (Delibes, Christensen), "Creatures of Prometheus" (Beethoven, Christensen), "Cycle" (Ernest Bloch, Bene Arnold), "The Eternal Idol" (Chopin, Michael Smuin), "Filling Station" (Virgil Thompson, Lew Christensen), "Firebird" (Stravinsky, Christensen), "Giselle" (Adam, Coralli), "Irish Fantasy" (Saint-Saens, Jacques d'Amboise), "La Bayadere" (Minkus, Christensen), "La Fille Mal Gardee" (Hertel, Jean Dauberval), "Les Bijoux du Mal" (Ibert, Christensen), "Les Sylphides" (Chopin, Michel Fokine), "Meditations" (Massenet, d'Amboise), "Mobile" (Khachaturian, Tomm Ruud), "Mozartiana" (Tchaikovsky, Christensen), "Nothing Doing Bar" (Milhaud, Christensen), "N.R.A." (Warner Jepson, Robert Gladstein), "Nutcracker" (Tchaikovsky, Christensen), "Paquita Pas de Deux" (Minkus, Christensen), "Pas de Dix from Raymonda" (Glazounov, Balanchine), "Pas de Six" (Nicolai, Christensen), "Pulcinella Variations" (Stravinsky, Smuin), "Romeo and Juliet Fantasy" (Tchaikovsky, Christensen), "Serenade" (Tchaikovsky, Balanchine), "Statements" (Copland, Ruud), "Swan Lake Act II" (Tchaikovsky, Christensen), "Symphony in C" (Bizet, Balanchine), "Three Movements for the Short Haired" (John Lewis, Lew Christensen), "You Are Love" (Jerome Kern, d'Amboise).

During the summer, the company presents a four week season in Aspen, Colorado.

"Square Dance" Top Right: Tomm Ruud, Janice James in "Giselle" (*Robert Clayton Photos*)

Janice James, Tomm Ruud in "Eternal Idol"
(*Martin Zwick Photo*)
Above: "Pulcinella Variations" (*Gary Horton Photo*)

Ballet Western Reserve in "The Bestiary"
(Dawn Perkins Photo)

Birmingham Civic Ballet in
"Mozart Divertimento"*(King Douglas Photo)*

Black Dance Workshop in "Masai"

BALLET WESTERN RESERVE
Youngstown, Ohio

Director-Choreographer, Michael Falotico; Choreographers, Marilyn Jones, Marilyn Kocinsky, Suzanne Thomas, Edward Myers, Valerie Deakin; Conductors, Franz Bibo, Michael Payne, C. Watson; Sets, Paul Kimpel, Russell Moore, Robert Eden, Richard Gullickson, Galen Elser; Costumes, Mel Juan, Laslow Myron, Bruce Mac, Roberta Johnson, Robert Elden, Georgann Sherwood; Lighting, Kenneth Lowther, Richard Nealy, Martha Bateson; Stage Managers, Galen Elser, Richard Nealy; Press, V. Friedman, C. McPhee, Jo Devine; Business Manager, Catherine McPhee; Company Manager, Roderic B. MacDonald; Executive Producers, Suzanne M. Frankle, Youngstown Symphony Ballet Guild

COMPANY

PRINCIPALS: Stephanie Dabney, Barbara Kohut, Amy Taylor, Robert Terleck
SOLOISTS: Cathy Frankle, Jacqueline Melnick, Robin Miller, Karen Szauter, Donald Tupper, Robert Tupper
CORPS DE BALLET: Lenore Pershing, Nancy Tiberio, Susan Tosi, Michelle Catoline, Lisa Devine, Karen George
GUEST ARTISTS: Christopher Lyall, Donna Baldwin, Brynar Mehl, Jean Anderson, Rita Brosh, Matthew Nash, David Lee, Nicholas Cate

REPERTOIRE

"Prologus" (Donizetti, Falotico), "End of the Morning" (Contemporary, Marilyn Jones), "Rustic Variations" (Adam, Galotico), "G and S for 8 + 2" (Sullivan, Falotico), "Giselle Act II" (Adam, Edward Myers), "Les Fetes Etranges" (Andres, Falotico), "Coronach" (Legley, Falotico), "Aurora's Wedding" (Tchaikovsky, Deakin), "Nutcracker" (Tchaikovsky, Sequoio-Falotico), "Pas de Cinq Classique" (Burgmuller, Falotico), "The Bestiary" (D'Indy, Falotico)
PREMIERES: "Homage to Haydn" (Haydn, Falotico), "Les Rendezvous" (Glazounov, Falotico), "Licorice Stick Frolic" (Weber, Falotico), "Faschings Terzett" (Beethoven, Falotico), "Mindscape" (Contemporary, Marilyn Jones), "Rarae Aves" (Various, Falotico)

BIRMINGHAM CIVIC BALLET
Birmingham, Alabama

Artistic Director-Choreographer, Alfonso Figueroa; Guest Choreographers, Jan Stripling, James Lewis; Costumes, Kristine Kaiser, Sandro LaFerla; Lighting, Walter Kaiser; Stage Managers, Walter Kaiser, Norton Owen; Press, June Cunniff, Cherie Woods

COMPANY

Katharine Anderson, Mary Deweese, Cynthia Ferguson, Alfonso Figueroa, Cythia Gray, James Lewis, Mary Ann Martin, Janet Moran, Jane Randolph, Marion Ransley, Karen Simmons, Kathryn Townsend, Vicky Valin, Vicki Vespaziani

REPERTOIRE

"Prokofiev Concerto" (Prokofiev, Figueroa), "Changes" (Brahms, Figueroa), "In Corte Sia" (Madrigals, Jan Stripling), "Nutcracker Pas de Deux" (Tchaikovsky), "Corsair Pas de Deux" (Drigo), "Don Quixote Pas de Deux" (Minkus)
PREMIERES: "Terpsichoros" (Mozart, Figueroa), "Primus" (Gassman, Figueroa), "Fantasy Dances" (Schumann, James Lewis)

BLACK DANCE WORKSHOP
Buffalo, N.Y.

Artistic Director-Choreographer, Carole Kariamu Welsh; Administrative Director, Glendora Johnson; Costume Designer, Carol Kariamu Welsh; Lighting Designer, Peter Gill; Press, Gail Wells, Yvonne James; Stage Manager, Stuart Keller

COMPANY

Carole Kariamu Welsh, Frances Hare, Yvonne James, Gaynell Sherrod, Christina Pressley, Herbert Tillman (Lead Drummer)
GUEST ARTIST: John Parks

REPERTOIRE

PREMIERES: "Journey; North" (Sound Track-Nina Simone-Otis Redding-Dakota Staton-Chambers Brothers, Carole Kariamu Welsh), "Masai" (Drums, Carole Kariamu Welsh), "Soba" (Drums, Chuck Davis), "New World Coming" (Barry White-Love Unlimited-Nina Simone, John Parks)

BOSTON BALLET
Boston, Massachusetts

Artistic Director, E. Virginia Williams; Executive Director, Ruth G. Harrington; Ballet Mistress, Sydney E. Leonard; Ballet Masters, James Capp, Samuel Kurkjian, Lorenzo Monreal; Regisseuse, Ellen O'Reilly; Choreographers in residence, Samuel Kurkjian, Alfonso Figueroa; Conductors, Arthur Fiedler, Michel Sasson; Lighting, Thomas Skelton, John W. Jacobson; General Manager, Michael B. Judson; Production Manager, Aloysius Petruccelli; Press, Elizabeth G. Dunton, Elinor Stout, Rosemary Polito

COMPANY

PRINCIPALS: David Brown, James Capp, Tony Catanzaro, Jerilyn Dana, Alfonso Figueroa, Woytek Lowski, Lorenzo Monreal, Ellen O'Reilly, Anamarie Sarazin, Robert Steele, Edra Toth, Laura Young
SOLOISTS: Elaine Bauer, Sanson Candelaria, David Drummond, Veronica Fell, Leo Guerard, Alphonse Poulin
CORPS DE BALLET: Kathryn Anderson, Carinne Binda, Miguel Angel Bolarin, Ron Cunningham, Kaethe Devlin, King Douglas, Mark Johnson, Walter Kaiser, Janet Moran, Stephanie Moy, Gigi Nactsheim, Clyde Nantais, Judith Shoaff, Ilene Strickler, Leslie Woodies

REPERTOIRE

"Allegro Brillante" (Tchaikovsky, Balanchine), "Coppelia" (Delibes, Williams after Ivanov-Cecchetti; Additional choreography, Samuel Kurkjian), "Donizetti Variations" (Donizetti, Balanchine), "Giselle" (Adam, Romanoff after Sergueff), "Rodeo" (Copland, deMille), "Speed Zone" (Hindemith, Kurkjian), "Swan Lake Act II" (Tchaikovsky, after Ivanov-Petipa), "Tarantella" (Gottschalk, Balanchine), "Adventures of Raggedy Ann 'n' Andy" (John Alden Carpender, Ron Cunningham), "Bach with Jacques" (Bach-Jacques Lussier, Tibor Zana), "Baroque Concerto" (Stolzel, Walker), "Don Quixote Pas de Deux" (Minkus, Lorenzo Monreal after Petipa), "Fall River Legend" (Gould, deMille), "Le Cygne" (Shankar, Bejart), "Spring Waters" (Rachmaninoff, Monreal after Messerer)
WORLD PREMIERE: "Jeu de Cartes" (Stravinsky, Alfonso Figueroa)

Right: "The Dolly Suite"
Top: Laura Young, Woytek Lowski in
"Donizetti Variations" (*King Douglas Photos*)

Leslie Woodies, Leo Guerard in "The People"
(*Dana Bisbee Photo*)

"Road of the Phoebe Snow"
(*Jack Mitchell Photo*)

BURLINGTON BALLET
Rancocas, N.J.

Artistic Director-Choreographer, Joan Kaletchitz Stebe; Business Manager, Madelyn Alexander Blair; Administrative Assistant, Eleanor H. Booth; Costume Designer, A. Christina Giannini

COMPANY

SOLOISTS: Deborah Dutton, Linda McMenamin, Dawn Tocci, Kim Geraghty, Trudy Cone
CORPS DE BALLET: Stacy Cross, Beth Kuzy, Julie Stebe, Suzanne Szepanski, Sue Frantz, Kathleen Nelboeck, Kelly Shaw, Saundra Shaw, Lisa Brodsky

REPERTOIRE

"Nocturne" (Chopin, Stebe), "Partheneion" (Researched by C. Sakellauiou, Stebe), "Ballade" (Chopin, Stebe), "Sesame Street Collage" (Stebe), "Confetti" (Stebe)
PREMIERES: "Waltz Bouquet" (Chopin, Stebe), "Kinetic Anemone" (Gwendolyn Watson, Stebe)

Ronald G. Williams Photo

Linda McMenamin in "Kinetic Anemone" (Burlington Ballet)

Jennifer Britton, Ann Simpson Sergent, Kim Pauley of Charleston Ballet in "Bouquet de Lilas"

CHARLESTON BALLET
Charleston, West Virginia

Director-Choreographer, Andre Van Damme; Stage Director, Strauss Wolfe; Lighting Director, William Lutman; President, Dr. Arnold C. Burke; Costumes, Maggy Van Damme

COMPANY

Names not submitted.

REPERTOIRE

PREMIERES: "Bouquet de Lilas" (Johannes Brahms, Andre Van Damme) with soloists Ann Simpson Sergent, "Storm" (Claude Debussy, Andre Van Damme) with soloist Julianne Kemp, "Madness" (Edward Grieg, Van Damme) with soloist Nor Brunschwyler, "Street Corner" (Andre Jolivet-improvisations, Van Damme)

Photo by Kern

Cathy Myers and Charleston Ballet Co. in "Cinderella"

CHARLESTON BALLET COMPANY
Charleston, S.C.

Artistic Director-Choreographer, Don Cantwell; Assistant Director, Robert Ivey; Sets, Bill Buggel, Robert Prengle

COMPANY

Martha League, Justin Geilfuss, Merran Funderburg, Venessa Perot, Evelyn Johnson, Ann Osborne, Maria Brown, Christine Cantwell, Lisa Moseley, Geormine Stanyard, Camilla Tezza, Ann Nast, Kris Pierce, Lisa Mason, Mary McKeever, Debbie Horton, Chris Harrelson, Steve Phlegar, Robert Ivey, Don Cantwell

REPERTOIRE

"Pas de Quatre" (Tchaikovsky, Cantwell), "Visions Fugitives" (Prokofiev, Cantwell), "Adagietto" (Mahler, Cantwell)
PREMIERES: "Hyperprism" (Edgar Varese, Don Cantwell), "The Red Shoes" (Brian Easdale, Cantwell)

Bill Buggel Photo

CHICAGO BALLET
Chicago, Illinois

Artistic Director, Ruth Page; Associate Artistic Director, Larry Long; Choreographers, Richard Arve, Frederick Ashton, Bill Evans, Larry Long, Ruth Page, George Skibine, Ben Stevenson; Conductors, Henry Brandon, Walter Hagen; Designers, Richard Arve, Alexandre Benois, Peter Brown, Bernard Dayde, Andre Delfau, Rolf Gerard, Ron Hodge, Sam Leve; Administrative Director, Gerald Ketelaar; Stage Manager, Peter Brown; Press, Christopher L. Watson

COMPANY

PRINCIPALS: Anna Baker, Dolores Lipinski, Orrin Kayan
CORPS DE BALLET: Ruby Aver, Birute Barodicaite, Tom Boyd, Jeannie Granger, Dawn-Marie Guch, Stephen Jenkins, Jerzy Koztowski, Antonio Mesa, Lee Michelson, Mary Nardi, Lynn Parkerson, Elyssa Paternoster, Kenneth Pierce, William Pironti, Charles Pizarro, Linda Riefsnyder, Robert Sullivan, Diana Turner, Barry Vancura, Victoria Vaslett
GUEST ARTISTS: Jean-Pierre Bonnefous, Kenneth Johnson, Patricia Klekovic, Rose Marie Menes, Patricia McBride, Paul Sutherland

REPERTOIRE

"Bachanalia" (Bach, Long), "Bolero" (Ravel, Page), "Idylle" (Serrette, Skibine), "The Nutcracker" (Tchaikovsky, Page after Ivanov-Petipa), "Romeo and Juliet" (Tchaikovsky, Page), "Three Preludes" (Rachmaninoff, Stevenson), "When Summoned" (Subotnik, Evans), "Carmen" (Bizet, Page), "Carmina Burana" (Orff, Page), "Catulli Carmina" (Orff, Page)
PREMIERES: "Collage" (Collage, Arve), "Monotones" (Satie, Ashton), "Raymonda" (Glazounov, Balanchine after Petipa)

Charles Schick, Patricia Klekovic
in "Carmina Burana"
(Chicago Ballet)

CINCINNATI BALLET COMPANY
Cincinnati, Ohio

Artistic Director, David McLain; Manager, Henry A. Young, Jr.; Assistant Artistic Director, David Blackburn; Administrative Assistant, Patricia C. Losey; Music Director, Carmon DeLeone; Production Coordinator-Resident Designer, Jay Depenbrock; Wardrobe Mistress, Mildred Benzing; Assistants to the Director, Natalie Huston, Sue Simpson; Sound, James Armstrong; Press, Stevens Nemo

COMPANY

Paula Davis, Diane Edwards, Colleen Giesting, Patrica Kelly, Carol Krajacic, Karen Kuertz, Steffi MacFarlane, Deborah McLaughlin, Ellen Moritz, Claudia Rudolf, Susan Shtulman, Alyce Taylor, Katherine Turner, Renee Hallman, Merritt Robinson, Robin Shimel, Lynn Ferszt, Karen Karibo, Deena Laska, Jacqualine Pagani, Marcia Sells, Ian Barrett, David Blackburn, Michael Bradshaw, Lawrence Jones, Thomas Kovaleski, Wayne Maurer, Kevin Ward, Michael DiMario

REPERTOIRE

"Antiche Arie E Danze" (Respighi, McLain), "Aubade" (Poulenc, Sabline), "The Beloved" (Hamilton, Horton-Truitte), "Clouds" (Dvorak, McLain), "Concerto" (Poulenc, McLain), "Concerto Barocco" (Bach, Balanchine), "Divertissement Classique" (Burgmuller, Jasinski), "Face of Violence" (Horton-DeLeone, Horton-Truitte-deLavallade), "Guernica" (DeLeone, Truitte), "Guitar Concerto" (Castelnuovo-Tedesco, McLain), "Pas de Quatre" (Pugni, Dolin-Markova), "Serenade" (Tchaikovsky, Balanchine), "Tribute to Jose Clemente Orozco" (Klaus, Horton-Truitte), "The Unicorn, the Gorgon, and the Manticore" (Menotti-Johnson), "Winter's Traces" (Verdi, McLain)
PREMIERES: "Et Cetera" (Palombo, Johnson, Weston), "The Firebird" (Stravinsky, Jasinski-Larkin after Fokine), "Frevo" (DeLeone, Horton-Truitte)

Lawrence Jones and Cincinnati Ballet
in "Frevo" Above: Susan Shtulman
in "Serenade"

CHRYSLER CHAMBER BALLET
Norfolk, Virginia

Artistic Director-Choreographer, Gene Hammett; Ballet Mistresses, Teresa Martinez, Susan Borree

COMPANY

SOLOISTS: Melissa Hoffer, Ralph Hewitt, Carter Cholson, Deborah Doughtery, Sandra Johnson
CORPS DE BALLET: Stacie Caddell, Nancy Cantin, Anna Maria Martinez, Wendy Wisoff, Loretta Dodd
GUEST ARTIST: Leigh Smartz

REPERTOIRE

"Swan Lake Act II" (Tchaikovsky, Hammett), "Afternoon of a Faun" (Debussy, Borree), "Jeux des Enfants" (Hammett), "Ecole de Ballet" (Offenbach, Hammett)

David Cuevas, Sandra Johnson and Chrysler Chamber Ballet in "Swan Lake Act II"

COLORADO BALLET COMPANY
Colorado Springs, Colorado

Artistic/Executive Director-Choreographer, Ilse Reese Gahart; Ballet Manager, Ben Gahart

COMPANY

PRINCIPALS: Pamela Benson, Mona Ketchersid
SOLOISTS: Debra Rich, Sybill Navas, Leslie Clark, Stephanie Ries, Meredith Houghton, Don Dayhoff
CORPS: Marie Burgess, Roger Butterfield, Tracie Ddaney, Bessie Frank, Avis Henthorne, Marna Lake, Marilyn Myers, Melissa McGill, Joanne McGraw, Leanne Pemberton, Melinda Sturgeon, Patricia Smith, Teri Sullivan, Charla Teale, Jane Wells

REPERTOIRE

"Chopin Festival" (Chopin, Gahart), "Don Quixote Pas de Deux" (Minkus, Paredes after Petipa), "Scheherazade" (Rimsky-Korsakov, Gahart), "The Planets" (Holst, Gahart), "The Firebird" (Stravinsky, Gahart), "Four Hungarian Dances" (Brahms, Gahart), "Cinderella" (Prokofiev, Gahart)

Left: Pamela Benson in "Cinderella"

CONTEMPORARY CIVIC BALLET
Royal Oak, Michigan

Founder-Artistic Director-Choreographer, Rose Marie Floyd

COMPANY

SOLOISTS: Alice Hlavaty, Kathleen Vander Velde, Julie Sasso, Cindy Wenson, Richard Newman, Michelle Gregory, Karen Couturier, Mary Nissley, Margie Osburn, Susan Wallstrom
CORPS: Jane Shaffmaster, Joan Wenson, Kimberly Thomson, Laura Brockett, Janine Meldrum, Michele Kapp, Martha Meek, Jane Sevald, Susan MacPhee, John Ligas, Dick Meldrum, Terry Butkovich, Annette Scese, Kathryn Acheson, Debbie Butkovich, Susan Ernstein, Karyn Thomson, Dana Blakley, Jeanne Osburn, Joe Nissley, Steve Nagel
GUEST ARTISTS: Gay Wallstrom, Tony Catanzaro, Ramon Segarra, Jan Hanniford, George Montalbano

REPERTOIRE

(All choreography by Rose Marie Floyd, except where noted) "Nutcracker Act III" (Tchaikovsky, Ramon Segarra-Floyd), "Midsummer Night's Dream" (Mendelssohn; Narration, Esther Frank), "Concerto Electro" (Hyman), "Capriccio Italian" (Tchaikovsky), "Selections from Oklahoma" (Rodgers-Hammerstein), "Oberon Overture" (Von Weber), "La Forza Destino" (Verdi), "Danse Macabre" (Saint-Saens), "Soirees Musicales" (Britton), "Ballet Parisienne" (Offenbach)
PREMIERES: "Coppelia" (Delibes, Tony Catanzaro-Floyd), "Bartered Bride" (Smetena), "Invitation to the Dance," "Fingal's Cave" (Mendelssohn), "Gayne Suite" (Khachaturian)

Contemporary Civic Ballet in "Bartered Bride"

DALLAS METROPOLITAN BALLET
Dallas, Texas

Artistic Directors-Choreographers, Ann Etgen, Bill Atkinson; Lighting-Production Manager, Jeannine Stegin; Costumes, A. Rozelle, Francis Machette; Company Manager, Wayne Pitts; Press, Dale Blair, Vaughn Allen

COMPANY

Mitzi Smith, Gail Peters, Susan Irons, Becky Blair, Jacquie Kessler, Cheryl Hartung, Tracey Forsyth, Megan Ready, Karen Stevens, Renee Pfrommer, Mary Hall, Martha Mullen, Suzanne Wagner, Trudi Perin, Trish Muller, Richard Conden, Sam Lopez, Mark Kessler, Mark Tatum, Enrique Juarez, Jerry Kelley, Scott Chapman, Stephen Haynes, Keri Wakser, Susan Parker, Elizabeth Booziotis, Suzie Blair, Kim Spratt, Jayme Cody, Arden Cronk, Jayne Schichil, Cynthia Norton, Lori Sirmen, Leslie McPhail, Mike Semmer

REPERTOIRE

"Wand of Youth" (Elgar), "La Valse" (Ravel, Marc Wilde), "Bouquet" (Auber), "Christina's World" (Collage, Norbert Vesak), "Country Garden" (Grainger), "Graduation Ball" (Strauss, Joseph Carrow after Lichine), "Pas de Russe" (Shostakovitch), "Coppelia" (Delibes, restaged by Robert Lunnon), "Sweet Echo" (Chabrier), "Gym Dandy" (Prokofiev)
PREMIERES: "Night before Christmas" (Adam), "Enamorati" (Wolf-Ferrari), "Roundrock" (Collage)

Members of
Dallas Metropolitan Ballet

Dancers' Workshop Company in "Mandala"

DANCERS' WORKSHOP COMPANY
San Francisco, California

DIRECTORIAL STAFF: Anna Halprin, Xavier Nash, John Gamble working collectively with Carl Levinson, Patric Hickey, Jim Nixon, Benito Santiago, Sioux Von Baeyer, Craig Van Collie, Peter Weiss

REPERTOIRE

"Trance Dance," "Rituals," "Male and Female Scores," "Female Ritual," "Paper Dance," "Mandala"

DELAWARE STATE BALLET
Dover, Delaware

Artistic Director-Choreographer, Harry Asmus; President, Marion Tracy; Press, Carolyn Brown; Lighting, Judith Haynes; Stage Manager, John Whetstone
COMPANY: Names not submitted
GUEST ARTISTS: Zhandra Rodriguez, John Prinz, Danny Levine

REPERTOIRE

"Le Corsaire," "The Poisoned Apple" (Prokofiev, Michael Lopuszanski), "Swan Lake" (Tchaikovsky, Asmus), "Peter and the Wolf" (Prokofiev, Lopuszanski), "The Nutcracker" (Tchaikovsky, Asmus), "Pas de Quatre" (Pugni, Asmus)
PREMIERES: "The Bachiana Suite" (Bach, Michael Lopuszanski), "Of Things Past" (Albeniz-Ravel-Torroba, Harry Asmus), "Rodrigo Suite" (Georg Handel, Harry Asmus)

Cheryl Miller of Delaware State Ballet
in "Of Things Past"

EGLEVSKY BALLET COMPANY
Massapequa, N.Y.

Artistic Director-Choreographer, Andre Eglevsky; Assistant Director, Ramon Segarra; Ballet Mistress, Leda Eglevsky; Costumes, Pat Niuccio, Dosi Sorokin; Sets, Thomas Shanton; Stage Manager, Robin DeMaggio; General Manager, Sofia Semler; Press, Dorothy Most

COMPANY

PRINCIPALS: Anna Aragno, Dermot Burke, Jane Miller, Leslie Peck, Jerry Schwender, Ramon Segarra, Deborah Weaver, Hector Zaraspe
SOLOISTS: Ronald Darden, Donna Grisez, Patrick Madden, Michelle Semler, Sally Silliman, Bronwyn Thomas
CORPS DE BALLET: Alice Cartwright, Joan Doberman, Charlene Dunn, Eric Emmanuele, Patricia Etzkorn, Jennifer Finnerty, Teresa Graziadei, Greg Ismaeloff, Adrian James, Deborah Lehwalder, Vladimir Levin, Leslie McGinn, Vesne Nikitovich, Deborah Salkoff, Lee Shein, Alicia Shurkin, Heather Steelman, James Sutton, Robert Woods
GUEST ARTISTS: Margot Fonteyn, Ivan Nagy, Ben Stevenson, Jonathan Watts

REPERTOIRE

"Tchaikovsky Pas de Deux" (Tchaikovsky, Balanchine), "Don Quixote Pas de Deux" (Minkus, Petipa), "Pas de Quatre" (Pugni, Dolin), "A La Francaix" (Balanchine), "Pas de Six" (Glazounov, Balanchine), "Coppelia" (Delibes, Eglevsky)
PREMIERES: "Sleeping Beauty" (Tchaikovsky, restaged by Andre Eglevsky), "Cinderella" (Prokofiev, restaged and choreographed by Andre Eglevsky and Ramon Segarra), "Preludes" (Rachmaninoff, Ben Stevenson), "Romance" (Dvorak, Jonathan Watts)

Ilona Lutomski of Elmira-Corning Ballet
in "La Fille Mal Gardee" Right Center:
150 Eglevsky Ballet in "Sleeping Beauty"

DISCOVERY DANCE GROUP
Houston, Texas

Director-Choreographer, Camille Long Hill; Choreographers Tess Blankinship, Lynn Reynolds, Valentine Boving, Ron Sequoio James Clouser; Press, Lee Hickle, Pam Stockman

COMPANY

Valentine Boving, Kathy Buck, Debbe Busby, Rick Durapo, Beth Ezzell, Erwin Gibaon, Kathy Guinn, Vicki Loftin, Cheryl McCollough, Kathleen Parker, David Quintero, Betty Reeves, Lynn Reynolds, Laticia Rodriguez, Pam Stockman, Pat Williams

REPERTOIRE

"Inhibitions" (Mingus), "2 Degrees East 3 Degrees West" (Lewis) "Sea Visions" (Garson), "Search" (Bartok), "A Time Remembered" (Ravel, Sequoio), "Web of Decision" (Fischer), "Out of Darkness" (Pink Floyd, Blankinship), "Jass Bit #2" (Drums)
PREMIERES: "Prelude" (Villa-Lobos, Ron Sequoio), "The Last Waltz" (Lacy, Valentine Boving), "The Families" (Faure, Lynn Reynolds), "Dance for Six" (Barron, Camille Hill), "Invocacion de los Dioses" (Ginastera, James Clouser), "Shades of Blue" (Weston, Camille Hill)

ELMIRA-CORNING BALLET
Elmira, N.Y.

Founder-Artistic Director-Choreographer, Mme. Halina; Conductors, Fritz Wallenburg, Theodore Hollenbach; Technical Director, Floyd Lutomski; Guest Choreographers, Michael Falotico, Henry Danton, Rochelle Zide, Val Deakin, James DeBolt, Paschal Guzman

COMPANY

PRINCIPALS AND SOLOISTS: Ginger Fancher, Deborah Salmirs, Debra Burgett, Steve Dickinson
CORPS: Stephanie Schmid, Dorothy Lindsay, Stacey Gorsky, Darlene Errett, Wendy Tuller, Elizabeth Howell, Joy Doane, Carla Chamberlain, Karen Minch, Jeanine Clate, Donna Gibson, Kathryn Smith, Sally Westphal, Gaylin Horton, Margaret Thompson, Julieanne Hughes, Kirsten Winsor, Maureen Dooley, Cathy Curran, Sally Updyke, Mary Lemark, Cathy Mason, Betsy Buch, Mary Ellen Hagy, Lindsay O'Connor
GUEST ARTISTS: Carmen Mathe, Eleanor D'Antuono, Ramon Segarra, William George, Diana Bayer, Martin Fredman, James DeBolt, Siuja Simonen, Rochelle Zide, Sonja Taverner, Richard Beatty, William Glassman, Ellen Everett, Veronique LaRoche, Richard Gradus, Paschal Guzman

REPERTOIRE

"La Fille Mal Gardee" (Herold, Deakin), "The Nutcracker" (Tchaikovsky, Halina), "Sleeping Beauty" (Tchaikovsky, Petipa), "Coppelia" (Delibes, Deakin-Ashton), "Bayadere" (Adam, Denton), "Mozartiana" (Mozart, DeBolt-Halina), "Karnival" (Arranged, Halina), "Snow Maiden" (Tchaikovsky, Halina), "Masquerade" (Khatchaturian, Halina)
PREMIERES: "Comedia del Arte" (Pouleng, Falotico), "Masque at Bergamasque" (Faure, Falotico), "Chinese Ballad" (Ketelbey, Halina), "Sylvia" (Delibes, Falotico-Halina)

Top Left: David Quintero, Pam Stockman
in "A Time Remembered"
(Discovery Dance Group)

ETHNIC DANCE ARTS COMPANY
Barnstable, Massachusetts

Artistic Director, La Meri; Administrative and Technical Director, A. L. Wendel; Stage Manager, Jack Vetorino

COMPANY

Jean Mellichamp, Cynthia Maddux, Amalie Hunter, Patricia Phillips, Vera Lynn Champlin, Barry Edson

REPERTOIRE

"Drishyakava" (Vivaldi, La Meri), "Bach-Bharata Suite" (Bach, La Meri), "Los Mantones" (Falla, La Meri), and divertissements: "Alarippu," "Natanam Adinar," "Tillana," "Urmya," "Kathak Mefil," "Nacni Nrrta," "Apsarases" from India, "Seguidillas Manchegas," "Fandanguillo," "Gitanerias," "Serenata," "Farruca," "Caracoles," "Zambra," "Valenciana," "Arin-arin," "Jota Aragenesa" from Spain, "Devil Dances," "Serimpi," "Kikuzukishi," "The Meeting," "Sita's Journey," "Yein Pwe" from the Orient, "Huayno," "Marineira," "Zandunga," "Tamberito," "Hoohene Keia" from the Occident

Images Photo

Ethnic Dance Arts Company in "Drishyakava"

FAIRMOUNT DANCE THEATRE
Novelty, Ohio

Artistic Director, Raymond Johnson; Rehearsal Director, John Magill; Technical Director, David Gotwald; Costumes Mistress, Inge Meyer; Company Manager, Ron Kumin

COMPANY

John Magill, Carter McAdams, Thom Scalise, Ellen Bryson, Elaine Florence, Joyce Zyznar, Jo Murray
GUEST ARTISTS: Sara Shelton, Laura Dean, Peggy Cicierska, James Waring, Bill Evans

REPERTOIRE

"Replay" (Rowan-Cowell, Ormiston), "Crazy Dog" (Pink Floyd, Shelton), "Pillow Dance" (Collage, Raymond Johnson), "Land Mark I" and "Land Mark II" (Arranged, Johnson), "Pedastal Imprints" (Balinese Gamelan, Johnson), "Harriet" (Arranged, Cicierska)
PREMIERES: "Birthspace" (Peggy Cicierska), "Moonlight Finaletto" (James Waring), "At the Edge" (Sara Shelton)

Fairmount Dance Theatre in "Pillow Dance"

Myron Howard Nadel
of Fine Arts Dance Theatre

FINE ARTS DANCE THEATRE
Milwaukee, Wisconsin

Director-Choreographer, Myron Howard Nadel; General Manager, Barbara Banasikowski-Smith; Choreographers, Carla Graham-White, Barbara Banasikowski-Smith
COMPANY: Names not submitted
GUEST ARTISTS: Kathryn Moriarty, Carla Graham-White

REPERTOIRE

"Animus" (Druckman, Nadel), "Slaughter on Tenth Avenue" (Rodgers, Nadel), "Russian Country Scene" (Folk, Carla Graham-White), "Blimpsville 3, Ecosphere" (Shankar, Barbara Banasikowski-Smith)

FLORIDA BALLET THEATRE
Tampa, Florida

Director, Richard Rader; Choreographer-in-residence, Frank Rey; Ballet Mistress, Betty Lee Rey; Stage Managers, Arthur C. Spanton, Helen Gonzalez; Lighting, Sydne Morris; Costumes, Betty L. Rey, Nancy Beronda, Mary Spanton

COMPANY

Sheri Brockmeier, Debi Gallo, Dawn Kersey, Teil Rey, Cathy Smith, Suzanne Spanton, Julie Beronda, Sandi Wargo, Cathy Wood, Debra Acosta, Teri Boynton, Roxane Cardoso, Kelly Clements, Lona Coonradt, Beth Dretzka, Karla LeDoux, Linda Lefler, Jan Leone, Bonnie Lowrie, Louis McDonald, Brenda Matistic, Diana Melon, Lili Morris, Jackie Page, April Pozzi, Tammy Pridgen, Veronica Reynolds, Desiree Rutkin, Victoria Reynolds, Irene Steele, Debbie White, Lydia Williams, Cricket Willis, Jennifer Woehlk, Angela Zummo, Rosella Cardoso, Beverly Gonzalez, Renee Roos, Debra Fasting
GUEST ARTISTS: Bill Martin-Viscount, Susana Benavides

REPERTOIRE

"Cinderella" (Prokofiev), "A Child Is Born" (Prokofiev), "Nutcracker" (Tchaikovsky), "Ballet Suite" (Shostakovich, Stigler), "And When She Was Good" (Prokofiev), "Accented Variations" (Gershwin, Rader), "Kaleidoscope" (Arranged), "Match Girl" (Chopin), "Via Victor" (Herbert), "Les Sylphides" (Chopin, Fokine-Martin-Viscount), "Folded, Spindled, and Mutilated" (Hayes, Rader), "Kid Stuff" (Arranged)
PREMIERES: "Brilliante" (Britten-Rossini, Rader), "Deja Vu" (Bolcom-Albright, Rey), "Embraces" (Lambert-Potter, Rey), "Song Fest" (Arranged, Rey)

Jinkey Gleaton, Sandi Wargo, Richard Rader
of Florida Ballet Theatre in "Embraces"

GEORGIA DANCE THEATRE
Augusta, Georgia

Formerly Augusta Ballet Theatre Company; Artistic Director-Choreographer, Frankie Levy; Ballet Mistress, Suzanne Denning; Assistant to the Director, Ann-Toni Estroff; Costumes and Sets, Claude Astin, Keith Cowling, Ann-Toni Estroff, Frankie Levy; Lighting, Ann-Toni Estroff; Sound, Bernard Chambers; Press, Nelson Danish

COMPANY

PRINCIPALS: Bebe Graham, Suzanne Denning, Dede Shiver, Martha Simkins, Cathy Adams
COMPANY: Lynn Harp, Ann Marie Schweers, Missy Tiller, Wanda McIntyre, Melissa Pierce, Tina Hagler, Keith Hendrix, Martha Teets, Michell Newman, Amy Winn, Alexandra Gibson
APPRENTICES: Suzanne Taylor, Joy Shapiro, Kim Kortick, Francine Wynn, Eileen Schweers, Amy Barksdale, Sharon Palmer, Velvie Ketch, Charlene Linder, Debra Berlin
GUEST ARTISTS: Edward Villella, Allegra Kent, Susan Hendl, Frank Ohman, Linda Yourth, Polly Shelton, Nolan T'sani, Bonnie Mathis, Dennis Wayne, Richard Rein

REPERTOIRE

"Baroque Six" (Teleman-Vivaldi), "Gypsy" (Gottschalk-Kay), "Mosaic" (Bruckner), "Venus and Adonis" (Greig), "Et Mors" (Saint-Saens), "First Day" (Gershwin), "Pas de Quatre" (Pugni), "Concerto" (Tchaikovsky), "Le Cirque" (Kabalevsky), "Classical Symphony" (Prokofiev), "Masquerade" (Khachaturian), "Chopin Today" (Chopin), "Summer Song" (Mozart), "The Little Match Girl" (Mahler), "Cinderella" (Prokofiev)

Nelson Danish Photo

Bebe Graham, Suzanne Denning, Dede Shiver
of Georgia Dance Theatre

GUS GIORDANO DANCE COMPANY
Evanston, Illinois

Artistic Director-Choreographer, Gus Giordano

COMPANY

Gus Giordano, Erik Geier, Debbie Hallak, Mary Beth Kisner, Pattie Obey, Clarence Teeters, Julie Walder

REPERTOIRE

"Judy" (Judy Garland), "American Heritage" (Traditional), "Fluctuation" (Bernstein, Kolb), "Glitzville, USA" (Rock 'n' Roll '50's, Hallak), "Back to Bach" (Bach, Giordano-Walder), "Menage" (Redding-Subotnick-Tchaikovsky, Evans-Petipa-Giordana), "Slaughter on Tenth Avenue" (Rodgers), "The Matriarch" (Iron Butterfly-Ingle), "Fancy Free" (Bernstein, Giordano-Walder), "Ragtime to Rock" (Traditional)
PREMIERES: "Solar Wind" (Pointer Sisters, Morgan), "The Rehearsal" (Cat Stevens, Giordano), "N.Y. Export, Op. Jazz" (Prince, Giordano)

Gus Giordano (C) and company

HAMPTON ROADS CIVIC BALLET
Hampton, Virginia

Directors-Choreographers, Edgerton Evans, Muriel Shelley Evans; Set Designers, Mary Beaven, Pat Masonis; Lighting, Patty Westfall, Tim Van Noys; Choreographers, Lisa Shaw, Joan Ashlyn; Stage Managers, C. O. Seaman, Stephanie Messick; Press, Marika Anthony, Susan McAllister

COMPANY

PRINCIPALS: Joan Ashlyn, Lisa Shaw, Debby Harrison, Danny Gunter
CORPS: Teresa Adams, Kitty Alvis, Kathy Ann Anthony, Lee Beaven, Kari Buttles, Joanne Crum, Michelle Cawthorn, Vicki Church, Lynne Davis, Darcy Evans, Ginger Gunter, Kathleen Harmon, Corinne Jantz, Sophia Jantz, Kathy Johnson, Cathy Kelly, Michele Lequeux, Susan McAllister, Tea Romano, Virginia Vaughan, Mary Vinosky, Cathy Welsh
GUEST ARTISTS: James Lewis, Rita Toy, Karoly Barta

REPERTOIRE

"Festival" (Various, Traditional), "Spectrum" (Shostakovitch, Edgerton Evans), "The Nutcracker" (Tchaikovsky, Petipa-Ivanov)
PREMIERES: "Les Ombres" (Shostokovitch, Muriel Shelley Evans), "Trois Encore" (Shostokovitch, Joan Ashlyn)

**Darcy Evans, Susan McAllister, Lisa Shaw
of Hampton Roads Civic Ballet in "Trois Encore"**
(*Joseph C. Fudge Photo*)

HARTFORD BALLET COMPANY
Hartford, Connecticut

Artistic Director, Michael Uthoff; Executive Director, Enid Lynn; Managing Director, James Hodson; Press, Raymond E. Byrne; Musical Director, Dr. Moshe Paranov; Assistant to Artistic Director, Lisa Bradley; Technical Director, Fred Thompson; Technical Assistant, David Owen; Assistant General Manager, Gary Lindsey; Wardrobe Mistress, Beulah Cole; Costumiere, Mary Wolfson; Lighting, Nicholas Lyndon, Jennifer Tipton; Sets, Anni Albers, Michael P. Duffy, Morton Fishman, James Steere; Costumes, Jose Coronado, Michael P. Duffy, Anny J., David James, Larry King, Pauline Lawrence, Alan Madsen, Peter Max, Carl Mitchell; Choreographers, Manuel Alum, Lois Bewley, Kathrine Gallagher, Doris Humphrey, Joyce Karpiej, Jose Limon, Enid Lynn, Mary Staton, Michael Uthoff

COMPANY

Jack Anderson, Kevin Aydelotte, Noble Barker, Leslie Craig, Charlotte Dickerson, Thomas Giroir, Judith Gosnell, Debra McLaughlin, John Perpener, Sandra Ray, Roland Roux, John Simone, Jeanne Tears, Robin Wagge, Brian Adams, Cathrine Chagnon, Joan Merrill, Deborah Whitehead
GUEST ARTIST: Lisa Bradley

REPERTOIRE

"Concerto for Harp" (Gliere, Karpiej), "Concerto Grosso" (Vivaldi, Uthoff), "Day on Earth" (Copland, Humphrey), "Dover Beach" (Barber, Lynn), "Dusk" (Satie, Uthoff), "Grandstand" (Compiled, Lynn), "History of America" (Compiled, Lynn), "La Malinche" (Lloyd, Limon), "Meatwaves" (Miller, Lynn), "Nutcracker" (Tchaikovsky, Lynn-Karpiej-Uthoff), "Peter and the Wolf" (Prokofiev, Uthoff), "Piece for One or More Dancers" (Gnazzo, Lynn), "Variations for Tape and Choreography" (Tal, Lynn), "Windsong" (Elgar, Uthoff), "Winter Dreams" (Tchaikovsky, Karpiej)
PREMIERES: "Brahms Variations" (Brahms, Uthoff), "Cantata" (Ginastera, Uthoff), "ChiaroScuro" (Parris, Staton), "Danza a Quattro" (Donizetti, Uthoff), "Deadlines" (Bach, Alum), "Marossezk Dances" (Kodaly, Uthoff), "Quartet in D Minor" (Schubert, Bewley), "Ten Seconds and Counting" (Uthoff), "F. Jasmine's Quiet Space" (Wakeman, Gallagher)

Kenn Duncan Photos

**"Brahms Variations" Above: Jack Anderson,
Lisa Bradley in "Quartet in D Minor"**

HOUSTON BALLET
Houston, Texas

Artistic Director, Mme. Nina Popova; General Director, Henry Holth; Conductors, Charles Rosekrans, Hugo Fiorato; Lighting Designer, Jennifer Tipton; Stage Manager, Patrick Ballard; Guest Choreographers, William Dollar, James Clouser, Frederic Franklin, May O'Donnell; Costumer, Brauna Ben-Shane; Ballet Master, Eugene Tanner; Press, Lawrence Watson

COMPANY

PRINCIPALS: Soili Arvola, Leo Ahonen, James DeBolt, Shirley McMillan, Leslie Peck, Jerry Schwender
SOLOISTS: Barbara Pontecorvo, Juliu Horvath, Denise Smokoski, Mary Margaret Holt
CORPS: Lisa Chalmers, Maureen Denman, Mary Jane Doornbos, Michaela Hughes, Natasha Lewczuk, Shirley New, Nancy Onizuka, Amanda Rivera, Colleen Robertson, Sheryl Rowland, Kathleen Weiss, Michele White, Brian Andrew, Dick Foose, Whit Haworth, Karl Lindholm, Jose Meier, John Murphy, Robert Raimondo, Larry Robertson
GUEST ARTISTS: Margot Fonteyn, Cynthia Gregory, Desmond Kelly, Allegra Kent, Gelsey Kirkland, Ted Kivitt, Helgi Tomasson, Edward Villella

REPERTOIRE

"Bachianas Brasilieras" (Villa-Lobos, Job Sanders), "Caprichos" (Bartok, Herbert Ross), "Concerto Barocco" (Bach, Balanchine), "Design with Strings" (Tchaikovsky, John Taras), "Flower Festival at Genzano Pas de Deux" (Helsted-Paulli, Bournonville), "Impressions" (Schuller, Sanders) "La Favorita Pas de Deux" (Donizetti, Arvola), "Le Combat" (de Banfield, Dollar), "Le Corsaire Pas de Deux" (Drigo, Petipa), "Napoli Act III" (Helsted-Gade-Paulli, Bournonville), "Opus '65" (Macero, Anna Sokolow), "Paquita" (Minkus, Petipa), "Pas de Dix" (Glazounov, Balanchine), "Protee" (Debussy, Lichine), "Tchaikovsky Pas de Deux" (Tchaikovsky, Balanchine), "The Nutcracker" (Tchaikovsky, Franklin), "Through a Glass Lightly" (Tape Collage, Clouser), "Waltz and Variations" (Glazounov, Balanchine), "Workout" (Shostakovich, Ann Etgen-Bill Atkinson)
PREMIERES: "Carmina Burana" (Orff, James Clouser), "Constantia" (Chopin, William Dollar), "Suspension" (Ray Green, May O'Donnell), "Homage" (Gounod, Frederic Franklin)

Left: "Paquita" Top: Soili Arvola, Leo Ahonen in "The Nutcracker" (Houston Ballet)

HOUSTON CONTEMPORARY DANCE THEATER
Houston, Texas

Founder-Artistic Director, Buddy Gurganus; General Manager, J. M. Arpad Lamell; Ballet Master, Eugene Collins; Technical Director, Terry Greene

COMPANY

Betty Dorsey, Tina Summers, Jorene Holas, Diane Aldis, Nancy Salomon, Valerie Means, Raymundo Sais, Richard Rock, Buddy Gurganus

REPERTOIRE

"Diminishing Landscape" (Jeff Duncan), "Terestrial Figure" (Jeff Duncan), "Warriors of the Rainbow" (Gurganus), "pigs 'n' things" (Gurganus), "Apocalypse" (Lucas Hoving), "Score" (Katherine Litz), "Flying down to Warsaw" (James Waring), "Lynchtown" (Charles Weidman), "Christmas Oratorio" (Weidman)
PREMIERES: "Para Ojos" (Raymundo Sais), "Trilogy" (Sais), "Social Graces" (Betty Dorsey), "Untitled Excerpts" (Nancy Salomon), "A Smile Is not Too Far Away" (Richard Rock), "A Time" (Eugene Collins), "Untitled Duet" (Collins), "Gymnetics" (Buddy Gurganus), "Nation on Wheels" (Gurganus), "Message from Sara" (Gurganus), "Dance out of Whack" (Gurganus)

Houston Contemporary Dance Theatre in "Northern Lights"

JACKSONVILLE BALLET THEATRE
Jacksonville, Florida

Artistic Director-Choreographer, Dulce Anaya; Assistant to the Director, Harriet Webb; President, Tom Schifanella; Choreographers, Haydee Gutierrez, Oleg Briansky, Richard Welch, Carl Ratcliff; Conductor, Willis Paige; Set Designers, Andrew Liliskis, Allison Mimaglia, Jerry Beebe; Costumes, Phil Phillips, Memphis Wood; Sound, Rush Bulloch; Stage Manager, Andrew Liliskis; Press, Muriel Kayter

COMPANY

Dulce Anaya (Prima Ballerina), Harriet Webb, Elaine Pennywitt, Anne Brown, Leslie Snow, Meme Menard, Mary C. Haut, Charmion Clark, Debbie Sidbury, Diane Collins, Cindy Crombie, Kathy Katibam, Sharon Campbell, Pattie Chipman, Kenley Jones, Pam Powers, Emilie Olsen, Wendy James, Billye Kay Kersey
GUEST ARTISTS: Edward Villella, Ted Kivitt, Alexei Yudenich, Barbara Sandonato, Adolfo Andrade, Ramon Segarra, Alexander Filipov, Haydee Gutierrez, Hilda Reverte, Art Hutchinson, Linda Willard Caddell

REPERTOIRE

"The Nutcracker" (Tchaikovsky, Anaya after Petipa), "Giselle" (Adam, Anaya after Coralli), "Carmina Burana" (Orff, Ratcliff), "Concerto" (Grieg, Anaya), "Aria" (Stravinsky, Gutierrez), "Tarantella" (Rossini, Anaya), "Ballet Fun" (Ponchielli, Anaya), "Red Mill" (Herbert), "Fledermaus" (Strauss), "Marriage of Figaro" (Mozart), "Carmen" (Bizet), "Firebird" (Stravinsky, Anaya), "Les Sylphides" (Chopin, Fokine), "Raggedy Rag" (Briansky), "Vida Efimera" (Sibelius, Anaya), "Grand Pas de Quatre" (Pugni, Lester), "Aurora's Wedding" (Tchaikovsky, Petipa), "The Statue" (Debussy, Welch)
PREMIÈRES: "Rhapsody in Blue" (Gershwin, Anaya), "Quartet" (Shostakovitch, Anaya), "Prince Igor" (Borodin, Fokine)

**Right Center: Harriet Webb and corps
in "Les Sylphides"**

**Kuni Dance Theatre Company
in "Song of Chain"**

INDIANA UNIVERSITY BALLET THEATER
Bloomington, Indiana

Artistic Director-Choreographer, Marina Svetlova; Conductor, Michael Kuttner; Choreographer, Dean Crane; Lighting, Allen R. White; Sets and Costumes, David Higgins, C. Mario Cristini, Max Rothlisberger; General Manager, Charles H. Webb; Artistic Director, Wilfred C. Bain; Executive Assistant, George Calder; Technical Director, Harold F. Mack; Press, Philip J. Stephenson, Hugh Hazelrigg; Technical Assistants, Fontaine Rodman, Jack Stewart; Stage Manager, Jean Sokol

COMPANY

Debbie Roshe, Rona Nereida, Debra Force, Jeanne Engel, Beth Golman, Judy Tevlin, Susan Holz, Kim Reifshneider, Marla Brattan, Homer Broaddus, Michael Tevlin, Chuck Frank, Natalie Sterba, Charles Jackson, Linda Adelkoff, Gina Brown, Deborah Champagne, Bonnie Feldman, Ellen Friedman, Linda Havas, Susan Jaffee, Elisabeth Mann, Cynthia Miles, Lisa Thompson, Sue Webster, Melodie Carr, Debra Force, Cynthia Hagburg, Kim Manlove, Barbara Parsons, Debbie Pigliavento, Cynthia Sparrenburger, Jan Carrington, Sam Cayne, Nick Humphrey, Nathan Montoya, Earl Tucker, Carlene Branmuller, Ione Cram, Jacki Garifo, Linda Havas, Janice Kurtz, Cynthia Luce, Catherine Metcalf, Pam Pfeiffer, Rebecca Wood, Jon Bunn, Mike Carter, Linda Cooper, Jan Curriden, David DeValera, Kathy Edwards, Paul Frederiksen, Charles Hammond, Jeff Hunter, Randy Hyman, Carol Imler, Steve Jamerson, Bobby Kittle, Rovin Lessel, Joel Richter, Linda Robinson, Anne Ziege, Pam Zylvestra, Polly Glassie, Julian Levene, Erika Matulich, Alice Reiselbach, Lee Buck

REPERTOIRE

"Pas de Quatre" (Pugni, Marina Svetlova-John Kriza after Dolin), "The Story of Judith" (Ernest Bloch, Dean Crane), "Firebird" (Stravinsky, Marina Svetlova-Dean Crane)

**Top Left: Judith Bratten, Homer Broaddus
in "Story of Judith"**

KUNI DANCE THEATRE COMPANY
Studio City, California

Artistic Director-Choreographer, Masami Kuni; Choreographers, Paul Edwards, Stephanie Romeo, Jo Ann Mayeda; Electronic Music, Ken Heller, Masami Kuni; Lighting, Larry Wiemer, Jerry McColgan; Costumes, Masami Kuni; Press, Paul Edwards; Stage Manager, Fred Sutton

COMPANY

Stephanie Romeo, Jo Ann Mayeda, Tomiyo Nagahashi, Valerie Sied, Miriam Tait, Linda Wojcik, Becky Wiemer, Susan Deppipo, Chris Drath, Janey McCoy, Paul Edwards, Lois Greyston, Henrietta Soloff, Chris Yamaga

REPERTOIRE

"Room" (Masami Kuni), "Song of Chain" (Kuni), and *premiere* of "Circle without Circumference" (Kuni)

LOUISVILLE BALLET COMPANY
Louisville, Kentucky

Artistic Directors-Choreographers, Richard Munro, Cristina Munro; Technical Director, Richard I. Mix; Vice President-Production, Mrs. Nancy Dysart; Press, Mrs. Betty Moore; Conductor, George Marriner Maull

COMPANY

Pam Baird, Carla Black, Karen Connelly, Lisa Campbell, Judy Eckman, Sherry Gilpin, Susie Heckard, Donna Hoess, Anabel Ishkanian, Chris Karibo, Laura Kmetz, Kimberly Krueger, Cindy Lewis, Terri Lewis, Lori Massie, Sharon McShane, Mary Means, Lynne Melillo, Colleen O'Callaghan, Lisa Patrick, Frances Penton, Gail Peterson, Mary Kay Quarles, Janet Shaffner, Jan Tabacheck, Therese Whitfill, Stan Bobo, Lee Brunner, Vincent Falardo, David Guffy, Douglas Maguire, Luther Nieh, David Thurmond, Greg Wolverton
GUEST ARTISTS: Edward Villella, Allegra Kent, Cynthia Gregory, Terry Orr

REPERTOIRE

"Nutcracker" (Tchaikovsky, Munro after Ivanov), "Les Sylphides" (Chopin, Fokine), "Swan Lake Act II" (Tchaikovsky, Bourmeister), "Grand Pas Des Fiancees" (Tchaikovsky, Carter), "Brahms Fantasie" (Brahms, Munro), "Pas de Quatre" (Pugni, after Lester), "Pas de Trois" (Tchaikovsky, Munro), "Jeux de Mer" (Ravel, Munro), "The Shakers" (Traditional, Humphrey), "Valse" (Gundle-Straus, Robert Barnett), premiere of "Peter and the Wolf" (Prokofiev, Mary Munro), and Pas de Deux: Don Quixote, Nutcracker, Le Corsair, Spring Waters, Sleeping Beauty, Peasant, Bluebird

Macon Ballet Guild
in "Peter and the Wolf"

LAKE CHARLES BALLET SOCIETY
FOR BALLET JOYEUX
Lake Charles, Louisiana

Artistic Director-Choreographer, Ida Winter Clarke; President, Mrs. Everett Scott; Assistant Director, Cissie Clarke; Production, Kitty Walker; Technical Director, Wayne Hine; Press, Kathleen Collins; Attractions, Mrs. James Leithead

COMPANY

Barbara Berger, Libby Tete, Cathy Hebert, Kay Beatty, Lee Anne Frederick, Polly Anderson, Phoebe Brian, Tamme Irby, Mary Abate, Beverly Facione, Vicki Lanza, Claudia Hart, Lisa Greenlee, Pat Scalisi, Anne Guillory, Renee Plauche, Claire Scobee, Mary Ferguson, Danny Martin, Jesse Dotty, Charles Newman, Johnny Painter

REPERTOIRE

"Nutcracker" (Tchaikovsky, Clarke), "Les Sylphides" (Chopin, Fokine), "Pas de Quatre" (Pugni, Petipa), "Don Quixote Pas de Deux" (Minkus, Petipa), "Les Patineurs" (Clarke), "Dancerscatter" (R. Englund), "Grand Tarantelle" (Gottschalk, Englund), "Divertissement D'Adam" (Adam, Segarra) "Holberg Variations" (Grieg, Segarra), "Fiddle Tunes" (Clarke), "Papillons" (Clarke), "La Guitarina" (Sequoio), "Peter and the Wolf" (Clarke), "Images of the Dance" (Clarke), "Le Corsaire" (Petipa), "Divertimento" (Clarke) PREMIERES: "Swan Lake Act II" (Tchaikovsky, Ashton after Ivanov), "Gyre & Gambol" (James Clouser), "Capriccio" (R. Englund)

Top Left: Cathy Hebert, Libby Tete, Kevin
Self in "Capriccio"

Louisville Ballet Company
in "Peter and the Wolf"

MACON BALLET GUILD
Macon, Georgia

Artistic Director-Choreographer, Gladys Lasky; President-Stage Director, Louis A. Friedel; Lighting, E. C. McMillan

COMPANY

Lesley Bower, Judy Friedel, Susan Bloodworth, Mary Holliday, Mary O'Shaughnessey, Becky Bartel, Melissa Garrette, Karen Hinson, Mary Virginia Kay, Lee Kinman, Edith Newton, Faye Orr, Fabia Rogers
PREMIERE: "Peter and the Wolf" (Prokofiev, Gladys Lasky; Scenery, B. R. Casey; Costumes, Gladys Lasky)

METROPOLITAN BALLET COMPANY
Bethesda, Maryland

Director-Choreographer, Charles Dickson; Assistant Director-Choreographer, Alan Woodard; Set and Lighting Design, Alan Rafel, Richard Hankins; Wardrobe Mistress, Gladys Fuller; Sound, Everett Fuller; Stage Manager, Richard Hankins; Guest teachers, Patricia Wilde, Sallie Wilson, Royes Fernandez, Ronald Emblem

COMPANY

PRINCIPALS: Maureen Gillen, Adrienne Subotnik, Elaine Browning, Laurie Zerkin, Ron Federico, Michael Kessler, James Mundell, Sidney Miller
SOLOISTS AND CORPS: Cathy Caplin, Dorothy Feulner, Anne Berry, Christine Feron, Andrea Wikner, Martha Allin, Isabelle Kay, Joni Kramer, Wendy Fuller, Susan L'Heureux, Lily Petrov, Sheila Thompson, Athena Smith, Michele Toohey, Jacqueline Reed, Carol Fonda, Holly Stern, Ann Stanley, Demetra Karousatos, Christine Philion, Ann Pflugshaupt, Georgina Slavoff, Shonna Wechsler, Wendy Carpenter, Peggy Steif, Virginia Furr, Lisa Green, Valerie Striar, Sally Schenkel, Connie Oxford

REPERTOIRE

"Snow Maiden" (Tchaikovsky, Dickson-Woodard), "Sylvia" (Delibes, Dickson-Woodard), "Britten Variations" (Britten, Woodard), "Waltz" (Tchaikovsky, Dickson), "Ballet Romantique" (Helsted, Woodard), "Pas de Deux" (Marcello, Dickson), "Tarantella" (Rossini-Respighi, Dickson)

Top Left: Metropolitan Ballet members in "Snow Maiden"

MIAMI BALLET COMPANY
Miami, Florida

Artistic Director-Choreographer, Thomas Armour; Co-Directors, Robert Pike, Renee Zintgraff, Martha Mahr; Choreographers, Ben Stevenson, Jean Paul Comelin, Robert Pike; Conductors, Peter Fuchs, Bruce Steeg; Sets and Costumes, Gerard Sibbritt, Edward Haynes, Norman McDowell; Lighting, Richard Mix; Stage Manager, Demetrio Menendez

COMPANY

Annemarie Amanzio, Cicely Balbin, Lupe Barroso, Betsy Bergner, Bettina Buckley, Cathy Contillo, Rio Cordy, Lucia Corsiglia, Vicki Eidenire, Ann England, Marianne Gordon, Lynn Huck, Clare Keane, Lisa Kott, Nanette Loren, Marlene Mouseur, Carol Raskin, Josephine Ramos, Marcia Sussman, Andrea Tiger, Joan Winters, Gary Fishman, Edward Bilanchone
GUEST ARTISTS: Karen Brock, Alba Calzada, Gaye Fulton, Charlene Gehm, Desmond Kelly, Ted Kivitt, Ben Stevenson, Kirk Peterson

REPERTOIRE

"Daughters of Mourning" (Martin, Comeline), "Paquita" (Minkus, Comelin after Mazilier), "Cinderella" (Prokofiev, Stevenson)
PREMIERES: "Suite de Ballet" (Burgmuller, Thomas Armour), "Daphnis and Chloe" (Ravel, Armour), "Tarantella" (Gottschalk-Kay, Robert Pike)

Nanette Loren and Miami Ballet in "Suite de Ballet"

Larry Yando and members of the Mid-Hudson Ballet Company

MID-HUDSON BALLET COMPANY
Poughkeepsie, N.Y.

Artistic Directors-Choreographers, Estelle & Alfonso; Sets, Lloyd Waldon, Ruth Waldon; Costumes, Olive Pearson

COMPANY

Larry Vando, Margo Scalzi, Eileen Bellizzi, Bettyjean Theyjohn, Sharon McDermott, Colleen Holt, Tracy Vita, Cindy Bonnett, Karen Cassetta, Janet Coppola, Cathy Cassetta, Mary Ann Fiorillo

REPERTOIRE

"High" (Entwhistle), "Spectrum" (Schubert), "The Waltz" (Kalman), "El Victorio Luis Alonso" (Giminez), "The Line" (Prado), "Pan" (Ravel)

MINNESOTA DANCE THEATRE
Minneapolis, Minnesota

Artistic Director-Choreographer, Loyce Houlton; Ballet Master, Keith Rosson; Technical Director, John Linnerson; Costume Designer, Judith Cooper; Lighting Design, Lance Olson; General Manager, Mary Anderson; Administrative Assistant, Karen Alnes; Press, Joanna Baymiller

COMPANY

Jon Benson, Michael Brown, Cynthia Carlson, Nancy Duncan, Marianne Greven, Michael Hackett, Peter Hauschild, Ronald Holbrook, Lise Houlton, Siri Kommedahl, Dana Luebke, Erin Luebke, Chris Lyman, Sandra Machala, Michael Simons, Roberta Stiehm, Andrew Thompson, Susan Thompson, David Voss, Wendy Wright
GUEST ARTISTS: Frank Bourman, William Dollar, Louis Falco, Ruth Ann Koesun, Jennifer Muller, Valentina Pereyaslavec, Michael Simms, Lar Roberson

REPERTOIRE

(All choreography by Loyce Houlton except where noted) "Ancient Air" (Crumb), "Apotheosis" (Busa), "Audition" (Dorati), "Billy the Kid" (Copland, Loring), "Bold and Brassy" (Bach), "Bone Lonely" (Barry), "Brandenburg" (Bach), "Caprice" (Schubert), "Caprichos" (Bartok, Ross), "Chronicles" (Bartok), "Cinders" (Joplin), "Collage" (Martin), "Le Combat" (deBanfield, Dollar), "Le Corsaire" (Drigo, Petipa), "Dinner Divertisements" (Scarlatti-Tommasini), "Distant Figures" (Elgar), "Don Quixote" (Minkus, Petipa), "Earthsong" (Copland), "Experiments I and II" (Penderecki, Koons), "Facade" (Walton, Ashton), "La Fille Mal Gardee" (Hertel, Nault), "Giselle Peasant Pas de Deux" (Adam, Coralli-Perrot), "Graduation Ball" (Strauss, Lichine), "Imprecis" (Ibert), "Insects and Lovers" (Bloch), "Liebeslieder Waltzes" (Brahms), "La Malinche" (Lloyd, Limon), "Mass" (Stravinsky), "Minkus Mix" (Minkus, Petipa), "Mythical Hunters" (Partos, Tetley), "Night Wind" (Pink Floyd, Caven), "November Steps" (Takemitsu), "Nutcracker Fantasy" (Tchaikovsky), "Paquita" (Minkus, Petipa), "Pas de Quatre" (Pugni, Dolin), "Les Patineurs" (Meyerbeer, Ashton), "Pi r2" (Varese, Bewley), "Present Laughter" (Roussel), "Rag Shapes" (Penderecki), "Raymonda" (Glazounov, Petipa), "La Recontre" (Sauguet, Lichine), "Revolutions" (Kraft), "Serenata Danzante" (Dvorak, Uthoff), "Slaughter on 10th Avenue" (Rodgers), "Sleeping Beauty Act III" (Tchaikovsky, Petipa), "The Killing of Susie Creamcheese" (Mothers of Invention), "Stages" (Alkan, Bourman), "Swan Lake Pas de Trois" (Minkus, Petipa), "Tactus" (Stravinsky), "Tenderplay" (Sibelius, Uthoff), "Terminal Point" (Cage), "Troth" (Brown), "Twisted Tree" (Tippet), "The Unicorn" (Menotti), "Wingborne" (Dvorak), "293.6" (Webern)
PREMIERES: "Diabolus" (Crumb, Houlton), "Notturno" (Mozart, Dollar), "Rose Adagio from Sleeping Beauty" (Tchaikovsky, Rosson after Petipa), "Tinsel Damsels" (Karlen, Koons)

Minnesota Dance Theatre in "Mythical Hunters"
Top: Marianne Greven, Andrew Thompson in "Sleeping Beauty"(*Myron Papiz Photos*)

Delia Weddington Stewart, Mark Hamilton
of Mississippi Coast Ballet

MISSISSIPPI COAST BALLET
Gulfport, Mississippi

Artistic Director-Choreographer, Delia Weddington Stewart; Choreographers, Christina Backstrom, Hazle White Shaw; Production Manager-Lighting, Bennie Stewart; Conductor, James Shannon

COMPANY

PRINCIPALS: Molly Johnson, Mark Hamilton, Christina Backstrom, Ellen Booth, Donna Ladner, Donna Martin, Julie Stewart, Jill Wilton, Barbara Titler, Kathleen Wade, Delia Stewart

REPERTOIRE

"Realities" (USM Jazz Lab Band, Delia Stewart), "Classical Suite" (Ravel, Stewart), "Woman's Suite" (The Flock, Christina Backstrom), "And It Goes On" (John Denver, Backstrom)

MUSIC IN MOTION DANCERS
Norfolk, Virginia

Director-Choreographer, Vija M. Cunningham; Choreographers, Gail Sedel, Heidi Robitshek; Lighting Designer-Company Manager-Stage Manager, Beth Hudson

COMPANY

Heidi Robitshek, Maggie Schmidt, Vija M. Cunningham, Ann John, Gail Sedel, Robin Kirby, Karen Booher, Monica Flitton, Frank Gruber

REPERTOIRE

"Rounds" (Diamond), "March of the Notes" (Purcell), "Ritma" (Brooks Gornto), "Song Medley" (Conger), "Dripsody" (LeCaine), "Swingcussion" (Dodds), "Peter and the Wolf" (Prokofiev), "Adventures in Color" (Rorem), "Line, Dot and Squiggle" (Diercks), "Impressions of Degas" (Chopin), "Composition in Four Dimensions" (Ives, Sedel), "Abstraction" (Sauter-Finnegan), "Dance" (Stravinsky), "Child's Spring" (Conger-Lohoefer), "Suite in Three Movements" (Martin, Sedel), "Bees" (Rice), "Season of Sounds" (Nature Sounds), "Mazurka" (Delibes, Robitshek), "Pizzicato Polka" (Delibes, Robitshek), "Idyl" (Walter-Olnick-Schaeffer)

NANCY HAUSER DANCE COMPANY
Minneapolis, Minnesota

Artistic Director, Nancy Hauser; Technical Director, Bruce Margolis; Managing Director, James W. Kerr; Music Director, Steve Kimmel; Associate Manager, Chyrll Weimar; Managerial Assistant, David Colacci; Costumer, Bev Sonen; Music School Director, Terry Tilley

COMPANY

Mary Cerny, Maria Cheng, Bruce Drake, Cassandra Davy, Lea Hall, Merile Halley, Heidi Jasmin, Gary Lund, Steve Potts, Marilyn Scher, Bev Sonen, Regina Wray

REPERTOIRE

"U.S. Folk" (Dylan-Margolis-Copeland-Howe-Steffe, Gail Turner), "Mandala" (Granros, Jerry Pearson), "Woman" (Paul Horn, Lea Hall), "Smile--God Loves You" (Ramayana Monkey Chat, Steve Potts), "Quantum" (Improvisation),
PREMIERES: "Pacifica" (Dennis Cochrane, Mary Cerny), "Partapartita" (Bach, Nancy Hauser), "Raingatherer" (Poem by Franklin Brainard, Mary Cerny), "Temporary Site" (Steve Kimmel, Viola Farber), "Dal-A-Bye" (Steve Kimmel, Heidi Jasmin)

Nancy Hauser Dance Company in "Partpapartita"
Top: in "Dal-A-Bye"

New England Dinosaur
in "Elliptic Spring"

NEW ENGLAND DINOSAUR
Lexington, Massachusetts

Artistic Director-Choreographer, Toby Armour; Company Manager, Margaret May Meredith; Associate Director, Lois Ginandes

COMPANY

Toby Armour, Betsy Mallinckrodt, Jean Churchill, Michael Mao, Bruce de Ste. Croix

REPERTOIRE

"Elliptic Spring" (air blowing, Armour), "Interlope," "Dinosaur Love I" (Voices, Armour), "Dinosaur Love II" (Tape, Armour), "Port de Bras for Referees" (Brown, Brown), "Ruby Turnpike" (Mozartvoice, Armour), "Novelty Sweets" (Joplin, Waring), "Social Dancing" (Popular, Armour), "Temptation" (Classic Tangos, Ginandes), "Winter Pavilion" (Sims, Ginandes), "Where the Wild Things Are" (Sims-narration, Armour after book by Maurice Sendak)

Marjorie Lenk Photo

159

NEW JERSEY DANCE THEATRE GUILD
Westfield, N.J.

Artistic Director, Alfredo Corvino; Ballet Mistress, Andra Corvino; Ballet Chairman, Patricia McCusker; Business Director, Jacquelynn Torcicollo; Administrative and Production Consultant, Yvette Cohen; Costumes, Gail Rae, Betty Krainatz, Marcella Corvino; Sets, Norman Cohen; Stage Managers, Verne Fowler, Jackie Lynn; President, Gertrude Weinberg; Choreographers, Alfredo Corvino, Andra Corvino, Charles Kelley, Sonia Dobrivinskaya, Francis Patrelle, Harry Asmus.

COMPANY

Linda Acker, Arminee Apelian, Laura Baldante, Felicia Battista, Geri Blyer, Deborah Bolanowski, Judy Bolanowski, Margaret Bonis, Eileen Byrne, Ruth Capaldo, Cindy Dern, Nancy Chismar, Cecily Douglas, Gina Greco, Beth Hnat, Joyce Kenny, Ellen Long, Joanne Long, Karen Lowande, Susan Margetts, Claire Miller, Mary Beth Nollstadt, Meg Potter, Jean Raison, Lori Richardson, Linda Rooney, Debra Sangivliano, Patricia Scarangello, Janice Sorrentino, Mary Stoltenberg, Deborah Strauss, Leslie Strauss, Lisa Torcicollo, Pixie Vivers

REPERTOIRE

"Nutcracker"(Tchaikovsky, Corvino after Ivanov), "Pas de Quatre" (Pugni, Dolin), "Don Quixote Pas de Deux" (Minkus, Petipa), "Dance of the Hours" (Ponchielli, Dobrovinskaya), "On the Pond" (Meyerbeer, Kelley), "Mission Accomplished" (Primrose, Kelley), "Roda-Roda" (Album for the Young, Asmus), "Beauty and the Beast" (Prokofiev, Patrelle), "Jazz Today" (Scorpio-Coffey, Kelley), and *premiere* of "It's Now" (Charles Kelley)

New Jersey Dance Theatre Guild in
"Beauty and the Beast"(*Roy Jones Photo*)

NORFOLK CIVIC BALLET
Norfolk, Virginia

Artistic Director-Choreographer, Gene Hammett; Ballet Mistresses, Teresa Martinez, Susan Borree; Drama Director, Penn Martin

COMPANY

SOLOISTS: Lorraine Graves, Deborah Dougherty, Melissa Hoffe, Sandra Flader, Janie Meredith, Laurie Carter, Carter Cholson, Ralph Hewitt, Lauren J. Eager
CORPS: Stacie Caddell, Nancy Cantin, Anna Maria Martinez, Wendy Wisoff, Loretta Dodd, Catherine Smith, Cheryl Donovan, Ginny Thumm, Renie Rhyder, Alexis Brown, Kim Fielding, Lynn Brehmer, Mary Bessesser, Kenne Marchbank, Ann Goldman, Lisa Rimkiv, Paige Fillion, Catherine Pugh, Patt Sawyer, Nancylew Guarnieri, Lori Buckley
GUEST ARTISTS: Glenn White, Dermot Burke, Charthel Arthur, Robert Estner, Carrol Sue Dodd, Leigh Smartz, Richard Prewitt, Richard Cacerces

REPERTOIRE

"Giselle Pas de Deux (Act I)" (Adam, White), "Giselle Act II" (Adam, Martinez), "Afternoon of a Faun" (Debussy, Borree), "Tchaikovsky Tribute" (Tchaikovsky, Borree), "Jeux des Enfants" (Hammett), "Hoppin' " (Anderson-Kerr, Eager), "Thru the Edge" (Barber, Lapouzanki), "Aurora's Wedding" (Tchaikovsky, Hammett-Martin)

Left: Lauren J. Eager

NORTH CAROLINA DANCE THEATRE
Winston-Salem, N.C.

Director, Robert Lindgren; Associate Director, Duncan Noble; General Manager, Janet Spencer; Designers, A. Christina Giannini; Lighting, Nananne Porcher; Artistic Consultant-Teacher, Sonja Tyven; Ballet Mistress, Sandra Williams; Press, Louise Bahnson; Technical Director, Lyn Caliva; Stage Manager, Bruce Tyrrell; Wardrobe Master-Graphics, Roland A. Guidry; Costume Supervisor, Evelyn Miller; Technician, Robert Gambrill

COMPANY

Sharon Filone, Kathleen Fitzgerald, Rodwic Fukino, Jan Horn, Cortlandt Jones, Lynn Keeton, Liz Kuethe, Warren Lucas, Marla Mann, Linda Miller, Nancy Miller, Jeff Satinoff, Michael Saunders, Gwen Spear, Gerald Tibbs

REPERTOIRE

"A Time of Windbells" (Norbert Vesak), "Adagio for Ten and Two" (Richard Gibson), "Bach: Brandenburg Three" (Charles Czarny), "Eye of Ice" (Richard Kuch), "Fugitive Visions" (Job Sanders), "La Malinche" (Jose Limon), "Mudai" (Kazuko Hirabayashi), "Myth" (Alvin Ailey), "Nutcracker Act II" (after Ivanov), "Raymonda Divertissements" (Balanchine-Danilova), "Symphony Thirteen" (Duncan Noble), "Vis-A-Vis" (Charles Czarny)
PREMIERES: "The Grey Goose of Silence" (Ann Mortifee, Norbert Vesak), "The Tempest" (Tchaikovsky, Duncan Noble)

North Carolina Dance Theatre
in "Adagio for Ten and Two"

NUTMEG BALLET COMPANY
Torrington, Connecticut

Artistic Director-Choreographer, Sharon E. Dante; Press, Norm St. Peter; Stage Managers, Beverly Zimmerman, Russell Ball; Coordinators and Costumes, Lenke, Claire LePage, JoAnn Morello

COMPANY

Denise LePage, Donna Neri, Debbie Tyczenski, Donna Bonasera, Charlene Jacobs, Darlene Jacobs, Jeanne Diorio, Cheryl Hart, Christina Andreoli, James Trimble, JoEllen Yadach, Julie Dancher, Anne Lawler
GUEST ARTISTS: Janet Shibata, Denise Warner, Jon Carrell, David Coll, Charles Ward, Richard Rock, Kenneth Hughs, Robin Wagge

REPERTOIRE

"The Nutcracker" (Tchaikovsky, Dante-Enid Lynn), "Switch to Bach" (Bach, Dante), "Rock" (Fifth Dimension, Dante), "Everyman's Day" (Moody Blues, Dante), "Etudes" (Mozart, Dante), "Don Quixote Pas de Deux," "Flower Festival Pas de Deux," "Black Swan Pas de Deux"
PREMIERES: "Holberg Suite" (Grieg, Dante), "On Our Way Back" (Medley, Dante), "Concerto Grosso" (Vivaldi, Michael Uthoff)

Jon Carrell and Nutmeg Ballet Company

ORLANDO BALLET COMPANY
Huntington, N.Y.

Director-Choreographer, Vincent Orlando; Producer, Sara Dean Orlando; Choreographer, James Pendill; Conductor, Michael Canipe; Costumes, Betty Orlando; Settings, Vincent Orlando; Lighting-Stage Manager, Mark Schlackman; Press, Virginia Page

COMPANY

Nina Bataller, Deborah Brennan, Jamie Diton, Lori Darley, Christopher Monks, Kathleen Keating, Lorna Glick, Leslie Perrell, Morna O'Riordan, Anita Jorgenson, George Stewart, Vincent Orlando, Jackie Riley, Julianne Brennan, Julie Josephson, Debbie Wilson, Jessica Teich
GUEST ARTISTS: Edward Villella, Allegra Kent

REPERTOIRE

"Froggs" (Satie, Pendill), "Trieme" (Gretry), "Mozart Variations" (Mozart), "Misa Criolla" (Ramirez), "Red Riding Hood" (without music), "Love and Other Things" (Judy Collins), "En Espana" (Granados)
PREMIERES: "Drummers and Mummers" (Stravinsky, James Pendill), "Acquiese" (Deutsch, Vincent Orlando)

OLYMPIA BALLET COMPANY
Olympia, Washington

Artistic Director-Choreographer, Virginia Woods; Conductors, C. Henry Howard, Gerald Wagner, Ken Olendorf; Art Director, Ray Gilliland; Costume Director, Clarice Campbell; Stage Manager, Chuck Foster; President, Barbara Olendorf; Secretary, Mrs C. Foster; Treasurer, Mrs. Homer Campbell

COMPANY

Debra Haverlock, Debi Campbell, Gail Tveden, Kathy Minnitti, Kendra Olendorf, Dan Heitzmann, Nancy Isely, Vicki Ross, Denise Egan, Stephen Burke, Sue Foster, Karen Ward, Gene Gylys, Ann Olson, Shirley Owens, Jade Yehle, Mary Ann Murphy, Jennifer Van Dijk, Nancy Heinrich

REPERTOIRE

"Nutcracker" (Tchaikovsky, Woods after Petipa), "Cinderella" (Prokofiev), "Wizard of Oz" (Various), "Gayne" (Khatchaturian, Flemming), "Madame Butterfly" (Puccini), "Jesus Christ Superstar" (Rice), "Spirituals" (Folk), "Entrance to Hades" (Hindemith), "Midsummer Night's Dream" (Mendelssohn, Zide), "Frankie and Johnny" (Gershwin), "Soliloquy" (Wagner), "Uirapuru" (Villa-Lobos), "The Seasons" (Wagner), "The Letter" (Wagner), "Heloise" (Wagner),
PREMIERES: "Coppelia" (Delibes, Virginia Woods), "Nostalgia '74" (Various, Woods)

Left: Debi Campbell, Doug Schmidt in "The Nutcracker" (*Greg Campbell Photo*)

Members of Orlando Ballet Company in "Mozart Variations"

Peninsula Ballet Theatre
in "The Class"(*Joey Tranchina Photo*)

PENINSULA CIVIC BALLET
Newport News, Virginia

Chairman, Mrs. William A. Lipscomb, Jr.; Artistic Director-Choreographer, Susan Borree; Artistic Adviser, Gene Hammett; Costumes, Renee Lampros Brown; Press, Mrs. William C. Harris, Richard W. Tripp, Jr.; Lighting, Edmund Tyler, Jr.; Stage Managers, Leonard Horne, Nick Codd; Make-up, Mrs. Julius W. Hatch; Costume Mistress, Mrs. Gerald P. Keating; Props, Mrs. Peter Mizelle; Choreographers, Susan Borree, Gene Hammett, Elbert Watson

COMPANY

PRINCIPALS: Alexis Brown, Lisa Headley, Richard Prewitt
SOLOISTS: Cheryl Ann Branscome, Donna Branscome, Melanie Davis, Edith Hatch, Jennifer Hines, Stephanie Hollingsworth, Shelley Martin, Lisa Nachman
CORPS: Carol Berry, Karen Copeman, Donna Fluharty, Vivian Kosic, Patricia Jourdan, Gigi Lovett, Lisa Smith, Marsha Smith, Yvonne Thomas, Pam Williams, Richard Hicks, Leonard Horn
APPRENTICES: Elizabeth Fluharty, Marcy Goldberg, Cathy Keating, Arna Heitman
GUEST ARTISTS: Glenn White, Marguerite Wesley White, Lorraine Graves, Richard Prewitt, David Cuevas

REPERTOIRE

"Pas de Quatre" (Pugni, Borree), "Le Corsair" (Drigo, Hammett), "Afternoon of a Faun" (Debussy, Borree), "La Fille Mal Gardee" (Herold-Lanchberry, Hammett), "Aurora's Wedding" (Tchaikovsky, Hammett-Borree), "Interplay Pas de Deux" (Gould, Borree)
PREMIERES: "Legend of Norway" (Grieg, Hammett), "Polonaise" (Chopin, Borree), "Moods 11" (Paul Simon-Isaac Hayes, Elbert Watson), "Jeux des Enfants" (Shostakovich, Hammett), "Greensleeves" (Debussy, Borree)

Right Center: Lisa Headley, Carter George
Cholson in "Aurora's Wedding"

Peoria Civic Ballet
in "The Nutcracker"

PENINSULA BALLET THEATRE
San Mateo, California

Director-Choreographer, Anne Bena; General Manager, Edward Bena; Stage Manager, Ken Rebman; Sets, Lila Vultee; Lighting David Arrow; Costumes, Lorraine Lehre, Mary Webb; Sound, Dick Wahlberg; Props, Kevin Simmers; Press, Alice Weiner

COMPANY

PRINCIPALS: Rosine Bena, Lorna Erker, Urs Frey, Sam Weber, Fred Williams
SOLOISTS: Jeannie Harriss, Mary Pat Robertson, Linda Triplet
CORPS: Loretta Bartlett, Sue Currall, Jill Donaldson, Alan Ebnother, Marilyn Gaddis, Leslie Gaumer, Kristin Laak, Bonnie Manzon, Cathleen McCarthy, Liz McCarthy, Robin Merrill, Sara Newton, Diana Riola, Anne Rosenberg, Maulie Sola, Gigi Stephansen, Tina Schucknecht, Marge Walsh, Beth Weiner

REPERTOIRE

"The Class" (Delibes, Rosine Bena), "Entre Cinq" (Faure, Antony Valdor), "Holberg Suite" (Greig, John Cranko), "Nutcracker" (Tchaikovsky, Anne Bena), "Paradox" (Kylian, Jiri Kylian), "Pas de Deux" (Tchaikovsky, Anne Bena), "Peasant Pas de Deux" (Burgmuller, Anne Bena), "Roundabout" (Arnold, Martin Buckner) "Valse" (Nicode, Robert Barnett), and *premiere* of "Poems of the Sea" (Block, Dick Ford)

PEORIA CIVIC BALLET
Peoria, Illinois

Co-Founders, Jack Slater, Shirley Pizer, Ann Salzenstein, Jack A. Coney, Daniel J. Steinberg; President, Dr. Hugh Statt; Artistic Director-Choreographer, Jack Slater; Musical Adviser-Conductor, Dr. Allen E. Cannon; Press, Bonnie White; Graphics, Marc Herr, Ann Bartel; Lighting, Jim Ludwig; Sound, Al Combs, Ken Dietsche; Production Manager, William Blake; Costumes-Wardrobe Mistress, Nellie Wiggins

COMPANY

Jack Slater, Sherrie Crenshaw, Renita Johnson, Diana Lippi, Sharon Moynihan, Paula Petrini, Mary Rochford, Shelly Fidler, Judy Hall, Lizann O'Donnell, Tanya Petrossian, Becky Steenrod, Jamie Cohen, Jerry Johnson, Darr Shelton

REPERTOIRE

"Waltz from Faust" (Gounod), "Gavotte" (Gould), "Hoedown" (Hayman), "Highlights from The Nutcracker" (Tchaikovsky), "Rachmaninoff's Variations on a Theme by Paganini" (Rachmaninoff, Slater-Loretta Rozak), "Aurora's Wedding" (Tchaikovsky, Slater-Elisa Stigler after Petipa), "Swan Lake" (Tchaikovsky, Slater-Ann Barzel after Petipa), "Les Sylphides" (Chopin, Slater after Fokine), "Spanish Suite" (Cani-Marquini-Bizet-Anderson, Slater-Rozak), "Frontier Fantasy" (Fiedler), "Ballet to Bacharach" (Bacharach), and *premiere* of "Paquita" (Minkus, Slater)

Peoria Journal Star Photo

PITTSBURGH BALLET THEATRE
Pittsburgh, Pennsylvania

Founder-Artistic Director-Choreographer, Nicolas Petrov; Ballet Master, Frano Jelincic; Music Director-Conductor, Dr. Michael Semanitzky; Music Coordinator, Phyllis Conner; Scenery and Costumes, Henry Heymann, Andre Delfau, Frank Childs; Lighting, Pat Simmons; Technical Director, Robert St. Lawrence; Company Manager, Rod J. Rubbo; Costume Coordinator, Stephen F. Petipas; Stage Manager, Larry Bussard; Business Manager, Mary Hakman; Press, Christine Hurst

COMPANY

PRINCIPALS: Dagmar Kessler, Patricia Klekovic, Gennadi Vostrikov, Alexander Filipov
SOLOISTS: Jordeen Ivanov, Jo Ann McCarthy, Dinko Bogdanic
CORPS: Suzanne Davis, Kristin Johnson, Jeanne Loomis, Susan O'Leary, Susan Perry, Betty Richmond, Laurie Savarino, Bruce Abjornson, Timothy Brown, Mark Diamond, Gregory Glodowski, Justin Glodowski, Roberto Munoz, Edward Stewart, James Reardon
GUEST ARTISTS: Leonide Massine, Frederic Franklin, Vitale Fokine, Milenko Banovitch, Ruth Page, John Taras, Alexander Minz, Peter Schaufuss, Orrin Kayan

REPERTOIRE

"Alice" (Collage, Page), "Cinderella" (Prokofiev, Petrov), "Coppelia" (Delibes, St. Leon), "Giselle" (Adam, Franklin), "Nutcracker" (Tchaikovsky, Petrov), "Romeo and Juliet" (Prokofiev, Petrov), "Swan Lake" (Tchaikovsky, Petrov-Franklin), "Bolero" (Ravel, Page), "Carmen" (Bizet, Page), "Gaite Parisienne" (Offenbach, Massine), "Georgian Suite" (Khatchaturian, Petrov), "Gopak" (Golperin, Petrov), "La Bayadere" (Minkus, Filipov), "Laurentia" (Krien, Minz), "Les Sylphides" (Chopin, Fokine), "Night on Bald Mountain" (Moussorgsky, Petrov), "Pas De Dix" (Glazounov, Balanchine), "Peter and the Wolf" (Prokofiev, Petrov), "Petrouchka" (Stravinsky, Fokine), "Romeo and Juliet" (Tchaikovsky, Page), "Scenes de Ballet" (Stravinsky, Petrov), "Soirees Musicales" (Britten, Petrov), "Spectre de la Rose" (von Weber, Fokine), "Suite de Danzes Moldaves" (Golperin, Petrov), "Variations for Five" (Chopin, Reardon), "Corsaire" (Drigo, Petipa), "Don Quixote" (Minkus, Gorsky), "Esmeralda Pas de Deux" (Pugni, Perrot), "Nocturne Pas de Deus" (Debussy, Bockman), "Spring Waters" (Rachmaninoff, Messerer)
PREMIERES: "Catulli Carmina," (Orff, Page), "Dahnanyi" (Dohnayi, Taras), "Beethoven's Ninth Symphony" (Beethoven, Petrov), "Contrast" (Fetler, Banovitch), "Jeu de Cartes" (Stravinsky, Petrov), "Rite of Spring" (Stravinsky, Petrov), "Romeo and Juliet" (Tchaikovsky, Petrov)

Michael Friedlander Photos

**Right: Dagmar Kessler, Nicolas Petrov
in "Coppelia" Top: "Contrasts"**

**Kenneth Johnson, Patricia Klekovic
in "Carmina Catulli"**

**Jo Ann McCarthy, Dinko Bogdanic
in "Cinderella"**

163

PHYLLIS ROSE DANCE COMPANY
Rockaway Park, N.Y.

Director-Choreographer, Phyllis Rose; Associate Director, Erick Hodges; Choreographers, Ricky Davenport, Erick Hodges, Diana Simkin; Costumes, Terry Leong; Lighting-Stage Manager, Deanna Wiener; Company Manager-Press, Virginia Page

COMPANY

Ricky Davenport, Esther Farmer, Nicholas Grant, Erick Hodges Adele LaTour, Elizabeth Price, Phyllis Rose, Diana Simkin, J. Edward Sydow

REPERTOIRE

"Diversions: 1, 2, 3, 4, 5, 6, 7," "Santanna" (Erick Hodges), "Ho!" "Pollution," "The Romp," "Trio for Four," "Cycle" (Nicholas Grant), "Journey into Satchiananda" (Ricky Davenport)

Ron Reagan Photo

Phyllis Rose Dance Company
in "Santana"

PILOBOLUS DANCE THEATER
Norwich, Vermont

Company Manager and Technical Director, Chris Ashe

COMPANY

Jonathan Wolken, Moses Pendleton, Michael Tracy, Martha Clarke, Alison Chase, Robby Barnett

REPERTOIRE

"Pilobolus" (Jon Appleton, Jonathan Wolken-Moses Pendleton-Steven Johnson), "Walklyndon" (Pilobolus Dance Theater), "Anaendrom" (Appleton, Pilobolus Dance Theater), "Anaendrom" (Appleton, Pilobolus Dance Theater), "Ocellus" (Jonathan Wolkin-Moses Pendleton, Wolken-Pendleton-Lee Harris-Bobby Barnett), "Spyrogyra" (Appleton, Walkon-Pendleton-Harris-Barnett), "Cameo" (Appleton, Alison Chase-Martha Clarke), "Ciona" (Appleton, Pilobolus Dance Theater), "Aubade" (Appleton, Martha Clarke-Robby Barnett), "Two Bits" (Choreography, Alison Chase-Martha Clarke)
PREMIERES: "Triptych" (Choreography, Martha Clarke-Robby Barnett), "Dispretzeled" (Steven Radecke, Alison Chase), "Pseudopodia" (Jonathan Wolken-Moses Pendleton, Jonathan Wolken), "Verticella" (Choreography, Moses Pendleton)

Tim Matson Photo

Pilobolus Dance Theatre
in "Spyrogyra"

PREMIERE DANCE ARTS COMPANY
Denver, Colorado

Artistic Director-Choreographer, Gwen Bowen; Conductor, Gordon Parks; Choreographers, Mark Schneider, Debra Norblom; Sets, Gwen Bowen, Mark Schneider; Costumes, Margaret Lenhart, Joan Cope; Lighting, Kathleen Caldwell; Props, Debra Totten, Joyce Rider; Press, Bonnie DiManna

COMPANY

SOLOISTS: Elaine Lenhart, Michelle Washington, Debra Norblom, Dixie Turnquist, Mark Schneider, Keith Kimmel
CORPS: Debra Andres, Suzanne Cacciatore, Carla Coose, Holly Cope, Chris Breed, Linda Jacoby, Irene Kropywiansky, Kathy Maurer, Cecilia Patkowsky, Colette Porter, Joyce Rider, Debra Totten, Douglas Bair, Steven Snyder

REPERTOIRE

"The Snow Maiden" (Glazounov, Bowen), "Moldovian Suite" (Traditional, John Landovsky), and *premiere* of "Heidi" (Selected, Gwen Bowen-Debra Norblom)

Premiere Dance Arts Company
in "The Snow Maiden"

ROYAL WINNIPEG BALLET
Winnipeg, Canada

Director, Arnold Spohr; Associate Director, Vernon Lusby; Production Coordinator, Richard Rutherford; Music Director, Neal Kayan; Ballet Master, Frank Bourman; Choreographer, John Neumeier; General Manager, Jim Cameron; Assistant General Manager-Company Manager, Peter Hawkins; Business Manager, Gloria P. Samoluk; Press, Maggie Morris; Stage Manager, Bill Riske; Technical Director, David Nelson; Regisseurs, Sheila MacKinnon, Terry Thomas; Pianist, Barbara Malcolm Riske; Concertmaster, Charles Dobias

COMPANY

PRINCIPALS: Ana Maria de Gorriz, Louise Naughton, Sylvester Campbell, Craig Sterling
SOLOISTS: Kimberley Graves, Bonnie Wyckoff, James Mercer, Terry Thomas, Anthony Williams
CORPS: Sheri Cook, Arleen Dewell, Kathleen Duffy, Frank Garoutte, Peter Garrick, Richard Gibbs, Erick Horenstein, David Hough, Bill Lark, Mary Neill, Victoria Pulkkinen, Patti Ross, Roger Shim, William Starrett, Jane Thelen, Trish Wilson
GUEST ARTISTS: Margot Fonteyn, Heinz Bosl, Laurel Benedict, Leo Ahonen, Soili Arvola

REPERTOIRE

"Meadow Lark" (Haydn, Feld), "What to Do Till the Messiah Comes" (Chilliwack-Syrinx-Werren, Vesak), "Pas de Deux Romantique" (Rossini, Carter), "Grand Pas Espagnol" (Moszkowski, Harkarvy), "Pulcinella Variations" (Stravinsky, Smuin), "Sleeping Beauty Excerpts" (Tchaikovsky, Slavin after Petipa), "Rodeo" (Copland, deMille), "Nutcracker" (Tchaikovsky, Neumeier), "Moncayo I" (Moncayo, Contreras), "Don Quixote Pas de Deux" (Minkus, Petipa), "Les Patineurs" (Mayerbeer, Ashton), "The Still Point" (Debussy, Bolender), "Eternal Idol" (Chopin, Smuin), "Sebastian" (Menotti, Butler), "Pas de Deux from Le Corsaire" (Drigo, Gorsky), "The Ecstasy of Rita Joe" (Mortifee, Vesak), "Variations on Strike Up the Band" (Lindup after Gershwin, Stone), "Pastiche" (Alonso, Ferran)
PREMIERES: "Etude: Printemps" (Krein-Yarulin-Minkus-Hertel, David Moroni), "Moments" (Antonin Dvorak, Larry Hayden), "The Game" (L. Stowkowski, Emerson-Lake & Palmer, John Neumeier)

Right: Bonnie Wyckoff, Anthony Williams in "Twilight" Top: Bonnie Wyckoff, Terry Thomas in "Rodeo"

Sheri Cook, James Mercer, Louise Naughton, Anthony Williams in "Grand Pas Espagnol"

"What to Do Till the Messiah Comes"

Director-Choreographer, Richard Arve
COMPANY: Richard Arve, Violetta Karosas, Mimi Rozak
REPERTOIRE: Not submitted

Left: Mimi Rozak, Richard Arve, Violetta Karosas in "Mandala"

SACRAMENTO BALLET
Sacramento, California

Artistic Director-Choreographer, Barbara Crockett; Associate Director, Jean-Paul Comelin; Personnel Director, Patti Cutting; Choreographers, Jean-Paul Comelin, Antony Tudor, Sophie Maslow, David Wood, Alan Howard, Lester Horton; Conductors, Harry Newstone, Daniel Kingman; Musical Consultant, Gaylen Hatton; Costume and Scenic Design, Don Ransom; Stage Managers-Lighting Designers, Bruce Kelley, Stephen Odehnal

COMPANY

Roberta Bader, Linda Brune, Leslie Crockett, Melinda Dobson, Cheryl Gomes, Valorie Kondos, Linda LeBarron, Margaret Luther, Diana Mark, Cindy Marvik, Leslie McBeth, Robyn Renollet, Andrew Rist, Peggy Sogorka, Teresa Stadler, Georgeanne Supple, Judith Supple, Heather Werby, Kim Willet, Roman Wright
GUEST ARTISTS: Marcia Haydee, Richard Cragun, Alba Calzada, Marjorie Mussman, Karen Goodman, Howard Sayette, Michael Onstad, Frank Hay, Charles Fuller, Earl Riggins

REPERTOIRE

"The Mute Wife" (Scarlatti, Howard), "Nutcracker" (Tchaikovsky, Crockett-Christensen), "Daughters of Mourning" (Martin, Comelin), "Fandango" (Soler, Tudor), "The Changelings" (Butterfield Blues, Wood), "A La Foire" (Schostakovich, Orejudos), "Hoedown" (Copland, Crockett)
PREMIERES: "Partita" (Bach, Comelin), "Folksay" (Traditional, Maslow), "The Beloved" (Hamilton, Horton), "Ballade" (Faure, Comelin)

Right: Marjorie Mussman, Jean-Paul Comelin in "The Beloved"

St. Louis Civic Ballet in "The Nutcracker"

SAINT LOUIS CIVIC BALLET
St. Louis, Missouri

Artistic Director-Choreographer-Designer, Stanley Herbertt; Stage Manager, Kenneth F. Kearney, Jr.; Press, Jane Maierhoffer; Ballet Mistresses, LaVerne Meyering, Betty McRoberts; Wardrobe, Mary Ann Grothe, Melva Jarrett, Marion Wehmueller; Repetiteur, Patty Corday; Props, Bernice MacKinnon, Pat Reifsteck, Jerry Schmidt; President, Mrs. Barbara Corday

COMPANY

Monica Albers, Christy Armantrout, Lauri Bartram, Amy Corday, Patty Corday, Karen Cracchiola, Linda Grimme, Judith Grothe, Mary Heidbreder, Michelle Jarrett, Linda Kean, Pat Kelsten, Tiffany Maierhoffer, Kathleen Massot, Tena Polukewich, Kim Reitz, Renee Vosevich, Kyle Wehmueller, Jim Akman, Tony Parise
GUEST ARTISTS: Tanju Tuzer, Patricia Machette

REPERTOIRE

"The Nutcracker" (Tchaikovsky), "While Paris Sleeps" (Traditional), "The Trunk" (Contemporary), "History of the Dance from Jig to Jet," "Crea-Ta-Dance," "Introduction" (Contemporary),

Mac Mizuki Photo

SAN FRANCISCO BALLET
San Francisco, California

Artistic Director, Lew Christensen; Associate Artistic Director, Michael Smuin; General Manager, Edward Reger; Marketing Director, Richard Haskins; Development, Ann Gralnek; Community Affairs, Penelope McTaggart; Production and Stage Manager, Parker Young; Choreographers, Lew Christensen, Michael Smuin; Conductors, Earl Bernard Murray, Dennis deCoteau; Costumes and Sets, Robert O'Hearn, Robert Fletcher, James Bodrero, Jose Varona, Marcos Paredes, Paul Cadmus, Richard Battle, Tony Duquette, Russell Hartley, Rouben Ter-Arutunian, Tony Walton, Ming Cho Lee, Paul Cadmus, Kurt Seligmann; Lighting, Jennifer Tipton, Gilbert Hemsley, Jr; Props, Robert Kirby; Costumes Mistress, Patricia Bibbins; Make-up, Leslie Sherman

COMPANY

Damara Bennett, Madeleine Bouchard, Maureen Broderick, Christine Busch, Gardner Carlson, Laurie Cowden, Allyson Deane, Odile deWitte, Nancy Dickson, Lisa DuClos, Michael Dwyer, Heidi Ellison, Betsy Erickson, Attila Ficzere, Alexander Filipov, Robert Gladstein, Michael Graham, Victoria Gyorfi, Jane Kelly, Sean Lavery, John McFall, Margaret McLaughlin, Lynda Meyer, Cynthia Meyers, Gary Moore, Anton Ness, Gina Ness, Anita Paciotti, Roberta Pfeil, Tina Santos, Daniell Simmons, Bojan Spassoff, Michael Thomas, Elizabeth Tienken, Paula Tracy, Michele Turetzky, Vane Vest, Gary Wahl, Diana Weber, Jerome Weiss, Kerry Williams
GUEST ARTISTS: Jean-Pierre Bonnefous, Liliana Cosi, Richard Cragun, Marcia Haydee, Niels Kehlet, Dagmar Kessler, Natalia Makarova, Patricia McBride, Peter Schaufuss

REPERTOIRE

"Airs de Ballet" (Gretry, Christensen), "The Beloved" (Hamilton, Horton), "Black Swan Pas de Deux" (Tchaikovsky, Petipa-Ivanov), "Celebration" (Luigini, Gladstein), "Con Amore" (Rossini, Christensen), "Don Quixote" (Minkus, Petipa), "Dying Swan" (Saint-Saens, Fokine), "Eternal Idol" (Chopin, Smuin), "Filling Station" (Thomson, Christensen), "Flower Festival" (Helsted-Paulli, Bournonville), "Four Temperaments" (Hindemith, Balanchine), "Jest of Cards" (Krenek, Christensen), "Jinx" (Britten, Christensen), "Legende" (Wienawski, Cranko), "Nutcracker" (Tchaikovsky, Christensen), "Pas de Quatre" (Pugni, Lester-Dolin) "Pulcinella Variations" (Stravinsky, Smuin), "Schubertiade" (Schubert, Smuin), "Serenade" (Tchaikovsky, Balanchine), "The Shakers" (Humphrey-Humphrey), "La Sonnambula" (Rieti, Balanchine), "Les Sylphides" (Chopin, Fokine), "Symphony in C" (Bizet, Balanchine), "Taming of the Shrew" (Stolze, Cranko), "Tchaikovsky Pas de Deux" (Tchaikovsky, Balanchine)
PREMIERES: "Cinderella" (Prokofiev, Christensen-Smuin), "Dance!!!!" (Ravel, Weiss), "Don Juan" (Rodrigo, Christensen), "For Valery Panov" (Rachmaninoff, Smuin), "Harp Concerto" (Reinecke, Smuin), "Mother Blues" (Russo, Smuin), "Portrait" (Satie, Moore), "Preludium" (Dag Wiren, Gladstein), "Tangents" (Bartok, Vest), "Tealia" (Holst, McFall)

Arne Folkedal Photos

Right: Vane Vest, Lynda Meyer in "Cinderella"
Top: Vane Vest, Diana Weber in "Harp Concerto"

"Mother Blues"

John McFall, Anita Paciotti
in "Don Juan"

167

SAN DIEGO BALLET COMPANY
San Diego, California

Artistic Directors, Sonia Arova, Thor Sutowski, Artistic Adviser, Jillana; Business Manager, Carlene Carroll; Technical Director, Bruce Kelley; Musical Director, Dr. Robert Emile

COMPANY

Jillana, Thor Sutowski, Robert Alwine, Dianne Brace, David Chastain, Susan Connor, Diana Culberston, Judith Emile, Seri Lueamrung, Gary Miner, Melissa Pieknik, Karen Schaefer, John Sladovic, Charles West, Antonette Yuskis

REPERTOIRE

(all choreography by Thor Sutowski except where noted) "A La Francaix" (Francaix, Balanchine), "Canzona" (Nordheim), "Dessins sur Bach" (Bach), "Dialogues and Images" (Stravinsky), "Georgian Suite" (Khachaturian, Arova), "Le Corsaire" (Drigo, Petipa), "Les Sylphides" (Chopin, Arova after Fokine), "Ouvertures Classiques" (Berlioz), "Ravel Concerto" (Ravel), "Raymonda" (Glazounov, Nureyev after Petipa), "Re-Sentiments" (Gould, Carroll), "Romeo and Juliet Pas de Deux" (Prokofiev), "Sand Song" (Messian), "Spring Waters" (Rachmaninoff, Messerer), "Stimmung" (Wagner), "Webern Pas de Deux" (Webern), "Romeo and Juliett" (Prokofiev, Arova-Sutowski after Lavrovsky), "The Nutcracker" (Tchaikovsky, Arova-Sutowski)

Jillana, Thor Sutowski
in "Holiday Dance Festival"

SAVANNAH BALLET GUILD
Savannah, Georgia

Director, Don Cantwell; Choreographers, Don Cantwell, Robert Ivey; Set and Lighting Designer, Don Cantwell; Costumes, Don Cantwell, Robert Ivey, Rosalie Cotler, Helen Glenn; Press, Alice Ashman; Artistic Directors, Madeleine Walker, Rosalie Cotler, Doris Martin, Lillian O'Donovan, Hilda DeLaGuardia

COMPANY

PRINCIPALS: Terri Lawless, Natalie W. Morgan, Lillian O'Donovan, Patricia Strong, Susan Murray Griffin, Anita Lane, Cynthia Huber, Beth Barrow, Kim Paddison, Molly Hale, Debra Letchworth, Rebecca Keating, Corbett Coleman, Tom Peak, Robert Hogue, Carter Judkins, Sally Nettles, Toni Walden, Lynn McElven, Ceil Adcock
SOLOISTS: Anne Smith, Cathy Myers
CORPS: Barbara Willowby, Kim Teague, Ann McGinty, Linda Eisenhard, Gaye Baxley, Jane Griffen, Erin McGinn, Pam Wade, Marissa Lee, Laurie Lee, Cinda Carlysle, Stacie Wong, Mary Stacy, Kay Roddenberry, Susan Spillance, Marie Powers, Julie Estus, Lauren Duffy, Shawn Doolan, Cathy Warlich, Debbie Pike, Karen Horst, Mires Rosenthal, Jr.

REPERTOIRE

"Soiree's Musicals" (Britten, Cantwell), "Waltz" (Strauss, Cantwell), "The Women" (Ravel, Ivey), and *premieres* of "Cinderella" (Prokofiev, Cantwell), "Swan Lake Act II" (Tchaikovsky, Cantwell-Ivey after Petipa)

Savannah Ballet Guild

SOUTH BEND CIVIC BALLET & DANCE COMPANY
South Bend, Indiana

Artistic Director-Choreographer, Marie Buczkowski; Choreographer, Ciretta Buczkowski

COMPANY

SOLOISTS: Ciretta Buczkowski, Ginger Flowers, Carolyn Gwyther, Janice Morrical, Christine Walkowiak, Barbara Zivitch

CORPS: names not submitted

REPERTOIRE: not submitted

PREMIERE: "Orpheus of the Underworld"

South Bend Civic Ballet
in "Orpheus of the Underworld"

SOUTHERN THEATRE BALLET
Jacksonville, Florida

Founder-Artistic Director-Choreographer, Marta Jackson; Guest Choreographer, Gayle Parmelee; Costumes, Mary Lovelace; Sets-Technical Director-Lighting, Nick Ciccarello, Samantha Laine; Ballet Mistresses, Sandy Barnert, Virginia Pelegrin, Lori Childers

COMPANY

Donald Van Vleet, Sandy Barnert, Debbie Greenberg, Virginia Pelegrin, Linda Bell, Caroline Lovelace, Linda Johnston, Gentry Linville, Caroline Faris, Joan Frazier, Shawn Nanney, Cindy Godsmith, Isabel Pelegrin, Cindy Steffey, Nancy Marley, Judy Marley, Kathy Bell, Susan Donziger, Pam Farber, Joy Farris, Sara Howell, Mary Saltmarsh, Sara Saltmarsh, Dona Cohan, Renatta Dendor, Yamille Diaz, Kathy Cogburn, Caroline Herbert, Susa de Hechavarria, Prisilla Hubbard, Martha Lovelace, Rosa Morales

REPERTOIRE

"Nutcracker" (Tchaikovsky, Parmelee), "Swan Lake Act II" (Tchaikovsky, Jackson after Petipa), "Grand Pas de Quatre" (Pugni, Jackson), "Aurora's Wedding" (Tchaikovsky, Jackson after Petipa), "El Amor Brujo" (deFalla, Jackson), "Rochene" (Glazounov, Jackson), "All Rights Reserved—even on the moon" (Satie, Parmelee), "Esprit" (Britten, Parmelee), "Isle of Loneliness" (Wagner, Jackson), "Solitude" (Ravel, Jackson)

Top Right: Southern Theatre Ballet
(Belton S. Wall Photo)

SUFFOLK CHILDREN'S THEATRE OF PERFORMING ARTS
Suffolk, Virginia

Artistic Director-Choreographer, Gene Hammett; Ballet Master, Ralph Hewitt; Company Manager, Patsy Barnes; General Administrator, W. T. Hawkins, Jr.

COMPANY

SOLOISTS: Dollicia Knight, Valerie Claude, Beth Pierce, Mary Stallings, Mary Daniel, Deanne Potter, Elizabeth Brothers, Cindy Shotten, Allison Draper, Tammy Shotten, Bonnie West CORPS: Janet Sawyer, Carolyn Hines, Paula White, Beth Hunter, Darnessa Hart, Joan Russell, Tonya Boone, Susan Branche, Jewel Williams

REPERTOIRE

"Classroom" (Herald, Hammett), "Christmas" (Anderson, Hammett), "Degas" (Offenbach, Hammett)

TANCE AND COMPANY
San Francisco, California

Artistic Director-Choreographer, Tance Johnson; Musical Director-Lighting Design, Carl Sitton; Stage Manager, Gerry Lochran; Costumes, Tance Johnson; Press, Lois Zanich

COMPANY

Evelyn Ante, Karen Brown, Annie Chang, Gina Bonati, Charlene Greene, Ron Levine, Diana Sanders, Ercilia Santos, Rosa Wang GUEST ARTISTS: Bruce Bain, Valerie Cook, Tripp Pierce, Susan Williams

REPERTOIRE

"Pavanne" (Faure, Johnson), "Interlude" (Rachmaninoff, Bruce Bain), "Introspections" (Varese, Susan Williams), "Mayazumi" (Mayazumi, Johnson), "Bailecito de Luces" (Los Calchakis, Johnson), "Lento" (Miyoshi, Rosa Wang), "Celebrate" (Contemporary Rock, Deborah Qaunain), "The Chase" (Rock, Evelyn Ante), "Now" (Collage, Johnson)

Pete Peters Photos

Rosa Wang in "Lento" Above: Tripp Pierce in "Now" (Tance and Company)

169

THEATRE BALLET OF SAN FRANCISCO
San Francisco, California

Artistic Director-Choreographer, Merriem Lanova; Stage Manager, Jack Green; Press, Kolmar Associates

COMPANY

Maria Balagot, Evelyne Bostok, Anita Bostok, Sonette Dhanda, Deborah Pitts, Patti Taylor, Jackie Tueller, Jean West, Jennifer Young, Maria deLarrazabal, Linda Montaner, Heidi Young, James Auwae, Thomas Hanner, Nicholas Pacana, Sylvio Briffa, Jeromy Switzer, Fred Tosi, Julian Montaner
GUEST ARTISTS: Helyn Douglas, Zina Bethune, David Panaieff, Alicia Colino

REPERTOIRE

"The Nutcracker" (Tchaikovsky), "Coppelia" (Delibes), "Grand Pas de Quatre" (Pugni), "Creole Trio" (Lanova), "Danse Macabre" (Feves), "Raymonda"
PREMIERES: "Many Faces of Carmen" (Bizet, James Kerber), "Salome" (Selected Rock, Kerber), "Command Performance" (Pugni, Lanova), "The American Dream" (Gottschalk, Lanova)

Zina Bethune, David Panaieff and Theatre Ballet of San Francisco in "The Nutcracker"

TOLEDO BALLET
Toledo, Ohio

Artistic Director-Choreographer, Marie Bollinger Vogt; Conductor, Serge Fournier; Costumes, Rosalind Glattes, Rose Glattes; President, Carol Van Sickle; Press, Darline Lehnkuhl

COMPANY

Craig Barrow, Polly Brandman, Kathy Carter, Suzanne Carter, Beth Glasser, Laura Hansen, Rebecca Hawkins, Hollis Hibscher, Judith Nasatir, Kim Parquette, Jean Peterson, Cris Phillips, Jill Putnam, Lisabeth Skalski, Mara Steinberg, Jo Anne Ullman, Laura Wade, Donna Wolff, Tracy Van Sickle
GUEST ARTISTS: Ruth Ann Koesun, Terry Orr, Soili Arvola, Leo Ahonen

REPERTOIRE

"Symphony for Fun" (Gillis), "Graduation Ball" (Strauss, Lichine), "Les Sylphides" (Chopin, Fokine), "Giselle" (Adam, Coralli-Perrot), "Nutcracker" (Tchaikovsky), "Les Patineurs" (Meyerbeer), "Water Music Suite" (Handel), and *premiere* of "Italian Symphony" (Mendelssohn, Marie Bollinger Vogt)

Mara Steinberg and Toledo Ballet in "Italian Symphony"

TULSA CIVIC BALLET
Tulsa, Oklahoma

Artistic Directors-Choreographers, Roman Jasinski, Moscelyne Larkin; President, Eugene A. Pelizzoni; Press, Betty Bradstreet; Manager, Charles Ellis; Conductor, Franco Autori; Sets, Kathryn Phelps, Albert Martin, Jerry Harrison; Costumes, Moscelyne Larkin, Mrs. L. E. Maines; Lighting, M. M. Donnelly

COMPANY

SOLOISTS: Kimberly Bell, Matthew Bridwell, Gail Gregory, Sheila McAulay, Cinda Potter, Edward Tuell, Cynthia Crews
CORPS: Janet Baumgart, Diane Bembeneck, Bonnie Boswell, Dorothy Bridwell, Lisa Collins, Barbara Crews, Kimberly Davis, Duncan Emanuel, Timothy Fox, Kirsten Hulebak, Kimmey Jin, Kimberly Jones, Jerri Kumery, Lisa Mahuron, Mary Beth Minor, Emily Palik, Julie Price, Hope Theodoris, Susie West, Gail White
APPRENTICES: Cynthia Ball, Ainsley Boles, Lynn Collins, Lisa Ferguson, Mary Catherine Fitzgerald, Peyton Foster, Julie Harris, Lisa Jackson, Tracy Lockwood, Allison Reid, Anita Scott, Kimberly Smiley, Annette Wean, Cheryl Willis, Chriss Witt
GUESTS in Mime Roles: Richard Latty, Penny Martin, Bob Barnes, Charles Ellis, J. Clyde Parker, Thom Weaver
GUEST ARTISTS: Cynthia Gregory, Ted Kivitt, Kay Mazzo, Peter Martins, Roman L. Jasinsky

REPERTOIRE

"The Nutcracker" (Tchaikovsky, Larkin-Jasinski after Ivanov), "Giselle" (Adam, Larkin-Jasinski after Sergeyev), "Tchaikovsky Pas de Deux" (Tchaikovsky, Balanchine)
PREMIERES: "Il Favorito" (Vivaldi, Jasinski), "L' Apres Midi d'un Faune" (Debussy, Larkin-Jasinski after Nijinski), "Spanish Dance Suite" (Moszkowski, Jasinski), "Concerto" (Mendelssohn, Jasinski)

Kimberly Bell, Roman Jasinski and Tulsa Civic Ballet in "Giselle"

UNIVERSITY CIVIC BALLET
El Paso, Texas

Artistic Director-Choreographer, Ingeborg Heuser; Ballet Mistresses, Debbie Moore, Renee Segapeli; Music Director, Laurence Gibson; President, James Anderson; Sets, William Kolliker, Arno Hansel, Bert Ronke, Reagan Cook; Costumes, Ingeborg Heuser; Lighting, Robin Quarm.

COMPANY

PRINCIPALS: Andre Harper, Debbie Moore, Renee Segapeli, Deitra Anthony, Joan Ferguson, Joni Gould, Linda Gudmundson, Kathi Henderson, Don Leghart, Roger Malone, Benjamin Marquez, Mary Scooley, Michael Stammer, Cristina Casas, Kim Cherry, Leticia Hernandez, Estella Levy, Cynthia Pashilk, Carol Schwarzkopf
GUEST ARTISTS: Oskar Antunez, Valentin Froman, Alfonso Hidalgo, David McNaughton, Hector Serrano

REPERTOIRE

"The Firebird" (Stravinsky, Heuser), "Chiarina" (Blacher, Heuser), "Cinderella" (Prokofiev, Martinez), "Romeo and Juliet" (Prokofiev, Gert Reinholm), "Pulcinella" (Stravinsky, Heuser), "Ballet of Carmen" (Schchedrin-Bizet, Heuser), "The Red Coat" (Nono, Reinholm), "Today and Tomorrow" (Bacharach, Heuser)

Renee Segapeli, Alfonso Hidalgo and members of
University Civic Ballet in "Carmen"

VALENTINA OUMANSKY DRAMATIC DANCE ENSEMBLE
Hollywood, California

Artistic Director-Choreographer, Valentina Oumansky; Lighting Designer, David Zacks; Manager, Marilyn Carter

COMPANY

Valentina Oumansky, Diana Black, Marilyn Carter, Bill Hogerheiden, Van Hurst, Melinda Plourde, Dellamaria Marino, Wendy Watson, and guest artist Fayard Nicholas

REPERTOIRE

"Conversations in Silence and Sound" (Klauss), "Adoration" (Hovhaness), "Homage to the Southwest Indian" (Stein), "God in a Box" (Berio), "Who Is Hieronymus?" (Broughton), "With Apologies to Aesop the Horse" (Stein), "In the Hills" (Hovhaness), "Ghazals" (Hovhaness), "Facade" (Sitwell-Walton), "El Popol Vuh" (Waldo)
PREMIERES: "Rin Tin Tin Superstar" (Hovhaness, Oumansky), "Afro-American Jazz Legend" (Compilation, Oumansky), "Cortez, the Conqueror" (Ginastera, Oumansky)

Valentina Oumansky Dramatic Dance Ensemble
in "God in a Box"

VIRGINIA BEACH CIVIC BALLET
Virginia Beach, Virginia

Artistic Director-Choreographer, Mieczyslaw Morawski; Stage Manager, Robert Weaver; Lighting, Maynard Allen; Sets, Robert Weaver; Sound, Ursula Jones; Press, Ruby Timlin; Costumes, Robert Weaver, Phyllis Hale, Donna McCloud; Coordinator, Phyllis Hale

COMPANY

PRINCIPALS: Debby Benvin, Shirley Oakes, Linda Searls, Petra Wirth, James Ambrose, John Medlin
CORPS: Vicki Anglin, Alison Edwards, Carolyn Jones, Ann Watkins, John Jones, Everett Ryder, Debbie Nonni, Cherie Ryder, Sherri Sellers, Dottie Watkins, Dale Anglin, Steve Hann, Alison Forst, Amanda Goldsmith, Lisa Hunt, Elizabeth Hurd, Trishia Meacham, Kelly Powell, Kim Powell, Ann Tate, Sabina Timlin, Joseph Timlin

REPERTOIRE

"Sleeping Beauty Pas de Deux" (Tchaikovsky, Morawski after Kirov-Petipa), "Awakening" (Hindemith-Bach, Baker), "Give It Up" (Redd-Kool, Benvin)
PREMIERES: "Ouverture to Ballet" (Selected, Morawski), "Chopin Suite" (Chopin, Morawski), "Beethoven's Fifth Symphony" (Beethoven, Morawski), "Greeting Polonaise" (Folkmusic, Morawski), "Trepak" (Tchaikovsky, Morawski), "Polka: Bumming Around" (Folkmusic, Morawski)

Ursula Jones Photo

Shirley Oakes, John Medlin, Ann Watkins
of Virginia Beach Civic Ballet in "Trepak"

Artistic Director, Erika Thimey; Choreographers, Erika Thimey, Sally Crowell; Stage and Light Directors, Robert Fabik, Jack Halstead; Narrators, Lee Reynolds, Carolyn Stewart, Karen Cross

COMPANY

Miriam Cramer, Sally Crowell, Julie Houghton, Stephen Johnson, E. Raye LeValley, Karen Murden, Carol O'Toole, Diana Parson

REPERTOIRE

"A Fear Not of One" (Lohoefer), "Of Our Air" (Chavez-Schostakovich), "Prediction" (Weather Report), "Folk Suite" (Traditional), "Night" (Santana), "Aesop Fables" (Lohoefer, Biase), "Ceremony of Carols" (Britten), "Psalm" (Ott), "Pieta" (Kreisler)

Left: Diana Parson, E. Raye LeValley of Washington Dance Theatre in "Ceremony of Carols"

WESTCHESTER BALLET COMPANY
Ossining, N.Y.

Artistic Director-Choreographer, Iris Merrick; Financial Director, Donald M. Rosenthal; Choreographers, Julia Levine, Edward Roll, Barry Edson; Set and Lighting Designers, Hallie Flanagan, David Auslander; Costumes, Janet Crapanzano, Jacqueline Stoner; Press, Gale Laurence, Marlene Offenberg

COMPANY

PRINCIPALS: Sue Crapanzano, Vivian Crapanzano, Lenore Meinel, Jan Rosenthal
SOLOIST: Paula Wandzilak, Maureen Moriarty, Elizabeth Wedge, Heather Behling, William Otto, David Otto, Laurie Beckett, Elizabeth Grusky
CORPS: Tracie Holmes, Sue Kenny, Faith Stevelman, Pamela Burton, Jane Brayton, Maria Tsu, Gail Greenstein, Elaine Seravalli, Nell Compo, Wereamantry, Deanne Lehman, Sue Cargill, Jill Robie, Erica Cargill, Patricia Morissey, Julie Wilde, Jill Offenberg, Laura Healy, Molly Jackson
GUEST ARTISTS: Jean-Pierre Frohlich, Charles Brideau, Daryl Gray, Barry Edson

REPERTOIRE

"Suite of Shubert Dances of Isadora Duncan," "Romeo and Juliet" (Tchaikovsky), "Giselle" (Adam), "Cinderella" (Prokofiev), "Le Retour" (Kabelevsky), "Holiday" (Anderson), "Sleeping Beauty" (Tchaikovsky), "Caprice" (Shostakovich), "Emperor Valse" (Strauss), "Peter and the Wolf" (Prokofiev), "Nutcracker" (Tchaikovsky), "East of the Sun" (Grieg), "Seasons" (Chausson), "Cry Baby Dolls" (Kabelevsky), "Come What May" (Reissager), "Star Maiden" (McDowell), "Dream Toy Shop" (Rossini-Britten), "Secret River" (Leyden), "Tarkus" (Emerson- Lake-Palmer), "Tailor and the Doll" (Britten)

Vivian Crapanzano, Daryl Gray of Westchester Ballet in "Cinderella"
(Curt R. Meinel Photo)

WETZIG DANCE COMPANY
Staten Island, N.Y.

Artistic Director, Betsy Wetzig; Choreographers, Betsy Wetzig, Peggy Hackney, Carol Boggs

COMPANY

Betsy Wetzig, Peggy Hackney, Kedzie Penfield, Pam Pilkenton, and guest artists Idelle Packer, Timothy Haynes

REPERTOIRE

PREMIERES: "Jonah" (Carl Michaelson, Betsy Wetzig; Sculpture, Richard Barnet), "Hello from Infinity" (Wetzig)

Wetzig Dance Company in "Hello from Infinity" *(Richard Barnett Photo)*

Alvin Ailey

Carolyn Adams

Joseph Albano

Maria Alba

Dick Andros

BIOGRAPHIES OF DANCERS AND CHOREOGRAPHERS

ABARCA, LYDIA. Born Jan. 8, 1951 in NYC. Studied at Fordham U., Harkness House. Debut 1968 with Dance Theatre of Harlem.

ADAIR, TOM. Born in Venus, Tex. Joined American Ballet Theatre in 1963, elevated to soloist in 1966.

ADAMS, CAROLYN. Born in N.Y.C. Aug. 16, 1943. Graduate Sarah Lawrence Col. Studied with Schonberg, Karin Waehner, Henry Danton, Wishmary Hunt, Don Farnworth. Member of Paul Taylor Co. since 1965. Director of Harlem Dance Studio.

ADAMS, DIANA. Born in Stanton, Va. Studied with Edward Caton, Agnes de Mille. Made professional debut in 1943 in "Oklahoma!" Joined Ballet Theatre in 1944. N.Y.C. Ballet 1950. Now ballet mistress-teacher at School of American Ballet. N.Y.C.

AHONEN, LEO. Born June 19, 1939 in Helsinki, Finland. Studied at Kirov Theatre. Scandinavian School of Ballet. Joined company and rose to principal. Appeared with Bolshoi Ballet. Joined National Ballet of Holland as dancer and ballet master; Royal Winnipeg Ballet 1966; San Francisco Ballet 1968. Since 1972 principal and teacher with Houston Ballet.

AIELLO, SALVATORE. Born Feb. 26, 1944 in N.Y. Attended Boston Cons. Studied with Danielian, Stanley Williams. Rosella Hightower, Professional debut with Joffrey Co. in 1964, subsequently with Donald McKayle, Pearl Lang, Patricia Wilde, Alvin Ailey, Harkness Ballet, and in Bdwy musicals. Joined Royal Winnipeg Ballet 1971. Promoted to principal 1972.

AILEY, ALVIN. Born Jan. 5, 1931 in Rogers, Tex. Attended UCLA. Studied with Lester Horton, Hanya Holm, Martha Graham, Anna Sokolow, Karel Shook, and Charles Wiedman. Debut 1950 with Lester Horton Dance Theatre, and became choreographer for company in 1953. Formed own company in 1958 and has toured U.S. and abroad. Now N.Y. City Center based.

AITKEN, GORDON. Born in Scotland in 1928. Joined Saddler's Wells Ballet in 1954. Soloist with Royal Ballet.

ALBA, MARIA. Born in China of Spanish-Irish parentage. Began studies in Russian School of Ballet, Peking. Moved to Spain, studied with Regla-Ortega, and La Quica. After professional debut in teens, became one of world's foremost Spanish dancers at 21. Toured with Iglesias Co., and Ballet Espagnol. With Ramon de los Reyes, formed company in 1964 that has toured U.S., S. America and Europe.

ALBANO, JOSEPH. Born Dec. 29, 1939 in New London, Conn. Studied with Vilzak, Legat, Bartholin, Hightower, Danielian, Graham, Weidman, and Limon. Performed with Charles Wiedman Co., Ballet Russe, Martha Graham, Joos-Leeder, N.Y.C. Ballet. Founder-artistic director-choreographer of Hartford Ballet Co., Established Albano Ballet 1971. First dancer to serve as Commissioner for Conn. Commission for the Arts.

ALBRECHT, ANGELE. Born Dec. 12, 1942 in Frieburg, Ger. Studied at Royal Ballet, and with Lula von Sachnowsky, Tatjani Granzeva, Rosella Hightower. Debut 1960 with Ntl. Theater Mannheim; Hamburg Staatsoper 1961–7; Ballet of 20th Century from 1967.

ALDOUS, LUCETTE. Born Sept. 26, 1938 in Auckland, N.Z. Studied at Royal Ballet School. Joined Rambert, London's Festival Ballet (1963), Royal Ballet (1966), Australian Ballet (1971).

ALENIKOFF, FRANCES. Born in N.Y.C.; graduate Bklyn Col. Studied with Graham, Limon, Horton, Anthony, Sanasardo, Humphrey, Sokolow, Barashkova, Dunham, Fort, Flores. Debut 1957. Since 1959 toured with own company, and as soloist. Has choreographed Bdwy musicals.

ALEXANDER, ROD. Born Jan. 23, 1922 in Colo. Studied with Cole, Holm, Maracci, Riabouchinska, Horton, Castle. Debut with Jack Cole Dancers, then in Bdwy musicals before forming own company and becoming choreographer for Bdwy and TV.

ALLEN, JESSICA. Born Apr. 24, 1946 in Bryn Mawr, Pa. Graduate UCol., NYU. Debut 1970 with Jean Erdman Dance Theatre. Also appeared with Gus Solomons, Matt Maddox.

ALONSO, ALICIA. Born Alicia Martinez, Dec. 21 in Havana: married Fernando Alonso. Studied with Federova, and Volkova, and at School of American Ballet. Made debut in musicals. Soloist with Ballet Caravan 1939–40. Ballet Theatre 1941. In 1948 formed own company in Havana. One of world's greatest ballerinas.

ALUM, MANUEL. Born in Puerto Rico in 1944. Studied with Neville Black, Sybil Shearer, Martha Graham, Mia Slavenska. Joined Paul Sanasardo Company in 1962, and is its assistant artistic director. Has appeared with The First Chamber Dance Quartet, and American Dance Theatre Co. Also teaches and choreographs, and formed own company 1972.

ALVAREZ, ANITA. Born in Tyrone, Pa. in 1920. Studied with Marth Graham, and appeared with her company 1936–41. Since 1941 has appeared in Bdwy musicals.

AMMANN, DIETER. Born Feb. 5, 1942 in Passau, Ger. Attended Essen Folkway School. Joined Stuttgart Ballet in 1965.

ANAYA, DULCE. Born in Cuba; studied with Alonso, at School of Am. Ballet: joined Ballet Theatre at 15, Ballet de Cuba where she became soloist. In 1957 was prima ballerina of Stuttgart Opera before joining Munich State Opera Ballet for 5 years, Hamburg Opera for 3. Returned to U.S. and joined Michael Maule's Dance Variations, Ballet Concerto. Founder-Director of Jacksonville (Fla.) Ballet Theatre since 1970.

ANDERSON, CAROLYN. Born Apr. 28, 1946 in Salt Lake City. Graduate Univ. Utah. Studied with William Christensen, Patricia Wilde, Peryoslavic, Cayton, Weisburger, Danilova, Vladimiroff. Principal dancer with Ballet West before joining Pa. Ballet as soloist.

ANDERSON, REID. Born Apr. 1, 1949 in New Westminster, BC, Can. Studied with Dolores Kirkwood, and Royal Ballet School. Appeared in musicals before joining London's Royal Opera Ballet 1967, Stuttgart Ballet 1969.

ANDERSSON, GERD. Born in Stockholm June 11, 1932. Pupil of Royal Swedish Ballet, and Lilian Karina. Joined company in 1948; became ballerina in 1958.

ANDROS, DICK. Born in Oklahoma City, March 4, 1926. Trained with San Francisco Ballet, American Theatre Wing, Ballet Arts, Met Ballet, Ballet Theatre, Ballet Russe. Has appeared with San Francisco Ballet, Irene Hawthorne, Marian Lawrence, John Beggs, Eve Gentry, Greenwich Ballet, Lehigh Valley Ballet, and Dance Originals. Now choreographs and operates own school in Brooklyn.

ANTONIO. Born Antonio Ruiz Soler Nov. 4, 1922 in Seville, Spain. Studied with Realito, Pericet, and Otero. Made professional debut at 7. Became internationally famous with cousin Rosario as "The Kids From Seville." Formed separate companies in 1950's, his becoming Ballets de Madrid. Made N.Y. debut in 1955 and has returned periodically.

ANTONIO, JUAN. Born May 4, 1945 in Mexico City. Studied with Xavier Francis, Am. Ballet Center, Ballet Theatre School. Made debut 1963 in Mexico with Bellas Artes, N.Y. debut 1964 with Ballet Folklorico, subsequently danced with Glen Tetley, Louis Falco, Pearl Lang, Gloria Contreras, and Jose Limon. Now associate director of Falco Co.

ANTUNEZ, OSKAR. Born Apr. 17, 1949 in Juarez, Mex. Studied with Ingeborg Heuser, and at Harkness School. Made debut with Les Grands Ballets Canadiens in 1968. Joined Harkness Ballet in 1968.

APINEE, IRENE. Born in Riga, Latvia where she began training at 11. Moved to Canada; founded school in Halifax. Became leading dancer with National Ballet of Canada, and in 1956 became member of Les Ballets Chiriaeff, now Les Grands Ballets Canadiens. Soloist with Ballet Theatre in 1959. Rejoined Les Grands Ballets in 1965.

APONTE, CHRISTOPHER. Born May 4, 1950 in NYC. Studied at Harkness House, and made debut in 1970 with the Harkness company.

ARMIN, JEANNE. Born in Milwaukee. Aug. 4, 1943. Studied with Ann Barzel, Stone and Camryn, Ballet Russe, and in Paris with Mme. Nora. Made debut with Chicago Opera Ballet in 1958, joined Ballet Russe (1959) American Ballet Theatre (1965). Has appeared on Bdwy.

ARMOUR, THOMAS. Born Mar. 7, 1909 in Tarpon Springs, Fla. Studied with Ines Noel Armour. Preobrajenska, Egorova. Debut with Ida Rubenstein, followed by Nijinska's company, Ballet Russe, Ballet Russe de Monte Carlo. Founder-Artistic Director Miami Ballet.

ARNOLD, BENE. Born in 1935 in Big Springs, Tex. Graduate UUtah. Trained with Willam, Harold, and Lew Christensen at San Francisco Ballet. Joined company in 1950, becoming soloist in 1952, Ballet Mistress 1960–63. Joined Ballet West as Ballet Mistress 1963.

AROVA, SONIA. Born June 20, 1927 in Sofia. Bulgaria. Studied with Preobrajenska; debut 1942 with International Ballet, subsequently appearing with Ballet Rambert, Met Opera Ballet, Petit's Ballet, Tokyo-Kamaski Ballet, Ballet Theatre, Ruth Page Ballet Co., Norwegian State Opera Ballet. Co-Director San Diego Ballet from 1971.

ARPINO, GERALD. Born on Staten Island, N.Y. Studied with Mary Ann Wells. May O'Donnell, Gertrude Shurr, and at School of American Ballet. Made debut on Bdwy in "Annie Get Your Gun." Toured with Nana Gollner, Paul Petroff Ballet Russe; became leading male dancer with Joffrey Ballet, and NYC Opera. Currently choreographer and assistant director of Joffrey Ballet and co-director of American Ballet Center.

ARTHUR, CHARTHEL. Born in Los Angeles. Oct. 8, 1946. Studied with Eva Lorraine, and at American Ballet Center. Became member of Joffrey Ballet in 1965.

ARVE, RICHARD. Born in Clemson, S.C. Studied with Graham, Cunningham, Joffrey, Hayden; soloist with Ruth Page Ballet, Chicago Opera Ballet, Flower Hujer, Phyllis Sabold, Erica Tamar, Maggie Kast. Now teaches, and director of Richard Arve Dance Trio.

ARVOLA, SOILI. Born in Finland; began ballet studies at 8; joined Finnish Ballet at 18; San Francisco Ballet 1968–72; Houston Ballet 1972–. Also choreographs and appears with Ballet Spectacular.

ASAKAWA, HITOMI. Born Oct. 13, 1938 in Kochi, Japan. Studied and made professional debut in Nishino Ballet 1957. Joined Ballet of 20th Century 1967.

ASAKAWA, TAKAKO. Born in Tokyo, Japan, Feb. 23, 1938. Studied in Japan and with Martha Graham. Has appeared with Graham Co., and with Alvin Ailey, Donald McKayle, and Pearl Lang, and in revival of "The King and I." Now permanent member of Graham company.

ASENSIO, MANOLA. Born May 7, 1946 in Lausanne, Switz. Studied at LaScala in Milan. Danced with Grand Theatre de Geneve (1963–4), Het Nationale Ballet (1964–6), NYC Ballet (1966–8), Harkness Ballet 1969–.

ASHLEY, FRANK. Born Apr. 10, 1941 in Kingston, Jamaica. Studied with Ivy Baxter, Eddy Thomas, Neville Black, Martha Graham. Has appeared with National Dance Theatre of Jamacia, Helen McGehee, Pearl Lang, Marth Graham, Yuriko, Eleo Pomare. Also choreographs.

ASHTON, SIR FREDERICK. Born in Guayaquil, Ecuador, Sept. 17, 1906. Studied with Massine and Marie Rambert. Joined Ida Rubinstein in Paris in 1927, but soon left to join Rambert's Ballet Club for which he choreographed many works, and danced. Charles Cochran engaged him to choreograph for his cabarets. In 1933 was invited to create works for the newly formed Vic Wells Co. and in 1935 joined as dancer and choreographer. Moved with company to Covent Garden, and continued creating some of world's great ballets. Was knighted in 1962; first man so honored for services to ballet. After serving as associate director of Royal Ballet, became its director with the retirement of Dame Ninette de Valois in 1963. Retired in 1970.

ASTAIRE, FRED. Born Frederick Austerlitz in Omaha, Neb. May 10, 1899. Began studying at 5; was in vaudeville with sister Adele at 7; Bdwy debut in 1916 in "Over The Top." Appeared in many musicals and films.

ATWELL, RICK. Born July 29, 1949 in St. Louis, Mo. Studied with Dokoudovsky, Mattox, Krassovska, and Wilde. Joined Harkness Ballet in 1967 after appearing in several musicals.

AUGUSTYN, FRANK. Born 1953 in Hamilton, Ont., Can. Studied at Ballet School of Canada. Joined Natl. Ballet of Canada in 1970, rising to principal in 1972.

av PAUL, ANNETTE. (Wiedersheim-Paul). Born Feb. 11, 1944 in Stockholm. Studied at Royal Ballet School, and made debut with Royal Opera House Ballet. Appeared with Royal Winnipeg Ballet before joining Harkness Ballet in 1966.

AYAKO. (See Uchiyama. Ayako)

BABILEE, JEAN. Born Jean Gutman Feb. 2, 1923 in Paris. Studied at School of Paris Opera. In 1945 became premier danseur in Les Ballets des Champs-Élysees. Toured with own company. Guest artist with ABT.

BAGNOLD, LISBETH. Born Oct. 10, 1947 in Bronxville, N.Y. UCLA graduate. Studied with Gloria Newman, Limon, Nikolais, Murray Louis. Joined Nikolais Dance Theatre in 1971.

BAILIN, GLADYS. Born in N.Y.C. Feb. 11, 1930. Graduate Hunter Col. Studied with Nikolais and joined his company in 1955. Has also appeared with Murray Louis and Don Redlich.

BAKER-SCOTT, SHAWNEEQUA. Born in Bronx; attended Hunter Col., CCNY. Studied with Holm, Humphrey-Wiedman, NDG, Ailey, Beatty, Holder, Clarke, Graham. Debut 1952 with Donald McKayle, subsequently with Destine, New Dance Group, Ailey, Marchant, Dancers Theatre Co., Eleo Pomare.

BALANCHINE, GEORGE. Born Georges Malitonovitch Balanchivadze in St. Petersburg, Russia on Jan. 9, 1904. Graduate Imperial School of Ballet. Debut 1915 in "Sleeping Beauty." Began choreographing while still in school. Left Russia in 1924 to tour with own company. Became associated with Diaghilev in Paris where he choreographed more than 10 works. Thence to Copenhagen as Ballet Master of Royal Dutch Ballet, then joined newly formed Russes de Monte Carlo. Formed Les Ballets in 1933 and toured Europe. Invited to establish school in N.Y., and in 1934 opened School of American Ballet, followed by American Ballet Co. Choreographed for Met (1935–8). Bdwy musicals, for such companies as Original Ballet Russe, Sadler's Wells Theatre Ballet, Ballet Russe de Monte Carlo, Ballet Theatre, and Ballet Society. Formed NYC Ballet which premiered in, 1948, and won international acclaim under his direction and with his brilliant choreography.

BALLARD, MICHAEL. Born July 17, 1942 in Denver, Colo. Studied with Nikolais and Louis at Henry Street Playhouse, and made professional debut with Alwin Nikolais Co. in 1966. Joined Murray Louis Co. in 1968.

BALOUGH, BUDDY. Born in 1953 in Seattle, Wash. where he began studying at 9. Trained at ABT School, and in 1970 joined Am. Ballet Theatre, rising to soloist in 1973. Also joined Ballet of Contemporary Art in 1973, for which he choreographs.

BANKS, GERALD. Born Feb. 4 in NYC. Attended CCNY, American Ballet Center. Joined Dance Theatre of Harlem 1969.

BARANOVA, IRINA. Born in Petrograd, Russia in 1919. Studied with Olga Preobrajenska. Soloist with Opera; Ballet Russe 1932–40; ballerina with Ballet Theatre 1941–2. More recently has been appearing in plays and musicals, and teaching at Royal Academy.

BARI, TANIA. formerly Bartha Treure). Born July 5, 1936 in Rotterdam. Studied with Netty Van Der Valk, Nora Kiss, Asaf Messerer. Joined Bejart's Ballet in 1955; principal from 1959.

BARKER, JOHN. Born in Oak Park, Ill., Nov. 20, 1929. Studied at Chicago U., and with Bentley Stone, Walter Camryn, Margaret Craske, Antony Tudor, Pierre Vladimiroff, Anatole Oboukoff, Valentina Perevaslavic, and Maria Nevelska. Made professional debut with Page-Stone Camryn Co. in 1951. Has appeared with Chicago Opera Ballet, Juilliard Dance Theatre, and Jose Limon Co.

BARNARD, SCOTT. Born Oct. 17, 1945 in Indianapolis, Ind. Graduate Butler U. Studied with Perry Bronson, Robert Joffrey, Gerald Arpino, Richard Englund, Hector Zaraspy. Debut 1963 with St. Louis Opera. Joined Joffrey Ballet in 1968.

BARNES, NERISSA. Born Feb. 2, 1952 in Columbus, Ga. Attended UIll. Debut 1969 with Julian Swain Inner City Dance Co. Joined Alvin Ailey company in 1972.

BARNETT, DARRELL. Born Sept. 24, 1949 in Miami, Okla. Attended Okla U. Studied with Mary Price, Ethel Winter, Betty Jones, Martha Graham. Debut in 1970 with Ethel Winter, subsequently with Yuriko, Mary Anthony, Pearl Lang, Erick Hawkins, Richard Gain, Kazuko Hirabayashi. Joined Harkness Ballet in 1971. Made soloist 1973.

BARNETT, ROBERT. Born May 6, 1925 in Okanogan, Wash. Studied with Nijinska, Egoroba, Preobrajinska, and at School of American Ballet. Made debut with Original Ballet Russe; joined NYC Ballet in 1950; Atlanta Ballet in 1958, and its director from 1963. Choreographs, and operates own school.

BARREDO, MANIYA. Born Nov. 19, 1952 in Manila, PI. Attended St. Paul Col., American Ballet Center. Debut 1965 with Philippine Harraya Dance Co. Joined Joffrey Ballet 1972.

BARTA, KAROLY. Born Aug. 5, 1936 in Bekescsaba, Hungary. Debut there at 11 with folk ensemble. Studied at Hungarian State Ballet Inst.; performed with Budapest opera and ballet. First choreographic work at 15. Joined Hungarian National Folk Ensemble before emigrating to U.S. in 1957. Attended Met Opera Ballet, and Stone-Camryn School. Joined Chicago Opera Ballet, and continued to choreograph for various groups. Co-founder of Hungarian Ballets Bihari for which he dances and choreographs, and was teacher-director for Birmingham Civic Ballet for 5 years.

Gerald Banks   Bene Arnold   Maurice Bejart   Soili Arvola   Paolo Bortoluzzi

BATES, JAMES. Born Feb. 8, 1949 in Dallas, Tex. Studied with Moreno, Nault, Danilova, Fallis, and Harkarvy. Joined Les Grands Ballets Canadiens in 1968.

BAUMAN, ART. Born in Washington, D.C. Studied at Juilliard, Met, and Martha Graham schools. Has danced with Lucas Hoving, Paul Sanasardo, Charles Weidman. Has choreographed numerous works and teaches. Is asst. director of DTW.

BAYS, FRANK. Born June 6, 1943 in Bristol, Va. Attended King Col. Studied with Perry Brunson, and at Am. Ballet Center. Debut with American Festival Ballet 1964; joined Joffrey Ballet 1965; First Chamber Dance Co. 1972.

BEALS, MARGARET. Born Mar. 5, 1943 in Boston. Studied with Mattox, Graham, Sanasardo, Slavenska. Has appeared in musicals, and with Valerie Bettis, Jean Erdman, Pearl Lang, Jose Limon, and Paul Sanasardo. Also choreographs, and performs in concert.

BEATTY, TALLEY. Made professional debut in Bdwy musicals. Joined Ballet Society in 1947. Has more recently toured, given solo performances, formed own company for which he choreographs, and teaches.

BECKER, BRUCE. Born May 28, 1944 in NYC. Graduate Utah State U. Studied at O'Donnell-Shurr, Graham, and Don Farnworth studios. Debut 1961 with Norman Walker, subsequently on Bdwy, with Tamiris-Nagrin, Limon, O'Donnell; joined Batsheva in 1969.

BECKLEY, CHRISTINE. Born Mar. 16, 1939 in Stanmore, Eng. Studied at Royal Ballet School, joined company and advanced to solo artist.

BEJART, MAURICE. Born Jan. 1, 1927 in Marseilles, France. Studied at Opera Ballet School, and with Leo Staats. Danced with Opera Ballet until 1945; Ballets de Roland Petit (1947–49); International Ballet (1949–50); Royal Swedish Ballet (1951–2). In 1954 organized Les Ballets de l'Etoile and debuted as choreographer. Company became Ballet Theatre de Maurice Bejart. In 1959 appointed director of Theatre Royale de la Monnaie, Brussels, and its name was changed to Ballet of the 20th Century.

BELHUMEUR, CHANTAL. Born Mar. 20, 1949 in Montreal, Can. Studied with Graham, Les Grands Ballets Canadiens and became member 1965; joined Eleo Pomare in 1971.

BELIN, ALEXANDRE. Born Apr. 3, 1948 in Mulhouse, France. Made debut in 1966 with Les Grands Ballets Canadiens.

BENJAMIN, FRED. Born Sept. 8, 1944 in Boston. Studied with Elma Lewis, ABT, Claude Thompson, Talley Beatty. Has danced in musicals, with Boston Ballet, and Talley Beatty Co. Also teaches and choreographs.

BENJAMIN, JOEL. Born Feb. 21, 1949 in NYC. Attended Juilliard, Columbia; studied with Alwin Nikolais, Martha Graham, and at American Ballet Center. Made debut in Paris in 1963. Formed own company in 1963. Director American Chamber Ballet.

BENNETT, CHARLES. Born in Wheaton, Ill. Studied with Bentley Stone, made debut with Ruth Page's Ballet before joining American Ballet Theatre. Member of NYC Ballet before formation of First Chamber Dance Quartet, now First Chamber Dance Co.

BENTLEY, MURIEL. Born in NYC. Studied with Tomaroff, Tarasoff, Swoboda, Fokine, Ruth St. Denis, Dolin and at Met Opera School. Made debut with Ruth St. Denis in 1931. Has appeared with Jose Greco 1936–7, at Met 1938–9; joined Ballet Theatre in 1940. Has since danced with Jerome Robbins' Ballets: U.S.A.

BERG, BERND. Born Nov. 20, 1943 in East Prussia. Began training at 11 in Leipzig. Joined Stuttgart Ballet in 1964; became soloist in 1967.

BERG, HENRY. Born in Chicago, Apr. 4, 1938. Studied with DeRea, Morrelli, Lew Christensen. Made professional debut with Ballet Alicia Alonso in 1958, subsequently joining San Francisco Ballet (1962), and Joffrey Ballet (1967).

BERGSMA, DEANNE. Born Apr. 16, 1941 in South Africa. Studied with Royal Ballet and joined company in 1958. Became soloist in 1962, principal in 1967.

BERIOSOVA, SVETLANA. Born Sept. 24, 1932 in Lithuania. Came to U.S. in 1940; studied at Vilzak-Shollar School. Debut with Ottawa Ballet Co. in 1947. Appeared with Grand Ballet de Monte Carlo 1947. Appeared with Grand Ballet de Monte Carlo 1947; Met Opera 1948; Sadler's Wells 1950, and became ballerina in 1954 with Royal Ballet.

BESWICK, BOB. Born Nov. 11, 1945 in San Francisco. Studied with Cunningham, Sokolow, Waring, Louis, Nikolais. Made debut in 1967 with Utah Repertory Dance Theatre, subsequently with Nikolais Co. Choreographer and teacher.

BETTIS, VALERIE. Born in 1920 in Houston, Tex. Studied with Hanya Holm. Debut with Miss Holm's company in 1937, and as a choreographer in 1941. Subsequently appeared as dancer-choreographer for several Bdwy productions, and own company that toured U.S. and abroad. Teaches in own studio in NYC.

BEWLEY, LOIS. Born in Louisville, Ky. Studied with Lilias Courtney. Made debut with Ballet Russe de Monte Carlo; subsequently with ABT, Ballets U.S.A., NYC Ballet.

BHASKAR. Born Bhaskar Roy Chowdhury in Madras, India, Feb. 11, 1930. Studied with G. Ellappa. Made debut in Madras in 1950 as concert dancer with own company which he brought to NYC in 1956. As dancer and/or choreographer, has appeared on Bdwy, and internationally; teaches.

BIEVER, KATHRYN. Born May 9, 1942 in Bryn Mawr, Pa. Studied in Ballet Russe School, Pa. Ballet School. Made debut in 1964 with American Festival Ballet before joining Pennsylvania Ballet. Joined Les Grands Ballets Canadiens 1972.

BIRCH, PATRICIA. Born in Englewood, N.J. Studied at School of Am. Ballet, Cunningham, and Graham schools. Made debut with Graham company. Has appeared in concert, on Bdwy, and with Donald Saddler, Valerie Bettis. Also choreographs.

BJORNSSON, FREDBJORN. Born in Copenhagen in 1926. Entered Royal Danish Ballet school 1935; graduated into company and became soloist in 1949; became one of great leading mimes and exponent of Bournonville style.

BLACKSTONE, JUDITH. Born May 10, 1947 in Iowa City, Iowa. Studied with Donya Feuer, Paul Sanasardo, Mia Slavenska, Karoly Zsedenyi. Debut with Sanasardo Co. in 1958.

BLAIR, DAVID. Born in Yorkshire, Eng. July 27, 1932. Trained at Royal Ballet School. Subsequently joined its company, rising to principal dancer in 1955. Honored by Queen Elizabeth with title Commander of the Order of the British Empire.

BLANKSHINE, ROBERT. Born Dec. 22, 1948 in Syracuse, N.Y. Studied at American School of Ballet. Professional debut in 1965 with Joffrey Ballet which he left in 1968. Joined Berlin Opera Ballet in 1970.

BOLENDER, TODD. Born in Canton, O. in 1919. Studied with Chester Hale, Vilzak, and at School of American Ballet. Soloist with Ballet Caravan in 1937, Littlefield Ballet in 1941; founder-director of American Concert Ballet in 1943; joined Ballet Theatre in 1944, Ballet Russe de Monte Carlo in 1945. First choreography in 1943. Became dancer-choreographer for Ballet Society, and has continued to choreograph for various companies; was director of Cologne and Frankfurt Opera Ballets.

BONNEFOUS, JEAN-PIERRE. Born Apr. 25, 1943 in Paris. Attended Paris Opera School of Dance. Made debut in 1964 with Opera Ballet and became premier danseur. Appeared with companies in Frankfort, Moscow, Milan, Berlin, Oslo, Toronto before joining NYC Ballet in 1970 as a principal.

BORIS, RUTHANNA. Born in 1918 in Brooklyn. Studied at Met Opera School, with Helene Veola, and Fokine. Member of American Ballet in 1935, Met soloist in 1936, and premiere danseuse 1939–43. Joined Ballet Russe de Monte Carlo in 1943. Has choreographed a number of works. Now teaches.

BORTOLUZZI, PAOLO. Born May 17, 1938 in Genoa, Italy. Debut 1958 with Italian Ballet. Joined Bejart Ballet in 1960, rising to principal dancer. Joined ABT in 1972 as principal.

BOUTILIER, JOY. Born in Chicago, Sept. 30, 1939. Graduate of U. Chicago. Studied at Henry St. Playhouse, and with Angelina Romett. Debut with Nikolais in 1964, subsequently with Mimi Garrard, Phyllis Lamhut, and Murray Louis. Has choreographed and appeared in own concerts.

BOWMAN, PATRICIA. Born in Washington, D.C. Studied with Fokine, Mordkin, Legat, Egorova, and Wallman. Ballerina at Roxy and Radio City Music Hall, with Mordkin Ballet in 1939, Ballet Theatre in 1940, and appeared with Chicago Opera, Fokine Ballet, and in musicals and operettas. Now teaches.

BRADLEY, LISA. Born in Elizabeth, N.J. in 1941. Studied at Newark Ballet Academy, American Ballet Center, and with Joyce Trisler. Appeared with Garden State Ballet before joining Joffrey Ballet in 1961. Invited to study classic roles with Ulanova. Joined First Chamber Dance Co. in 1969; Hartford Ballet 1972.

BRASSEL, ROBERT. Born Nov. 3, in Chicago. Attended Ind. U., American Ballet Center. Trained with Robert Joffrey, Hector Zaraspe, Lillian Morre. Joined Joffrey Ballet in 1965, ABT in 1968.

BRIANSKY, OLEG. Born in Brussels Nov. 9, 1929. Studied with Katchourovsky, Gsovsky, Volkova. Joined Les Ballets des Champs-Elysees; became lead dancer in 1946. Subsequently with Ballets de Paris, London Festival Ballet, Chicago Opera Ballet. Formed own company, and teaches.

BRIANT, ROGER. Born May 4, 1944 in Yonkers, N.Y. Studied at Joffrey Center, Martha Graham Studio, O'Donnell-Shurr Studio. Has appeared on Bdwy, and with Martha Graham, Glen Tetley, Donald McKayle, Norman Walker companies.

BROCK, KARENA. Born Sept. 21, 1942 in Los Angeles. Studied with Lanova, Lichine, Riabouchinska, DuBoulay, and Branitzska. Danced with Natl. Ballet of Netherlands before joining American Ballet Theatre in 1963. Became soloist in 1968, principal 1973. Has appeared in musicals and films.

BROOKS, ROMAN. Born July 5, 1950 in Millington, Tenn. Attended Harbor-Compton Jr. Col. Studied with Eugene Loring. Joined Dance Theatre of Harlem 1973.

BROWN, CAROLYN. Born in Fitchburg, Mass. in 1927. Graduate of Wheaton College. Studied with Marion Rice, Margaret Craske, Antony Tudor and Merce Cunningham. Professional debut with Cunningham in 1953 and appeared in almost entire repertoire of the company in roles she created. Left company in 1973 to choreograph.

BROWN, KELLY. Born Sept. 24, 1928 in Jackson, Miss. Studied with Bentley Stone, Walter Camryn. Made professional debut with Chicago Civic Opera Ballet in 1946; soloist with Ballet Theatre (1949–1953). Has since appeared in films, musicals, and on TV.

BROWN, LAURA. Born Sept. 1, 1955 in San Francisco, Cal. Studied at Ballet Celeste, San Francisco Ballet. Joined Dance Theatre of Harlem 1972.

BROWN, SANDRA. Born Jan. 6, 1946 in Ft. Wayne, Ind. Studied with Tudor, Craske, Graham, Limon. Made Debut in Juilliard concert in 1967, subsequently dancing with DTW, James Clouser, James Waring, and Lucus Hoving.

BRUHN, ERIK. Born Oct. 3, 1928 in Copenhagen. Attended Academie of Royal Danish Theatre, and received training with Royal Danish Ballet with which he made his debut in 1947. Became its leading male dancer, and has appeared on tour with the company, and as guest soloist with all leading companies throughout the world. For brief period was a principal dancer with American Ballet Theatre, and a permanent guest artist. Is considered one of world's greatest classical dancers. Appointed Director of Ballet of Royal Swedish Opera in 1967. Retired in 1972. Resident Producer National Ballet of Canada 1973.

BRYANT, HOMER. Born Mar. 29, 1951 in St. Thomas, VI. Attended Adelphi U. Debut 1970 with Manhattan Festival Ballet; Joined Dance Theatre of Harlem 1973.

BUCHTRUP, BJARNE. Born Aug. 11, 1942 in Copenhagen. Studied with Birger Bartholin. Leon Danielian. Appeared in musicals before joining West Berlin Ballet Co. in 1963. Danced with Manhattan Festival Ballet (1965–66) and joined American Ballet Theatre in 1967.

BUIRGE, SUSAN. Born in Minneapolis, June 19, 1940. Graduate of U. Minn. Studied at Juilliard, Henry St. Playhouse, Conn. College. Made professional debut with Nikolais Co. in 1964. Has also appeared with Murray Louis, Mimi Garrard, Bill Frank, Juilliard Dance Ensemble, and Jose Limon. Also choreographs, and teaches.

BUJONES, FERNANDO. Born Mar. 9, 1955 in Miami, Fla. Attended Cuban Ntl. Ballet School, School of American Ballet, Juilliard. Debut 1970 with Eglevsky Ballet, followed by Ballet Spectacular 1971–2, American Ballet Theatre 1972. Raised to soloist 1973.

BURKE, DERMOT. Born Jan. 8, 1948 in Dublin, Ire. Studied at Royal School of Dance. Appeared with Royal Concert Group before joining Joffrey Company in 1966, National Ballet 1972.

BURR, MARILYN. Born Nov. 20, 1933 in New South Wales. Studied at Australian Ballet School; made debut with Ntl. Ballet Co. in 1948. Joined London Festival Ballet in 1953 as soloist; became ballerina in 1955. Joined Hamburg State Opera Co. in 1963. Had danced with Natl. Ballet of Wash.

BUSSEY, RAYMOND. Born Mar. 8, 1946 in Pawtucket, R. I. Studied with Perry Brunson, Tupine, and at Joffrey School. Made professional debut with American Festival Ballet in 1962. Joined Joffrey Company in 1964.

BUSTILLO, ZELMA. Born in Cartagena, Columbia, but came to N.Y.C. at 6. Graduate HS Performing Arts. Appeared with Thalia Mara's Ballet Repertory, at Radio City Music Hall, with American Festival Ballet, Joffrey Ballet Co. (1965), National Ballet (1970).

BUTLER, JOHN. Born in Memphis, Tenn., Sept. 29, 1920. Studied with Martha Graham and at American School of Ballet. Made debut with Graham company in 1947. Appeared in Bdwy musicals before becoming choreographer. Formed own company with which he toured.

CALDWELL, BRUCE. Born Aug. 25, 1950 in Salt Lake City, U. Studied with Bene Arnold, Willam Christensen at UUtah. Joined Ballet West in 1967; became principal in 1973.

CALZADA, ALBA. Born Jan. 28, 1947 in Puerto Rico. UPR graduate. Studied in San Juan and made debut with San Juan Ballet in 1964. Was guest with Eglevsky and Miami Ballets before joining Pa. Ballet. in 1968. Now a principal.

CAMMACK, RICHARD L. Born Oct. 24, 1945 in Knoxville, Tenn. Graduate Butler U. Studied at Harkness House, American Ballet Theatre School. Joined ABT in 1969.

CAMPANERIA, MIGUEL. Born Feb. 5, 1951 in Havana, Cuba. Studied at Ntl. Ballet of Cuba, and made debut with company in 1968. Joined Harkness Ballet and became soloist in 1973.

CAMPBELL, SYLVESTER. Born in Oklahoma. Joined NY Negro Ballet 1956, and subsequently Het Netherlands Ballet 1960, Ballet of 20th Century, Royal Winnipeg Ballet 1972.

CAMRYN, WALTER. Born in Helena, Mont, in 1903. Studied with Bolm, Maximova, Swoboda, Novikoff, and Muriel Stuart. Appeared with Chicago Civic Opera Ballet. Page-Stone Ballet, and Federal Theatre as premier danseur and choreographer. Teacher at Stone-Camryn School, Chicago. Has choreographed more than 20 ballets.

CANDELARIA, SANSON. Born July 13, 1947 in Albuquerque, NMex. Joined Les Grands Ballets Canadiens 1965, Lisbon's Gulbenkian Ballet 1969, American Classical Ballet 1971, Boston Ballet 1972.

CARAS, STEPHEN. Born Oct. 25, 1950 in Englewood, N.J. Studied at American Ballet Center, School of American Ballet. Made debut in 1967 with Irene Fokine Co. Joined N.Y.C. Ballet in 1969.

CARLSON, CAROLYN. Born in Oakland, Calif., Mar. 7, 1943. Graduate of U. Utah. Studied at San Francisco Ballet School, and Henry St. Playhouse. Professional debut in 1965 with Nikolais Co. Has also appeared with Murray Louis, and in New Choreographers Concert.

CARROLL, ELISABETH. Born Jan. 19, 1937 in Paris. Studied with Sedova, Besobrasova. Made debut in 1952 with Monte Carol Opera Ballet; joined Ballet Theatre in 1954, Joffrey Ballet in 1962, and Harkness Ballet in 1964.

CARTER, RICHARD. Became principal male dancer of San Francisco Ballet in 1958. With wife, Nancy Johnson, performed in more than fifty countries around the world. Was director and premier danseur of the San Diego Ballet Co. for which he created 14 ballets. Now with San Francisco Ballet.

CARTER, WILLIAM. Born in 1936 in Durant, Okla. Studied with Coralane Duane, Carmalita Maracci. Joined American Ballet Theatre in 1957, N.Y.C. Ballet in 1959. Helped to organize and appeared since 1961 with First Chamber Dance Co. Joined Martha Graham Co. 1972, ABT 1972.

CARTIER, DIANA. Born July 23, 1939 in Philadelphia, Pa. Studied with Tudor, Doubrouska, Balanchine, Joffrey, Griffith, and Brunson, Debut 1960 with Met Opera Ballet, subsequently with John Butler, N.Y.C. Opera Ballet, Zachary Solov, and Joffrey Ballet since 1961.

CASEY, SUSAN. Born in April 1949 in Buffalo, N.Y. Studied at Ballet Russe, and Harkness Schools, and with Kravina, Danielian, Shollar, Vilzak, and Volkova. Joined American Ballet Theatre in 1965; became its youngest soloist in 1969.

CASTELLI, VICTOR. Born Oct. 9, 1952 in Montclair, N.J. Studied at Newark Ballet Acad., School of American Ballet. Appeared with Garden State Ballet, and Eglevsky Ballet before joining NYC Ballet in 1971.

CATANZARO, TONY. Born Nov. 10, 1946 in Bklyn. Studied with Normal Walker, Sanasardo, Danielian, Lillian Moore, Lang, Joffrey, Jaime Rogers. Debut 1968 in musicals, subsequently appearing with Norman Walker, Harkness Youth Ballet, N.J. Ballet, Boston Ballet; joined Joffrey in 1971. Returned to Boston Ballet 1973.

Bjarne Buchtrup　　**Elisabeth Carroll**　　**Dermot Burke**　　**Lili Cockerille**　　**Elie Chaib**

CATON, EDWARD. Born in St. Petersburg, Russia. Apr. 3, 1900 Studied at Melidova's Ballet School, Moscow, and made professional debut in 1914. Joined Max Terptzt Co. (1918), Ourkransky-Pavley Co. (1919), Pavlova (1924), Chicago Opera Ballet (1926), American Ballet (1934), Catherine Littlefield (1935), Mikhail Mordkin (1938), Ballet Theatre (1940), retired in 1942 to become teacher and choreographer.

CAVRELL, HOLLY. Born Sept. 2, 1955 in NYC. Attended Hunter Col., studied with Pearl Lang, Patsy Birch, Rod Rodgers, Alwin Nikolais, American Dance Center, Debut 1972 with Ballet Players; Joined Martha Graham Co. 1973.

CEBRON, JEAN. Born in Paris in 1938. Made debut in 1956 in London. Joined Joos Folkwangballet. Tours world in concert.

CESBRON, JACQUES. Born May 10, 1940 in Angers, France. Studied at Paris Opera Ballet School, and joined company in 1958. Member of Harkness Ballet before becoming soloist with Pennsylvania Ballet in 1966. Left in 1969.

CHAIB, ELIE. Born July 18, 1950 in Beirut, Lebanon. Began studies in Beirut in 1966. Made debut 1969 as soloist with Beirut Dance Ensemble. Came to U.S. in 1970; appeared in Joffrey's "Petrouchka," Chamber Dance Ensemble before joining Paul Taylor Co. 1973.

CHAMBERLIN, BETTY. Born Nov. 10, 1949 in Madison, Wisc. Studied with Armour, LaVerne, Nault, Skibine, and at ABT. Joined American Ballet Theatre in 1969.

CHAMPION, GOWER. Born in Geneva, Ill., June 22, 1920. After appearing in vaudeville, night clubs, and on Bdwy, made debut as choreographer for "Lend An Ear" in 1946. Is now in great demand as choreographer and director of musicals, and films.

CHARLIP, REMY. Born Jan. 10, 1929 in Brooklyn, NY. Attended Cooper Union, Reed Col. Studied at New Dance Group, with Merce Cunningham, Jean Erdman. Appeared with Cunningham for 11 years. Now choreographs.

CHASE, DAVID. Born June 18, 1948 in Mill Valley, Cal. Graduate URochester. Studied with Walter Nicks, Karl Shook, Graham School, Joffrey School, Nadia Potts, Norbert Vesak. Debut 1971 with Norbert Vesak, subsequently with Walter Nicks Co., Kazuko Hirabayashi; joined Martha Graham Co. 1972.

CHASE, LUCIA. Born March 24, 1907 in Waterbury, Conn. Studied at Theatre Guild School, and with Mikhail Mordkin. Became member of his company and danced title role in "Giselle" in 1937. Was principal dancer with Ballet Theatre when it was founded in 1939. In 1945 became co-director with Oliver Smith of American Ballet Theatre. In recent years has appeared only with her company in "Fall River Legend." "Swan Lake," and "Las Hermanas."

CHAUVIRE, YVETTE. Born Apr. 22, 1917 in Paris. Studied at Paris Opera School. Appeared with Paris Opera Ballet, London Festival Ballet, Royal Ballet (1959). In 1963 appointed director of Paris Opera Ballet School.

CHIRIAEFF, LUDMILLA. Born in 1924 in Latvia. Began training at early age in Berlin with Alexandra Nicolaieva. Joined de Basil's Ballets Russe, was soloist with Berlin Opera Ballet, and prima ballerina at Lausanne Municipal Theatre. Opened own academy in Geneva and choreographed for Ballet des Arts, Geneva. Moved to Canada in 1952 and organized own company, ultimately leading to her being founder and artistic director of Les Grands Ballets Canadiens.

CHOUTEAU, YVONNE. Born in Ft. Worth, Tex. in 1929. Studied with Asher, Perkins, Vestoff, Belcher, Bolm, at Vilzak-Shollar School of American Ballet. Made debut as child in American Indian dance company at Chicago's 1933 Fair. Joined Ballet Russe de Monte Carlo in 1943. Now teaches, makes guest appearances, and is Co-Director of Okla. Civic Ballet.

CHRISTENSEN, HAROLD. Born Dec. 24 in Brigham City, Utah. Studied with Balanchine. Appeared with Met Opera Ballet (1934), Ballet Caravan, San Francisco Opera Ballet, San Francisco Ballet. Retired to teach and direct San Francisco Ballet School.

CHRISTENSEN, LEW. Born May 9, 1906 in Brigham City, Utah. Studied with uncle Lars Christensen at American School of Ballet. Performer and choreographer since 1934, on Bdwy, for Met Opera, Ballet Caravan, American Ballet Co., and N.Y.C. Ballet. In 1938, with brothers Harold and William, founded San Francisco Ballet; has been general director since 1951.

CHRISTENSEN, WILLAM. Born Aug. 27, 1902 in Brigham City, Utah. Studied with uncle Lars Christensen, Nescagno, Novikoff, and Fokine. Made debut with Small Ballet Quartet in 1927, subsequently becoming choreographer, ballet master, director and teacher. With brothers Harold and Lew, formed San Francisco Ballet which he directed until 1951 when he established School of Ballet at U. of Utah. Is director-choreographer for Utah Civic Ballet which he organized in 1952, now Ballet West.

CHRISTOPHER, ROBERT. (formerly Robert Hall). Born Mar. 22, 1942 in Marion, Md. Studied with Harry Asmus, Vincenzo Celli, Celo Quitman. Made debut in 1960 with National Ballet of Venezuela; subsequently with Stuttgart Ballet, ABT, Anne Wilson, Valerie Bettis, Sophie Maslow; soloist and ballet master for Garden State Ballet, and appears with Downtown Ballet.

CHRYST, GARY. Born in LaJolla, Calif. Studied with Walker, Hoving, Limon, Jaime Rogers, Nina Popova, ABC. Debute at 16 with Norman Walker, subsequently with McKayle, Washington Ballet, N.Y.C. Opera, before joining Joffrey Ballet in 1968.

CLARE, NATALIA. Born in Hollywood, Calif. Studied with Nijinska, Egorova; joined de Basil's Ballet Russe, then Markova-Dolin Co., Ballet Russe de Monte Carlo. In 1956, established school in North Hollywood, and founded Ballet Jeunesse for which she is artistic director and choreographer.

CLARKE, THATCHER. Born Apr. 1, 1937 in Springfield, Ohio. Made professional debut with Met Opera Ballet in 1954, subsequently joined Ballet de Cuba, Ballet Russe de Monte Carlo, San Francisco Ballet, and American Ballet Theatre. Has appeared in several musicals.

CLAUSS, HEINZ. Born Feb. 17, 1935 in Stuttgart. Studied at Stuttgart Ballet School, and with Balanchine. Joined Stuttgart Ballet in 1967 after appearing with Zurich Opera Ballet, and in Hamburg.

CLEAR, IVY. Born in Camden, Maine, Mar. 11, 1948. Studied at Professional Children's School of Dance and School of American Ballet. Made professional debut in 1963 with N.Y.C. Ballet. Soloist with Joffrey Ballet from 1965 to 1969.

CLIFFORD, JOHN. Born June 12, 1947 in Hollywood. Studied at American School of Dance and School of American Ballet. Appeared with Ballet of Guatemala and Western Ballet before joining N.Y. City Ballet in 1966. Soloist since 1969. Has choreographed 7 works for the company, in addition to works for other companies. Left in 1974 to become artistic director-choreographer for Los Angeles Ballet.

CLOUSER, JAMES. Born in 1935 in Rochester, N.Y. Studied at Eastman School of Music, Ballet Theatre School. Joined ABT in 1957, Royal Winnipeg Ballet in 1958, rising to leading dancer in 1959, subsequently choreographed, composed and designed for it, and became ballet master and assistant director. Has appeared in concert, taught, and tours with wife Sonja Zarek. Ballet master for Houston Ballet.

COCKERILLE, LILI. Born in Washington, D.C. Studied at Fokine School. Wash. School of Ballet and School of American Ballet. Made professional debut with N.Y.C. Ballet in 1963, joined Harkness Ballet in 1964, Joffrey Co. in 1969.

COFFMAN, VERNON. Born Dec. 5, 1947 in Tucson, Ariz. Studied with Lew and Harold Christensen. Made professional debut with San Francisco Ballet in 1964. Joined Joffrey Ballet in 1966, and American Ballet Theatre in 1967.

COHAN, ROBERT. Born in N.Y.C. in 1925. Soloist with Martha Graham Co. Opened own school in Boston, joined faculty of Harvard's Drama Center, made solo tours here and abroad, taught in Israel and choreographed for Batsheva Co. Now director of London Contemporary Dance Theatre.

COHEN, ZE'EVA. Born Aug. 15, 1940 in Israel. Studied at Juilliard, and appeared with its Dance Ensemble. Joined Anna Sokolow Co. 1961, subsequently with Pearl Lang, and in solo concerts. Choreographs and teaches.

COLEMAN, LILLIAN. Born Nov. 21, 1949 in N.Y.C. Attended SUNY, Harkness School. Made debut with New Dance Group.

COLL, DAVID. Born Mar. 20, 1947 in Chelsea, Mass. Studied with Vilzak, Nerden, Van Muyden, Fallis, Christensen. Made debut in 1965 with San Francisco Ballet. Joined American Ballet Co. in 1969. ABT in 1970. Became soloist in 1972.

COLLIER, LESLEY. Born Mar. 13, 1947 in Kent, Eng. Studied at Royal Academy of Dancing, Royal Ballet School. Joined Royal Ballet in 1965.

COLLINS, JANET. Born in New Orleans in 1917. Studied with Carmalita Maracci, Bolm, Lester Horton, Slavenska and Craske. Appeared in solo concerts before becoming premiere danseuse of the Met Opera Ballet (1951–54). Now teaches.

COLTON, RICHARD. Born Oct. 4, 1951 in N.Y.C. Attended Hunter Col., ABT School, American Ballet Center. Debut 1966 with James Waring Co.; joined Joffrey Ballet 1972.

COMELIN, JEAN-PAUL. Born Sept. 10, 1936 in Vannes, France. Studied at Cons. of Music and Art; made debut with Paris Opera Ballet in 1957. Soloist for London Festival Ballet in 1961, principal in 1962. Joined National Ballet for 1967, Pa. Ballet in 1970; Left in 1972.

CONDODINA, ALICE. Born in Phildelphia; graduate of Temple U. Studied with Tudor, Zaraspe, Danielian, and at Met Opera Ballet, Ballet Theatre, and American Ballet Schools. Danced with Ruth Currier, Lucas Hoving, Sophie Maslow, Jack Moore, and Jose Limon Companies. Director-choreographer for own company since 1967.

CONOVER, WARREN. Born Feb. 5, 1948 in Philadelphia, Pa. Studied with Peter Conlow, Harkness House. Debut 1966 with Pa. Ballet. Subsequently with Harkness Ballet, Eglevsky Ballet, Niagara Ballet, Richmond Ballet; joined ABT 1971, soloist 1973.

CONRAD, KAREN. Born in 1919 in Philadelphia. Made debut with Littlefield Ballet (1935–7), subsequently with Mordkin Ballet, and Ballet Theatre. Retired in 1946 and opened school in Atlanta.

COREY, WINTHROP. Born in 1947 in Washington, D.C. Studied with Ntl. Ballet and appeared with company. Joined Royal Winnipeg Ballet in 1966; Ntl. Ballet of Canada 1972; principal 1973.

CORKLE, FRANCESCA. Born Aug. 2, 1952 in Seattle, Wash. Studied with Virginia Ryan, Perry Brunson, Robert Joffrey. Joined Joffrey Ballet in 1967.

CORKRE, COLLEEN. Born in Seattle, Wash. and began training at 4. Debut with Chicago Opera Ballet. Dancer and choreographer for several musicals. Formed own company that tours every season.

CORVINO, ALFREDO. Born in Montevideo, Uruguay, where he studied with Alberto Poujanne. Also studied with Margaret Craske, Antony Tudor. Was premier danseur, assistant ballet master, and choreographer for Municipal Theatre, Montevideo. Appeared with Jooss Ballet, Ballet Russe de Monte Carlo, Metropolitan Opera Ballet. Juilliard dance faculty since 1952.

COSI, LILIANA. Born in Milan, and entered LaScala School in 1950. Was exchange artist with Bolshoi; made debut as prima ballerina in 1965 in "Swan Lake" with Bolshoi. Named prima ballerina of LaScala in 1968, and Assoluta in 1970. Has appeared as guest artist with many companies.

COWEN, DONNA. Born May 2, 1949 in Birmingham, Ala. Studied with Gage Bush, Richard Englund, School of American Ballet, Joffrey. Made debut in 1968 with Huntington Dance Ensemble; joined Joffrey Ballet in 1969.

CRAGUN, RICHARD. Born in Sacramento, Cal. Studied in London's Royal Ballet School and in Denmark. Joined Stuttgart Ballet in 1962 and quickly emerged as principal.

CRANE, DEAN. Born Jan. 5, 1932 in Logan, Iowa. Made professional debut at 14 as aerialist with Pollock Circus. Studied with Nimura, Dokoudovsky, Tudor and Petroff. Became first dancer and choreographer with Ballet Arts Co. Has also appeared on Bdwy and in clubs.

CRASKE, MARGARET. Born in England. Studied with Cecchetti. Appeared with Diaghilev Ballets Russe, de Valois group. Became Ballet Mistress for Ballet Theatre in 1946, subsequently joined Met Opera Ballet School staff and became its assistant director. Currently with Manhattan School of Dance.

CRAVEY, CLARA. Born July 1, 1950 in West Palm Beach, Fla. Trained at Harkness School, and made debut with company in 1968.

CRISTOFORI, JON. Born in Buzzard's Bay, Mass., and began training at 15. Became lead student dancer in National Ballet of Wash., and toured with it until joining Joffrey Ballet. Left in 1969.

CROLL, TINA. Born Aug. 27, 1943 in N.Y.C. Bennington Col. graduate. Studied with Cunningham, Fonaroff. Debut 1964 in Kaufmann Hall. Has danced and choreographed for DTW since 1965. Formed own company in 1970 for which she choreographs.

CROPLEY, EILEEN. Born Aug. 25, 1932 in London. Studied with Sigurd Leeder, Maria Fay, Martha Graham, Don Farnworth. Made debut in 1966 with Paul Taylor Co.

CUNNINGHAM, JAMES. Born Apr. 1, 1938 in Toronto, Can. Graduate UToronto, London Academy Dramatic Arts. Studied at Martha Graham School. Choreographed for and performed with own company from 1967.

CUNNINGHAM, MERCE. Born Apr. 16 in Centralia, Wash. Studied at American School of Ballet. Professional debut as soloist with Martha Graham in 1940; with company through 1945. Began choreographing in 1946; in 1952 formed own company that has toured extensively every year. Teaches in his N.Y.C. studio.

CUNNINGHAM, RON. Born in Chicago; graduate Roosevelt U. Studied with Robert Lunnon, Eric Braun, Wigman, Cunningham, Humphrey, Weidman. Debut 1965 with Martha Graham. Subsequently with Lucas Hoving, Kazuko Hirabayashi, Daniel Nagrin, Lotte Goslar, Zena Bethune, Ballet Concepts, Boston Ballet 1972.

CURRIER, RUTH. Born in 1926 in Ashland, Ohio. Studied with Doris Humphrey and Elsa Kahl. Made debut in 1949 with American Dance Festival. Soloist with Jose Limon Co. 1949–63. Since 1956 has been director-choreographer for own company which has toured U.S. Also teaches.

d'AMBOISE, JACQUES. Born July 28, 1934 in Dedham, Mass. Joined N.Y. Ballet at 15 after 7 years at School of American Ballet; rapidly rose to premier danseur in 1953. Has appeared in films and on TV and choreographed.

DANA, JERILYN. Born in Portland, Me., where she began dancing at 6. Studied with Boston Ballet, and graduated into company. Became soloist in 1969.

DANIAS, STARR. Born Mar. 18, 1949 in N.Y.C. Studied at School of Am. Ballet. Debut 1968 with London Festival Ballet, subsequently joined Joffrey Ballet in 1970.

DANIELIAN, LEON. Born Oct. 31, 1920 in N.Y.C. Studied with Mordkin and Fokine. Debut with Mordkin Ballet in 1937. Appeared with Original Ballet Russe, Ballet Russe de Monte Carlo, Ballet Theatre, Ballet des Champs Elysees, and San Francisco Ballet. Was choreographer-director of Ballet de Monte Carlo. Now with American Ballet Theatre School.

DANIELS, DANNY. Born in 1924 in Albany, N.Y. Studied with Thomas Sternfield, Jack Potteiger, Vincenzo Celli, Elisabeth Anderson-Ivantzova, Anatole Vilzak. Appeared in musicals, as soloist with orchestras, and Agnes de Mille Dance Theatre before becoming choreographer for TV and Bdwy musicals.

DANILOVA, ALEXANDRA. Born Nov. 20, 1906 in Peterhof, Russia. Graduate of Imperial School of Ballet, and became member of company. Subsequently with Balanchine's company, Les Ballets Russes de Diaghilev, Ballet Russe de Monte Carlo (both de Basil's and Massine's). Made N.Y.C. debut in 1948 at Met with Massine's company. Has appeared with and choreographed for N.Y.C. Ballet. In 1954 formed and toured with own company, The Concert Dance Group; choreographer for Met 1961–62. Now teaches.

DANTE, SHARON. Born Jan. 8, 1945 in Torrington, Conn. Graduate UHartford. Studied with Graham, Limon, Weidman, ABT School. Appeared with Charles Weidman, Larry Richardson, Rudy Perez, Jose Limon. Founder-Director of Nutmeg Ballet.

D'ANTUONO, ELEANOR. Born in 1939 in Cambridge, Mass. Danced with Ballet Russe de Monte Carlo for 6 years before joining Joffrey Ballet in 1960. Became member of American Ballet Theatre in 1961; principal since 1963.

Warren Conover   **Colleen Corkre**   **Leon Danielian**   **Starr Danias**   **Charles Dickson**

DAVIDSON, ANDREA. Born in 1955 in Montreal, Can. Studied at Ntl. Ballet School, and joined company in 1971; Promoted to soloist in 1972.

DAVIS, MARTHA HILL. Born in East Palestine, O. Graduate Columbia, NYU. Debut with Martha Graham (1929–31). Director of Dance, Bennington (1934–42), NYU (1930–51), Juilliard since 1951. Founder Conn. Col. School of Dance and American Dance Festival.

DAVIS, ROBERT. Born March 13, 1934 in Durham, N.C. Studied at Wash. School of Ballet, and with Fokine, Franklin, and Joffrey. Debut in 1960 and has appeared as principal dancer with Washington Ballet, National Ballet of Canada, and Joffrey Ballet. Is also director and choreographer.

DEAN, LAURA. Born Dec. 3, 1945 on Staten Island, NY. Studied with Lucas Hoving, Muriel Stuart, Matt Mattox, Martha Graham, American Ballet Center, Mia Slavenska. Appeared with Paul Taylor, Paul Sanasardo. Formed own company in 1971.

DeANGELO, ANN MARIE. Born Oct. 1, 1952 in Pittston, Pa. Trained at San Francisco Ballet School and made debut with its company in 1970. Joined Joffrey 1972.

DE BOLT, JAMES. Born in Seattle, Wash. Studied with Marian and Illaria Ladre, and at U. Utah. Debut with Seattle's Aqua Theatre. Joined Joffrey Ballet in 1959, subsequently with N.Y.C. Opera Ballet, N.Y.C. Ballet 1961, Manhattan Festival Ballet 1965. Is also a costume designer and choreographer. Re-joined Joffrey Co. in 1968. Currently premier danseur with Oslo's Den Norske Opera.

DE GANGE, ANN. Born Sept. 22, 1952 in New London, Conn. Juilliard graduate. Studied with Corvino, Tudor, McGehee, Winters. Debut 1971 with Kazuko Hirabayashi, subsequently with Martha Graham Co. from 1972.

DE JONG, BETTIE. Born in Sumatra, and moved to Holland in 1947. Made debut with Netherlands Pantomime Co. Studied with Martha Graham and joined company; subsequently with Pearl Lang and Lucas Hoving. Joined Paul Taylor in 1962.

DELAMO, MARIO. Born during January 1946 in Havana, Cuba. Studied with May O'Donnell, Gertrude Shurr, Norman Walker. Debut 1966 with Norman Walker Co.; Glenn Tetley 1969; Ailvin Ailey 1970; Martha Graham Co. 1972.

DELANGHE, GAY. Born Aug. 21, 1940 in Mt. Clemens, Mich. Studied at Severo School. Professional debut in 1960 and toured with "The Dancemakers." Choreographer, performer and teacher since 1965. Joined Lucas Hoving Co. in 1969.

de LAPPE, GEMZE. Born Feb. 28, 1922 in Woodhaven, Va. Attended Hunter Coll. and Ballet Arts School. Studied with Duncan, Fokine, Nimura, Caton, and Nemtchinova. Has appeared with Ballet Theatre and Agnes de Mille Dance Theatre and in Bdwy productions.

de LAVALLADE, CARMEN. Born March 6, 1931 in Los Angeles. Attended LACC, and studied with Lester Horton. Professional debut with Horton Dance Theatre. Bdwy debut in 1954. Has appeared with John Butler, Met Opera, de Lavallade-Ailey, Donald McKayle, and Ballet Theatre.

DELZA, SOPHIA. Born in N.Y.C. Studied in China. Professional debut 1953 in program of Chinese dances. Has toured world in concert, and been choreographic consultant for Met Opera, LCRep. Theatre, and Bdwy musicals.

de MAYO, FRED DOUGLASS. Studied at Abbey Theatre, and with Fokine, Youskevitch, Pereyaslavec, and in Paris with Preabrajenska. Appeared with National Ballet, Met. Opera Ballet. Founder of Newburgh Ballet. Now Director of Dance at West Point, and teaches at New Paltz SUNY.

de MILLE, AGNES. Born in N.Y.C. in 1909. Graduate of UCLA. Studied with Kosloff, Rambert, Karsavina, Tudor, Sokolova, Caton, Craske, Stroganova, and Dolmetsch. Debut in 1928 in own dance compositions and toured with them in Europe. Became leading choreographer for Bdwy. Created first ballet "Black Ritual" for Ballet Theatre in 1940. In 1953 organized Agnes de Mille Dance Theatre which toured U.S. Has also choreographed for Ballet Russe de Monte Carlo, and Royal Winnipeg Ballet.

DENARD, MICHAEL. Born Nov. 5, 1944 in Dresden, Germany. Studied in Toulouse and Paris. Has appeared with Berlin Opera, and Paris Opera Ballets, with Bejart, and joined ABT (1971) as principal.

DENVERS, ROBERT. Born Mar. 9, 1942 in Antwerp. Studied with Nora Kiss, Tania Grantzeva, Peretti; joined Bejart's Ballet in 1963; Ntl. Ballet of Canada.

De SOTO, EDWARD. Born Apr. 20, 1939 in The Bronx. Attended Juilliard, AADA, New Dance Group Studio. Danced with Gloria Contreras, Judith Willis, Sophie Maslow, Art Bauman, Valerie Bettis, before joining Limon Co. in 1966.

DESTINE, JEAN-LEON. Born in Haiti, March 26, 1928. Attended Howard U. Made professional debut at Jacob's Pillow in 1949. Formed own company and has toured U.S., Europe, and Japan. Also teaches.

DIAMOND, MATTHEW. Born Nov. 26, 1951 in N.Y.C. Attended CCNY. Debut 1967 with Matteo and the Indo-American Dance Co. Subsequently with Norman Walker, N.Y.C. Opera, Louis Falco.

DI BONA, LINDA. Born July 21, 1946 in Quincy, Mass. Studied at Boston Ballet School and made debut with company in 1965. Joined Harkness Ballet 1972.

DICKSON, CHARLES. Born June 30, 1921 in Bellwood, Pa. Studied with Fokine, Massine, Dolin, Tudor, Volkova, Preobrajenska, Egorova, Balanchine, Volkova, Markova, Loring, Nijinska. Debut 1938 with Ballet Russe de Monte Carlo; AmBalTh 1940–42; Alicia Alonso Ballet 1952–55; Borovansky Ballet of Australia 1955–58; ballet master London Festival Ballet 1958–61; artistic director-ballet master Ballet Municipal de Santiago 1963–76; from 1971 director Metropolitan Academy, and Metropolitan Ballet Co.

DISHONG, ZOLA. Born Aug. 4, 1945 in Albany, Cal. Studied with Lew Christensen, Anatole Vilzak, Michael Lland, Patricia Wilde. Debut 1962 with San Francisco Ballet, subsequently with ABT 1967.

DITSON, ANNE. Born Dec. 20, 1944 in Baton Rouge, La. UCLA graduate. Studied with Dunham, Nikolais, Murray Louis. Made debut in 1968 with UCLA Dance Co. Joined Murray Louis in 1971.

DOBRIEVICH, LOUBA. Born Feb. 9, 1934 in Bajina Basta, Yugoslavia. Studied at Belgrade Academy of Dance. Debut 1954 with Opera Zagreb; subsequently with Paris Theatre Ballet 1958, Maurice Bejart Co. from 1959.

DOBRIEVICH, PIERRE. Born Dec. 27, 1931 in Veles, Yugoslavia. Studied at Etudes de Droit. Debut 1955 with Opera Zagreb; subsequently with Paris Theatre Ballet 1957, Ludmila Cherina 1958, Les Etoiles de Paris 1959, Maurice Bejart from 1960.

DOKOUDOVSKY, VLADIMIR. Born in 1922 in Monte Carlo. Studied with Preobrajenska; made debut at 13; became soloist with Ballet Russe de Monte Carlo, Mordkin Ballet, Ballet Theatre. Premier danseur with Original Ballet Russe (1942–52). Has choreographed several ballets. Now teaches.

DOLIN, ANTON. Born Sydney Francis Patrick Chippendall Healey-Kay in Slinfold, Sussex, Eng. July 27, 1904. Studied with Astafieva, Nijinska. With Diaghileff Company 1921–9, principal dancer with Sadler's Wells 1931–5. Ballet Russe 1946–8. Founder, director, and dancer with Markova-Dolin Co. 1935–8, 1945, 1947–8. Danced, restaged, and choreographed for Ballet Theatre from inception to 1946. 1949 organized and danced with London Festival Ballet until 1961. Currently artistic adviser of Les Grands Ballets Canadiens.

DOLLAR, WILLIAM. Born Apr. 20, 1907 in East St. Louis, Mo. Studied with Fokine, Mordkin, Balanchine, Vladimiroff, and Volinine. Lead dancer with Philadelphia Opera, American Ballet 1936–7, Ballet Caravan 1936–8, Ballet Theatre 1940, American Ballet Caravan 1941, New Opera Co. 1942, Ballet International 1944, ballet master for American Concert Ballet 1943, Ballet Society 1946, Grand Ballet de Monte Carlo 1948, N.Y.C. Ballet. Has choreographed many works, and teaches.

DONN, JORGE. Born Feb. 28, 1947 in Buenos Aires. Attended School of Teatro de Colon. Appeared in musicals before joining Bejart Ballet in 1963, rising to leading male dancer.

DORADO, THIERRY. Born in 1950 in Paris, France. Studied with Nina Tikanova, Paris Opera School. Debut with Paris Opera Ballet; appeared with Nice Opera Ballet, Ballets de Roland Petit, Stuttgart (1969–70). Joined Ballet West as principal 1973.

DOUGLAS, SCOTT. Born June 16, 1927 in El Paso, Tex. Studied with Lester Horton and Ruth St. Denis. Appeared with San Francisco Ballet, Ballets U.S.A., John Butler, Ballet Theatre, Nederlands National Ballet, Glen Tetley Co.

DOWELL, ANTHONY. Born in London Feb. 16, 1943. Studied with June Hampshire, entered Royal Ballet School at 10. Debut as hunter in "Swan Lake" at Covent Garden Opera House. Joined Sadler's Wells Opera Ballet, and Royal Ballet in 1961. Is now a principal.

DOYLE, DESMOND. Born June 16, 1932 in South Africa. Joined Royal Ballet in 1951. Became soloist in 1953; is now a principal and teacher.

DRAPER, PAUL. Born 1909 in Florence, Italy. Began studies at early age, and became tap soloist, elevating it to ballet-tap concert form. Made debut in 1932 in London. Continues to give solo performances, teaches, and is photographer.

DRIVER, SENTA. Born Sept. 5, 1942 in Greenwich, Conn. Graduate Bryn Mawr, Ohio State U. Studied with Don Farnworth, and at O'Donnell-Shur Studio. Joined Paul Taylor Company in 1967.

DU BOULAY, CHRISTINE. Born in 1923 in Ealing, Eng. Trained in Sadler's Wells Ballet School. Soloist with International Ballet before joining Sadler's Wells. Settled in U.S. in 1950, and with husband, Richard Ellis, became founders and directors of Illinois Ballet Co.

DUBREUIL, ALAIN. Born in Monte Carlo, Mar. 4, 1944. Studied at mother's ballet school until awarded scholarship at Arts Educational School (1960). Joined London Festival Ballet in 1962 and became soloist in 1964.

DUDLEY, JANE. Dancer-choreographer. Born in N.Y.C. in 1912. Studied with Martha Graham, Hanya Holm, Louis Horst. Leading dancer with Graham Co. (1937–44). With Sophie Maslow and William Bales, formed concert Dance Trio. Retired in 1954 to teach.

DUELL, DANIEL. Born Aug. 17, 1952 in Rochester, NY. Attended Fordham U., School of American Ballet. Debut 1971 with Edward Villella Co., subsequently with Eglevsky Ballet, Dayton Ballet, Lincoln Center Repertory Dancers.

DUFFY, DIANE. Born in Philadelphia, Pa. Studied at Pa. Ballet Sch., Harkness House. Debut at 15 with Pennsylvania Ballet; joined Harkness, National, Eliot Feld Ballet (1973).

DUNCAN, JEFF. Born Feb. 4, 1930 in Cisco, Tex. Attended N. State U., studied with Holm, Nikolais, Limon, Cunningham, Schwetzoff, Tomkins, Joffrey. Assistant to Doris Humphrey and Anna Sokolow. Debut 1952 at Henry St. Playhouse. Has appeared with New Dance Group, Juilliard Dance Theatre, Anna Sokolow, Jeff Duncan Dance Co., and is founder-director of Dance Theatre Workshop. Has also appeared in Bdwy musicals.

DUNHAM, KATHERINE. Born June 22, 1912, in Chicago. Debut with Chicago Opera Co. in 1933. Bdwy debut 1940 in "Cabin In The Sky." Formed own company for which she choreographed; toured with it in 1943, and subsequently in 57 other countries. Founded Katherine Dunham School of Cultural Arts in N.Y.C. in 1943.

DUNNE, JAMES. Born in Waldwick, N.J. Studied with Irene Fokine, and at School of American Ballet, Harkness House. Joined Harkness Ballet for 4 years, then Joffrey Ballet.

EBBELAAR, HAN. Born Apr. 16, 1943 in Hoorn, Holland. Studied with Max Dooyes and Benjamin Harkarvy. Danced with Nederlands Dans Theater before joining American Ballet Theatre in 1968 as soloist; promoted to principal in 1969, Dutch Natl. Ballet (1970).

EBBIN, MICHAEL. Born June 5, 1945 in Bermuda. Studied at Patricia Gray's, National Ballet, American Ballet Center, and Harkness Schools. Has danced with Eleo Pomare, Cleo Quitman, Australian Dance Theatre, Anna Sokolow, Talley Beatty, and Rod Rodgers companies, and appeared on Bdwy. Joined Ailey company 1972.

EDWARDS, LESLIE. Born Aug. 7, 1916 in Teddington, Eng. Studied with Marie Rambert and at Sadler's Wells School. Debut 1933 with Vic-Wells Ballet, subsequently joined Ballet Rambert, Royal Ballet, Now teaches and makes guest appearances.

EGLEVSKY, ANDRE. Born in Moscow Dec. 21, 1917. Received training in France. At 19 joined Rene Blum's Ballet de Monte Carlo. Came to U.S. in 1937, and after appearing with all major companies, joined Ballet Theatre. In 1947 appeared with Grand Ballet du Marquis de Cuevas. In 1950 joined N.Y.C. Ballet and danced leading male roles until 1958, also created "Scotch Symphony" and other ballets for the company. In 1955, with his wife, prima ballerina Leda Anchutina, opened school in Massapequa, L.I., and in 1960 formed local classical ballet company which he directs.

EISENBERG, MARY JANE. Born Mar. 28, 1951 in Erie, Pa. Attended Hunter, New School. Studied at Graham, ABT, Harkness schools. Debut 1969 with Glen Tetley, subsequently with Keith Lee, Contemporary Dance Ensemble, Louis Falco.

ELLIS, RICHARD. Born 1918 in London. At 15 joined Vic-Wells Ballet which became Sadler's Wells Ballet. Important member of company until 1952. After touring U.S. with company in 1949–50, settled in Chicago. With wife, Christine Du Boulay, became founders and co-directors of Illinois Ballet Co.

ENCKELL, THOMAS. Born in Helsinki, Finland, Oct. 14, 1942. Studied with Margaret Craske. Professional debut with Met Opera Ballet in 1962. Joined Finnish Natl. Opera Ballet 1965. Manhattan Festival Ballet 1966.

ENGLUND, RICHARD. Born in Seattle, Wash. Attended Harvard, Juilliard. Studied with Tudor, Graham, Volkova. Appeared with Limon, Met Opera, Natl. Ballet of Canada, ABT, and in musicals. Currently teaches and choreographs.

ENTERS, ANGNA. Dancer, choreographer, and mime was born in 1907 in N.Y.C. Created own style of dance and pantomime that she has performed all over the world. Is also a writer and painter.

ERDMAN, JEAN. Born in Honolulu, Hawaii. Graduate of Sarah Lawrence College (1938). Studied at Bennington, American School of Ballet, Hisamatsu, Martha Graham, Pukui and Huapala Hawaiian Dance Schools. Professional debut 1938 with Martha Graham, and as a choreographer in 1942. Organized own company in 1950, and made annual tours through 1960. World tour 1963–5 with "The Coach With The Six Insides" which she conceived and staged. Head of NYU Dance Dept. for 5 yrs.

ERICKSON, BETSY. Born in Oakland, Cal. Attended Cal. State U., San Francisco Ballet School. Debut with San Francisco Ballet. Joined American Ballet Theatre 1967; returned to SF Ballet 1973.

ESTELLE & ALFONSO. Born in N.Y.: trained with Haakon, Mattox, Juarez, LaSylphe, Nettles, Chileno, Wills, Thomas. Toured widely as team. Currently operate school in Poughkeepsie, N.Y., and artistic directors for Mid-Hudson Regional Ballet.

ESTNER, ROBERT. Born in North Hollywood, Calif. Attended Los Angeles City Valley Jr. Col. Studied with Robert Rossalatt, Natalie Clare, Andre Tremaine, Carmalita Maracci, and at ABC. Appeared with Ballet Concerto, Pacific Ballet, Ballet La Jeunesse, before joining Joffrey Co.

EVANS, BILL. Born Apr. 11, 1946 in Lehi, Utah. Graduate Univ. Utah. Studied at Harkness House, American Dance Center, ABT School. Made debut in 1966 with Ruth Page Ballet. Joined Repertory Dance Theatre in 1967 as dancer and choreographer.

EVERETT, ELLEN. Born in Springfield, Ill. June 19, 1942. Studied in Chicago and School of American Ballet. Professional debut 1958 with Ruth Page's Chicago Opera Ballet. Soloist with American Ballet Theatre from 1967. Raised to principal 1973. Has also appeared on Bdwy.

FADEYECHEV, NICOLAI. Born in Moscow in 1933. Studied at Bolshoi School and joined company in 1952; became soloist in 1953, and subsequently premier danseur.

FAISON, GEORGE. Born Dec. 21, 1945 in Washington, D.C. Attended Howard U. Studied with Louis Johnson, Claude Thompson, Alvin Ailey, Dudley Williams, Elizabeth Hodes. Appeared on Bdwy and with Universal Dance Experience (1971).

FALCO, LOUIS. Born in N.Y.C.; studied with Limon, Weidman, Graham, and at American Ballet Theatre School. Has danced, choreographed, and toured with Jose Limon Co., choreographed for other groups, and own company.

FALLET, GENEVIEVE. Born Aug. 2, 1943 in Switzerland. Studied at Royal Ballet, and with Yuriko, Cunningham, Wagoner, DTW. Has danced with London and Paris companies, with Frances Alenikoff, and solo.

FALLIS, BARBARA. Born in 1924 in Denver, Colo. Moved to London in 1929. Studied at Mona Clague School. Vic-Wells and Vilzak-Shollar Schools. Debut 1938 in London. With Vic-Wells Ballet 1938–40; Ballet Theatre in 1941; Ballet Alicia Alonso (1948–52), N.Y.C. Ballet (1953–58). Now teaches.

FARBER, VIOLA. Born in Heidelberg. Ger., Feb. 25, 1931. Attended American U. and Black Mt. College. Studied with Katherine Litz, Merce Cunningham, Alfredo Corvino, and Margaret Craske. Debut 1952 with Merce Cunningham, subsequently with Paul Taylor, and Katherine Litz. More recently, choreographing, and guest artist with Merce Cunningham.

| **Jeff Duncan** | **Senta Driver** | **Eliot Feld** | **Ellen Everett** | **Frederic Franklin** |

FARRELL, SUZANNE. Born Roberta Sue Ficker Aug. 16, 1945 in Cincinnati. Began ballet studies in Cincinnati, subsequently attending School of American Ballet. After 15 months joined N.Y.C. Ballet, and became a principal dancer in 1965. Joined National Ballet of Canada in 1970, Bejart (1970).

FAXON, RANDALL. Born Sept. 26, 1950 in Harrisburg. Pa. Studied with Elizabeth Rockwell. Martha Graham, Paul Sanasardo, Alfredo Corvin, and at Juilliard. Debut 1969 with Ethel Winter; joined Lucas Hoving in 1970.

FEIGENHEIMER, IRENE. Born June 16, 1946 in N.Y.C. Attended Hunter Col. Studied with Holm, Graham, Cunningham, ABC. Debut 1965 with Met Opera Ballet, subsequently danced with Merry-Go-Rounders, Ruth Currier, Anna Sokolow, Cliff Keuter, Don Redlich.

FELD, ELIOT. Born 1943 in Brooklyn. Studied with Richard Thomas and at School of American Ballet. Appeared with N.Y.C. Ballet, and on Bdwy before joining American Ballet Theatre in 1963. Co-founder (1969), director, dancer, and choreographer for American Ballet Co. Rejoined ABT in 1971. Debuted Eliot Feld Ballet 1974.

FERNANDEZ, ROYES. Born July 15, 1929 in New Orleans. Studied with Lelia Hallers and Vincenzo Celli. Appeared with Ballet Russe, Markova-Dolin, Ballet Alicia Alonso, de Cuevas' Ballet, before joining Ballet Theatre. Premier danseur since 1957. Retired in 1973 to teach. Has appeared with several companies as guest artist.

FIBICH, FELIX. Born May 8, 1917 in Warsaw, Poland; attended dance and theatre schools, and made professional debut there in 1936. Became dancer-choreographer in 1939. Formed own company that has toured widely with Israeli and Chassidic dancers. Also teaches.

FIFIELD, ELAINE. Born in Sydney, Aust. Studied at Sadler's Wells, RAD. Debut 1948 with Sadler's Wells Co., subsequently appeared with Royal Ballet, Australian Ballet.

FIGUEROA, ALFONSO. Born May 24, 1947 in N.Y.C. Graduate Boston Cons. Studied with Virginia Williams, Thomas-Fallis, Pearl Lang. Debut 1967 with Boston Ballet; subsequently Pearl Lang, American Ballet 1968, Alvin Ailey 1970, Boston Ballet 1971.

FILIPOV, ALEXANDER. Born Mar. 19, 1947 in Moscow. Studied at Leningrad Kirov School. Debut with Moiseyev Ballet, defected and appeared with Pa. Ballet, Eglevsky Ballet, ABT (1970), Pittsburgh Ballet 1971, San Francisco Ballet 1974.

FISHER, NELLE. Born Dec. 10, 1920 in Berkeley, Cal. Appeared with Martha Graham Co., in Bdwy musicals; choreographs and teaches.

FITZGERALD, HESTER. Born Oct. 1, 1939 in Cleveland, O. Trained with Nedjedin, Levinoff, and at Ballet Russe, American, and Ballet Theatre schools. Debut with Ballet Russe 1956; subsequently with N.Y.C. Ballet, ABT, and Harkness Ballet.

FLINDT, FLEMMING. Born Sept. 30, 1936 in Copenhagen. Entered Danish Royal Ballet School at 10; became member at 18. Invited by Harald Lander to appear in London; returned to Danish Ballet and became leading dancer before joining Paris Opera as danseur etoile, and choreographing. Ranks among world's greatest male dancers, and has achieved recognition as choreographer. Became director of Royal Danish Ballet in 1966.

FONAROFF, NINA. Born in N.Y.C. in 1914. Studied with Martha Graham, at School of American Ballet. Danced with Graham (1937–46) before forming own company in 1945. Is now teacher-choreographer.

FONTEYN, MARGOT. Born May 18, 1919 in Surrey, Eng. Began training at 14 with Astafieva, and a few months later entered Sadler's Wells School. Solo debut with company in 1934 in "The Haunted Ballroom." In 1935, succeeded to ballerina roles of Markova. Unrivaled in roles of Aurora and Chloe. Made Dame of British Empire by Queen Elizabeth. Guest star of Royal Ballet, and considered Prima Ballerina Assoluta of the world.

FOREMAN, LAURA. Born in Los Angeles. U. Wisc. graduate. Danced with Tamiris-Nagrin, Marion Scott, Harriet Anne Gray, Ann Halprin. Director of Laura Foreman Dance Company; Founder/Director of Choreographers Theatre/ChoreoConcerts; director New School Dance Dept.

FOSSE, BOB. Born in Chicago June 23, 1927. Appeared in musicals before becoming outstanding choreographer for Bdwy, films, and TV.

FOSTER, RORY. Born Feb. 3, 1947 in Chicago, Ill. Attended Ill. Benedictine Col. Studied with Robert Lunnon, Doreen Tempest, Vincenzo Celli. Debut 1962 with Allegro American Ballet; joined American Ballet Theatre 1970.

FOWLER, TOM. Born Feb. 18, 1949 in Long Beach, Cal. Graduate U. Cin. Studied with David Howard, Claudia Corday, David McLean, Margaret Black, Richard Thomas, Harkness House. Debut 1971 with American Ballet Company.

FRACCI, CARLA. Born Aug. 20, 1936 in Milan, Italy. Began training at 8 at La Scala with Edda Martignoni, Vera Volkova, and Esmee Bulnes. Became prima ballerina of La Scala in 1958; joined London Festival Ballet as guest artist. Now permanent guest artist with American Ballet Theatre.

FRALEY, INGRID. Born Nov. 1, 1949 in Paris, France. Studied at San Francisco Ballet, and made debut with company in 1964. Subsequently with Kiel-Lubeck Opera Ballet, Fokine Ballet, Eglevsky Ballet, joined American Ballet Theatre 1969.

FRANKEL, EMILY. Born in N.Y.C. Studied with Weidman, Holm, Graham, Craske, Tudor, and Daganova. Professional debut 1950. Founder, director, choreographer, and dancer with Dance Drama Co. since 1955. Has made 8 transcontinental tours, a State Dept. sponsored tour of Europe, and British Arts Council tour of England and Scotland.

FRANKLIN, FREDERIC. Born in Liverpool, Eng. in 1914. Studied with Legat, Kyasht, and Pruzina. Made debut as child dancer; went to London at 17; appeared in music halls, night clubs, and musicals before joining Markova-Dolin Co. 1935–7. Premier danseur with Ballet Russe de Monte Carlo from 1938; became its ballet master in 1944. Artistic adviser ABT (1961). Since 1962 director of National Ballet.

FREDERICK, JULIA. Born in Boston. Studied and performed with Boston Ballet, Harkness Ballet, N.Y.C. Ballet. Also danced with Penn. Ballet, Garden State Ballet, and N.Y.C. Opera Co. Resident soloist with Hartford Ballet.

FREEDMAN, LAURIE. Born July 7, 1945 in N.Y.C. Graduate Bennington Col. Studied with Graham, Cunningham, Zena Rommett. Debut 1967 with Merry-Go-Rounders, subsequently with Batsheva Dance Co. (1968).

FREEMAN, FRANK. Born July 16, 1945 in Bangalore, India. Studied at Royal Ballet School. Joined company in 1963. Joined London Festival Ballet as soloist in 1971.

FUENTE, LUIS. Born in 1944 in Madrid where he began studies at early age. Joined Antonio's Ballets de Madrid in 1963; Joffrey Ballet 1964–1970. National Ballet (1970) as principal; London Festival Ballet 1972.

FUERSTNER, FIONA. Born Apr. 24, 1936 in Rio de Janeiro. Attended San Francisco State College. Studied at San Francisco Ballet School (debut with company 1952). School of American Ballet, Ballet Rambert, Royal Ballet, Ballet Theatre schools. Has danced with Les Grands Ballets Canadiens, San Francisco, N.Y.C. Center, and Philadelphia Opera ballet companies. Principal dancer with Pennsylvania Ballet. Became Ballet Mistress in 1974.

GABLE, CHRISTOPHER. Born 1940 in London, began studies at Royal Ballet School. At 16 joined Sadler's Wells Opera Ballet, and next year Covent Garden Opera Ballet. In 1957 became member of Royal Ballet and at 19 advanced to soloist. Retired in 1967 to act.

GAIN, RICHARD. Born in Belleville, Ill. Jan. 24, 1939. Studied with Lalla Baumann, and Martha Graham. Professional debut with St. Louis Municipal Opera, followed by musicals. Became member of Graham Co. in 1961, also danced with Jazz Ballet Theatre, Lotte Goslar, Sophie Maslow, and Pearl Lang, and formed concert group "Triad" that performed in N.Y. and on tour. Joined Joffrey Co. in 1964; ABT in 1967. Teaches at N.C. School of Arts.

GARDNER, BARBARA. Born June 7, 1940 in Lynbrook, NY. Graduate Stanford U. Studied with Wigman, Sanasardo, Cunningham. Has appeared with Nikolais, Marion Scott, Phoebe Neville, Elina Mooney, and her own company. Also teaches.

GARRARD, MIMI. Born in Gastonia, N.C. Attended Sweet Briar College. Studied at Henry St. Playhouse, with Julia Barashkova, Angelina Romet. Has appeared with Alwin Nikolais and Murray Louis companies, and own company for which she choreographs.

GARTH, MIDI. Born in N.Y.C. Studied with Francesca de Cotelet, Sybil Shearer, Louis Horst. Has choreographed and performed solo concerts in N.Y. and on tour. Also teaches.

GARY, M'LISS. Born Nov. 8, 1951 in Lisbon, Port, Graduate Natl. Ballet Academy. Studied with Oleg Tupine, Richard Thomas, Barbara Fallis. Debut 1969 with National Ballet, joined American Ballet Co. in 1971.

GAYLE, DAVID. Born July 10, 1942 in Yorkshire, Eng. Appeared in Covent Garden opera ballets before joining Royal Ballet. Left in 1970 to teach in Buffalo.

GENNARO, PETER. Born 1924 in Metairie, La. Studied at American Theatre Wing. Debut with Chicago San Carlo Opera 1948, and Bdwy bow same year. After several musicals and TV, choreographed "Seventh Heaven" in 1955. Is much in demand as dancer and choreographer on television.

GENTRY, EVE. Born Aug. 20, in Los Angeles. Used own name Henrietta Greenhood until 1945. Studied with Holm, Graham, Humphrey, Weidman, Tamiris, Barashkova, at Ballet Arts Studio, and American Ballet Center. Debut with Hanya Holm. Since 1949, director-choreographer-soloist with own company.

GERMAINE, DIANE. Born July 5, 1944 in N.Y.C. Studied with Martha Graham. May O'Donnell, Norman Walker, Paul Sanasardo. Debut with Sanasardo in 1963. Has appeared in concert with Norman Walker, and teaches.

GEVA, TAMARA. Born 1908 in St. Petersburg, Russia. Studied at Maryinsky Theatre. Joined Diaghilev. Came to U.S., signed by Ziegfeld, subsequently appeared in musicals and films and with American Ballet.

GIELGUD, MAINA. Born Jan. 14, 1945 in London. Studied with Karsavina, Idzikovski, Egorova, Gsovsky, Hightower. Debut 1961 with Petit Ballet, subsequently with Ballet De Marquis de Cuevas, Miskovitch, Grand Ballet Classique, joined Bejart Ballet in 1967.

GILPIN, JOHN. Born in 1930 in Southsea, Eng. Was child actor; joined Ballet Rambert 1945, London's Festival ballet 1950, becoming artistic director and principal dancer. Guest artist with ABT and Royal Ballet. Resigned as artistic director Festival Ballet but remains premier danseur.

GIORDANO, GUS. Born July 10, 1930 in St. Louis. Graduate U. Mo. Debut at Roxy N.Y.C., 1948, subsequently appeared in musicals on TV before becoming choreographer. Currently director of Giordano Dance Studio in Evanston, Ill., and his own company.

GLADSTEIN, ROBERT. Born Jan. 16, 1943 in Berkeley, Calif. Attended San Francisco State College, and studied at San Francisco Ballet School. Became member of San Francisco Ballet in 1960 and choreographed 13 ballets. Joined American Ballet Theatre in 1967, became soloist in 1968. Rejoined S.F. Ballet 1970.

GLASSMAN, WILLIAM. Born 1945 in Boston and began dance studies at 7. Scholarship to School of American Ballet. Studied with Alfredo Corvino and Margaret Craske. Appeared in musicals, with N.Y.C. and on TV, before joining American Ballet Theatre in 1963. Promoted to soloist 1965. Now with Niagara Frontier Ballet.

GLENN, LAURA. Born Aug. 25, 1945 in N.Y.C. Graduate Juilliard. Joined Limon Co. in 1964. Has also performed with Ruth Currier, Sophie Maslow, Valerie Bettis, and Contemporary Dance Sextet.

GLUCK, RENA. Born Jan. 14, 1933. Juilliard graduate. Studied with Graham, Tudor, Horst, Blanche Evans. Founding member of Batsheva Dance Co. in 1963. Also choreographs.

GLUSHAK, NANETTE. Born Dec. 31, 1951 in NYC. Studied at School of Am. Ballet. Made debut with American Ballet Theatre in 1967. Promoted to soloist 1973.

GODREAU, MIGUEL. Born Oct. 17, 1946 in Ponce, P.R. Studied at Joffrey Ballet Center, School of American Ballet, Ballet School, and with Martha Graham. Debut 1964 with First American Dance Co., subsequently with Ailey, McKayle, and Harkness Ballet. After appearing on Bdwy, organized and danced with own company in 1969. Returned to Ailey Co. in 1970. Left to appear in London. Now principal with Birgit Cullberg Co. in Sweden.

GOLLNER, NANA. Born 1920 in El Paso, Texas. Studied with Kosloff. Soloist with American Ballet 1935, de Basil's Ballet Russe 1935–6. Blum's Ballet Russe 1936–7. Ballet Theatre 1939–48. Only American to achieve rank of ballerina in foreign country.

GOODMAN, ERIKA. Born Oct. 9 in Philadelphia. Trained at School of American Ballet, and American Ballet Center. Debut with N.Y.C. Ballet 1965. Appeared with Pa. Ballet, and Boston Ballet before joining Joffrey Ballet in 1967.

GOPAL, RAM. Born Nov. 20. Hindu dancer, came to U.S. in 1938, and with own company has toured world as its soloist. Operates own school.

GORDON, LONNY JOSEPH. Born in Edinburg, Tex. Graduate of U.Tex and U.Wisc. Studied at Grand Kabuki Theatre in Tokyo, and with Koisaburo Nishikawa, Richo Nishikawa. Has given solo performances throughout Japan and U.S.

GORDON, MARVIN. Born in N.Y.C. Graduate Queens Col. Studied with New Dance Group, Met Opera Ballet, Graham, Humphrey, and Weidman. Appeared on Bdwy and TV, in concert with Doris Humphrey, and Pearl Lang. Choreographed before becoming founder-director of Ballet Concerts, that has appeared in N.Y. and on tour throughout U.S.

GOSLAR, LOTTIE. Born in Dresden, Ger. Studied at Mary Wigman School. Toured Europe as dance mime before coming to U.S. in 1937. Formed own pantomime company for tours of U.S. and Europe. Also teaches.

GOTSHALKS, JURY. Born in Riga, Latvia. Studied at Latvian Natl. Ballet School. Appeared with National Ballet of Canada, Les Grands Ballets Canadiens, N.Y.C. Opera. Since 1968, teacher at U.Wisc., and director of Milwaukee Ballet.

GOVRIN, GLORIA. Born Sept. 10, 1942 in Newark, N.J. Studied at Tarassof School, American Ballet Academy, School of American Ballet. Joined N.Y.C. Ballet in 1957. Promoted to soloist at 19.

GOYA, CAROLA. Born in N.Y.C. Studied with Fokine, Otero, LaQuica, Maria Esparsa. Danced with Met Opera before solo debut as Spanish dancer in 1927. Appeared with Greco before partnership with Matteo in 1954.

GRAHAM, MARTHA. Born May 11, 1893 in Pittsburgh. Studied at Denishawn School of Dance; made debut with its company in 1919, and danced with them until 1923. First choreographed and appeared in N.Y.C. in a program of 18 original works in 1926, followed by annual concerts until 1938. A founder of Bennington (Vt.) Dance Festival where she staged several premieres of her works. Formed own company with which she has made numerous successful tours throughout world. Founded Martha Graham School of Contemporary Dance in 1927, and remains its director. Has created over 100 dances.

GRANT, ALEXANDER. Born Feb. 22, 1925 in Wellington. New Zealand. Entered Sadler's Wells School in 1946, and five months later joined company. Has created more major roles than any other male dancer with Royal Ballet.

GRAY, DIANE. Born May 29, 1944 in Painesville, Ohio. Attended Juilliard. Studied with Graham, Tudor, Youskevitch, Schwezoff, Melikova, Hinkson, Winter, McGehee, Ross. Debut 1964 with Martha Graham Co. Has also appeared with Helen McGehee, Yuriko, Pearl Lang, Sophie Maslow, Jeff Duncan.

GRECO, JOSE. Born Dec. 23, 1919 in Montorio-Nei-Frentani, Compobasso, Italy. Studied with Mme. Veola in N.Y.C. Argentinita and La Quica in Madrid. Debut as soloist 1935 with Salmaggi Opera Co. Partner with La Argentinita 1943–4. Pilar Lopez 1946–8, before organizing own company in 1949, with which he has become internationally famous.

GREENFIELD, AMY. Born July 8, 1940 in Boston. Studied with Graham, Cunningham, Fonaroff, Robert Cohan, American Ballet Center. Made debut in 1965. Has appeared in concert and with DTW.

GREGORY, CYNTHIA. Born July 8 in Los Angeles where she studied with Lorraine, Maracci, Panaieff, and Rossellat. Danced with Santa Monica Civic Ballet, L.A. Civic Light Opera in 1961 joined San Francisco Ballet, subsequently S.F. Opera Ballet, and American Ballet Theatre in 1965, became principal in 1968.

GREY, BERYL. Born in Highgate, England, June 11, 1927. Began studies at Sadler's Wells Ballet School, and at 15 danced "Swan Lake" with its company. Left in 1957 but returned for guest appearances. Appointed in 1966 to head Arts Education School, London. Director London Festival Ballet, made Commander British Empire in 1973.

GRIFFITHS, LEIGH-ANN. Born Dec. 5, 1948 in Johannesburg, S.A. Studied at Royal Ballet School. Joined Stuttgart Ballet in 1968.

GRIGOROVICH, YURI. Born in Leningrad Jan. 2, 1927. Graduated from Leningrad Ballet School and became one of leading soloists with Kirov Co. In 1964 became choreographer for Moscow Bolshoi Ballet Co.

GROMAN, JANICE. Born in New Britain, Conn. Joined N.Y.C. Ballet at 16. Later with ABT, and First Chamber Dance Quartet.

Diane Gray

Richard Gain

Janice Groman

John Hiatt

Marcia Haydee

GUERARD, LEO. Born Jan. 18, 1937 in Boston, Mass. Studied at School of American Ballet. Debut 1952 with ABT; subsequently with Grand Ballet de Cuevas 1957, Skandinavian Ballet 1960, Royal Winnipeg Ballet 1963, Western Theatre Ballet 1964, Intl. Ballet Caravan 1968, Boston Ballet 1968.

GUNN, NICHOLAS. Born Aug. 28, 1947 in Bklyn. Studied with Ellen Segal, Helen McGehee, June Lewis, Don Farnworth. Appeared with Stuart Hodes Co. Joined Paul Taylor Co. in 1969.

GUTELIUS, PHYLLIS. Born in Wilmington, Del. Studied with Schwetzoff, Tudor, Graham. Joined Graham Company in 1962. Has appeared on Bdwy, with Glen Tetley, Yuriko, Sophie Maslow, John Butler.

GUTHRIE, NORA. Born Jan. 2, 1950 in N.Y.C. Studied with Marjorie Mazia, Martha Graham, and at NYU. Debut 1970 with Jean Erdman Co.

GUZMAN, PASCHAL. Born in Arecibo, P.R. Attended Harkness, National Ballet, Graham, Dalcroze schools. Debut 1964 with National Ballet, subsequently with Baltimore Ballet, Washington Dance Repertory, Penn. Ballet, New America Ballet, Ballet Concerto, Downtown Ballet.

GYORFI, VICTORIA. Born in Wenatchee, Wash. Studied at San Francisco Ballet, and made debut with its company. Appeared with Munich Ballet, Bayerische Staats Oper, and returned to SF Ballet.

HAAKON, PAUL. Born in Denmark in 1914 Studied at Royal Danish Ballet School, with Fokine, Mordkin, and at School of American Ballet. Debut with Fokine in 1927. Danced and toured with Anna Pavlova. Became premier danseur with American Ballet in 1935. Appeared in musicals and nightclubs. In 1963 became ballet master and instructor of Jose Greco Co.

HALL, YVONNE. Born Mar. 30, 1956 in Jamaica, WI. Studied at Dance Theatre of Harlem and made debut with company in 1969.

HAMILTON, PETER. Born in Trenton, N.J. Sept. 12, 1915. Attended Rutgers. Danced in Broadway musicals before becoming choreographer and teacher.

HAMMONS, SUZANNE. Born Aug. 26, 1938 in Oklahoma City. Attended San Francisco Ballet, American Ballet Center, and Harkness schools. Debut in 1958 with San Francisco Ballet; subsequently joined Harkness, and Joffrey Ballet companies.

HANITCHAK, LEONARD R., JR. Born July 24, 1944 in Oklahoma City. Studied with Ethel Butler, Graham, and Cunningham. Has danced with DTW, and Rudy Perez Co.

HANKE, SUSANNE. Born in 1948 near Berlin. Studied with Anneliese Morike, Anne Woolliams, and at Royal Ballet School. Debut 1963 in Wuerttemberg State Theatre Ballet. Joined Stuttgart Ballet in 1966.

HARKAVY, BENJAMIN. Born in N.Y.C. in 1930. Studied with Chaffee, Caton, Preobrajenska, and at School of Am. Ballet. Made debut with Bklyn. Lyric Opera, for which he also choreographed. Opened school in 1955 and formed concert group. Ballet master for Royal Winnepeg, and Nederlands Ballet. Artistic Director of Pa. Ballet 1972.

HARKNESS, REBEKAH. Born in St. Louis, Mo. Promoted American dancers for several years before establishing Harkness Ballet in 1965, and Harkness Ballet School.

HARPER, LEE. Born Nov. 10, 1946 in Hickory, N.C. Juilliard graduate. Studied with Tudor, Limon, Koner, Lindgren, Cunningham, Alvin Ailey.

HARPER, MEG. Born Feb. 16, 1944 in Evanston, Ill. Graduate of U. Ill. Studied with Merce Cunningham and made professional debut with his company in 1968.

HARRIS, RANDAL. Born in Spokane, Wash. Attended Pacific Lutheran U. Studied with Joffrey, Edna McRae, Jonathan Watts ABC. Joined Joffrey Ballet in 1970.

HART, DIANA. Born Apr. 21, 1952 in Lansing, Mich. Attended Juilliard, and Martha Graham schools. Made debut 1973 with Graham Company. Has also appeared with Saeko Ichinohe Co.

HART, JOHN. Born in London in 1921. Studied with Judith Espinosa, and at Royal Acad. Joined Sadler's Wells in 1938, and rose to principal. Became ballet master in 1951, asst. director in 1962.

HARVEY, DYANE. Born Nov. 16, 1951 in Schenectady, N.Y. Studied with Marilyn Ramsey, Paul Sanasardo. Appeared with Schenectady Ballet, Dance Uptown, Miguel Godreau, Eleo Pomare, Movements Black, Story Time Dance Theatre.

HARWOOD, VANESSA. Born June 14, 1947 in Cheltenham, Eng. Studied with Betty Oliphant, Ntl. Ballet School, Rosella Hightower. Debut 1965 with National Ballet of Canada; became principal in 1970.

HASH, CLAIRE RISA. Born May 18, 1946 in Norwich, Conn. Studied at U. Colo. and NYU. Debut 1970 with Jean Erdman Co.

HAUBERT, ALAINE. Born in N.Y.C. Attended U. Utah. Studied with Helen Averell, Raoul Pause, Kira Ivanovsky, Dorothy Dean, Alan Howard, William Griffith. Debut with Monterey Peninsula Ballet, subsequently with Pacific Ballet, ABT, Joffrey Ballet.

HAUPERT, LYNN. Born Aug. 16, 1954 in Syracuse, NY. Studied with Paul Sanasardo, Dance Theatre of Harlem. Debut 1972 with Paul Sanasardo Dance Co.

HAWKINS, ERICK. Born in Trinidad, Colo. Studied at School of American Ballet. Appeared with American Ballet 1934–7, Ballet Caravan 1936–9, and with Martha Graham, before becoming choreographer, teacher, and director of his own company.

HAYDEE, MARCIA. Born April 18, 1940 in Rio de Janeiro. Studied at Royal Ballet School, London. Debut with Marquis de Cuevas Ballet. Joined Stuttgart Ballet in 1961, becoming its prima ballerina.

HAYDEN, MELISSA. Born in Toronto, Can. April 25, 1923, where she received early training before becoming charter member of N.Y.C. Ballet in 1949. Has appeared with Natl. Ballet of Canada, Ballet Theatre, and Royal Ballet. In great demand as educator and lecture-demonstrator. Has also appeared on Bdwy. Director "Ballet Festival." Retired 1973 to teach.

HAYMAN-CHAFFEY, SUSANA. Born Jan. 31, 1948 in Tenterden, England, Studied at Sadler's Wells School, and with Lepeshinskaya, Graham, Cunningham. Made debut in 1968 with Merce Cunningham.

HAYWARD, CHARLES SUMNER. Born May 2, 1949 in Providence, R.I. Attended Juilliard. Debut in 1968 with Jose Limon Company.

HEINEMAN, HELEN. Born Aug. 13, 1947 in Highland Park, Ill. Attended Hunter Col. Studied with Sybil Shearer, Mme. Swoboda. Debut 1963 with National Ballet; became soloist before leaving in 1966. Ballet Russe 1967; Nederlands Dans Theater 1968–9; Harkness Ballet 1970.

HELPMANN, ROBERT. Born April 9, 1909 in Mt. Gambier, Austl. Attended King Alfred Col.; studied with Laurent Novikov. Debut in Austl. musicals; in 1933 joined Sadler's Wells (now Royal Ballet), and rose to soloist from 1933–50. Became choreographer, and created ballet "Hamlet" in 1942. Recently has devoted time to acting, guest performances, and directing Australian Ballet. Made Commander of British Empire in 1964.

HERBERTT, STANLEY. Born in Chicago in 1919. Studied with Tudor, Caton, Ivantzova. Member of Polish Ballet, Littlefield, Chicago and San Carlo Opera Ballets before joining Ballet Theatre in 1943. Founder-Director of St. Louis Ballet. Also teaches and choreographs.

HERMANS, EMERY. Born June 25, 1931, in Seattle. Studied with Vaunda Carter, and at Henry St. Playhouse. Debut 1968 with Nikolais Co. Has danced with Carolyn Carlson, Al Wunder, and in own works.

HIATT, JOHN. Born Oct. 5, 1939 in St. George, U. Studied at UUtah, and became charter member and principal of Ballet West in 1963.

HIGHTOWER, ROSELLA. Born Jan. 30, 1920 in Ardmore, Okla. Studied at Perkins School. Appeared with Ballet Russe de Monte Carlo 1938–41. Ballet Theatre 1941–5. Markova-Dolin 1946. Original Ballet Russe 1946–7. Teaches in Cannes and makes guest appearances.

HILL, CAROLE. Born Jan. 5, 1945 in Cambridge, Eng. Studied at Royal Ballet School and made debut with Royal Ballet Co. in 1962.

HILL, MARTHA. (see DAVIS, MARTHA HILL)

HINKSON, MARY. Born in Philadelphia, March 16, 1930. Graduate of U. Wisc. Studied with Graham, Horst, Shook, June Taylor, Schwezoff. Debut with Graham Co. in 1952, and still appears as soloist. Also danced with John Butler, N.Y.C. Opera, and N.Y.C. Ballet.

HOCTOR, HARRIET. Born in Hoosick Falls, N.Y. Studied with Tarasov, Chalif, Dolin, Legat. Danced in vaudeville, theater, and films before opening own school in Boston in 1941, where she teaches.

HODES, STUART. Born in 1924. Studied with Graham, Lew Christensen, Ella Daganova, and at School of American Ballet. Leading dancer with Graham (1947–58), appeared in Bdway musicals, and as soloist in own works. Choreographer and instructor with Harkness Ballet. Now teaches, and heads NYU Dance Dept.

HOFF, ALEXIS. Born Aug. 31, 1947 in Chicago. Studied with Melba Cordes, Betty Gour, Edna MacRae and at Stone-Camryn School. Made debut with Chicago Lyric Opera Ballet in 1961. Joined Harkness Ballet in 1965, becoming soloist in 1968.

HOFF, STEVEN-JAN. Born June 24, 1943, in Hilversum, Holland. Studied at Amsterdam Academie of Dance. Appeared in musicals before joining American Ballet Theatre in 1966. Became soloist in 1969. Joined Garden State Ballet 1970. Formed own "Film and Dance Theatre" in 1971.

HOFFMAN, PHILLIP. Born in Rochester. N.Y. Attended Miami Dade Jr. Col. Studied with Thomas Armour, and at Harkness House, ABC. Joined Joffrey Ballet in 1969.

HOGAN, JUDITH. Born Mar. 14, 1940 in Lincoln. Neb. Studied with Martha Graham. Made debut with Bertram Ross in 1964. Danced with Glen Tetley before joining Graham Co. in 1967.

HOLDEN, RICHARD. Born Aug. 8 in Braintree, Mass. Graduate of London Inst. of Choreology. Appeared with George Chaffee Ballet, Met Opera, Ballets Minerva. Choreologist for Harkness Ballet, and director of Tucson Civic Ballet.

HOLDEN, STANLEY. Born in London, Jan. 27, 1928. Studied with Marjorie Davies Romford. Made professional debut in 1944 with Royal Ballet and remained until 1969. Now teaches, and makes guest appearances.

HOLDER, CHRISTIAN. Born in Trinidad. Studied in London, and with Martha Graham, Bella Malinka, ABC, Joined Joffrey Ballet.

HOLDER, GEOFFREY. Born in Port-of-Spain, Trinidad, Aug. 1, 1930. Attended Queens Royal College. With brother's dance company in Trinidad, later its director. With own company, made first U.S. appearance in 1953. Besides touring, and giving annual concerts with his group, has appeared on Bdwy, with Met opera, and John Butler Co., also choreographs and designs.

HOLM, HANYA. Born in 1898 in Worms-am-Rhine, Germany. Attended Hoch Conserv., Dalcroze Inst., Wigman School. U.S. debut with own company in 1936, followed by annual performances and transcontinental tours. Came to U.S. in 1931 to found N.Y. Wigman School of Dance which became her school in 1936. Has choreographed musicals and operas in U.S. and London.

HOLMES, GEORGIANA. Born Jan. 5, 1950 in Vermont. Studied with Pauline Koner, Duncan Noble, Job Sanders, Boston School of Ballet. Debut 1969 with Norman Walker; subsequently with Pearl Lang, Louis Falco, Paul Sanasardo.

HONDA, CHARLOTTE. Born June 2, 1940 in San Jose, Calif. Graduate Ohio State U. Studied with Cunningham, Graham, Hoving, Limon, Sanasardo, Farnworth. Debut in 1967 with Larry Richardson; subsequently with Katherine Litz, ChoreoConcerts, and Laura Foreman.

HORNE, KATHRYN. Born in Ft. Worth, Tex., June 20, 1932. Studied with Margaret Craske, Anthony Tudor. Debut 1948 with Ft. Worth Opera Ballet. Appeared with American Ballet Theatre as Catherine Horn (1951–56), a principal dancer Met Opera Ballet (1957–65), Manhattan Festival Ballet (1963–8), also ballet mistress and teacher for MFB.

HORVATH, IAN. Born in Cleveland, O., June 3, 1945. Studied with Danielian, Joffrey. Appeared in musicals, and on TV before joining Joffrey Ballet. With ABT from 1967, soloist in 1969.

HOSKINS, PAUL. Born Sept. 5, 1952 in Collinsville, Ill. Attended Southern Ill. U. Studied with Katherine Dunham. Joined Alvin Ailey Co. 1972.

HOVING, LUCAS. Born in Groningen, Holland. Attended Dartington Hall, and Kurt Jooss School. Professional debut with Kurt Jooss Ballet in 1942. Has appeared with Graham, Limon, and his own company. Has also appeared in Bdwy musicals.

HOWARD, ALAN. Born in Chicago. Studied with Edna MacRae and in Europe. Joined Ballet Russe de Monte Carlo in 1949 and became premier danseur. Appeared with N.Y.C., and Met Opera Ballets before being appointed director of Academy of Ballet in San Francisco. Founded and is artistic director of Pacific Ballet.

HOWELL, JAMES. Born in Yakima, Wash. Attended U. Wash. Studied with Else Geissmar, Martha Graham, Doris Humphrey, Mary Wigman, Margaret Craske, Alfredo Corvino, Robert Joffrey. Original member of Joffrey Ballet.

HUANG, AL. Born in Shanghai, came to U.S. in 1955. Attended Oregon State U., Perry-Mansfield School, graduate UCLA and Bennington. Studied with Carmelita Maracci. Appeared with Lotte Goslar before forming own co., with which he tours when not teaching.

HUGHES, KENNETH. Born in Virginia; attended NC School of Arts, School of Am. Ballet. Debut 1969 with American Classical Ballet; subsequently with Lar Lubovitch, American Classical Ballet, Les Grands Ballets Canadiens, ABT 1972.

HUJER, FLOWER. Born in Hollywood, Calif. Studied with Theodore Kosloff, Charles Weidman. Has toured in solo concerts and choreographs.

HUNTER, JENNY. Born Aug. 20, 1929 in Modesto, Calif. Studied with Merce Cunningham, Charles Weidman, Marjorie Sheridan. Debut 1951 with Halprin-Lathrop Co. With Dancers' Workshop Co. until 1958 when she left to found, direct, and choreograph for own company, Dance West.

HYND, RONALD. Born in London, April 22, 1931. Studied with Marie Rambert, Angela Ellis, Volkova Idzikowski, and Pereyaslavee. Professional debut 1949 with Ballet Rambert. Joined Royal Ballet in 1951, and graduated from corps to principal dancer.

INDRANI. Born in Madras, India. Studied with Pandanallur Chokkalingam Pillai, Sikkil Ramaswami Pillai, Devas Prasad Das, Narasimha. First dancer to present Orissi classic dance outside India. Tours extensively in solo and with company.

ISAKSEN, LONE. Born Nov. 30, 1941 in Copenhagen where she studied with Edithe Feifere Frandson. Accepted in Royal Danish Ballet School at 13. In 1959 joined group organized by Elsa Marianne Von Rosen and Allan Fredericia, and shortly elevated to soloist. In 1961 studied at Joffrey's American Ballet Center, and appeared with his company. In 1965 joined Harkness Ballet, and became one of its principal dancers until 1970, when she joined Netherlands Natl. Ballet.

ISRAEL, GAIL. Born in Paterson, N.J. Studied with Alexandra Fedorova. Rose to soloist with Ballet Russe before joining American Ballet Theatre in 1962.

JACKSON, DENISE. Born in N.Y.C.: attended ABC. Danced with N.Y.C. Opera Ballet, joined Joffrey Ballet in 1969.

JAGO, MARY. Born in 1946 in Henfield, Eng. Trained at Royal Ballet School. Joined Covent Garden Opera Ballet in 1965; Natl. Ballet of Canada 1966; now a principal.

JAMES, JANICE. Born Feb. 14, 1942 in Salt Lake City, U. Studied with William and Lew Christensen; Joined NYC Ballet in 1963; joined Ballet West 1965, and is now a principal, and teacher.

JAMISON, JUDITH. Born in 1944 in Philadelphia. Studied at Judimar School, Phila. Dance Acad., Joan Kerr's School, Harkness School, and with Paul Sanasardo. Debut 1965 with ABT. Joined Ailey Co. in 1965, Harkness Ballet in 1966, and rejoined Ailey 1967.

JAYNE, ERICA. Born Aug. 8, 1945 in Amersham, Eng. Studied at Royal Ballet School, RAD. Debut 1962 with Royal Opera Ballet. Currently principal with Les Grands Ballets Canadiens.

JEANMAIRE, RENEE ZIZI. Born Apr. 29, 1924 in Paris. Studied at L'Opera de Paris with Volinine, and with Boris Kniaserf. Debut with Ballet de Monte Carlo in 1944. Joined Ballet Russe de Colonel de Basil (1945–47), Petit's Ballets de Paris in 1948. Has appeard in musicals and films.

JENNER, ANN. Born March 8, 1944 in Ewell, Eng. Began studies at 10 with Royal Ballet School. Debut with Royal Ballet in 1962. Became soloist in 1966, principal in 1970.

JENSEN, CHRIS. Born Jan. 24, 1952 in Los Angeles, Cal. Studied with Albert Ruiz, Harriet DeRea, Carmelita Maracci, and at School of Am. Ballet. Debut 1970 with Ballet du Grand Theatre de Geneve; joined Harkness Ballet 1972.

JERELL, EDITH. Studied with Antony Tudor, Margaret Craske, Dokoudovsky, Brenna, Pereyaslavee, Joffrey, Popova, Gentry, Norman Walker, Nona Schurman, Nancy Lang. Lazowski, Dunham, and Nimura. Appeared with Met Opera Ballet as principal or solo dancer for 10 years. Is now teacher, concert and guest artist.

JHUNG, FINIS. Born May 28, 1937 in Honolulu where he began training. Gradute of U. Utah. Appeared on Bdwy before joining San Francisco Ballet in 1960. Advanced to soloist then joined Joffrey Ballet in 1962. Joined Harkness Ballet as soloist in 1964. Now teaches.

JILLANA. Born Oct 11, 1936 in Hackensack. N.J. After studying from childhood at School of American Ballet, joined N.Y.C. Ballet in teens, rising rapidly to ballerina. With ABT (1957–8) returned to NYCB (1959). Retired in 1966. Is active in teaching and touring U.S. Artistic Adviser for San Diego Ballet.

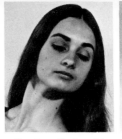

| Ian Horvath | Mary Jago | Robert Joffrey | Krystyna Jurkowski | Jonas Kage |

JOFFREY, ROBERT. Born Dec. 24, 1930 in Seattle, Wash. Began studies with Mary Ann Wells, later attended School of American Ballet, and studied with May O'Donnell and Gertrude Shurr. Debut as soloist with Petit's Ballets de Paris. Appeared with O'Donnell company, and taught at HS Performing Arts and Ballet Theatre School before starting his own American Ballet Center in 1950. Formed first company in 1952 that was resident co. of N.Y. Opera, and made tours in his own works in the U.S. and abroad. Reorganized group appeared in 1965 and has been internationally acclaimed. Is now City Center Company.

JOHNSON, BOBBY. Born Oct. 26, 1946 in San Francisco. Studied at Harkness House and with Joffrey, Mattox, Jack Cole, Fokine. Has appeared on Bdwy and with Fred Benjamin Co.

JOHNSON, LOUIS. Born in Statesville, N.C. Studied with Doris Jones, Clara Haywood, and at School of American Ballet. Debut with N.Y.C. Ballet in 1952. Appeared in musicals before forming, choreographing for, and dancing with own group. Teaches, and on staff of Negro Ensemble Co.

JOHNSON, NANCY. Born in 1934 in San Francisco. Studied with Harold and Lew Christensen at San Francisco Ballet School, eventually becoming principal dancer of S.F. Ballet Co. With Richard Carter, toured world, appearing in fifty nations. Was prima ballerina with San Diego Ballet Co.

JOHNSON, PAMELA. Born in Chicago where she studied with Richard Ellis and Christine Du Boulay. Made debut with their Illinois Ballet Co. Joined Joffrey Ballet in 1966, American Ballet Theatre 1972.

JOHNSON, RAYMOND. Born Sept. 9, 1946 in N.Y.C. Graduate Queens Col. Studied with Alwin Nikolais, Murray Louis, Gladys Bailin, Phyllis Lamhut. Debut 1963 with Nikolais, joined Murray Louis in 1968; subsequently with Rod Rodgers, Joy Boutilier, Rudy Perez. Also teaches and choreographs.

JOHNSON, VIRGINIA. Born Jan. 25, 1950 in Washington, DC. Attended NYU, Washington School of Ballet. Debut 1965 with Washington Ballet; joined Capitol Ballet 1968: Dance Theatre of Harlem 1971.

JOHNSON, WILLIAM. Born Aug. 13, 1943 in Ashland, Kan. Attended San Francisco City Col., SF Ballet School. Debut 1961 with San Francisco Ballet; joined NYC Ballet 1970.

JONES, BETTY. Born in Meadville, Pa. Studied with Ted Shawn, Alicia Markova, La Meri, Doris Humphrey, and Jose Limon. Debut 1947 with Limon Co. and toured world with it. Has own lecture-performance, and teaches master classes throughout U.S. Has appeared in Bdwy musicals.

JONES, MARILYN. Born Feb. 17, 1940 in Newcastle, Australia. Studied with Tessa Maunder, Lorraine Norton, Royal Ballet School. Debut 1956 with Royal Ballet, subsequently with Borovansky Ballet, Marquis de Cuevas, London Festival, and Australian Ballets.

JONES, SUSAN. Born June 22, 1952 in York, Pa. Studied at Washington School of Ballet. Joined Joffrey company 1968, NYC Opera Ballet 1969, Am. Ballet Theatre 1971.

JORGENSEN, NELS. Born in New Jersey in 1938. Studied with Rose Lischner, and toured with her co. before beginning studies at School of American Ballet in 1953. Appeared in musicals and on TV before joining Joffrey Ballet as soloist in 1958. Artistic director Louisville Ballet.

JURKOWSKI, KRYSTYNA. Born June 15, 1954 in Nottingham, Eng. Appeared with Joffrey II, NJ Ballet, before joining City Center Joffrey Ballet in 1973.

KAHN, WILLA. Born May 4, 1947 in NYC. Attended Bklyn Col., CCNY. Studied with Paul Sanasardo, Mia Slavenska, Karoly Zsedbnyi. Debut 1959 with Paul Sanasardo Dance Co.

KAIN, KAREN. Born in 1952 in Hamilton, Ontario, Can. Trained at Ntl. Ballet School, and joined Ntl. Ballet of Canada in 1969; promoted to principal in 1971.

KARNILOVA, MARIA. Born in Hartford, Conn., Aug. 3, 1920. Studied with Mordkin, Fokine, Charisse, and Craske. First appeared with Met corps de ballet (1927–34). Became soloist with Ballet Theatre, and Met Opera Ballet. Recently in several Bdwy musicals.

KATAYEN, LELIA. Born in N.Y.C.: studied with Francesca de Cotelet, Sybil Shearer, Nanette Charisse, Joseph Pilates. In 1960 formed Katayen Dance Theatre Co, for which she is director-choreographer. Head of Southampton College Dance Dept.

KATO, MIYOKO. Born Sept. 26, 1943 in Hiroshima, Japan. Studied at Tachibana Ballet School. Made U.S. debut in 1965 with Met. Opera Ballet Member of Harkness Ballet.

KAYE, NORA. Born in N.Y.C. Jan. 17, 1920. Studied at Ballet School of Met Opera, and with Michel Fokine. Debut at 7 with Met's children's corps de ballet. Joined American Ballet Theatre as soloist in 1940 and N.Y.C. Ballet in 1950. Now assistant to her husband, choreographer Herbert Ross.

KEAN, FIORELLA. Born in Rome, Italy. Studied at Royal Acad., Sadler's Wells. Debut 1946 with Sadler's Wells Ballet; Sadler's Wells Ballet 1948–54; teacher 1959–69. Ballet Mistress Juilliard (1966–69), Dance Rep. Co. (1969–72), Ailey Co. (1972–3); ABT (1973).

KEHLET, NIELS. Born in 1938 in Copenhagen where he began studies at 6, subsequently going to Royal Danish Ballet School. Teachers include Vera Voklova, Stanley Williams, Nora Kiss, and Melissa Hayden. First solo at 16 in Royal Danish Ballet's "Sleeping Beauty." Made concert tour of Africa, and guest artist with de Cuevas' Ballet, London Festival Ballet, and ABT (1971).

KEHR, DOLORES. Born May 11, 1935 in Boston. Studied with Fokine, Danielian, Doukodovsky, Vikzak. Made debut in 1952 with Ballet Russe; former ballerina with National Ballet. Now has school in Ft. Lauderdale. Fla., and is director of "Classiques."

KELLY, DESMOND. Born in 1945 in Bulawayo, Rhodesia. Studied at London's Royal Acad. Joined London Festival Ballet, becoming principal in 1963; subsequently with New Zealand Ballet, Zurich Opera Ballet, National Ballet 1968, Royal Ballet as principal in 1970.

KELLY, GENE. Born Aug. 23, 1912 in Pittsburgh. Graduate of U. Pittsburgh. Teacher and choreographer before appearing in Bdwy musicals and films. Currently choreographing and directing films.

KELLY, KAREN. Born Feb. 1, 1951 in Philadelphia. Trained at Thomas-Fallis School. Debut 1969 with American Ballet Co.

KENT, ALLEGRA. Born Aug. 11, 1938 in Los Angeles where she began her studies. At 13 went to School of American Ballet, and 2 years later joined N.Y.C. Ballet. Quickly rose to one of company's leading ballerinas.

KENT, HELEN. Born Dec. 30, 1949 in N.Y.C. U. Wisc. graduate. Studied with Waring, Cunningham, Nikolais. Made debut in 1971 with Murray Louis Co.

KENT, LINDA. Born Sept. 21, 1946 in Buffalo, N.Y. Juilliard graduate. Studied with Graham, Limon, Sokolow, Craske, Corvino, Tudor, Joined Alvin Ailey Co. in 1968.

KESSLER, DAGMAR. Born in 1946 in Merchantville. N.J. Studied with Thomas Cannon. Joined Penn. Ballet 1965, Hamburg State Opera 1966, London's Festival Ballet in 1967, Pittsburgh Ballet 1973.

KEUTER, CLIFF. Born in 1940 in Boise, Idaho. Studied with Welland Lathrop, Graham, Farnworth, Slavenska, Sanasardo. Debut in 1962 with Tamiris-Nagrin Co. Formed own company in 1969 for which he choreographs.

KIDD, MICHAEL. Born in N.Y.C. Aug. 12, 1919. Attended City College, and School of American Ballet. Studied with Blanche Evan, Ludmilla Scholler, Muriel Stewart, and Anatole Vitzak. Appeared as soloist with Ballet Caravan in 1938, and with Eugene Loring Co. Solo dancer with Ballet Theatre (1942–47), before becoming popular choreographer for musicals and films.

KIM, HAE-SHIK. Born Apr. 29, 1944 in Seoul, Korea. Graduate of Ewha U. Studied at Royal Ballet, London. Made debut in 1959 with Lim Sung Nam: subsequently with Zurich Opera Ballet (1967) and from 1969 with Les Grands Ballets Canadiens; promoted to soloist in 1970.

KIMBALL, CHRISTINA. Born Dec. 22, 1954 in Otsu, Japan. Debut 1972 with Alvin Ailey Co.

KINCH, MYRA. Born in Los Angeles. Graduate of U. of Calif. Solo and concert dancer, and choreographer of satirical ballets. Also teaches.

KING, BRUCE. Born in Oakland, Calif. Graduate of U. Calif. and NYU. Studied at Holm, Met Opera Ballet and Cunningham Schools. Debut 1950 with Henry St. Playhouse Dance Co. Toured with Merce Cunningham and is choreographer and teacher.

KIRKLAND, GELSEY. Born in 1953 in N.Y.C. Joined N.Y.C. Ballet in 1968, promoted to soloist in 1969, principal in 1972. Joined ABT 1974.

KIRPICH, BILLIE. Born in N.Y.C., graduate of NYU. Studied with Graham, and at American School of Ballet. Debut 1942 with Pittsburgh Dance Co. Has appeared with New Dance Group, NYC Opera Ballet, on TV, and in musicals.

KITCHELL, IVA. Born in Junction City, Kan., March 31, 1912. Appeared with Chicago Opera Ballet before making solo debut as dance satirist in 1940. Has continued as concert artist and teacher.

KIVITT, TED. Born in Miami, Fla., Dec. 21, 1942. Studied with Alexander Gavriloff, Thomas Armour, Jo Anna Kneeland, and George Milenoff. Debut 1958 in night club revue. Appeared in Bdwy musicals before joining American Ballet Theatre in 1961. Elevated to soloist in 1964, principal dancer in 1967.

KNAPP, MONICA. Born Jan. 23, 1946 in Germany. Made debut in 1963, and appeared with several companies before joining Stuttgart Ballet in 1971.

KNOBLAUCH, CHRISTINE. Born Feb. 25, 1949 in St. Louis, Mo. Made debut in 1966 with St. Louis Municipal Opera. Subsequently joined National Ballet, and Harkness Ballet.

KOESUN, RUTH ANN. Born May 15, 1928 in Chicago. Studied with Suoboda, Nijinksa, Tudor, and Stone-Camryn. Debut with Ballet Theatre in 1946, and became one of its principal dancers. Retired in 1968 but makes guest appearances.

KOLPAKOVA, IRINA. Born in 1933 in Leningrad. Studied with Kirov company and made debut at 18. Elevated to principal ballerina. Now prima ballerina for Leningrad Kirov Co.

KONDRATYEVA, MARINA. Born Feb. 1, 1933 in Kazan, Russia. Enrolled in Bolshoi School in 1943; graduated into company in 1953. One of company's principal ballerinas.

KONER, PAULINE. Born 1912 in NYC. Studied with Fokine, Michio Ito, Angel Cansino. Debut 1926 with Fokine Ballet. Debut as choreographer-solo dancer 1930. Formed own company (1949–1964). In addition to solo-performances, now teaches and choreographs.

KONING, LEON. Born July 5, 1947 in Zandvoort, Netherlands. Studied with Peter Leoneff, Benjamin Harkarvy, Richard Gibson, Hans Brenner. Debut 1967 with Netherlands Dance Theater.

KOSMINSKY, JANE. Born in Jersey City, N.J. in 1944. Attended Juilliard, CCNY. Debut 1960 with May O'Donnell. Joined Paul Taylor Co. in 1965. Has appeared with Helen Tamiris, Daniel Nagrin, and Norman Walker.

KRASSOVSKA, NATHALIE. Born June 3,1918 in Leningrad. Studied with Preobrajenska, Fokine, Massine, Balanchine, and Nijinska. Prima ballerina with Ballet Russe de Monte Carlo and London Festival Ballet. Currently teaches and dances with Dallas Civic Ballet, and appears with other companies as guest artist.

KRIZA, JOHN. Born Jan. 15, 1919 in Berwyn, Ill. Attended Cicero Jr. Coll., Stone-Camryn School, and studied with Dolin, Vladimeroff, Pereyaslavec, Tudor, and Craske. Danced with WPA Ballet 1938–9, joined American Ballet Theatre in 1940, becoming one of its most popular soloists. Currently its assistant director.

KRONSTAM, HENNING. Born in Copenhagen in 1934. Studied at Royal Danish Ballet School and joined company in 1952. Became premier danseur in 1956. Has appeared as guest artist with many companies.

KRUPSKA, DANIA. Born Aug. 13, 1923 in Fall River, Mass. Studied with Ethel Phillips, and Mordkin Ballet Schools. Began dancing at 6 in Europe as Dania Darling. On return to U.S., joined Catherine Littlefield Ballet. Became member of American Ballet Co. in 1938. More recently has been busy as choreographer.

KUCHERA, LINDA M. Born Jan. 28, 1952 in Monongahela, Pa. Studied at Wash. School of Ballet. Debut 1970 with NYC Opera Ballet; Joffrey II 1970, Ballet Brio 1972–3, ABT 1973.

KUNI, MASANI. Started career in Japan at 13. Gained international fame in solo recitals throughout Europe. Graduate of German Dance College, and studied with Mary Wigman and Max Terpis. Has taught and choreographed in Berlin, London, Copenhagen, Italy, Argentina, and Israel. Is currently director of Kuni Inst. of Creative Dance in Tokyo and Los Angeles.

LAERKESEN, ANNA. Born in 1942 in Copenhagen. Studied at Royal Danish Ballet School and joined company in 1959. Became soloist in 1961.

LaFONTSEE, DANE. Born Nov. 9, 1946 in Lansing, Mich. Studied at School of Am. Ballet. Debut in 1966 with National Ballet; joined Pa. Ballet in 1967, promoted to soloist in 1972.

LAING, HUGH. Born in 1911 in Barbados, B.W.I. Studied in London with Craske and Rambert. Long career with Ballet Rambert, and Ballet Theatre, before joining N.Y.C. Ballet in 1950. Now a commercial photographer.

LA MERI. Born Russell Meriwether Hughes in Louisville, Ky., May 13, 1899. Professional debut in 1928. Annual tours throughout world until 1957. Established Ethnologic Dance Center and Theater in 1943, which she closed in 1956, and retired in 1960. Has written several books on dance, and teaches. Organized Festival of Ethnic Dance 1970.

LAMHUT, PHYLLIS. Born Nov. 14, 1933 in N.Y.C. where she began her studies in Henry St. Settlement Playhouse. Also studied with Cunningham, and at American Ballet Center. Debut in title role of Nikolais' "Alice in Wonderland." In 1957 gave concert of own works, and has appeared with Murray Louis. In addition to dancing, teaches and choreographs.

LAMONT, DENI. Born in 1932 in St. Louis, Mo. Appeared in musicals before joining Ballet Russe de Monte Carlo in 1951, Ballet Theatre 1953, N.Y.C. Ballet in 1954, now soloist.

LANDER, TONI. Born June 19, 1931 in Copenhagen, and studied there with Leif Ornberg, and in School of Royal Danish Ballet. Became member of its company at 17. In 1951, joined Paris Opera Ballet. Later joined London Festival Ballet, Ballet Theatre Francais. ABT in 1960 becoming principal ballerina. Rejoined Royal Danish 1971.

LANDON, JANE. Born Jan. 4, 1947 in Perth, Australia. Attended Royal Ballet School, London. Joined company in 1963 rising to principal dancer in 1969. Member of Stuttgart Ballet from 1970.

LANG, HAROLD. Born Dec. 21, 1920 in Daly City, Calif. Debut with S.F. Opera Co., subsequently dancing with Ballet Russe de Monte Carlo, and Ballet Theatre. More recently has appeared in musicals, and teaches.

LANG, PEARL. Born May 29, 1922 in Chicago. Attended U. of Chicago, and studied at Frances Allis, Martha Graham, American Ballet, Nenette Charisse, and Vicente Celli Schools. Debut with Ukrainian Folk Dance Co. in 1938, subsequently appearing with Ruth Page, Martha Graham companies before forming her own. Became active choreographer and teacher and has appeared on Bdwy.

LANNER, JORG. Born Mar. 15, 1939 in Berlin. Studied with Kurt Jooss, Nora Kiss, Menia Martinez. Debut 1958 in Ballet Babilee; joined Bejart in 1959.

LANOVA, MERRIEM. Born in California. Attended San Francisco State, and U. Cal. Studied with Nijinska, Lichine, Danilova, and at School of Am. Ballet, and Ballet Arts. Appeared with Ballet International, and Ballet Russe de Monte Carlo. Now operates own school, choreographs for and directs Ballet Celeste International.

LAPZESON, NOEMI. Born in Buenos Aires, Argentina, June 28, 1940. Studied at Juilliard, and with Corvino, Tudor, Limon, Nikolais, and Graham. Debut in Buenos Aires in 1955. Has appeared with Yuriko, Sophie Maslow, Helen McGehee, Bertram Ross, and Martha Graham. Has appeared in several musicals, and teaches.

LARSEN, GERD. Born in Oslo in 1921. Studied with Tudor. Debut with London Ballet, followed with Ballet Rambert, International Ballet, Sadler's Wells (now Royal) becoming soloist in 1954. Also teaches.

LATIMER, LENORE. Born July 10, 1935 in Washington, D.C. Graduate Juilliard. Joined Jose Limon Co. in 1959. Has appeared with Valerie Bettis, Anna Sokolow. Also teaches.

LAYTON, JOE. Born May 3, 1931 in N.Y.C. Studied with Joseph Levinoff. Bdwy debut in 1947. After many musicals, joined Ballet Ho de George Reich in Paris (1945–6). Returned to N.Y. and has become popular director and choreographer.

LECHNER, GUDRUN. Born Nov. 7, 1944 in Stuttgart, Ger. Studied at Stuttgart, and Royal Ballet School, London. Debut 1962 with Stuttgart Ballet.

LEDIAKH, GENNADI. Born in 1928 in Russia. Entered Bolshoi School in 1946, and was graduated into company in 1949.

LEE, ELIZABETH. Born Jan. 14, 1946 in San Francisco. Studied with Harriet DeRea, Wilson Morelli, Richard Thomas. Debut 1964 with Pennsylvania Ballet. Joined American Ballet Theatre in 1967. American Ballet Co. 1969. Rejoined ABT in 1971; Eliot Feld Ballet 1974.

LEE, KEITH. Born Jan. 15, 1951 in the Bronx. Studied at Harkness, and Ballet Theatre Schools. Has danced with Norman Walker, Harkness Youth Co., and own company. Joined ABT in 1969; became soloist in 1971.

LEES, MICHELLE. Born Mar. 18, 1947 in Virginia. Studied at Wash. School of Ballet. Made debut 1964 with National Ballet.

LEIGH, VICTORIA. Born July 3, 1941, in Brockton, Mass. Studied with Georges Milenoff and at JoAnna-Imperial Studio. Debut 1958 with Palm Beach Ballet. Joined American Ballet Theatre in 1961, and became soloist in 1964.

Monika Knapp

Toni Lander

Susan Lovelle

Michelle Lucci

Peggy Lyman

LELAND, SARA. Born Aug. 2, 1941 in Melrose, Mass. Studied with E. Virginia Williams, Robert Joffrey, and at School of Am. Ballet. Debut with New England Civic Ballet, and subsequently with N.Y.C. Opera (1959), Joffrey Ballet (1960), N.Y.C. Ballet from 1960. Appointed principal in 1972.

LERNER, JUDITH. Born in Philadelphia, Dec. 30, 1944. Attended Hunter College, American Ballet School, Ballet Theatre School, and studied with Nenette Charisse and Antony Tudor. Debut as soloist with Eglevsky Ballet in 1961, and joined American Ballet Theatre same year.

LESINS, MARCIS. Born Jan. 6, 1946 in Neustadt, WGer. Studied with Elisabeth Curland, Helen Uraus-Natschewa, Leonid Gonta. Debut 1963 with Munich Opera Ballet; joined Stuttgart Ballet 1970.

LEVINE, MICHELLE. Born Jan. 24, 1946 in Detroit, Mich. NYU graduate. Studied with Nenette Charisse, Gladys Bailin, Jean Erdman. Debut 1970 with Erdman Co.

LEVINS, DANIEL. Born Oct. 7, 1953 in Ticonderoga, N.Y. Studied at HS Performing Arts, N.Y. School of Ballet. Debut in 1969 with American Ballet Co. Joined ABT in 1971, promoted to soloist in 1972, principal 1973.

LEWIS, DANIEL. Born July 12, 1944 in Bklyn. Juilliard graduate. Joined Limon Co. in 1963. Has appeared with Ruth Currier, Felix Fibich, Anna Sokolow companies.

LEWIS, JAMES J. Born July 30, 1946 in Denver, Colo. Graduate U. Mich. Studied with Sandra Severo. Debut 1969 with Boston Ballet. Joined American Ballet Co. in 1970.

LEWIS, MARILYN. Born June 15, 1947 in Winnipeg, Can. Attended United Col. Debut in 1966 with Royal Winnipeg Ballet; subsequently with Deutsche Operam Phein, and Wuppertal Opera in Germany, Netherlands Dans Theatre.

LIEPA, MARIS. Born July 27, 1930 in Riga, Latvia. Studied at Riga, and Bolshoi schools. Joined Bolshoi in 1961, quickly rising to principal.

LINDEN, ANYA. Born Jan. 3, 1933 in Manchester, Eng. Studied in U.S. with Theordore Koslov, entered Sadler's Wells School in 1947; joined company (now Royal) in 1951; ballerina in 1958. Now retired.

LINDGREN, ROBERT. Born in 1923 in Vancouver, Can. Studied with Vilzak, Swoboda, Preobrajenska. Joined Ballet Russe in 1942, N.Y.C. Ballet in 1957. Retired to teach.

LINN, BAMBI. Born in Brooklyn. April 26, 1926. Studied with Mikhail Mordkin, Helen Oakes, Hanya Holm, Agnes de Mille, and Helene Platava. Debut 1943 in "Oklahoma!" Subsequently danced with Ballet Theatre, Met Opera Ballet, Dance Jubilee Co., and American Ballet Co.

LISTER, MERLE. Born in Toronto, Can., where she began training and had own dance troupe. After moving to N.Y.C., organized dance company in 1964 with which she has appeared in N.Y. and on tour. Also teaches.

LITZ, KATHERINE. Born in 1918 in Denver, Colo. Studied with Humphrey, Weidman, Horst, Platova, Thomas. Debut with Humphrey-Weidman Co. in 1936. Soloist with Agnes de Mille Co. (1940–42), and in Bdwy musicals. Debut as choreographer in 1948 in Ballet Ballads, followed by solo and group works. Also teaches.

LLAND, MICHAEL. Born in Bishopville, S.C. Graduate U.S. Car. Studied with Margaret Foster. Debut 1944 in "Song of Norway." Joined Teatro Municipal Rio de Janeiro (1945), ABT (1948) rising to principal in 1957, Ballet Master Houston Ballet (1968), ABT (1971).

LOKEY, BEN. Born Dec. 15, 1944 in Birmingham, Ala. Graduate U. Utah. Studied with Wm. Christensen, Caton, Peryoslavic, Weisberger, Morawski, Patricia Wilde. Made debut in 1966. Principal with Ballet West, and soloist with Pa. Ballet.

LOMBARDI, JOAN. Born Nov. 18, 1944 in Teaneck, N.J. Parsons graduate. Studied with Raoul Gelebert, Igor Schwezoff, Paul Sanasardo, Richard Thomas. Debut 1967 with Sanasardo Co. Has appeared with N.Y.C. Opera Ballet, and John Butler.

LOMMEL, DANIEL. Born March 26 in Paris. Studied with Joseph Lazzini, Nora Kiss. Made debut in 1966 with Grand Ballet Marquis de Cuevas. Joined Bejart Ballet in 1967 and is now a principal dancer.

LORING, EUGENE. Born in Milwaukee in 1914. Studied at School of American Ballet, and with Balanchine, Muriel Stuart, Anatole Vilzak, and Ludmilla Schollar. Debut 1934 in "Carnival." Subsequently with Met Opera Ballet, and Ballet Caravan, for whom he choreographed and starred in "Billy The Kid." Has become a leading choreographer for all media. Owns and operates American School of Dance in Hollywood.

LORRAYNE, VYVYAN. Born April 20, 1939 in Pretoria, South Africa. Entered Royal Ballet School in 1956 and company in 1957. Became principal in 1967.

LOSCH, TILLY. Born in Vienna, Aust., Nov. 15, 1907. Studied ballet with Vienna State Opera, later becoming its premiere danseuse. Toured Europe as dance soloist, and with Harold Kreutzberg. Joined Balanchine Ballets in Paris, and later formed own company "Les Ballets." In additon to choreographing, has appeared on Bdwy and is successful painter.

LOUIS, MURRAY. Born Nov. 4, 1926 in N.Y.C. Graduate of NYU. Studied with Alwin Nikolais, and made debut in 1953. Has appeared annually in concerts and on tour with Nikolais, and own company, for which he also choreographs. Co-director of Chimera Foundatuon for Dance.

LOUTHER, WILLIAM. Born 1942 in Brooklyn. Attended Juilliard. Studied with Kitty Carson, Martha Graham, May O'Donnell, Antony Tudor, Gertrude Schurr. Debut with O'Donnell Co. in 1958. Has appeared in musicals, and in Donald McKayle Co. Joined Graham Co. in 1964. Artistic director Batsheva Co. 1972.

LOVE, EDWARD. Born June 29, 1950. Graduate Ohio U. Debut 1973 with Alvin Ailey Dance Theatre.

LOVELLE, SUSAN. Born May 22, 1954 in NYC. Attended Barnard, SUNY. Studied at Dance Theatre of Harlem, and made debut with company in 1968.

LOWSKI, WOYTEK. Born Oct. 11, 1939 in Brzesc, Poland. Studied in Warsaw and Leningrad. Debut 1958 with Warsaw Ballet, joined Bejart Ballet 1966, Cologne Ballet 1971, Roland Petit Co. in 1972; Boston Ballet 1973 as premier danseur.

LOYD, SUE. Born May 26, 1940 in Reno, Nev. Studied with Harold and Lew Christensen, Vilzak, Danielian, Zerapse, Bruson, and Joffrey. Debut with San Francisco Ballet in 1954. Joined Joffrey Ballet in 1967.

LUBOVITCH, LAR. Born in Chicago; attended Art Inst., U. Iowa, Juilliard, ABT School, and studied with Martha Graham, Margaret Black. Debut 1962 with Pearl Lang, subsequently with Glen Tetley, John Butler, Donald McKayle, Manhattan Festival Ballet, Harkness, before forming own company. Also designs and choreographs for other companies.

LUCAS, JONATHAN. Born Aug. 14, 1922 in Sherman, Tex. Gradute of Southern Methodist U. Studied at American Ballet School. Debut 1945 in "A Lady Says Yes," followed by many Bdwy musicals. Became choreographer in 1956.

LUCCI, MICHELLE. Born Apr. 26, 1950 in Buffalo, NY. Studied at Banff School, with Joffrey, Caton, Lazowski, and Harkarvy. Debut 1968 with Royal Winnipeg Ballet. Joined Pennsylvania Ballet in 1969.

LUDLOW, CONRAD. Born in Hamilton, Mont. in 1935. Began studies in San Francisco, and became member of its ballet company where he attained rank of soloist before joining N.Y.C. Ballet in 1957. Retired in 1973.

LUPPESCU, CAROLE. Born April 18, 1944 in Brooklyn. Attended Ind. U. Studied at Met Opera Ballet School. Joined Pennsylvania Ballet in 1964. Has performed with Ballet Rambert. Now retired.

LUSBY, VERNON. Born in New Orleans, La. Studied with Leila Haller, Dolin, Caron, Craske, Nijinska, Tudor. Appeared with ABT, Grands Ballets de Marquis de Cuevas, Natl. Ballet of Brazil. Also dancer and choreographer on Bdwy. Now associate director Royal Winnipeg Ballet.

LYMAN, PEGGY. Born June 28, 1950 in Cincinnati, Ohio. Studied at Stone-Camryn, Martha Graham, and Joffrey schools. Debut 1969 with NYC Opera Ballet. Joined Martha Graham Co. in 1973.

LYNN, ENID. Born in Manchester, Conn. Studied with Joseph Albano, Martha Graham, Sigurd Leeder. Director-Choreographer for Hartford Modern Dance Theatre, and Hartford Ballet.

LYNN, ROSAMOND. Born Dec. 31, 1944 in Palo Alto, Calif. Studied with Bill Griffith, Vincenzo Celli, Richard Thomas, Patricia Wilde. Debut 1964 with Philadelphia Lyric Opera, subsequently with ABT (1965), Alvin Ailey Co. (1970)

MacDONALD, BRIAN. Born May 14, 1928 in Montreal, Canada where he began choreographing for television. In 1958 became choreographer for Royal Winnipeg Ballet, and commuted to Norwegian and Royal Swedish Ballets where he held positions as director. Joined Harkness Ballet as director in 1967, left in 1968.

MacLEARY, DONALD. Born in Iverness, Scot., Aug. 22, 1937. Trained at Royal Ballet School. Joined company in 1954, became soloist in 1955 and premier danseur in 1959. Has partnered Beriosova on most of her appearances.

MacMILLAN, KENNETH. Born Dec. 11, 1930 in Scotland. Studied at Sadler's Wells and joined company (now Royal) in 1948. Debut as choreographer with Sadler's Wells Choreographers Group in 1953 with "Somnambulism." Subsequently created dances for Theatre Ballet, Royal Ballet, American Ballet Theatre, Royal Danish Stuttgart, and German Opera Ballet. Perhaps most famous are "Romeo and Juliet" and "The Invitation." Director Royal Ballet from 1970.

MADSEN, EGON. Born Aug. 24, 1944 in Copenhagen. Appeared with Pantomime Theatre and Scandinavian Ballet before joining Stuttgart Ballet in 1961. Promoted to soloist in 1963. Now principal.

MADSEN, JORN. Born Dec. 7, 1939 in Copenhagen. Studied at Royal Danish Ballet School; joined company in 1957; appointed soloist in 1961. Guest with Royal Ballet in 1965. Now retired.

MAGALLANES, NICHOLAS. Born Nov. 27 in Chihuahua, Mex. Studied at School of American Ballet. Danced with Littlefield Ballet, American Ballet Caravan, Ballet Russe de Monte Carlo. Principal dancer with N.Y.C. Ballet from its inception in 1946.

MAGNO, SUSAN. Born in 1946 in Melrose, Mass. Studied with Margaret Craske, Alice Langford, Virginia Williams. Appeared with Boston Ballet before joining Joffrey Ballet in 1965. Lar Lubovitch Co. in 1972.

MAHLER, RONI. Born in N.Y.C. in 1942. Studied with Maria Swoboda and at Ballet Russe School. Debut with Ballet Russe de Monte Carlo in 1960. Joined National Ballet in 1962 and became leading soloist in 1963. Joined ABT as soloist in 1969.

MAKAROVA, NATALIA. Born Nov. 21, 1940 in Leningrad. Studied at Kirov School and joined company in 1959. Had triumph with her first "Giselle" in 1961. Defected in 1970 and joined ABT in 1970 as principal, making debut in "Giselle."

MANN, BURCH. Born in Texas: Studied with Adolph Bolm, Mordkin, and Fokine. Operates studio in Pasadena, Calif. Organized "Burch Mann Concert Group" that has become The American Folk Ballet.

MARCEAU, MARCEL. Born March 22, 1923 in Strasbourg, France. Studied with Charles Dullen and Etienne Decroux. Debut with Barrault-Renaud Co. in 1946. In 1947 formed own company, and among other works, presented "Bip" with whom he has become identified. Subsequently toured Europe, and U.S.

MARCHOWSKY, MARIE. Studied with Martha Graham: became member of company 1934-40. With own company, and as soloist, performing own choreography, has appeared in U.S. and abroad.

MARINACCIO, GENE. Born 1931 in Newark, NJ. Studied with Bupesh Guha, Michael Brigante. Appeared with Lichine's Ballet, Petit's Ballet de Paris, Ballet Russe Monte Carlo, Ballet de Cuba. Now teaches and formed own company American Concert Ballet.

MARKO, IVAN. Born Mar. 29, 1947 in Hungary. Studied at Allami Ballet Intezet. Debut 1967 with Budapest Opera Ballet. Joined Ballet of 20th Century 1968.

MARKOVA, ALICIA. Born in London, Dec. 1, 1910. Studied with Seraphine Astafieva and Enrico Cecchetti. Appeared with Diaghilieff Ballet (1925-29). Vic-Wells Ballet (1932-5), Markova-Dolin Ballet (1935-7), Monte Carlo Ballet Russe (1938-41), prima ballerina Ballet Theatre (1941-5). Original Ballet Russe 1946, Markova-Dolin Co. (1947-8), co-founder and prima ballerina London Festival Ballet (1950-2), and has appeared as guest artist with companies throughout the world. Director of Met Opera Ballet 1963-9. Teaches at U. Cinn.

MARKS, BRUCE. Born in N.Y.C. in 1937 and studied at Met Opera School of Ballet with Tudor and Craske. Joined Met Opera Ballet in 1957, rising to rank of first dancer; joined American Ballet Theatre in 1961 as a principal dancer, and became premier danseur. Appeared as guest in 1963 with Royal Swedish Ballet, and in 1965 with London Festival Ballet. Joined Royal Danish Ballet in 1971; ABT 1974 summer season.

MARKS, J. Born in Los Angeles, Feb. 14, 1942. Founder of San Francisco Contemporary Dancers Foundation. Has choreographed over 200 works. Founder-Director of First National Nothing.

MARSICANO, MERLE. Born in Philadelphia. Studied with Ethel Phillips, Mordkin, Ruth St. Denis, Mary Wigman, Martha Graham, Louis Horst. Debut with Pennsylvania Opera. Since 1952 has presented own program of solos which she choreographs.

MARTIN, KEITH. Born June 15, 1943 in Yorkshire, Eng. Joined Royal Ballet School in 1958 and company in 1961. Appointed soloist in 1967. Joined Pa. Ballet in 1971, and now a principal.

MARTIN, YON. Born Sept. 12, 1945 in Washington, D.C. Studied with Erika Thimey, Paul Sanasardo, and at Washington School of Ballet. Debut with Dance Theatre of Wash. Joined Sanasardo Co. in 1966.

MARTINEZ, ENRIQUE. Born 1926 in Havana, Cuba where he studied with Alonso and danced with Ballet Alicia Alonso. In addition to appearing with American Ballet Theatre has created several ballets, and in 1964 served as ballet master of Bellas Artes Ballet de Mexico.

MARTINEZ, MENIA. Born Sept. 27, 1938 in Havana, Cuba. Studied at Alonso School. Made debut with Alicia Alonso Ballet in 1959; subsequently with Bolshoi (1965), Kirov (1966), and Bejart from 1969.

MARTINS, PETER. Born 1947 in Copenhagen. Trained at Royal Danish Ballet School and joined company in 1965. Granted leave to appear with N.Y.C. Ballet. Joined company in 1970 as principal.

MARTIN-VISCOUNT, BILL. Born in Winnipeg, Can. Began study at 12 with Royal Winnipeg Ballet, subsequently studied at Royal Ballet, American Ballet Theatre, and Bolshoi Schools. Joined Royal Winnipeg Ballet in 1959; took leave to appear with London Festival Ballet, and returned in 1962. Appeared with Joffrey as principal in 1969, Rio de Janeiro Ballet in 1970. In demand as guest artist with regional companies. Artistic director Memphis Ballet 1974.

MASLOW, SOPHIE. Born in N.Y.C. where she studied with Blanche Talmund, and Martha Graham. Joined Graham company and became soloist. Debut as choreographer 1934. Joined Jane Dudley, William Bales to form Dudley-Maslow-Bales Trio. Helped found American Dance Festival at Conn. College. Has choreographed and appeared in many of her works. On Board of Directors and teaches for New Dance Group Studio.

MASON, KENNETH. Born April 17, 1942 in Bartford, Eng. Attended Royal Ballet School and joined company in 1959. Became principal in 1968.

MASON, MONICA. Born Sept. 6, 1941 in Johannesburg, S.A. Studied at Royal Ballet School, and joined company in 1958, rising to soloist, and principal in 1967.

MASSINE, LEONIDE. Born in Moscow, Aug. 9, 1896. Studied at Imperial Ballet School and with Domashoff Checchetti, and Legat. Discovered by Diaghilev; joined his company in 1914; became principal dancer and choreographer; Ballet de Monte Carlo 1932-41; Ballet National Theatre 1941-4, organized Ballet Russe Highlights 1945-6; subsequently appearing as guest artist and/or choreographer with almost every important company, and in films.

MATHIS, BONNIE. Born Sept. 8, 1942 in Milwaukee, Wisc. Attended Juilliard. Studied with Tudor and Anderson. Performed with Radio City Ballet, Paul Taylor, Norman Walker, before joining Harkness Ballet. ABT (1971) as soloist.

MATTEO (VITTUCCI). Born in Utica, N.Y. Graduate of Cornell. Studied at Met Opera School, with La Meri, LaQuica, Esparsa, Azuma, Guneya, Balasaraswati. Member Met Opera Ballet (1947-51); solo debut in 1953; formed partnership with Carola Goya in 1954. Teaches, and organized Indo-American Dance Group with which he appears.

MATTHEWS, LAURENCE. Born in Hollywood, Cal. Studied with Lew and Harold Christensen, Anatole Vizak, Ted Howard, Paul Curtis, Richard Gibson, Royal Cons. Den Hag. Debut with San Francisco Ballet 1968. Joined Penn. Ballet 1973 as soloist.

MATTOX, MATT. Born Aug. 18, 1921 in Tulsa, Okla. Attended San Bernardino College; studied with Ernest Belcher, Nico Charisso, Eugene Loring, Louis Da Pron, Evelyn Bruns, Teddy Kerr, and Jack Cole. Debut 1946 in "Are You With It?," subsequently appearing in many musicals. First choreography in 1958 for "Say, Darling," followed by several Bdwy productions, and Met Opera Ballet.

MAULE, MICHAEL. Born Oct. 31, 1926 in Durban, S.Af. Studied with Vincenzo Celli and made debut in 1946 in "Annie Get Your Gun." Joined Ballet Theatre, then Ballet Alicia Alonso (1949-50), N.Y.C. Ballet (1950-53), Ballets; U.S.A. (1959), Ballet Ensemble (1960-61). In 1964 organized own touring group. Now teaches.

MAULE, SARA. Born June 27, 1951 in Tokyo, Japan. Studied at UCal., San Francisco Ballet School. Joined SFB in 1965; became soloist 1970; Am. Ballet Theatre 1972.

MAXIMOVA, YEKATERINA. Born in Russia in 1939. Entered Bolshoi School to 10, and joined company in 1958, rising to ballerina.

MAXWELL, CARLA. Born Oct. 25, 1945 in Glendale, Calif. Juilliard graduate; debut 1965 with Limon Co. (now soloist), also appears with Louis Falco, and in concert with Clyde Morgan.

Monica Mason

Bruce Marks

Jolinda Menendez

Jack Moore

Lynda Meyer

MAYBARDUK, LINDA. Born in1951 in Orlando, Fla. Studied at Natl. Ballet School of Canada and graduated into company in 1969; promoted to soloist.

MAZZO, KAY. Born Jan. 17, 1947 in Chicago. Studied with Bernadene Hayes, and at School of American Ballet. In 1961 appeared with Ballets U.S.A. before joining N.Y.C. Ballet corps in 1962, became soloist in 1965, ballerina in 1969.

McBRIDE, PATRICIA. Born Aug. 23, 1942, in Teaneck, N.J., and studied at School of American Ballet. Joined N.Y.C. Ballet in 1959 and became principal dancer before leaving teens; ballerina in 1961.

McFALL, JOHN. Born in Kansas City, Mo.; studied at San Francisco Ballet, and joined company in 1965.

McGEHEE, HELEN. Born in Lynchburg, Va. Graduate Randolph-Macon College. Studied at Graham School and joined company; became first dancer in 1954. Among her choreographic works are "Undine," "Metamorphosis," "Nightmare," "Cassandra," and "Oresteia." Also teaches, and dances with own company.

McKAYLE, DONALD. Born in N.Y.C., July 6, 1930. Attended NYCC; studied at New Dance Group Studio, Graham School, with Nenette Charisse, Karel Shook, and Pearl Primus. Debut with New Dance Group in 1948, subsequently appeared with Dudley-Maslow-Bales, Jean Erdman, N.Y.C. Dance Theatre, Anna Sokolow, and Martha Graham. Formed own company in 1951, and in addition to choreographing, teaches.

McKINNEY, GAYLE. Born Aug. 26, 1949 in NYC. Attended Juilliard. Made debut 1968 with Dance Theatre of Harlem.

McLERIE, ALLYN ANN. Born Dec. 1, 1926 in Grand Mere, Can. Studied with Nemchinova, Caton, De Mille, Yeichi Nimura, Holm, Graham, and Forte. First performed in ballet corps of San Carlo Opera in 1942. Bdwy debut 1943 in "One Touch of Venus" followed by many musicals. Now in films.

MEAD, ROBERT. Born April 17, 1940 in Britol, Eng. Studied at Royal Ballet School, and joined company in 1958. Made principal dancer in 1967. Joined Hamburg Opera Ballet in 1971.

MEDEIROS, JOHN. Born June 5, 1944 in Winston Salem, N.C. Studied at Boston Cons., with Ailey, Beatty, and Segarra. Has appeared in musicals and with Alvin Ailey Co.

MEEHAN, NANCY. born in San Francisco. Graduate U. Cal. Studied with Halprin, Lathrop, Graham, and Hawkins. Debut 1953 with Halprin company. Joined Erick Hawkins in 1962.

MEISTER, HANS. Born in Schaffhausen on the Rhine. Studied at Zurich Opera Ballet, Royal Ballet, Leningrad Kirov Schools. Joined Ntl. Ballet of Canada 1957; Met Opera Ballet (1962–6); Zurich Opera 1966; founder-member Swiss Chamber Ballet; now principal and teacher for Finnish Natl. Opera Ballet.

MENENDEZ, JOLINDA. Born Nov. 17, 1954 in NYC. Studied at Ntl. Academy of Ballet. Made debut with Ballet Repertory Co. Joined American Ballet Theatre 1972.

MERCIER, MARGARET. Born in Montreal. Studied at Sadler's Wells School, graduating into company in 1954. Joined Les Grands Ballets Canadiens in 1958; Joffrey Ballet 1963; Harkness Ballet 1964.

MERRICK, IRIS. Born in 1915 in N.Y.C. Studied with Fokine, Fedorova, Vladimiroff Decroux, Egorova. Is now director and choreographer of Westchester Ballet Co. which she founded in 1950.

MEYER, LYNDA. Born in Texas. Studied at San Francisco Ballet School and joined company in 1962. Became principal dancer in 1966.

MILLER, BUZZ. Born in 1928 in Snowflake, Ariz. Graduate Ariz. State College. Debut 1948 in "Magdalena." In addition to Bdwy musicals, has appeared with Jack Cole Dancers, Ballets de Paris, and is choreographer.

MILLER, JANE. Born Mar. 19, 1945 in NYC. Studied at School of American Ballet. Debut 1964 with Pennsylvania Ballet; subsequently with Harkness Ballet, National Ballet.

MINAMI, ROGER. Born in Hawaii, reared in Calif. Left Long Beach State College to attend Eugene Loring's American School of Dance. Became member of Loring's Dance Players, and now teaches in Loring's school.

MITCHELL, ARTHUR. Born in N.Y.C. Mar. 27, 1934. Studied at School of American Ballet. Joined N.Y.C. Ballet in 1955 and rapidly rose to principal. Was choreographer at Spoleto, Italy, Festival for one season. Founder-director-choreographer for Dance Theatre of Harlem.

MITCHELL, JAMES. Born Feb. 29, 1920 in Sacramento, Calif. Graduate of LACC. Debut 1944 in "Bloomer Girl." Joined Ballet Theatre in 1950, subsequently danced with Met Opera, De Mille Dance Theatre, and on Bdwy.

MITCHELL, LUCINDA. Born Feb. 18, 1946 in Takoma Park, Md. Graduate Smith Col. Studied with Martha Graham. Debut 1970 with Bertram Ross Co.; Kazuko Hirabayashi Dance Theatre 1971; Martha Graham Co. 1972.

MLAKAR, VERONIKA. Born in 1935 in Zurich, Switzerland. Appeared with Roland Petit, Ruth Page, Milorad Miskovitch, Janine Charat, John Butler, and Jerome Robbins before joining American Ballet Theatre in 1964.

MOFSIE, LOUIS. Born in N.Y.C., May 3, 1936. Graduate of SUNY at Buffalo. Training on Hopi and Winnebago Indian reservations. Debut at 10. In 1950, organized, directed and appeared with own group performing native Indian dances, both in N.Y.C. and on tour.

MOLINA, JOSE. Born in Madrid, Spain, Nov. 19, 1937. Studied with Pilar Monterde. Debut 1953 with Soledad Mirales Co., subsequently joined Pilar Mirales, Jose Greco, and in 1962 premiered own company in the U.S. Has since made international tours.

MONCION, FRANCISCO. Born in Dominican Republic, July 6. Studied at School of American Ballet. Danced with New Opera Co., Ballet International, Ballet Russe de Monte Carlo, and Ballet Society which became N.Y.C. Ballet. Is now a principal. First choreographic work "Pastorale" performed by company in 1957. Is also a painter.

MONK, MEREDITH. Born Nov. 20, 1943 in Lima, Peru. Graduate of Sarah Lawrence. Studied with Tarassova, Slavenska, Cunningham, Graham, Mata and Hari. Debut 1964, subsequently choreographed for herself and company.

MONTALBANO, GEORGE. Born in Bklyn. Studied with Mme. Deinitzen, Natalia Branitska., ABC. Appeared with Westchester Ballet, and in musicals, before joining Joffrey Ballet; Eliot Feld Ballet 1974.

MONTERO, LUIS. Born in Granada in 1939. Debut at 15 with Mariemma company. Joined Pilar Lopez, then Jose Greco, Victor Albarez. Became first dancer with Jose Molina Bailes Espanoles in 1961; also choreographs for company.

MOONEY, ELINA. Born Nov. 28, 1942 in New Orleans. Attended Sara Lawrence Col. Studied with Evelyn Davis, Weidman, Cunningham, Tamiris, Sanasardo. Debut 1961 with Tamiris-Nagrin Co., subsequently with Weidman, Marion Scott, Paul Sanasardo, Cliff Keuter, Don Redlich, and own company.

MOORE, GARY. Born Jan. 29, 1950 in Washington, D.C. Studied with Mavis Murry, Tania Rousseau, Oleg Tupine. Debut with Harkness Youth Co. in 1969, after which joined Pa. Ballet.

MOORE, JACK. Born Mar. 18, 1926 in Monticello, Ind. Graduate U. Iowa. Studied at Graham School, School of American Ballet, Conn. College, and Cunningham Studio. Debut 1951, subsequently with Nina Fonaroff, Helen McGehee, Pearl Lang, Katherine Litz, Martha Graham, Anna Sokolow, and NYC Opera, in musicals, and his own works annually since 1957. Has taught at Conn. College, Bennington, Juilliard, UCLA, and Adelphi.

MORALES, HILDA. Born June 17, 1946 in Puerto Rico. Studied at San Juan Ballet School and American School of Ballet. Debut with N.Y.C. Ballet, then joined Penn. Ballet in 1965, becoming principal. Guest with Les Grands Ballets Canadiens, ABT 1973 as soloist.

MORAWSKI, MIECZYSLAW. Born Jan. 1, 1932 in Wilno, Poland. Studied at Warsaw Ballet School, Bolshoi and Kirov schools, and graduated as teacher. Now director of Virginia Beach Ballet.

MORDAUNT, JOANNA. Born Feb. 13, 1950 in London. Trained at Royal Ballet School; joined company in 1968; London Festival Ballet in 1970.

MORDENTE, TONY. Born in Brooklyn in 1935. Studied with Farnworth. Has appeared on Bdwy and TV, and been assistant to Gower Champion and Michael Kidd. Has also directed and choreographed musicals.

MORE, VICTORIA. Born in Los Angeles. Attended School of American Ballet. Debut with N.Y.C. Opera and joined Joffrey Ballet in 1969.

MORGAN, CLYDE. Born Jan. 30, 1940 in Cincinnati. Graduate Cleveland State Col. Studied at Bennington, Karamu House, Ballet Russe, New Dance Group. Debut 1961 with Karamu Dance Theatre; joined Limon 1965 (now soloist), also appears with Anna Sokolow, Pearl Lang, Olatunji, and in concert with Carla Maxwell.

MORGAN, EARNEST. Born Dec. 3, 1947 in Waihjwa, Hawaii. Attended Northwestern U. Studied with Jene Sugano, Gus Giordano, Ed Parish. Debut 1966 with Gus Giordano Co., subsequently in musicals before joining Paul Taylor Co. in 1969.

MORGAN, VICTORIA. Born Mar. 18, 1951 in Salt Lake City, U. Graduate UUtah with training under William Christensen. Joined Ballet West in 1970; principal since 1972.

MORRIS, MARNEE. Born Apr. 2, 1946 in Schenectady, N.Y. Studied with Phyllis Marmein, Cornelia Thayer, Vladimir Dokoudovsky, and at School of Am. Ballet. Joined N.Y.C. Ballet in 1961. Is now a soloist.

MORRIS, MONICA. Born Sept. 23, 1946 in Eustis, Fla. Attended Oglethorpe U. Debut 1966 with Harkness Ballet; subsequently with Martha Graham Co., Paul Taylor Co. 1972.

MOYLAN, MARY ELLEN. Born in 1926 in Cincinnati. Studied at School of American Ballet, and made debut at 16 as leading dancer in operetta "Rosalinda." In 1943 joined Ballet Russe de Monte Carlo as soloist. In 1950 became ballerina with Ballet Theatre. Retired in 1957.

MUELLER, CHRISTA. Born Dec. 20, 1950 in Cincinnati, O. Studied with Merce Cunningham, Ben Harkarvy, Harkness House. Debut 1972 with Dance Repertory Co. Joined Alvin Ailey Co. 1973.

MULLER, JENNIFER. Born Oct. 16, 1944 in Yonkers, N.Y. Graduate Juilliard. Studied with Limon, Graham, Lang, Tudor, Corvino, Craske, Horst, Sokolow. Has danced with Pearl Lang, Sophie Maslow, N.Y.C. Opera, Frances Alenikoff, Louis Falco. Member of Jose Limon Company from 1963. Teaches, and choreographs. Associate director of Falco Co.

MUMAW, BARTON. Born in 1912 in Hazelton, Pa. Studied with Ted Shawn; debut with Shawn's company in 1931 and danced with group until it disbanded. Now makes guest appearances, teaches, and appears in musicals.

MUNRO, RICHARD. Born Aug. 8, 1944, in Camberley, Eng. Trained at Hardie Ballet School. Debut with Zurich Opera Ballet, subsequently with London Festival Ballet, American Ballet Co. Now co-director of Louisville Ballet and teaches.

MURPHY, SEAMUS. Born in Hong Kong. Attended Juilliard. Appeared on Bdwy before forming own company. Also teaches.

MURRAY-WHITE, MELVA. Born May 24, 1950 in Philadelphia, Pa. Attended Md. State, Ohio State U. Studied with Marion Cuyjet, Bettye Robinson. Debut 1971 with Dance Theatre of Harlem.

MUSGROVE, TRACI. Born Feb. 7, 1948 in Carlysle, Pa. Graduate SMU. Studied with Graham, Limon, Hoving, Kuch, Yuriko. Debut 1970 with Yuriko, subsequently with Pearl Lang, Martha Graham.

MUSIL, KARL. Born Nov. 3, in Austria. Studied at Vienna State Opera School; joined company in 1953; promoted to soloist in 1958. Has appeared as guest artist with many companies.

MUSSMAN, MARJORIE. Born Feb. 19, 1943 in Columbus, O. Attended Smith College, and Sorbonne, Paris. Studied with Reznikoff, Marmein, Limon, and Joffrey. Debut with Paris Festival Ballet in 1964, and U.S. debut with Jose Limon in 1964. Member of Joffrey Ballet 1965. Currently with First Chamber Dance Co.

NAGRIN, DANIEL. Born May 22 in N.Y.C., graduate of CCNY. Studied with Graham, Tamiris, Holm, and Sokolow. Debut in 1945 in "Marianne," followed by several Bdwy musicals and choreography for Off-Bdwy productions. Now appears in solo concerts, and teaches.

NAGY, IVAN. Born Apr. 28, 1943 in Debrecen, Hungary. Studied at Budapest Opera Ballet School and joined company. Came to U.S. and National Ballet in 1965. One season with N.Y.C. Ballet; joined ABT in 1968 as soloist. Became principal in 1969.

NAHAT, DENNIS. Born Feb. 20, 1947 in Detroit, Mich. Studied at Juilliard. Debut 1965 with Joffrey Ballet. Appeared and choreographed on Bdwy before joining ABT in 1968; Soloist 1970, Principal 1973.

NAULT, FERNAND. Born Dec. 27, 1921 in Montreal, Can. Studied with Craske, Tudor, Preobrajenska, Volkova, Pereyaslavic, Leese. Debut with American Ballet Theatre in 1944, for which he has been ballet master 20 years. Artistic Director of Louisville Ballet, and associate director of Les Grands Ballets Canadiens.

NEARHOOF, PAMELA. Born May 12, 1955 in Indiana, Pa. Studied at American Ballet Center, Sulik School. Joined Joffrey Ballet 1971.

NEARY, PATRICIA. Born Oct. 27, 1942 in Miami, Fla. Studied with Georges Milenoff and Thomas Armour, at Natl. Ballet School, School of American Ballet. From 1962 to 1968 was soloist with N.Y.C. Ballet. Now makes guest appearances. Co-director Berlin State Opera Ballet 1970. Director Le Grand Theatre du Geneve 1972.

NEELS, SANDRA. Born Sept. 21, 1942 in Las Vegas, Nev. Studied with Nicholas Vasilieff, Martha Nishitani, Richard Thomas. Debut with Merle Marsicano in 1962. Teacher at Cunningham School since 1965.

NELSON, Ted. Born May 17, 1949 in San Pedro, Cal. Studied at San Francisco Ballet, School of American Ballet. Debut 1970 with San Francisco Ballet. Joined Joffrey Ballet 1973.

NERINA, NADIA. Born Oct. 21, 1927 in Cape Town, South Africa where she received training. Joined Sadler's Wells Ballet in 1946, subsequently becoming one of its leading ballerinas. Now retired.

NEUMEIR, JOHN. Born Feb. 24, 1942 in Milwaukee. Studied at Stone-Camryn, and Royal Ballet (London) schools, and with Sybil Shearer, Vera Volkova. Debut 1963 with Sybil Shearer. With Stuttgart Ballet from 1963. Director Frankfurt Opera Ballet 1969; Hamburg Opera Ballet 1973.

NICKEL, PAUL. Born in Detroit, Mich. Debut with N.Y.C. Ballet. Joined American Ballet Theatre in 1961, became soloist in 1967.

NIGHTINGALE, JOHN. Born Oct. 21, 1943 in Salisbury, Southern Rhodesia. Studied at London School of Contemporary Dance. Joined Paul Taylor Company in 1967.

NIKOLAIS, ALWIN. Born Nov. 25, 1912 in Southington, Conn. Studied with Graham, Humphrey, Holm, Horst, Martin, and at Bennington Summer Dance School. Professional debut 1939. Designs, composes, and choreographs for own company that tours U.S. and abroad. Was co-director of Henry St. Playhouse School of Dance and Theatre. Now co-director of Chimera Foundation for Dance.

NILES, MARY ANN. Born May 2, 1933 in N.Y.C. Studied with Nenette Charisse, Ernest Carlos, Frances Cole, and Roye Dodge. Appeared with American Dance Theatre in U.S. and Europe. Was half of Fosse-Niles dance team that toured U.S. and appeared in Bdwy musicals. Currently teaching, dancing and choreographing.

NILLO, DAVID. Born July 13, 1917 in Goldsboro. N.C. Debut with Ballet Theatre in 1940, then with Ballet Caravan, and Chicago Opera Ballet before appearing in and choreographing musicals.

NIMURA, YEICHI. Born in Suwa, Japan March 25, 1908. First appeared with Operetta Taza. Soloist Manhattan Opera House 1928. Choreographed for musicals and Met Opera. Currently teaches.

NOBLE, CHERIE. Born Dec. 11, 1947 in Philadelphia. Studied with Ethel Phillips, Michael Lopuszanski, Edmund Novak, Pa. Ballet School. Debut with Novak Ballet in 1961 before joining Pennsylvania Ballet in 1962. Now retired.

NUCHTERN, JEANNE. Born in N.Y.C. Nov. 20, 1939. Studied with Craske, and Graham. Debut 1965 in "The King and I" followed by appearances with Martha Graham. Yuriko, Sophie Maslow, and Bertram Ross.

NUREYEV, RUDOLF. Born Mar. 17, 1938 in Russia; reared in Tartary, Bashkir. Admitted to Kirov Ballet school at 17; joined company and became premier danseur. Defected during 1961 appearance in Paris. Invited to join Royal Ballet as co-star and partner of Margot Fonteyn. Has choreographed several ballets. Considered by many as world's greatest male dancer.

O'BRIEN, SHAUN. Born Nov. 28, 1930. Studied with Fokine, Schwezoff, Diaghilev, Balanchine, School of American Ballet. Debut 1944 with Ballet International, subsequently with Ballet for America, Grand Ballet de Monte Carlo, Ballet Da Cuba, Conn. Ballet. N.Y.C. Ballet from 1949.

ODA, BONNIE. Born Sept. 15, 1951 in Honolulu, Hawaii. Graduate UHawaii. Apeared with UHawaii Dance Theater (1968–73), Ethel Winter (1971), Met. Opera Ballet (1971). Joined Martha Graham Co. 1973.

O'DONNELL, MAY. Born in Sacramento, Calif., in 1909. Debut with Estelle Reed Concert Group in San Francisco; lead dancer with Martha Graham Co. 1932–44. Formed own school and company for which she dances and choreographs.

OHARA, ORIE. Born June 18, 1945 in Tokyo. Studied at Tokyo Ballet School. Debut 1960 with Tokyo Ballet before joining Bejart Ballet.

OHMAN, FRANK. Born Jan. 7, 1939 in Los Angeles. Studied with Christensens in San Francisco, and appeared with S.F. Ballet. Joined N.Y.C. Ballet in 1962. Now soloist.

OLRICH, APRIL. Born in Zanzibar, E. Africa in 1931. Studied with Borovsky, and Tchernicheva. Joined Original Ballet Russe in 1944. Appeared on Bdwy.

ONSTAD, MICHAEL. Born Feb. 18, 1949 in Spokane, Wash. Studied with Robert Irwin, Anatol Joukowski, William Christensen, Gordon Paxman, Philip Keeler. Joined Ballet West as soloist in 1966.

Iva Murray-White   Michael Onstad   Mary Ann Niles   Marcos Paredes   Bonnie Oda

ORIO, DIANE. Born Feb. 9, 1947 in Newark, N.J. Trained at Newark Ballet Academy, School of American Ballet, American Ballet Center. Joined Joffrey Ballet in 1968.

ORMISTON, GALE. Born April 14, 1944 in Kansas. Studied with Hanya Holm, Shirlee Dodge, and at Henry St. Playhouse. Debut 1966 with Nikolais Co. Appeared with Mimi Garrard, and formed own company in 1972.

ORR, TERRY. Born Mar. 12, 1943 in Berkeley, Calif. Studied at San Francisco Ballet School; joined company in 1959; American Ballet Theatre in 1965, became principal in 1972.

OSATO, SONO. Born Aug. 29, 1919 in Omaha, Neb. Studied with Egorova, Oboukhoff, Caton, Bolm and Bernice Holmes. Member of corps de ballet and soloist with Ballet Russe de Monte Carlo (1934–40), Ballet Theatre (1940–43), followed by Bdwy musicals.

OSSOSKY, SHELDON. Born Brooklyn, June 10, 1932. Attended Juilliard, and studied with Nikolais, Graham, Limon, Tudor, and Craske. Debut 1950, subsequently appeared in musicals and with Pearl Lang, Sophie Maslow, Fred Berke, and at Henry St. Playhouse.

OSTERGAARD, SOLVEIG. Born Jan. 7, 1939 in Denmark. Studied at Royal Danish Ballet School; joined company in 1957; appointed soloist in 1962.

OUMANSKY, VALENTINA. Born in Los Angeles; graduate of Mills College. Studied with Oumansky, de Mille, Vladimiroff, Horst, Cunningham, Graham, and Maracci. Debut with Marquis de Cuevas' Ballet International, subsequently in Bdwy musicals, before devoting full time to choreography, concert work, and teaching.

OWENS, HAYNES. Born in Montgomery, Ala. Studied with Elinor Someth, Molly Brumbly; appeared with Montgomery Civic Ballet. Attended ABC, and joined Joffrey Ballet in 1966.

OXENHAM, ANDREW. Born Oct. 12, 1945 in London, Eng. Studied with Gwenneth Lloyd, Rosella Hightower, Franchetti. Debut 1964 with Ntl. Ballet of Canada; joined Stuttgart Ballet 1969; National Ballet of Canada 1973 as soloist.

PADOW, JUDY. Born Jan. 10, 1943 in N.Y.C. Studied with Don Farnworth, Marvis Walter, Trisha Brown Schlicter, Ann Halprin. Has danced with Yvonne Rainer, and in own pieces.

PAGE, ANNETTE. Born Dec. 18, 1932 in Manchester, Eng. Entered Royal Ballet School in 1945, and joined company in 1950. Became ballerina in 1959. Has toured with Margot Fonteyn, and made guest appearances at Stockholm's Royal Opera. Retired in 1967.

PAGE, RUTH. Born in Indianapolis, Ind. Studied with Cecchetti, Bolm, and Pavlowa. Debut 1919 with Chicago Opera Co. Toured S. America with Pavlowa, leading dancer on Bdwy, and premier danseuse with Met Opera. Danced with Diaghilev Ballet Russe, and Ballet Russe de Monte Carlo. Formed own company with Bently Stone and toured U.S., Europe, and S. America for 8 years. In Chicago, has been first dancer, choreographer, director for Allied Arts, Grand Opera Co., Federal Theatre, Ravinia Opera Festival. Currently ballet director of both Chicago Opera Ballet and Lyric Opera of Chicago.

PANAIEFF, MICHAEL. Born in 1913 in Novgorod, Russia. Studied with Legat, Egorova. Debut with Belgrade Royal Opera Ballet, becoming first dancer in two years; later joined Blum Ballet, Ballet Russe, and Original Ballet Russe. Now has school and performing group in Los Angeles.

PANOV, VALERY. Born in 1939 in Vilnius, Lithuania. Made debut at 15. Joined Leningrad Maly Ballet 1958; Kirov 1963 and became its lead dancer.

PAPA, PHYLLIS. Born Jan. 30, 1950 in Trenton, N.J. Studied at Joffrey, Harkness, and Ballet Theatre schools. Debut with Harkness Ballet in 1967. Joined ABT in 1968. Royal Danish Ballet 1970.

PAREDES, MARCOS. Born in Aguascalientes, Mex. Trained at Academia de la Danza. Danced with Ballet Contemperaneo, and Ballet Classico de Mexico before joining American Ballet Theatre in 1965. Became soloist 1968, principal 1973.

PARK, MERLE. Born Oct. 8, 1937 in Salisbury, Rhodesia. Joined Sadler's Wells (now Royal) Ballet in 1954, becoming soloist in 1958. Now a leading ballerina.

PARKER, ELLEN. Born Feb. 18 in Columbus, O. Attended N.C. School of Arts, and U. Pa. Studied with Josephine Schwarz, Oleg Briansky, Deborah Jowitt, Job Sanders, Pauline Koner, Duncan Noble, Edward Caton. Appeared in musicals before joining Pa. Ballet in 1968,; left in 1972.

PARKES, ROSS. Born June 17, 1940 in Sydney, Australia. Studied with Valrene Tweedie, Peggy Watson, Audrey de Vos, Martha Graham. Debut 1959 with Ballet Francais. Has danced with Ethel Winter, Bertram Ross, Helen McGehee, Marcha Graham, Sophie Maslow, Glen Tetley, Mary Anghony, Carmen de Lavallade, Jeff Duncan companies. Joined Pennsylvania Ballet in 1966; Martha Graham 1973.

PARKINSON, GEORGINA. Born Aug. 20, 1938 in Brighton, Eng. Studied at Sadler's Wells School. Joined Royal Ballet in 1957, became soloist in 1959. Now a principal ballerina.

PARKS, JOHN E. Born Aug. 4, 1945 in the Bronx. Studied at Julliard. Teacher-dancer-choreographer for Movements Black: Dance Repertory Theatre. Joined Alvin Ailey Co. in 1970.

PARRA, MARIANO. Born in Ambridge, Pa. Mar. 10, 1933. Studied with La Meri, Juan Martinez, La Quica, and Luisa Pericet in Spain. Debut 1957. Has organized and appeared with own company in N.Y.C. and on tour.

PATAROZZI, JACQUES. Born Apr. 28, 1947 in Ajallio, France. Studied with Paul Sanasardo and joined his company in 1972.

PAUL, MIMI. Born in Nashville, Tenn., Feb. 3, 1943. Studied at Washington (D.C.) School of Ballet and School of American Ballet. Debut 1960 in N.Y.C. Ballet in "Nutcracker." Joined ABT in 1969.

PENNEY, JENNIFER. Born Apr. 5, 1946 in Vancouver, Can. Studied at Royal Ballet School, London, and graduated into company. Is now a principal.

PEREZ, RUDY. Born in N.Y.C. Studied with New Dance Group, Graham, Cunningham, Hawkins, Anthony, Artist-in-residence Marymount Manhattan Col., on faculty at DTW. Choreographer-Director Rudy Perez Dance Theatre, and artist-in-residence at Marymount Manhattan Col.

PERI, RIA. Born Aug. 20, 1944 in Eger, Hungary. Trained at Hungary State Ballet School, London Royal Ballet School. Debut 1964 with Royal Ballet.

PERRY, PAMARA. Born Feb. 8, 1948 in Cleveland, Ohio. Studied at School of American Ballet. Debut 1966 with Western Ballet Association of Los Angeles. With Eglevsky Ballet (1966–7), joined Joffrey Ballet in 1967. Retired in 1969.

PERRY, RONALD. Born Mar. 17, 1955 in NYC. Studied at Dance Theatre of Harlem, and made debut with company in 1969.

PERUSSE, SONIA. Born in 1954 in Longueil, Quebec, Can. Attended Ntl. Ballet School, and graduated into company in 1972. Promoted to soloist 1973.

PETERS, DELIA L. Born May 9, 1947 in N.Y.C. Attended School of American Ballet. Joined N.Y.C. Ballet in 1963.

PETERSON, CAROLYN. Born July 23, 1946 in Los Angeles. Studied with Marjorie Peterson, Irina Kosmouska, Carmelita Maracci, and at School of American Ballet. Debut 1966 with N.Y.C. Ballet.

PETERSON, STANZE. Born in Houston, Tex. Has appeared with Syvilla Fort, Edith Stephen, Charles Weidman, Eve Gentry, and Gloria Contreras. In 1963 organized Stanze Peterson Dance Theatre with which he has appeared in N.Y.C. and on tour.

PETIT, ROLAND. Born in Paris Jan. 13, 1924. Studied at Paris Opera School; became member of corps in 1939, and began choreographing. In 1945 was co-founder, ballet master, and premier danseur of Les Ballets des Champs-Elysees. In 1948 formed own company Les Ballets de Paris, for which he danced and choreographs.

PETROFF, PAUL. Born in Denmark: Studied with Katja Lindhart; Debut 1930 with Violet Fischer. Became premier danseur of de Basil's Ballet Russe; later joined Original Ballet Russe, Ballet Theatre (1943) and International Ballet. Now teaches.

PETROV, NICOLAS. Born in 1933 in Yugoslavia; studied with Ureobrajenska, Gsowsky, Massine. Appeared with Yugoslav Ntl. Theatre, Ballet de France, Theatre d'Art Ballet; lead dancer with Massine Ballet. Came to U.S. in 1967 and founded Pittsburgh Ballet Theatre; also teaches.

PHIPPS, CHARLES. Born Nov. 23, 1946 in Newton, Miss. Studied with Graham, Cunningham, and at Ballet Theatre School. Debut 1968 with Pearl Lang, subsequently with Louis Falco, Lucas Hoving.

PIERSON, ROSALIND. Born in Salt Lake City. Bennington graduate. Studied at Thomas-Fallis School, American Ballet Center. Has appeared with Ruth Currier, Charles Wiedman, Ballet Concepts, Anne Wilson, DTW, Garden State Ballet.

PIKSER, ROBERTA. Born Sept. 3, 1941 in Chicago. Graduate U. Chicago. Studied with Erika Thimey, Paul Sanasardo. Debut 1951 with Dance Theatre of Washington; subsequently with Edith Stephen, Paul Sanasardo, Eleo Pomare.

PLATOFF, MARC. Born in Seattle, Wash., in 1915. Debut with de Basil's Ballet Russe; soloist with Ballet Russe de Monte Carlo 1938–42 and choreographed for them. As Marc Platt made Bdwy bow in 1943, subsequently in and choreographing for films. Was director of Radio City Ballet.

PLEVIN, MARCIA. Born Oct. 26, 1945 in Columbus, O. Graduate U. Wisc. Studied with Lang, Graham, Cohan, Yuriko. Debut 1968 with Pearl Lang, subsequently with Sophie Maslow. New Dance Group, Ethel Winter.

PLISETSKAYA, MAYA. Born in Russia Nov. 20, 1925. Began studies at Moscow State School of Ballet at 8 and joined Bolshoi company in 1943, rising to premiere danseuse. Internationally famous for her "Swan Lake." Awarded Lenin Prize in 1964. In addition to dancing with Bolshoi, is now teaching. Considered one of world's greatest ballerinas.

PLUMADORE, PAUL. Born Nov. 5, 1949 in Springfield, Mass. Studied at NYU and with Kelly Holt, Jean Erdman, Nenette Charisse, Gladys Bailin. Debut 1969 with Katherine Litz, with Jean Erdman in 1970, and in concert.

POMARE, ELEO. Born in Cartagena, Colombia Oct. 22, 1937. Studied with Jose Limon, Luis Horst, Curtis James, Geoffrey Holder, and Kurt Jooss. In 1958 organized and has appeared with the Eleo Pomare Dance Co. in N.Y.C., abroad, and on tour in the U.S.

POOLE, DENNIS. Born Dec. 27, 1951 in Dallas, Tex. Trained at Harkness School, and joined company in 1968; soloist 1970; National Ballet 1971–74 as principal.

POPOVA, NINA. Born in 1922 in Russia. Studied in Paris with Preobrajenska and Egorova. Debut 1937 with Ballet de la Jeunesse. Later with Original Ballet Russe, Ballet Theatre, and Ballet Russe de Monte Carlo. Now teaches.

POSIN, KATHRYN. Born Mar. 23, 1944 in Butte, Mont. Bennington graduate. Studied with Fonaroff, Cunningham, Graham, Thomas-Fallis. Debut with Dance Theatre Workshop in 1965. Has danced with Anna Sokolow, Valerie Bettis, Lotte Goslar, American Dance Theatre, and in own works.

POWELL, GRAHAM. Born in Cardiff, Wales. Aug. 2, 1948. Studied at Royal Ballet School; joined company in 1965, then Australian Ballet

POWELL, ROBERT. Born in Hawaii in 1941; graduate of HS Performing Arts. Has been featured dancer with all major American modern dance companies, and appeared with N.Y.C. Opera Ballet. Soloist with Graham Co., associate artistic director 1973.

PRICE, MARY. Born May 20, 1945 in Fort Bragg, N.C. Graduate U. Okla. Studied with Mary Anthony, Martha Graham. Debut 1970 with Mary Anthony, subsequently with Pearl Lang, Richard Gain, Larry Richardson.

PRIMUS, PEARL. Born Nov. 29, 1919 in Trinidad, B.W.I. N.Y. Debut at YMHA in 1943; first solo performance 1944. Has since choreographed and performed in West Indian, African, and primitive dances throughout the world. Also teaches.

PRINZ, JOHN. Born in Chicago May 14, 1945. Studied with Comiacoff, Allegro School, American Ballet Center, School of American Ballet. Joined N.Y.C. Ballet in 1964; Munich Ballet, then ABT in 1970. Appointed principal in 1971.

PROKOVSKY, ANDRE. Born Jan. 13, 1939 in Paris, and achieved recognition in Europe with Grand Ballet du Marquis de Cuevas and London Festival Ballet; made world tour with "Stars of the French Ballet." Joined N.Y.C. Ballet as principal dancer in 1963; London's Festival Ballet in 1967.

PROVANCHA, LEIGH. Born Mar. 22, 1953 in St. John's, Newfoundland. Studied at Wash. Ntl. School of Ballet, NC Sch. of Arts, Sch. of Am. Ballet. Debut 1972 with Ballet Repertory Co. Joined ABT 1973.

QUITMAN, CLEO. Born in Detroit. Attended Weinstein U. Studied with Martha Graham, Alfredo Corvino, Maria Nevelska. Formed N.Y. Negro Ballet Co. that toured Europe. Had appeared with Joffrey Ballet and is founder-director-choreographer of Cleo Quitman's Dance Generale.

RADIUS, ALEXANDRA. Born July 3, 1942 in Amsterdam, Holland. Studied with Benjamin Harkarvy. Debut with Nederlands Dans Theatre in 1957. Joined American Ballet Theatre in 1968 as soloist. Became principal in 1969. Joined Dutch National Ballet in 1970.

RAINER, YVONNE. Born in 1934 in San Francisco. Studied with Graham, Cunningham, Halprin, Stephen. Has performed with James Waring, Aileen Passloff, Beverly Schmidt, Judith Dunn. Started Judson Dance Workshop in 1962, and choreographs for own company.

RAINES, WALTER. Born Aug. 16, 1940 in Braddock, Pa. Attended Carnegie-Mellon U. Studied at Pittsburgh Playhouse, School of American Ballet, Dance Theatre of Harlem. Debut 1952 with Pittsburgh Opera Ballet; subsequently with Pennsylvania Ballet 1962, Stuttgart Ballet 1964, Dance Theatre of Harlem 1969.

RALL, TOMMY. Born Dec. 27, 1929 in Kansas City, Mo. Attended Chouinard Art Inst. Studied with Carmelita Maracci, David Lichine, and Oboukhoff of School of American Ballet. Joined Ballet Theatre in 1944, and became soloist in 1945. Has appeared in musicals, films, and choreographed for TV.

RAPP, RICHARD. Born in Milwaukee, Wisc. Studied with Adele Artinian, Ann Barzel, School of American Ballet. Joined N.Y.C. Ballet in 1958; became soloist in 1961.

RAUP, FLORITA. Born in Havana, Cuba; attended school in Springfield, O. Has studied with Holm, Limon, Humphrey, Tamiris, and Julia Berashkova. Debut in 1951. Has appeared in concert and with own group since 1953, in N.Y.C. and on tour.

REBEAUD, MICHELE. Born Jan. 24, 1948 in Paris, France. Debut 1972 with Paul Sanasardo Co.

REDLICH, DON. Born in Winona, Minn., Aug. 17, 1933. Attended U. Wisc., studied with Holm, and Humphrey. Debut in 1954 musical "The Golden Apple." Has danced with Hanya Holm, Doris Humphrey, Anna Sokolow, Murray Louis, John Butler, and in own concert program. Is teacher, choreographer, and tours with own Co.

REED, JANET. Born in Tolo, Ore., Sept. 15, 1916. Studied with William Christensen, Tudor, and Balanchine. Member of San Francisco Ballet 1937–41, Ballet Theatre 1943–6, N.Y.C. Ballet from 1949. Has been teaching since 1965.

REESE, GAIL. Born Aug. 13, 1946 in Queens, N.Y. Studied with Syvilla Fort, Hector Zaraspe, Marianne Balin. Debut with Cleo Quitman in 1967, and then with Talley Beatty, Lar Lubovitch, and Alvin Ailey from 1970.

REID, ALBERT. Born July 12, 1934 in Niagara Falls, N.Y. Graduate Stanford U. Studied with Nikolais, Cunningham, Lillian Moore, Richard Thomas, Margaret Craske. Debut 1959 with Nikolais Co., with Murray Louis, Erick Hawkins, Katherine Litz, and Yvonne Rainer.

REIN, RICHARD A. Born May 10, 1944 in N.Y.C. Attended Adelphi U. School of Am. Ballet. Debut 1965 with Atlanta Ballet, subsequently with Ruth Page's Chicago Ballet, Pa. Ballet, joined ABT in 1970, Pa. Ballet 1973.

REMINGTON, BARBARA. Born in 1936 in Windsor, Can. Studied with Sandra Severo, School of American Ballet, Ballet Theatre School, Royal Ballet. Joined Royal Ballet in 1959, followed by American Ballet Theatre, Joffrey Ballet.

RENCHER, DEREK. Born June 6, 1932 in Birmingham, Eng. Studied at Royal Ballet school and joined company in 1952, rising to soloist and principal in 1969.

REVENE, NADINE. Born in N.Y.C. Studied with Helen Platova. In musicals before joining Ballet Theatre. Subsequently member of N.Y.C. Ballet, prima ballerina of Bremen Opera in Germany, and First Chamber Dance Quartet. Joined Pa. Ballet in 1970 as soloist. Now assistant ballet mistress.

REY, FRANK. Born in 1931 in Tampa, Fla. Made debut with Chicago Opera Ballet. Founder-Director Florida Dance Camp, Choreographer-in-residence for Florida Ballet Theatre. Is noted as choreographer for outdoor dramas.

REYES, RAMON DE LOS. Born in Madid and started dancing at 9. Debut at 17 after studying with Antonio Marin. Formed own company and toured Spain, Europe, and U.S. Joined Ximenez-Vargas Co., later Roberto Iglesias Co. as leading dancer. With Maria Alba, formed Alba-Reyes Spanish Dance Co. in 1964.

REYN, JUDITH. Born Dec. 28, 1943 in Rhodesia. Studied at Royal Ballet School, London, and joined company in 1963. Member of Stuttgart Ballet since 1967.

RHODES, CATHRYN. Born in 1958 in Westchester, NY. Studied with Iris Merrick, Don Farnsworth, at Manhattan Ballet School, Manhattan School of Dance, Am. Ballet Theatre School. Joined ABT 1973.

| Nicolas Petrov | Gail Reese | Luis Rivera | Zhandra Rodriguez | Bertram Ross |

RHODES, LAWRENCE. Born in Mt. Hope, W. Va., Nov. 24, 1939. Studied with Violette Armand. Debut with Ballet Russe de Monte Carlo. Joined Joffrey Ballet in 1960, Harkness Ballet in 1964. Became its director in 1969. Joined Netherlands National Ballet in 1970, Pa. Ballet 1972. Appeared with Eliot Feld Ballet 1974.

RIABOUCHINSKA, TATIANA. Born May 23, 1916 in Moscow. Studied with Alexandre Volinin, and Mathilda Kchesinska. Debut in London in 1932. With Monte Carlo Ballet Russe de Basil (1933–43), Ballet Theatre, London Festival Ballet, Theatre Colon (Buenos Aires, 1946–47). Also appeared in musicals. Now teaches.

RICHARDSON, DORENE. Born in N.Y.C., Oct. 5, 1934. Studied at NYU and Juilliard. Debut in 1953. In addition to musicals has appeared with Natanya Neumann, Sophie Maslow, Donald McKayle, and Alvin Ailey.

RICHARDSON, LARRY. Born Jan. 6, 1941 in Minerva, O. Graduate of Ohio State U. Studied with Louis Horst, Jose Limon. Has danced at Kauffman Hall, Hunter College, in musicals, and with Pearl Lang. Also choreographs and tours own company.

RIVERA, CHITA. Born in 1933 in Washington, D.C. Studied at School of American Ballet. Has become popular star of musicals, and TV.

RIVERA, LUIS. Born in Los Angeles. Studied with Michael Brigante, Martin Vargas, Luisa Triana, Mercedes & Albano, Alberto Lorca. Appeared with several companies before forming his own.

ROBBINS, JEROME. Born Oct. 11, 1918 in N.Y.C. Attended NYU. Studied with Daganova, Platova, Loring, Tudor, New Dance League, and Helen Veola. Debut in 1937 with Sandor-Sorel Co. Subsequently in musicals before joining Ballet Theater in 1940, for which he first choreographed "Fancy Free." Joined N.Y.C. Ballet in 1949 and became its associate artistic director in 1950. Formed Ballets: U.S.A. which toured Europe and U.S. (1958–1961). Has choreographed and directed many Bdwy productions and ballets.

ROBERSON, LAR. Born May 18, 1947 in Oakland, Calif. Attended Cal. State College, and Graham School. Debut 1968 with Sophie Maslow Company. Joined Graham Company in 1969. Also appeared with Pearl Lang.

ROBINSON, CHASE. Born in Panama City, Fla. Graduate of Fla. State U. Studied with Aubry Hitchins, Don Farnworth. Debut in 1956. Has since appeared with Natl. Ballet of Canada, Joffrey Ballet, Limon, Graham, Lang, Butler, Cunningham, and Hoving. Also teaches.

ROBINSON, NANCY. Born Aug. 28, 1945 in Los Angeles. Studied with Andre Tremaine, Michael Panaieff, San Francisco Ballet, joining company in 1960, becoming soloist in 1964. Joined American Ballet Theatre in 1967, Joffrey Co. in 1968.

RODGERS, ROD. Born in Detroit where he began his studies. Member of Erick Hawkins Dance Co., and dance supervisor of Mobilization for Youth project. Has also appeared in concert of own works and with own company for which he choreographs.

RODHAM, ROBERT. Born Sept. 2, 1939 in Pittston, Pa. Studied with Barbara Weisberger, Virginia Williams, and at School of American Ballet. Joined N.Y.C. Ballet in 1960. Ballet master, choreographer, and principal with Pennsylvania Ballet from 1963.

RODRIGUEZ, ZHANDRA. Born Mar. 17, 1947 in Caracas. Ven. Debut 1962 with Ballet National Venezuela; joined American Ballet Theatre in 1968; soloist 1970, principal 1973.

ROHAN, SHEILA. Born Nov. 20, 1947 in Staten Island, N.Y. Studied with Vincenzo Celli, Phil Black, James Truitte. Debut 1970 with Dance Theatre of Harlem.

ROMANOFF, DIMITRI. Born in Tsaritzin, Russia. Came to U.S. in 1924 to attend Stanford U. and study with Theodore Kosloff. First dancer with American Ballet Theatre when it was organized in 1940. Now directs school in San Jose, Calif.

ROMERO, RAFAEL. Born Apr. 2, 1945 in Puerto Rico. Studied at School of American Ballet, Natl. Ballet, and American Ballet Center. Has appeared with Ballets de San Juan, Westchester Ballet, Pilar Gomez, National Ballet, Joffrey Ballet, N.Y.C. Opera Ballet (1970).

RON, RACHAMIM. Born Nov. 15, 1942 in Cairo. Studied with Gertrude Kraus. Donald McKayle, Glen Tetley, Pearl Lang, Martha Graham. Debut 1963 with Batsheva Dance Co. of Israel. Joined Donald McKayle Co. in 1967 and Martha Graham in 1968. Rejoined Batsheva 1970.

ROOPE, CLOVER. Born 1937 in Bristol, Eng. Studied at Royal Ballet School and joined company in 1957. Debut as choreographer in 1958. Also appeared with Helen McGehee.

ROSARIO. Born Rosario Perez in Seville Nov. 11, 1920. Cousin of Antonio with whom she achieved international fame. Studied with Realito. With Antonio, became known as "The Kids From Seville" and toured world together until they separated in 1952. Formed own company, but changed to dance recitals. Has returned to guest star with Antonio and his Ballets de Madrid.

ROSS, BERTRAM. Born in Brooklyn, Nov. 13, 1920. Leading male dancer of the Martha Graham Co., appeared in almost every work in the active repertoire. Has appeared with own company and choreography. Teaches at Graham School, Julliard, and Neighborhood Playhouse.

ROSS, HERBERT. Born May 13, 1927 in Brooklyn. Studied with Doris Humphrey, Helene Platova, and Laird Leslie. Debut in "Follow the Girls" in 1944. In 1950 choreographed and appeared with Ballet Theatre in "Caprichos," subsequently choreographing for Bdwy musicals, Met Opera Ballet, American Ballet Theatre, and danced with own company in 1960.

ROSSON, KEITH. Born Jan. 24, 1937 in Birmingham, Eng. Studied at Royal Ballet School. Joined Covent Opera Ballet in 1954 and Royal Ballet in 1955. Became soloist in 1959, and principal dancer in 1964.

ROTANTE, THEODORE. Born Feb. 23, 1949 in Stamford, Conn. Studied with Nenette Charisse, Kelly Holt, Jean Erdman, Gladys Bailin, Matt Mattox, Donald McKayle. Debut in 1970 with Jean Erdman Dance Theatre.

ROTARDIER, KELVIN. Born Jan. 23, 1936 in Trinidad, W. I. Studied at London's Sigurd Leder School, Jacob's Pillow, and International School of Dance. Appeared in musicals before joining Alvin Ailey Co. in 1964.

ROZOW, PATRICIA. Born Feb. 18, 1947 in Brooklyn, NY. Graduate Butler U. Studied at Harkness School. Joined Ballet West in 1969. Promoted to soloist in 1971; principal in 1973.

RUDKO, DORIS. Born Oct. 18, in Milwaukee. Graduate U. Wisc. Studied with Humphrey, Weidman, Limon, Graham, Holm, Horst, Daganova, Platova, Joffrey, and Fonaroff. Debut on Bdwy 1946 in "Shooting' Star." Concert performer and choreographer since 1947. Formed own company in 1957. Is also a teacher.

RUUD, TOMM. Born in 1943 in Pasadena, Cal. Graduate UUtah. Studied with William Christensen, Bene Arnold, Gordon Paxman. Joined Ballet West 1963; made soloist 1965, principal 1969. Teaches and makes guest appearances with other companies.

RUIZ, BRUNILDA. Born in Puerto Rico June 1, 1936. Studied with Martha Melincoff, and Robert Joffrey before joining his touring group in 1955, and his company in 1961. Appeared with Philadelphia and N.Y.C. Opera companies. Joined Harkness Ballet in 1964.

RUSHING, SHIRLEY. Born in Savannah, Ga. Attended Julliard, Bklyn Col. Studied with O'Donnell, Shurr, Bronson, Limon, Tudor, Graham. Has appeared with Eleo Pomare, Rod Rodgers, Louis Johnson, Gus Denizulu.

RUSSELL, PAUL. Born Mar. 2, 1947 in Texas. Studied at School of American Ballet, Dance Theatre of Harlem. Debut 1970 with Hartford Ballet; subsequently with Garden State Ballet, Syracuse Ballet Theatre; joined Dance Theatre of Harlem 1971.

SABLE, SHERRY. Born Sept. 4, 1952 in Philadelphia. Studied at Phila. Dance Academy, Graham School. Debut 1970 with Pearl Lang, subsequently with DTW, Richard Gain.

SABLINE, OLEG. Born in 1925 in Berlin. Studied with Preobrajenska, Egorova, Colinine, Ricaus; danced with Grand Ballet de Monte Carlo, l'Opera Comique Ballet, Grand Ballet du Marquis de Cuevas. Came to U.S. in 1958. Formed and toured with own group Ballet Concertante. Currently teaches.

SADDLER, DONALD. Born Jan. 24, 1920 in Van Nys, Calif. Attended LACC. Studied with Maracci, Dolin, and Tudor. Debut in 1937, subsequently appearing with Ballet Theatre (1940–3, 1946–7), and in Bdwy musicals. First choreography "Blue Mountain Ballads" for Markova-Dolin Co. in 1948. Performed with own company in 1949. Assistant artistic director of Harkness Ballet 1964–1970. Has choreographed several Bdwy productions.

SAMPSON, RONDA CAROL. Born June 26, 1953 in Roanoke, Va. Made debut with Atlanta Ballet in 1968. Joined Dance Theatre of Harlem in 1969.

SAMPSON, ROSLYN. Born May 8, 1955 in Nashville, Tenn. Appeared with Atlanta Ballet; joined Dance Theatre of Harlem 1969.

SANASARDO, PAUL. Born Sept. 15, 1928 in Chicago. Attended Chicago U. Studied with Tudor, Thimey, Graham, and Slavenska. Debut in 1951 with Wrika Thimey Dance Theatre; subsequently with Anna Sokolow, and Pearl Lang. In 1958 established, and directs Studio For Dance, a school for his own company that presents concerts throughout the U.S., Canada, and BWI. Choreographer and dancer on TV. Director of Modern Dance Artists (N.Y.C.), and School of Modern Dance (Saratoga, N.Y.).

SANCHEZ, MIGUEL. Born Feb. 21, 1951 in Puerto Rico. Studied at School of American Ballet, and with Anne Wooliams. Debut 1969 with Stuttgart Ballet. Is guest artist with Ballets de San Juan, P.R.

SANDERS, JOB. Born in Amsterdam in 1929. Studied with Gavrilov, and at School of American Ballet. Debut with Ballet Society. Subsequently with Ballet Russe de Monte Carlo, ABT, Ruth Page's Ballet, American Festival Ballet, Netherlands Ballet, Netherlands Dance Theatre. Began choreographing in 1956. Also teaches.

SANDONATO, BÁRBARA. Born July 22, 1943 in Harrison, N.Y. Studied at Lorna London School, and School of American Ballet. Debut with N.Y.C. Ballet, danced with Gloria Contreras Co., before joining Pennsylvania Ballet in 1964 and rising to principal; Canadian Ntl. Ballet 1972–3; returned to Pa. Ballet 1973.

SANTANGELO, TULY. Born May 30, 1936 in Buenos Aires. Studied at Opera Theatre, with Martha Graham, Alwin Nikolais. Debut 1956 with Brazilian Co., subsequently with Nikolais, Don Redlich (1970).

SAPIRO, DANA. Born Jan. 2, 1952 in N.Y.C. Studied with Karin Irvin, Joffrey, and at American Ballet Center. Debut 1970 with Joffrey Ballet. Joined Alvin Ailey company 1972.

SAPPINGTON, MARGO. Born in Baytown, Tex., July 30, 1947. Studied with Camille Hill, Matt Mattox, and at American Ballet Center. Debut with Joffrey Ballet in 1965. Also appeared in musicals, and choreographs.

SARRY, CHRISTINE. Born in Long Beach, Calif. in 1947. Studied with Silver, Howard, Maracci, Oumansky, Fallis, Thomas. Joined Joffrey Ballet in 1963. American Ballet Theatre in 1964. American Ballet Co. (1969), rejoined ABT as soloist in 1971; Eliot Feld Ballet 1974.

SARSTADT, MARIAN. Born July 11, 1942 in Amsterdam. Studied at Scapino School, with Mme. Nora, Audrey de Vos. Debut in 1958 with Scapino Ballet. Joined de Cuevas Co. in 1960. Netherlands Dance Theatre in 1962.

SATO, SHOZO. Born May 18, 1933 in Kobe, Japan. Graduate Tokyo U. Debut with Classical Ballet in 1948. Has appeared around the world in concert and lecture demonstrations since 1964.

SAUL, PETER. Born Feb. 10, 1936 in N.Y.C. Studied with Craske, Tudor, and Cunningham. Appeared with Met Opera Ballet 1956–7, International Ballet 1960–61, American Ballet Theatre 1962–4, Les Grands Ballets Canadien 1964–5, Merce Cunningham 1966–7.

SCHAFER, RICHARD. Born Dec. 27, 1952 in Denver, Col. Studied at Sch. of Am. Ballet, Ntl. Sch., with Vera Volkova, Maggie Black, and David Howard. Debut 1972 with ABT.

SCHANNE, MARGRETHE. Born in Copenhagen Nov. 21, 1921. Graduate of Royal Danish Ballet school; joined company, in mid-1940's, rapidly rising to premiere danseuse and the epitome of the Bournonville style. Briefly joined Petit's Ballets des Champs-Elysses in Paris and in 1947 made London debut with it before returning to Royal Danish Ballet where she became synonymous with "La Sylphide." Made N.Y. debut in it in 1956, and danced in it for her farewell performance in N.Y. and Copenhagen in 1966. Now teaches.

SCHEEPERS, MARTIN. Born in 1933 in Arnheim, Holland. Studied with Georgi, Adret, Crofton, Lifar, Gsovsky, Kiss. Debut in 1948 with Amsterdam Opera. Joined Champs-Elysses and London Festival Ballets before American Ballet Theatre in 1960.

SCHORER, SUKI. Born in Cambridge, Mass. Attended U. Cal. Studied at San Francisco Ballet School and joined company. In 1959 joined N.Y.C. Ballet, becoming soloist in 1963, ballerina in 1969. Retired in 1971 and teaches.

SCHRAMEK, TOMAS. Born in Bratislave, Czech. Began training at 9. Graduate Musical and Theatrical Academy. Joined Slovak Character Dance Co. 1959, rising to principal. Left Czech. in 1968 to join National Ballet of Canada. Promoted to principal 1973.

SCHULKIND, MARCUS. Born Feb. 21, 1948 in N.Y.C. Graduate Goddard Col. Studied at Juilliard. Debut 1968 with Pearl Lang, then with Norman Walker, Felix Fibich; joined Batsheva in 1970.

SCOTT, MARION. Born July 24, 1922 in Chicago. Studied with Graham, Humphrey, Weidman, Horst, Tamiris, and Slavenska. Debut with Humphrey-Weidman Co. in 1942. Worked with Tamiris, and in 1964 formed own company for which she choreographs. Also teaches.

SCOTT, WILLIAM. Born Nov. 3, 1950 in N.Y.C. Studied with Martha Graham, Harkness House, Richard Thomas. Debut 1968 with Harkness Youth Co. Joined Dance Theatre of Harlem in 1970. Is also ballet master and teacher.

SEGARRA, RAMON. Born Nov. 26, 1939 in Mayaguez, P.R. Studied with Chafee, Malinka, Moore, Pereyaslavec, Vilzak, Oboukoff, Vladimiroff, Eglevsky, and Zaraspe. Debut 1954 with Ballet Chafee, subsequently appearing as soloist with May O'Donnell Co. (1956–8), Ballet Russe de Monte Carlo (1958–61), N.Y.C. Ballet (1961–4), and ballet master of Ailey Co. from 1970. Ballet Master Hamburg Stage Opera Ballet 1972; Ballet Hispanico 1972.

SEKIL, YAROSLAV. Born in Ukrania in 1930. Entered Bolshoi School in 1949, and joined company in 1951. Became one of leading character dancers.

SELLERS, JOAN. Born Sept. 21, 1937 in N.Y.C. Studied with Graham, Cunningham, Thomas, Fallis, Farnworth. Debut 1960 with Dance Theatre, subsequently with DTW, James Cunningham Co.

SERAVALLI, ROSANNA. Born March 9, 1943 in Florence, Italy. Trained and performed in Italy before joining American Ballet Theatre in 1963.

SERGAVA, KATHERINE. Born in Tiflis, Russia. Studied with Kehessinska, Fokine, Kyasht, Mendes. Danced with Mordkin Ballet, Ballet Theatre (1940), Original Ballet Russe. More recently appeared in musicals.

SERRANO, LUPE. Born Dec. 7, 1930 in Santiago, Chile. Studied in Mexico City with Dambre and joined Mexico City Ballet Co. Organized Mexican Academy of Modern Dance. After studying with Celli and Tudor, performed with Ballet Russe, and Ballet Theatre (since 1953).

SETTERFIELD, VALDA. Born Sept. 17, 1934 in Margate, Eng. Studied with Rambert, Karsavina, Waring, Cunningham. Debut with Ballet Rambert in 1955. Since, with James Waring, Aileen Pasloff, Katherine Litz, David Gordon, Merce Cunningham.

SEYMOUR, LYNN. Born in 1939 in Wainwright. Alberta, Canada. Studied at Royal Ballet School, London graduating into company. Besides appearances as dramatic ballerina with Royal Ballet, has made guest appearances with Stuttgart, and Canadian National Ballet. Guest artist with Ailey Co. 1970–71. Rejoined Royal Ballet 1970.

SHANG, RUBY. Born 1950 in Tokyo where she began studies at 6. Attended Pembroke Col. Studied with Julie Strandberg, Martha Graham, Iehige Reiko. Joined Paul Taylor Co. in 1971.

SHANKAR, UDAY. Born in Udayapur, India, in 1902. Had such success helping his father produce Hindu plays and ballets, that Anna Pavlova requested his help, and he appeared with her in "Radha-Krishna." At her insistence, pursued dance career. Organized own company and toured U.S. in 1931, 1952, 1962, and 1968. Has been more responsible than any other dancer for arousing interest in Indian dance.

SHAW, BRIAN. Born June 28, 1928 in Golear, Yorkshire, Eng. At 14 entered Sadler's Wells School, and joined company 2 years later, becoming one of Royal Ballet's outstanding principal dancers.

SHEARER, MOIRA. Born in Dunfermline, Scotland. Jan. 17, 1926. Studied with Legat and Preograjenska; joined International Ballet at 15, transferring to Sadler's Wells and became ballerina in 1944. More recently has appeared on stage and films.

SHEARER, SYBIL. Born in Toronto, Can. Studied in France and Eng. Before forming and choreographing for own group, danced with Humphrey Weidman Co., and Theatre Dance Co. Also teaches.

SHELTON, SARA. Born Dec. 17, 1943. Studied at Henry St. Playhouse. Debut 1966 with Bill Frank Co., subsequently with Nikolais, Louis Murray, Mimi Garrard, Raymond Johnson. Also teaches and choreographs.

SHERWOOD, GARY. Born Sept. 24, 1941, in Swindon, Eng. Studied at Royal Ballet School; joined company in 1961; Western Theatre Ballet 1965; London's Festival Ballet 1966; returned to Royal Ballet in 1967.

SHIMIN, TONIA. Born Sept. 16, 1942 in N.Y.C. Attended Met Opera Ballet, Royal Ballet, Graham schools. Debut 1965 with Martha Graham, subsequently with Pearl Lang, Gus Solomons, Anna Sokolow, Mary Anthony.

nda Carol Sampson　　Richard Schafer　　Christine Sarry　　William Scott　　Trinette Singleton

SHIMOFF, KAREL. Born in Los Angeles where she began studies with Irina Kosmovska. Appeared with L.A. Junior Ballet and N.Y.C. Ballet's "Nutcracker" in L.A. in 1961. Studied at School of American Ballet, and joined N.Y.C. Ballet for 2 years, before returning as principal dancer with Ballet of Los Angeles.

SHULER, ARLENE. Born Oct. 18, 1947 in Cleveland, O. Studied at School of American Ballet, and American Ballet Center. Debut with N.Y.C. Ballet in 1960, and joined Joffrey Ballet in 1965.

SHURR, GERTRUDE. Born in Riga, Latvia. Studied at Denishawn, and with Humphrey, Weidman, and Graham. Has appeared with Denishawn Co., Humphrey-Weidman Concert Co., and Martha Graham. Now teaches.

SIBLEY, ANTOINETTE. Born in Bromley, Eng., Feb. 27, 1939. Studied at Royal Ballet School, and made debut with them in 1956, becoming soloist in 1959, principal in 1960.

SEIGENFELD, BILLY. Born Oct. 15, 1948 in Mt. Vernon, N.Y. Graduate Brown U. Studied with Nikolais. Debut 1970 with Don Redlich Co., subsequently with Elina Mooney.

SIMMONS, DANIEL. Born in Edinburg, Tex. Studied at Pan American U., San Francisco Ballet School. Debut with SF Ballet 1967.

SIMON, VICTORIA. Born in 1939 in N.Y.C. Studied at School of American Ballet, American Ballet Center, Ballet Theatre School. Joined N.Y.C. Ballet in 1958, promoted to soloist in 1963.

SIMONE, KIRSTEN. Born July 1, 1934 in Copenhagen. Studied at School of Royal Theatre; made debut with Royal Danish Ballet in 1952, subsequently becoming principal dancer. Has appeared with Ruth Page Opera Ballet, Royal Winnipeg Ballet, Royal Swedish Ballet.

SIMONEN-SVANSTROM, SEIJA. Born in Helsinki, Finland, Sept. 7, 1935. Studied at Finnish Natl. Opera Ballet School, and with Nikitina, Baltazcheva, Semjonowa, Lopuchkina, Karnakoski, Stahlberg, Northcote, Franzel, and Craske. Debut 1952 with Helsinki Natl. Opera. Has appeared with Finnish Natl. Ballet, and London Festival Ballet.

SINGLETON, SARAH. Born Apr. 21, 1951 in Morgantown, WVa. Graduate Stephens Col. Studied with Susan Abbey, Rebecca Harris, Karel Shook, Paul Sanasardo. Debut 1972 with Sanasardo Dance Co.

SINGLETON, TRINETTE. Born in Beverly, Mass., Nov. 20, 1945. Studied with Harriet James, and at American Ballet Center. Debut with Joffrey Ballet in 1965.

SIZOVA, ALLA. Born in Moscow in 1939. Studied at Leningrad Ballet School. Joined Kirov Co. in 1958, and became its youngest ballerina.

SKIBINE, GEORGE. Born Jan. 17, 1920 in Russia. Studied with Preobrajenska, and Oboukhoff. Debut with Ballet de Monte Carlo in 1937, and with company until 1939. Original Ballet Russe (1939-40). American Ballet Theatre (1940-1942). Marquis de Cuevas Grand Ballet (1947-56), Theatre National de Opera Paris (1956-64), artistic director of Harkness Ballet 1964-66. Currently works with regional companies.

SLAVENSKA, MIA. Born in 1916 in Yugoslavia. At 12 made debut and toured Europe with Anton Vyanc, subsequently with Lifar and Dolin, and prima ballerina with Ballet Russe de Monte Carlo, before forming own company Ballet Variant that toured Americas and Europe. Has worked with many regional companies, toured with Slavinska-Franklin Co. Currently teaches at UCLA.

SLAYTON, JEFF. Born Sept. 5, 1945 in Richmond, Va. Attended Adelphi U. Studied with Merce Cunningham and made debut with his company in 1968. Appears with Viola Farber Co.

SLEEP, WAYNE. Born July 17, 1948 in Plymouth, England. Attended Royal Ballet School, and was graduated into the company in 1966.

SMALL, ROBERT. Born Dec. 19, 1949 in Moline, Ill. UCLA graduate. Studied with Gloria Newman. Murray Louis, Nikolais, and at Am. School of Ballet. Debut in 1971 with Murray Louis Co.

SMALLS, SAMUEL. Born Feb. 17, 1951 in N.Y.C. Attended CCNY. Studied with Lester Wilson, Jamie Rodgers, Harkness House. Debut 1969 with Dance Theatre of Harlem.

SMUIN, MICHAEL. Born Oct. 13, 1929 in Missoula, Mont. Studied with Christensen brothers, William Dollar and Richard Thomas. Joined San Francisco Ballet in 1957, and made choreographic debut in 1961. Has choreographed for Harkness and Ballet Theatre. A principal with American Ballet Theatre since 1969. Associated director San Francisco Ballet 1973.

SOKOLOW, ANNA. Born in 1912 in Hartford, Conn. Studied with Graham and Horst. Became member of Graham Co. but left to form own in 1938. Internationally known as choreographer, and her works include many modern classics. Formed Lyric Theatre Co. in Israel in 1962. Has taught at major studios and universities, and choreographed for Broadway, TV, and opera.

SOLINO, LOUIS. Born Feb. 7, 1942 in Philadelphia. Studied with Graham, O'Donnell, Schurr, Walker, Anthony, Farnworth. Has performed with Glen Tetley, Mary Anthony, Sophie Maslow, Norman Walker, Arthur Bauman, Seamus Murphy, and Jose Limon.

SOLOMON, ROBERT. Born Feb. 13, 1945 in The Bronx. Studied at Henry Street Playhouse. Has appeared with Henry Street Playhouse Company, and Nikolais.

SOLOMON, RUTH. Born June 10, 1936 in N.Y.C. Studied with Jean Erdman and joined company in 1957, still appears with her between teaching. Now head of Dance-Theatre program at U. Cal. at Santa Cruz.

SOLOMONS, GUS, Jr. Born in Boston where he studied with Jan Veen and Robert Cohan. Danced with Donald McKayle, Joyce Trisler, Pearl Lang, Martha Graham, Merce Cunningham. Formed own company in 1971.

SOLOV, ZACHARY. Born in 1923 in Philadelphia. Studied with Littlefield, Preobrajenska, Carlos, Holm, and Humphrey and at American Ballet School. Debut with Catherine Littlefield Ballet Co. Later joined American Ballet, New Opera Co., Loring Dance Players, and Ballet Theatre. In 1951 became choreographer for Met Opera Ballet. Toured own company 1961-1962. Also appeared on Bdwy and with regional companies.

SOLOVYOV, YURI. Born Aug. 10, 1940. Graduated from Leningrad Ballet School and into Kirov Co. in 1958. Has become one of its leading soloists.

SOMBERT, CLAIRE. Born in 1935 in Courbevoie, France. A pupil of Brieux, made debut in 1950. Has appeared with Ballets de Paris. Ballets Jean Babilee, Miskovitch Co. Toured U.S. with Michel Bruel.

SOMES, MICHAEL. Born Sept. 28, 1917 in Horsley, Eng. Attended Sadler's Wells School; joined company (now Royal) in 1937, and became lead dancer in 1938. For many years, partner for Margot Fonteyn, and creator of many famous roles. In 1962 appointed assistant director of company, and still performs character roles.

SORKIN, NAOMI. Born Oct. 23, 1948 in Chicago. Studied at Stone-Camryn School. Debut with Chicago Lyric Opera Ballet in 1963. Joined ABT in 1966; promoted to soloist in 1971. Joined San Francisco Ballet 1973.; Eliot Feld Ballet 1974.

SPASSOFF, BOJAN. Born in Oslo, Norway. Appeared with Ntl. Ballet of Holland, Royal Danish Ballet, ABT, and joined San Francisco Ballet 1973.

SPOHR, ARNOLD. Born in Saskatchewan, Can. Joined Winnipeg company in 1945, rising to leading dancer, and appeared in England partnering Markova. Began choreographing in 1950. In 1958 was appointed director of Royal Winnipeg Ballet for which he choreographs.

SPURLOCK, ESTELLE. Born May 9, 1949 in Jersey City, N.J. Graduate Boston Cons. Studied with Sonia Wilson, Lar Lubovitch, James Truitte. Debut 1971 with Alvin Ailey Co.

STACKHOUSE, SARAH. (formerly Sally). Born in Chicago, Graduate U. Wisc. Studied with Arrby Blinn, Steffi Nossen, Perry-Mansfield School, John Begg, Limon, Graham, and Nagrin. Joined Limon company in 1959. Also appeared with Alvin Ailey Co. Teaches at Juilliard and Conn. College.

STARBUCK, JAMES. Born in Albuquerque, New Mex. Attended College of Pacific. Debut 1934 with Ballet Modern, subsequently appearing with San Francisco Opera Ballet. Ballet Russe de Monte Carlo (1939–44). On Bdwy in musicals before first choreography for "Fanny." Has since choreographed and directed for theatre and TV.

STEELE, MICHAEL. Born in Roanoke, Va. Studied at American Ballet School, and made debut with N.Y.C. Ballet.

STEELE, ROBERT. Born June 22, 1946 in Erie, Pa. Attended Boston Cons. Studied with Statia Sublette, Virginia Williams, Stanley Williams, Vera Volkova. Debut 1974 with Boston Ballet; subsequently with Pennsylvania Ballet 1964, American Festival Ballet 1965, Royal Danish Ballet 1966, Boston Ballet 1968.

STEFANSCHI, SERGIU. Born Mar. 2, 1941 in Roumania. Graduate of Academie Ballet. Debut 1962 with Bucharest Opera Ballet; subsequently with Theatre Francais de la Dance, National Ballet of Canada 1971 as principal.

STEPHEN, EDITH. Born in Salamanca, N.Y. Studied with Doris Humphrey, Jose Limon, Mary Wigman, Rudolf Laban. Debut in 1962 with own company and choreography. Has toured U.S. and Europe.

STEVENSON, BEN. Born April 4 in Portsmouth, Eng. Was principal dancer for many years with London's Festival Ballet. Retired to teach but makes guest appearances. Directed Harkness Youth Co. Now with National Ballet.

STEWART, DELIA WEDDINGTON. Born in Meridian, Miss. Studied at Ballet Arts Center, Ballet Theatre, and International Dance Schools. Appeared in Bdwy musicals. Director of Dixie Darling Dance Group. In 1963 became artistic director of Mississippi Coast Ballet.

STIRLING, CRISTINA. Born May 22, 1940 in London. Trained at Audrey de Vos and Andrew Hardie School. Debut with Sadler's Wells Opera Ballet, Subsequently with Netherlands Ballet, London Festival Ballet, American Ballet Co. Now co-director of Louisville Ballet and teacher.

STONE, BENTLEY. Born in Plankinston, S.Dak. Studied with Severn, Caskey, Albertieri, Novikoff, and Rambert. After dancing in musicals joined Chicago Civic Opera, becoming premier danseur. Also danced with Ballet Rambert, Ballet Russe, and Page-Stone Ballet for which he choreographed many works.

STRICKLER, ILENE. Born July 5, 1952 in NYC. Studied at Met Opera Ballet School. Debut 1969 with Manhattan Festival Ballet; subsequently with Yuriko Co., Boston Ballet 1973.

STRIPLING, JAN. Born Sept 27, 1940 in Essen, Ger. Studied with Volkova, Tudor, Jooss, Hoving, and Jean Lebron. Joined Stuttgart Ballet in 1963.

STROGANOVA, NINA. Born in Copenhagen, and studied at Royal Danish Ballet with Preobrajenska and Dokoudovsky. Appeared with Ballet de L'Opera Comique Paris, Mordkin Ballet, National Ballet Theatre, de Basil's Original Ballet Russe, Ballet Russe de Monte Carlo, and Danish Royal Ballet. Was co-director and ballerina of Dokoudovsky-Stroganova Ballet. Is now a teacher.

STRUCHKOVA, RAISSA. Born in 1925 in Moscow; graduate of Bolshoi School in 1944. Became soloist in 1946 with company; now a prima ballerina. Has appeared in almost every ballet performed in Bolshoi.

SULTZBACH, RUSSELL. Born in Gainesville, Fla. Studied at Royal School, and American Ballet Center. Debut 1972 with Joffrey Ballet.

SUMNER, CAROL. Born Feb. 24, 1940 in Brooklyn. Studied with Eileen O'Connor and at School of American Ballet. Joined N.Y.C. Ballet, becoming soloist in 1963.

SURMEYAN, HAZAROS. Born in 1942 in Yugoslavia. Began training at 13. Made debut with Skopje Opera Ballet; subsequently with Belgrade Opera Ballet, Mannheim Opera Ballet, Cologne Opera Ballet. Joined National Ballet of Canada in 1966. Is now a principal and teacher.

SUTHERLAND, DAVID. Born Sept. 18, 1941 in Santa Ana, Cal. Studied with Michel Panaieff, Aaron Girard. Debut 1959 with Ballet de Cuba. Joined Stuttgart Ballet in 1965.

SUTHERLAND, PAUL. Born in 1935 in Louisville, Ky. Joined Ballet Theatre in 1957, subsequently dancing with Royal Winnipeg Ballet, and Joffrey Ballet. Rejoined American Ballet Theatre as soloist in 1964; promoted to principal 1966; Harkness in 1969, Joffrey 1971.

SUTOWSKI, THOR. Born in Trenton, NJ. in Jan. 1945. Studied with Rosella Hightower, Franchette, Williams, Franklin, Tupine, Pereyaslavec. Debut with San Diego Ballet; then with San Francisco Ballet, National Ballet, Hamburg Opera Ballet, Norwegian Opera Ballet where he became premier soloist. Now co-director of San Diego Ballet.

SUZUKI, DAWN. Born in Slocan, B.C., Can. Graduate U. Toronto; studied at Canadian Royal Academy of Dance, Banff and Martha Graham Schools. Debut with Yuriko in 1967, followed by performances with Pearl Lang. Joined Graham Co. in 1968.

SVETLOVA, MARINA. Born May 3, 1922 in Paris. Studied with Trefilova, Egorova, and Vilzak. With Original Ballet Russe (1939–41). Ballet Theatre (1942), prima ballerina Met Opera Ballet (1943–50), N.Y.C. Opera (1950–52), own concert group (1944–58), and as guest with most important European companies, Artistic Director of Dallas Civic Ballet; choreographer for Dallas, Seattle, and Houston Operas; Teaches at Indiana U.

SWANSON, BRITT. Born June 6, 1947 in Fargo, N.Dak. Studied at S.F. Ballet Sch., N.Y. School of Ballet. Debut 1963 with Chicago Opera Ballet, subsequently with S.F. Ballet, on Bdwy, with Paul Sanasardo, Paul Taylor (1969).

TALLCHIEF, MARIA. Born Jan. 24, 1925 in Fairfax, Okla. After studying with Nijinska, joined Ballet Russe de Monte Carlo in 1942, and became leading dancer. In 1948 joined N.Y.C. Ballet as prima ballerina, and excelled in classic roles. Has appeared as guest artist with Paris Opera and other European companies. Retired in 1965.

TALLCHIEF, MARJORIE. Born Oct. 19, on Indian reservation in Oklahoma in 1927. Studied with Nijinska, and Lichine, Debut with American Ballet Theatre in 1945, subsequently with Marquis de Cuevas Ballet (1947–56), Theatre National Opera de Paris (1956–64), Harkness (1964), and Harkness Ballet in 1964. Resigned in 1966. Now teaches.

TALMAGE, ROBERT. Born June 24, 1943 in Washington, D.C. Attended S.F. State Col. Studied with Eugene Loring. Appeared with Atlanta Ballet, in musicals, before joining Joffrey Ballet in 1968.

TANNER, RICHARD. Born Oct. 28, 1949 in Phoenix, Ariz. Graduate U. Utah. Studied at School of Am. Ballet. Made debut with N.Y.C. Ballet in 1968.

TARAS, JOHN. Born in N.Y.C. Apr. 18, 1919. Studied with Fokine, Vilzak, Shollar, and at School of American Ballet. Appeared in musicals and with Ballet Caravan, Littlefield Ballet, American Ballet, and Ballet Theatre with which he became soloist, ballet master, and choreographed first ballet "Graziana" in 1945. Joined Marquis de Cuevas' Grand Ballet in 1948. Returned to N.Y.C. Ballet in 1959 as assistant to Balanchine. Has created and staged ballets for companies throughout the world.

TAVERNER, SONIA. Born in Byfleet, Eng., in 1936. Studied at Sadler's Wells, and joined company before moving to Canada where she became member of Royal Winnipeg Ballet, developing into its premiere danseuse. Joined Pa. Ballet as principal in 1971; left in 1972.

TAYLOR, BURTON. Born Aug. 19, 1943 in White Plains, N.Y. Studied with Danielian, and at Ballet Theatre School. Debut with Eglevsky Ballet in 1959 before joining American Ballet Theatre, Joffrey Co. in 1969.

TAYLOR, JUNE. Born in 1918 in Chicago. Studied with Merriel Abbott. Debut in "George White's Scandals of 1931." Choreographer for June Taylor Dancers and director of own school.

TAYLOR, PAUL. Born in Allegheny County, Pa., July 29, 1930. Attended Syracuse U., Juilliard., Met Opera Ballet, and Graham Schools. Studied with Craske and Tudor. Member of Graham Co. for 6 years, and appeared with Merce Cunningham, Pearl Lang, Anna Sokolow, and N.Y.C. Ballet. In 1960 formed and choreographs for own company that tours U.S. and Europe annually.

TCHERINA, LUDMILLA. Born in Paris in 1925. Trained with d'Allesandri, Clustine, Preobrajenska. Has appeared with Monte Carlo Opera, Ballets des Champs-Elysees. Nouveau Ballet de Monte Carlo. Toured with own company, and now appears in films.

TCHERKASSKY, MARIANNA. Born 1955 in Glen Cove, N.Y. Studied with her mother Lillian Tcherkassky; made debut with Eglevsky Ballet; joined ABT in 1970; soloist in 1972.

TENNANT, VERONICA. Born Jan. 15, 1947 in London, Eng. Studied in Eng., and Ntl. Ballet School of Canada. Debut 1964 with Ntl. Ballet of Canada., and rapidly rose to principal.

TETLEY, GLEN. Born Feb. 3, 1926 in Cleveland, Ohio. Attended Franklin and Marshall College, and NYU graduate. Studied with Holm, Graham, Tudor, and Craske. Debut in 1946 in "On The Town," subsequently with Hanya Holm (1946–9), John Butler (1951–9), N.Y.C. Opera (1951–66), Robert Joffrey (1955–6), Martha Graham (1957–60). American Ballet Theatre (1958–60), Ballets; U.S.A. (1960–1), Nederlands Dans Theatre (1962–5). Formed own company in 1961, and choreographs. Director of Stuttgart Ballet 1974.

THARP, TWYLA. Graduate Barnard College. Studied with Collonette, Schwetzoff, Farnworth, Louis, Mattox, Graham, Nikolais, Taylor, and Cunningham. Debut with Paul Taylor in 1965. Has organized, choreographed, and appeared with own company in N.Y.C. and on tour.

THOMAS, ROBERT. Born Mar. 5, 1948 in Iowa City. Studied with Anne Kirksen, and at Harkness School. Joined Harkness Ballet in 1968. Joffrey Ballet 1970.

THOMPSON, BASIL. Born in Newcasle-on-Tyne, Eng. Studied at Sadler's Wells. Joined Covent Garden Ballet in 1954, the Royal Ballet, ABT in 1960. Currently ballet master of Joffrey Ballet.

| Cristina Stirling | Hazaros Surmeyan | Edra Toth | Martine Van Hamel | Michael Uthoff |

THOMPSON, CLIVE. Born in Kingston, Jamaica, B.W.I., Oct. 20. Studied with and joined Ivy Baxter's Dance Co. Attended Soohih School of Classical Dance, and University College of West Indies. In 1958 represented Jamaica at Federal Festival of Arts. Won Jamaican award for choreography and contribution to dance. Came to U.S. in 1960, studied with Graham, and joined company in 1961. Also with Talley Beatty, Pearl Lang, Yuriko, Geoffrey Holder, and Alvin Ailey.

THORESEN, TERJE. Born in 1945 in Stockholm. Debut in 1959. Appeared with Royal Dramatic Theatre, Stockholm Dance Theatre, Syvilla Fort African Dance Group.

TIMOFEYEVA, NINA. Born in 1935 in Russia. Entered Leningrad Ballet School and graduated into Kirov Co. in 1953. Joined Bolshoi in 1956 and is a principal ballerina.

TIPPET, CLARK. Born Oct. 5, 1954 in Parsons, Kan. Trained at National Academy of Ballet. Made debut with American Ballet Theatre 1972.

TOMASSON, HELGI. Born Oct. 8, in Reykjavik, Iceland. Studied with Sigidur Arman, Erik Bidsted, Vera Volkova, and American Ballet School. Debut in Copenhagen's Pantomine Theatre in 1958. In 1961 joined Joffrey Ballet; Harkness Ballet in 1964; N.Y.C. Ballet in 1970, becoming principal.

TORRES, JULIO. Born in Ponce, PR. Attended NY High School of Performing Arts. Appeared with Jose Greco, Carmen Amaya, Vienna Volksopera, Pilar Lopez. Founder-Director-Choreographer of Puerto Rican Dance Theatre.

TOTH, EDRA. Born in 1952 in Budapest, Hungary. Trained with Alda Marova, E. Virginia Williams. Joined Boston Ballet in 1965, rising to principal.

TOUMANOVA, TAMARA. Born in 1919. Protege of Pavlowa; danced first leading role with Paris Opera at 10; ballerina with Ballet Russe de Monte Carlo at 16. Joined Rene Blum Co. in 1939; returned to Paris Opera in 1947, and to London with de Cuevas Ballet in 1949. More recently in films.

TRACY, PAULA. Born Feb. 25 in San Francisco where she studied with Lew and Harold Christensen. Debut with San Francisco Ballet in 1956. Joined American Ballet Theatre in 1967, San Francisco Ballet 1973.

TRISLER, JOYCE. Born in Los Angeles in 1934. Graduate of Juilliard. Studied with Horton, Maracci, Tudor, Holm, Joffrey, Caton. Debut with Horton Co. in 1951. Became member of Juilliard Dance Theater, and performed with own group, for which she choreographed. Has also choreographed for musicals and operas. Now teaches.

TROUNSON, MARILYN. Born Sept. 30, 1947 in San Francisco. Graduated from Royal Ballet School and joined company in 1966.

TUDOR, ANTONY. Born Aug. 4, 1908 in London. Studied with Marie Rambert, and made debut with her in 1930, when he also choreographed his first work. Joined Vic-Wells Ballet (1933-5), and became choreographer. Formed own company, London Ballet, in N.Y. in 1938. In 1940 joined American Ballet Theatre as soloist and choreographer. Has produced ballets for N.Y.C. Ballet, Theatre Colon, Deutsche Opera, and Komaki Ballet. Was in charge of Met Opera Ballet School (1957-63); artistic director Royal Swedish Ballet 1963-64. Considered one of world's greatest choreographers. Associate director Am. Ballet Theatre 1974.

TUNE, TOMMY. Born Feb. 28, 1939 in Wichita Falls, Tex. Graduate UTex. Has been featured dancer in films and on Bdwy.

TUPINE, OLEG. Born in 1920 aboard ship off Istanbul. Studied with Egorova and made debut with her company. Joined Original Ballet Russe in 1938, Markova-Dolin Co. in 1947. Ballet Russe de Monte Carlo in 1951, then formed own company. Now teaches.

TURKO, PATRICIA. Born May 22, 1942 in Pittsburgh. Studied at School of American Ballet. Danced with Pittsburgh and Philadelphia Opera companies and in musicals before joining Pennsylvania Ballet in 1964. Now retired.

TURNEY, MATT. Born in Americus, Ga. Joined Martha Graham Co. in 1951. Also danced with Donald McKayle, Alvin Ailey, Paul Taylor, and Pearl Lang.

TUROFF, CAROL. Born Jan. 14, 1947 in New Jersey. NYU graduate; studied with Jean Erdman, Erick Hawkins. Debut 1968 with Hawkins Co., subsequently appearing with Jean Erdman, and in concert.

TUZER, TANJU. Born May 17, 1944 in Istanbul, Turkey. Trained at State Conservatory. Made debut with Turkish State Ballet 1961. Joined Hamburg State Opera Ballet 1969, Harkness Ballet 1972.

UCHIDA, CHRISTINE. Born in Chicago, Ill. Studied with Vincenzo Celli, School of American Ballet, American Ballet Center. Debut 1972 with Joffrey Ballet.

UCHIYAMA, AYAKO. Born in Japan in 1925. Began studies in Tokyo with Masami Kuni, Aiko Yuzaki and Takaya Eguchi. In 1950 organized Uchiyama Art Dance School. Awarded scholarship to study in U.S. with Graham, Horst, Limon, Cunningham, Joffrey, Ballet Russe School, and Luigi's Jazz Center. Has given many concerts and recitals in Japan, and U.S. under sponsorship of Japan and Asia Societies.

ULANOVA, GALINA. Born in Russia, Jan. 8, 1910. Studied with Vagonova. Graduate of Leningrad State School of Ballet. Joined Bolshoi Company and became Russia's greatest lyric ballerina. Now in retirement, but coaches for Bolshoi.

ULLATE, VICTOR. Born in Spain. Studied with Rosella Hightower, Maria de Avila. Debut with Antonio. At 18 joined Bejart Ballet.

UTHOFF, MICHAEL. Born in Santiago, Chile, Nov. 5, 1943. Graduate of U. Chile. Studied at Juilliard, School of American Ballet, American Ballet Center, and with Tudor, and Limon. Debut with Limon's company in 1964. Appeared with American Dance Theatre before he joined Joffrey Ballet in 1965, First Chamber Dance Co. (1969) Presently Artistic Director of Hartford Ballet, and teacher at SUNY in Purchase N.Y.

VALDOR, ANTONY. Began career with Marquis de Cuevas Company, subsequently appearing with Jose Torres' Ballet Espagnol, Opera de Marseille, Theatre du Chatelet, Theatre Massimo de Palermo. Currently ballet master of San Francisco Ballet.

VALENTINE, PAUL. Born March 23, 1919 in N.Y.C. Began career at 14 with Ballet Russe de Monte Carlo, subsequently as Val Valentinoff with Fokine Ballet, and Mordkin Ballet. Since 1937 has appeared in theatre, TV, and night clubs.

VAN DYKE, JAN. Born April 15, 1941, in Washington, D.C. Studied with Ethel Butler, Martha Graham, Merce Cunningham, and at Conn. College, Henry St. Playhouse, Dancer-choreographer-director of Church St. Dance Co., and appeared with DTW.

VAN HAMEL, MARTINE. Born Nov. 16, 1945 in Brussels. Attended Natl. Ballet School of Canada. Debut 1963 with Natl. Ballet of Can. Guest with Royal Swedish Ballet, Royal Winnipeg Ballet, Joffrey Ballet, before joining ABT. Became soloist in 1971, principal 1973.

VARDI, YAIR. Born May 29, 1948 in Israel. Studied at Batsheva Dance Studio, and joined Batsheva Dance Co.

VARGAS, GEORGE. Born Apr. 19, 1949 in Barranquilla, Col. Studied with Thomas Armour, School of American Ballet. Debut 1968 with Eglevsky Ballet; joined Boston Ballet 1969.

VASSILIEV, VLADIMIR. Born in Russia 1940. Studied at Bolshoi School and joined company in 1958, becoming soloist in 1959, then principal.

VEGA, ANTONIO. Born in Huelva, Spain. Studied with Pericet and Antonio Marin. Has performed with Jose Molina, Luisillo, Mariemma, Antonio, and Jose Greco. Joined Ballet Granada in 1968 as soloist.

VERDON, GWEN. Born Jan. 13, 1926 in Culver City, Calif. Studied various styles of dancing, including ballet with Ernest Belcher and Carmelita Maracci. Danced with Aida Brodbent company, and Jack Cole. Became assistant choreographer to Cole on several films, before becoming star in Bdwy musicals.

VERDY, VIOLETTE. Born in Brittany, Dec. 1, 1933. Debut in 1944 with Roland Petit. Has appeared with major European ballet companies, including England's Royal Ballet, Petit's Co., and Paris Opera Ballet. Joined ABT in 1957, N.Y.C. Ballet in 1958 as a principal.

VERE, DIANA. Born Sept. 29, 1942 in Trinidad. Studied at Royal Ballet School; joined company in 1962; promoted to soloist in 1968, principal 1970.

VERED, AVNER. Born Feb. 3, 1938 in Israel. Debut 1965 with Bertram Ross, subsequently with Joffrey Ballet, Pearl Lang.

VERSO, EDWARD. Born Oct. 25, 1941 in N.Y.C. Studied with Vincenzo Celli. Appeared on Bdwy and with Ballets U.S.A., before joining American Ballet Theatre in 1962, Joffrey Ballet in 1969. Directs his own school, and Festival Dance Theatre in N.J.

VEST, VANE. Born in Vienna. Studied with Larry Boyette. Debut with Denver Civic Ballet; subsequently with Ballet Theatre Players, ABT 1968, San Francisco Ballet 1972.

VETRA, VIJA. Born Feb. 6 in Latvia. Studied in Vienna, and India. Debut 1945 in Burgtheatre, Vienna. Since 1955 has toured world in solo concerts, and teaches in own N.Y. studio.

VIKULOV, SERGEI. Trained at Leningrad Ballet School. Joined Kirov Company in 1956.

VILLELLA, EDWARD. Born Oct. 1, 1936, in Bayside, Queens, N.Y. Began studies at School of American Ballet at 10. Graduate of Maritime College. Joined N.Y.C. Ballet in 1957, and rapidly rose to leading dancer. First male guest artist to appear with Royal Danish Ballet. Appeared in N.Y.C. Center productions of "Brigadoon," and on TV. Recently choreographed for N.Y.C. Ballet and own ensemble.

VODEHNAL, ANDREA. Born in 1938 in Oak Park, Ill. Studied at Ballet Russe School, and School of American Ballet, and with Semenova and Danilova. Joined Ballet Russe de Monte Carlo in 1957, and became soloist in 1961. Joined National Ballet in 1962 as ballerina.

VOLKOVA, VERA. Born in St.Petersburg, Russia. Studied with Maria Romanova, Agrippina Vaganova. During revolution, moved to China and danced with George Goncharov, with International Ballet (1941). Opened London studio in 1943. Since 1952, teacher and artistic adviser for Royal Danish Ballet.

VOLLMAR, JOCELYN. Entered native San Francisco Ballet School at 12 and joined company at 17 in 1943. Later with N.Y.C. Ballet, American Ballet Theatre, de Cuevas Ballet, and Borovansky Australian Ballet. Rejoined S.F. Ballet in 1957, and has choreographed several ballets.

VON AROLDINGEN, KARIN. Born July 9, 1941 in Germany. Studied with Edwardova, Gsovsky. Debut 1958 in Frankfurt. Joined N.Y.C. Ballet in 1961, soloist 1967, principal 1972.

VONDERSAAR, JEANETTE. Born May 17, 1951 in Indianapolis, Ind. Trained at Harkness School, and made debut with company in 1969.

WAGNER, RICHARD. Born Jan. 30, 1939 in Atlantic City, N.J. Studied with Antony Tudor. Debut with Ballet Russe de Monte Carlo in 1957; joined American Ballet Theatre in 1960, and Harkness Ballet in 1964 as dancer and choreographer.

WAGONER, DAN. Born July 13, 1932 in Springfield. W.Va. Attended U.W.Va. Studied with Ethel Butler, Martha Graham. Debut 1958 with Graham, subsequently with Merce Cunningham, Paul Taylor, and in own choreography and concerts.

WALKER, DAVID HATCH. Born Mar. 14, 1949 in Edmonton, Can. Studied at Natl. Ballet School. Toronto Dance Theatre, Martha Graham. Debut 1968 with Ballet Rambert, London, subsequently with Donald McKayle, Lar Lubovitch, Martha Graham.

WALKER, NORMAN. Born in N.Y.C. in 1934. Studied at HS Performing Arts. Appeared with May O'Donnell, Yuriko, Pauline Koner, and Pearl Lang. Began choreographing while in army, and afterward taught at Utah State U., Choreographed for musicals and festivals throughout U.S. Now appears with own company, and choreographs for it as well as others. Also teaches, and was artistic director of Batsheva Co.

WALL, DAVID. Born in London, March 15, 1946. Attended Royal Ballet School, and made debut with company in 1962. Now a principal.

WALLSTROM, GAY. Born Mar. 9, 1949 in Beumont, Tex. Studied at American Ballet Center and joined Joffrey Ballet in 1968.

WARD, CHARLES. Born Oct. 24, 1952 in Los Angeles, Cal. Studied with Audrey Share, Stanley Holden, Michael Lland, Ballet Theatre School, Gene Marinaccio. Debut 1970 with Houston Ballet; joined ABT 1972.

WARDELL, MARCIA JEAN. Born Dec. 22, 1948 in Lansing, Mich. Studied with Elizabeth Wiel Bergmann, Betty Jones, Ethel Winter, Alfredo Corvino, Murray Louis, Nikolais, Gladys Bailin. Debut in 1971 with Murray Louis Co.

WARNER, DENISE. Born Mar. 24, 1951 in Meriden, Conn. Studied with Vera Nikitins, American Ballet Theatre School. Debut 1968 with Hartford Ballet; joined ABT 1972.

WARREN, GRETCHEN. Born Apr. 7, 1945 in Princeton, N.J. Attended Aparri School, School of Ballet, Royal Ballet, and National Ballet Schools. Debut in 1964 with Covent Garden Opera Ballet; subsequently with Icelandic Natl. Opera Ballet, National Ballet (1964–5), Pa. Ballet from 1965. Made soloist in 1968.

WARREN, VINCENT. Born Aug. 31, 1938 in Jacksonville, Fla. Studied at Ballet Theatre School. Debut 1957 with Met Opera Ballet, subsequently with Santa Fe Opera, James Waring, Aileen Pasloff, Guatemala Natl. Ballet, Penn. Ballet, Cologne Opera Ballet, Les Grands Ballets Canadiens.

WATANABE, MIYOKO. Born in Japan and began training at 6. Joined all-girls Kabuki Troupe and became one of its leading performers. Came to U.S. in 1960 as announcer-interpreter for Kabuki troupe, and remained to perform in concert and teach classic Japanese dances.

WATTS, JONATHAN. Born in 1933 in Cheyenne, Wyo. Studied with Joffrey, Shurr, and O'Donnell. Debut with Joffrey before joining N.Y.C. Ballet in 1954, Australian Ballet 1962, and Cologne Opera Ballet as premier danseur in 1965. Now director Am. Ballet Center.

WAYNE, DENNIS. Born July 19, 1945 in St. Petersburg, Fla. Debut 1962 with Norman Walker Co.; subsequently with Harkness Ballet 1963, Joffrey Ballet 1970.

WEBER, DIANA. Born Jan. 16, in Passaic, N.J. Studied at Ballet Theatre School. Joined ABT in 1962; became soloist in 1966; San Francisco Ballet 1973.

WEIDMAN, CHARLES. Born July 22, 1901, in Lincoln, Neb. Studied at Denishawn School, with Frampton, and Humphrey. Debut with Martha Graham in "Xochitl." Toured with Denishawn Dancers for 8 years. In 1929, with Doris Humphrey, established school and concert company. In 1948, formed own company "Theatre Dance." Was choreographer for N.Y.C. Opera Co., and Bdwy productions. In 1960, established Expression of Two Arts Theatre with weekly performances.

WEISS, JEROME. Born in Florida; graduate Juilliard. Debut with Miami Ballet; subsequently with Atlanta Ballet, Netherlands Dans Theatre 1968, Harkness Ballet 1971, San Francisco Ballet 1973.

WELCH, GARTH. Born Apr. 14, 1936 in Brisbane, Aust. Studied with Phyllis Danaher, Victor Gzovsky, Anna Northcote, Zaraspe, Martha Graham. Debut 1955 with Borovansky Ballet, subsequently with Western Theatre Ballet, Marquis de Cuevas Ballet, Australian Ballet (1962).

WELLS, BRUCE. Born Jan. 17, 1950 in Tacoma, Wash. Studied with Patricia Cairns, Banff School, School of American Ballet. Joined N.Y.C. Ballet in 1967, dancing soloist and principal roles since 1969.

WELLS, DORREN. Born June 25, 1937 in London. Studied at Royal Ballet School and made debut with company in 1955, rising to ballerina.

WENGERD, TIM. Born Jan. 4, 1945 in Boston. Graduate U. Utah. Studied with Elizabeth Waters, Yuriko, Ethel Winter, Merce Cunningham, Viola Farber, Donald McKayle. Debut in 1966 with Ririe-Woodbury Co. Dancer-choreographer with Repertory Dance Theatre from 1966. Joined Graham Co. 1972.

WESCHE, PATRICIA. Born Oct. 13, 1952 in West Islip, N.Y. Attended American Ballet Theatre School. Debut 1969 with ABT.

WESLOW, WILLIAM. Born Mar. 20, 1925 in Seattle, Wash. Studied with Mary Ann Wells. Appeared on Bdwy and TV before joining Ballet Theatre in 1949. Joined N.Y.C. Ballet in 1958.

WHELAN, SUSAN. Born Feb. 26, 1948 in N.Y.C. Studied with Eglevsky, at Ballet Theatre, and Harkness schools. Joined Harkness Ballet in 1966, ABT 1971.

WHITE, FRANKLIN. Born in 1924 in Shoreham, Kent, Eng. After 3 years with Ballet Rambert, joined Royal Ballet in 1942. Is also well known as lecturer on ballet.

WHITE, GLENN. Born Aug. 6, 1949 in Pittsburg, Calif. Studied at Norfolk Ballet Academy. American Ballet Center, Debut 1968 with N.Y.C. Opera, joined Joffrey Company in 1969.

WHITE, ONNA. Born in 1925 in Cape Breton Island, Nova Scotia. Debut with San Francisco Opera Ballet Co. Became assistant choreographer to Michael Kidd, and subsequently choreographer for Bdwy, Hollywood, and London productions.

WHITENER, WILLIAM. Born Aug. 17, 1951 in Seattle, Wash. Studied with Karen Irvin, Mary Staton, Hector Zaraspe, Perry Brunson. Debut 1969 with City Center Joffrey Ballet.

WILDE, PATRICIA. Born in Ottawa, Can. July 16, 1928 where she studied before joining Marquis de Cuevas' Ballet International and continuing studies at School of American Ballet. Joined N.Y.C. Ballet in 1950 and became one of its leading ballerinas, having danced almost every role in the company's repertoire. Director of Harkness School. Now teaches. Ballet mistress for ABT.

WILLIAMS, ANTHONY. Born June 11, 1946 in Naples, Italy. Studied with Virginia Williams and Joffrey. Debut 1964 with Boston Ballet. Joined Joffrey company 1968; rejoined Boston Ballet in 1969. Soloist with Royal Winnipeg Ballet 1973.

WILLIAMS, DANIEL. Born in 1943 in San Francisco. Studied with Welland Lathrop, Gloria Unti, May O'Donnell, Gertrude Shurr, Nina Fonaroff, Wishmary Hunt, Paul Taylor. Joined Taylor's company in 1963 and appears in most of its repertoire.

Charles Ward   **Kerry Williams**   **William Whitener**   **Rochelle Zide**   **Alexei Yudenich**

WILLIAMS, DEREK. Born Dec. 14, 1945 in Jamaica, WI. Studied at Harkness House, Martha Graham School. Debut with Jamaican Ntl. Dance Co. Joined Dance Theatre of Harlem 1968.

WILLIAMS, DUDLEY. Born in N.Y.C. where he began dance lessons at 6. Studied with Shook, O'Donnell, Tudor, Graham, and at Juilliard. Has appeared with May O'Donnell, Martha Graham, Donald McKayle, Talley Beatty, and Alvin Ailey from 1964.

WILLIAMS, KERRY. Born in Philadelphia; studied at San Francisco Ballet School, and made debut with company. Joined American Ballet Co., and returned to SF Ballet in 1972.

WILLIAMS, STANLEY. Born in 1925 in Chappel, Eng. Studied at Royal Danish Ballet and joined company in 1943. Became soloist in 1949. Teacher and guest artist since 1950. Ballet master and leading dancer with Ballet Comique (1953–4). Knighted by King of Denmark. Since 1964, on staff of School of Am Ballet.

WILSON, ANNE. Born in Philadelphia. Graduate of U. of Chicago. Studied with Foline, Tudor, Weidman, Elizabeth Anderson, Etienne Decroux, and Heinz Poll. Debut 1940 with American Ballet Theatre. Also with Wiedman, and in 1964 formed own co. Noted for solo concert-lecture "The Ballet Story" which she has toured extensively.

WILSON, JOHN. Born in 1927 in Los Angeles. Studied with Katherine Dunham. Toured with Harriette Ann Gray, appeared in concert with own group, and Joyce Trisler. Joined Joffrey Ballet in 1956, Harkness Ballet in 1964.

WILSON, PAUL. Born Oct. 19, 1949 in Carbondale, Pa. Attended Jersey City State Col. Studied with Zena Rommett, Wilson Morelli, Charles Weidman. Joined Weidman company 1971.

WILSON, SALLIE. Born Apr. 18, 1932 in Ft. Worth, Tex. Studied with Tudor and Craske. Joined American Ballet Theatre in 1959, and in 1963 became principal dancer. Has also appeared with Met Opera and N.Y.C. Ballets.

WILSON, ZANE. Born Feb. 25, 1951 in Elkton, Md. Attended UMd. Trained at Harkness School and joined Harkness Ballet in 1970.

WINTER, ETHEL. Born in Wrentham, Mass., June 18, 1924. Graduate of Bennington College, Soloist with Martha Graham Co. since 1964. Has taught Graham Method in various schools in Eng. and appeared as lecture-demonstrator. Her own choreography has received recognition, and is included in repertoire of Batsheva Co. Also appeared with N.Y.C. Opera, and Sophie Maslow.

WOLENSKI, CHESTER. Born Nov. 16, 1931 in New Jersey. Attended Juilliard, and American School of Ballet. Debut 1956 with Jose Limon, subsequently with Anna Sokolow, Donald McKayle, John Butler, American Dance Theatre, Juilliard Dance Theatre, Jack Moore, Bill Frank and Ruth Currier. Also appeared in musicals.

WONG, MEL. Born Dec. 2, 1938 in Oakland, Cal. Graduate UCLA. Studied at Academy of Ballet. SF Ballet School, School of Am. Ballet, Cunningham Studio. Debut in 1968 with Merce Cunningham Co.

WOOD, DONNA. Born Nov. 21, 1954 in NYC. Joined Alvin Ailey Dance Theatre 1972.

WOODIN, PETER. Born in Tucson, Ariz. Graduate Wesleyan U. Debut 1971 with Lucas Hoving Co.; subsequently with Utah Repertory Dance Theatre, Gus Solomons, Chamber Arts Dance Players, Alvin Ailey Dance Theatre 1973.

WRIGHT, REBECCA. Born Dec. 5, 1947 in Springfield, Ohio. Studied with David McLain and Josephine Schwarz. Joined Joffrey Ballet in 1966.

YOHN, ROBERT. Born Sept. 23, 1943 in Fresno, Calif. Studied at Fresno State Col., New Dance Group, and with Charles Kelley, Perry Brunson. Has appeared with New Dance Group, Bruce King, and joined Erick Hawkins Company in 1968.

YOUNG, CYNTHIA. Born Dec. 16, 1954 in Salt Lake City, U. Studied with Carol Reed, Ben Lokey, William Christensen, Anatole Vilzak, Gordon Paxman. Joined Ballet West in 1970; promoted to soloist 1973; principal 1974.

YOUNG, GAYLE. Born Nov. 7, in Lexington, Ky. Began study with Dorothy Pring at U. Calif. Studied at Ballet Theatre School, and joined Joffrey Ballet. Appeared on Bdwy and with N.Y.C. Ballet before joining American Ballet Theatre in 1960. Became principal in 1964.

YOUSKEVITCH, IGOR. Born in Moscow, Mar. 13, 1912. Studied with Preobrajenska. Debut in Paris with Nijinska company; joined De Basil's Ballet, then, Ballet Russe de Monte Carlo. In 1946 became premier danseur with Ballet Theatre. Currently operating own school in N.Y.

YOUSKEVITCH, MARIA. Born Dec. 11, 1945 in N.Y.C. Studied with father, Igor Youskevitch, and made debut with his company in 1963. Appeared with Met Opera Ballet before joining American Ballet Theatre in 1967. Promoted to soloist 1973.

YUAN, RINA. Born Oct. 9, 1947 in Shanghai, China. Attended Juilliard, Martha Graham School. Debut 1969 with Pearl Lang; subsequently Yuriko 1970, Chinese Dance Co. 1972, Alvin Ailey Co. 1972.

YUDENICH, ALEXEI. Born July 5, 1943 in Sarajevo, Yugoslavia. Studied at Sarajevo Opera Ballet School, and made debut with company. Guest artist with Sagreb Opera Ballet before joining Pennsylvania Ballet in 1964 as principal dancer; retired in 1973 and now teaches.

YURIKO. Born Feb. 2, 1920 in San Jose, Calif. Began professional career at 6 with group that toured Japan for 7 years. Studied with Martha Graham, and joined company in 1944, becoming soloist, and choreographer. Formed own company in 1948 with which she has appeared in N.Y. and on tour. Also appeared in musicals.

ZAMIR, BATYA. Studied with Alwin Nikolais, Gladys Bailin, Phyllis Lamhut, Murray Louis, Mimi Garrard, Rachel Fibish, Joy Boutilier, and in own concerts and choreography. Also teaches.

ZHDANOV, YURI. Born in Moscow in 1925. Began career at 12 before attending Bolshoi School. Joined Company in 1944, became Ulanova's partner in 1951. Is now retired.

ZIDE, ROCHELLE. Born in Boston, Ap. 21, 1938. Studied with Hoctor, Williams, Pereyaslavec, Joffrey, Danielian, and at Ballet Russe School. Debut in 1954 with Ballet Russe de Monte Carlo, subsequently appearing with Joffrey Ballet (1958), Ballets U.S.A. (1961), American Dances (1963), N.Y.C. Opera Ballet (1958–63), Ballet Spectaculars (1963), and became ballet mistress of Joffrey Ballet in 1965.

ZIMMERMANN, GERDA. Born Mar. 26, in Cuxhaven, Ger. Studied with Georgi, Wigman, Horst, Zena Rommett. Soloist with Landestheater Hannover 1959–62. Choreographer from 1967. Solo recitals in U.S. from 1967 and in Ger. Formed Kammertanz Theatre. Teaches.

ZITO, DOROTHY. Born in Jersey City, N.J. Attended Juilliard. Studied at Graham, Harkness schools, and N.Y. School of Ballet. Debut 1969 with New Dance Group, subsequently with Pearl Lang.

ZOMPAKOS, STANLEY. Bron in N.Y.C. May 12, 1925. Studied with Balanchine and at School of American Ballet. Debut 1942 with New Opera Co. In Bdwy musicals, with Ballet Russe de Monte Carlo (1954–6), and became artistic director of Charleston, S.C., Civic Ballet.

ZORINA, VERA. Born Jan. 2, 1917 in Berlin, Ger. Studied with Edwardova, Tatiana and Victor Gsovsky, Dolin, and Legat. Debut 1930 in Berlin. Toured with Ballet Russe de Monte Carlo (1934–6). Made N.Y.C. debut in "I Married An Angel" in 1938. Joined Ballet Theatre in 1943. Subsequently, appeared in Bdwy productions, films.

ZORITCH, GEORGE. Born in Moscow June 6, 1919. Studied in Lithuania, Paris, and N.Y., with Preobrajenska, Vilzak, Vladimiroff, and Oboukhoff. Debut 1933 with Ida Rubenstein Co. in Paris. Joined de Basil Ballet Russe 1936. Ballet Russe de Monte Carlo 1938, Grand Ballet de Marquis de Cuevas (1951–8), Marina Svetlova Co. (1961), then formed own company. A favorite teacher and choreographer for regional ballet companies. Operates own school in Los Angeles.

OBITUARIES

ANDERSON-IVANTZOVA, ELISABETH, late 70's, teacher and former dancer, died Nov. 10, 1973 in her NYC home. Moscow-born, she became a member of the Bolshoi, and was made a ballerina in 1917. After coming to the U.S., she opened her studio in 1937 and helped produce many ballet stars. She was the widow of operatic tenor and coach Ivan Ivantzoff. No reported survivors.

ANTONOVA, HELENE A., 75, co-director of the Wilmington, Del., Academy of Dance, died in October 1973. She was born in St. Petersburg, Russia, and studied ballet there. She had been a member of the Diaghilev, Ida Rubenstein, Nijinska, and Ballets Russes companies. She opened the Academy in 1956. A daughter survives.

BAIM, JOAN, 41, former member of Martha Graham's company, died of cancer July 11, 1973. She is survived by her husband, playwright Neil Simon, and two daughters.

BOSKOVIC, NATALIA, 62, former prima ballerina of the Royal Yugoslav Ballet, and the Belgrade State Opera, died June 30, 1973 in NYC following a heart attack. She had also danced with the Diahgilev, and Pavlova companies. She emigrated to the U.S. in 1950, and became active as a teacher. Surviving is her husband, Ljubischa Vido, and a sister.

CANNELL, KATHLEEN EATON, 83, dance critic, died May 19, 1974 in Boston. She joined the staff of the Christian Science Monitor in 1948, after serving as fashion correspondent in Paris for the New York Times. A sister survives.

COLE, JACK, 60, choreographer, teacher, and former dancer, died Feb. 17, 1974 in Los Angeles. He made his debut with the Denishawn company, subsequently dancing with Shawn's Men Dancers, Doris Humphrey, and Charles Weidman, before forming his own group. After appearing in night clubs and on Broadway, and choreographing for several musicals, he went to Hollywood where he choreographed for films for over 20 years. He was teaching at UCLA when he died. His Bdwy credits as a choreographer include "Magdalena," "Alive and Kicking," "Kismet," "Jamaica," "Foxy," "Kean," and "Man of La Mancha." For films he choreographed "Gilda," "Some Like It Hot," "Gentlemen Prefer Blondes," "The Jolson Story," and "Kismet." A son survives.

CRANKO, JOHN, 45, one of the world's leading choreographers, former dancer, and director of the Stuttgart Ballet, died June 26, 1973 aboard a plane from Philadelphia to Stuttgart. Death was from asphyxia by stomach inhalation while under sedation. South African by birth, at 19 he joined Sadler's Wells Ballet, and became resident choreographer of Sadler's Wells Ballet Theatre in 1950. Ten years later he began his association with the Stuttgart Ballet which he built into one of the world's great companies. He was especially noted for his "story" ballets, such as "Eugene Onegin," "Romeo and Juliet," and "The Taming of the Shrew." For the theatre he wrote, directed and choreographed three revues: "Cranks," "Keep Your Hair On," and "New Cranks." He had just completed his third U.S. tour with his company.

FEALY, JOHN, 44, dancer, choreographer, teacher and Dance Magazine correspondent from Mexico, died May 17, 1974 in The Hague, Neth., after being struck by a car. Brooklyn-born, he moved to Mexico in 1954 where he was soloist with Xavier Francis' Nuevo Teatro de Danza for many years. He also performed regularly as guest artist with Ballet Nacional. In 1967 he began working with, and choreographing for the New Ballet Independiente. He was in the Netherlands to stage one of his ballets, "Arioso," for Nederlands Dans Theater. His "Voices" is in the Ailey company repertoire. Surviving are his mother and four brothers.

FERGUSON, HOWARD, 78, national executive secretary of Dance Masters of America, died Jan. 18, 1974, in a NYC hotel while attending a meeting of the organization's advisory board. After World War I he established his own dance studio in Elmira, NY. He retired from teaching in 1962. His widow survives.

FOKINE, LEON, 68, teacher, and former dancer, died Nov. 20, 1973 in his NYC home. Born in Leningrad, he studied at the Maryinsky, now the Kirov Ballet School. He taught at the Cuban Ballet School (1956–8), and at the Harkness Ballet School, from which he retired in 1967. For several years he had his own school in Washington, D.C. He was a nephew of the late Michel Fokine. No reported survivors.

FRAMPTON, ELEANOR, 77, teacher, critic, and former dancer, died Oct. 8, 1973 in her home in Cleveland Heights, O. She had appeared with ballet companies around the world, and had also been in musicals and vaudeville. She was dance critic for the Plain Dealer. No reported survivors.

GOTH, TRUDY, 60, writer on dance, and a former dancer and producer, died May 12, 1974 of cancer in her Florence, Italy home. Born in Germany, she came to The States in the 1940's. She was a modern dancer, and appeared as a soloist. In 1946 she founded the Choreographers Workshop where she produced experimental works. She wrote for Dance News, Dance Magazine, Opera News, and Variety. She was buried on the Island of Elba. Her mother survives.

GSOVSKY, VICTOR, 72, choreographer, teacher, and former dancer, died during April 1974 of leukemia in Hamburg, Ger. Born and trained in St. Petersburg, Russia, he moved to Germany in 1925. He became ballet master of Berlin State Opera. In 1937 he joined the Markova-Dolin troupe in London. Subsequently he became ballet master for the Paris Opera, Ballets des Champs-Elysees, and London's Metropolitan Ballet. His works include "Hamlet," "Road to Light," and "The Pearl." He was married to Tatiana Gsovska.

JACKSON, LAWRENCE, 53, among the best jazz tap dancers in the world, died Apr. 2, 1974 of cancer in a NYC hospital. Began his career at 11 in vaudeville as "Baby Laurence." He had appeared with many bands, on tv, and with Josephine Baker at the Palace. No reported survivors.

LIEPA, ALFA, 50, Lithuanian-born teacher and former dancer, died Apr. 19, 1974 at his home in North Miami, Fla. He emigrated to NY in 1948. He founded the Ballet Art School of North Miami in 1967. He had appeared with such companies as Germany Lassell Opera Company of Austria, Agnes deMille company, Royal Winnipeg Ballet, Janine Charrat Company of France. No reported survivors.

JOHNSON, JULIE, 71, former dancer, and wife of former Senator George Murphy, died Sept. 28, 1973 of a heart ailment in her Beverly Hills home. She taught her husband how to dance and together, they became a vaudeville team that toured the U.S. and Europe. In addition to her husband, a son, and daughter survive.

MAKLETZOVA, XENIA, 81, former ballerina, died May 18, 1974 at her home in Long Beach, NY. She was born in St. Petersburg, and studied at the Bolshoi school. She became a soloist before joining Maryinsky Ballet. Later she became prima ballerina with Diaghilev's company, and rejoined the Maryinsky in 1917. After dancing in the Orient for eight years, she came to the U.S. in 1926 to tour with Michail Mordkin's company.

NEUMANN, NATANYA, 50, teacher and former member of Martha Graham's company, died Apr. 23, 1974 in a NYC hospital. Surviving are her husband, Harold P. Manson, and two sons.

RITCHIE, CARL, 64, former dancer, and later a Hollywood agent, died of a massive heart attack March 16, 1974 in Hollywood. Began his career as a "hoofer" in the 1920's. Later formed a dance team with Margie Rich whom he married. Surviving is his widow.

ST. DENIS, BROTHER, age unreported, dancer and stage manager for his sister, the late Ruth St. Denis, died Nov. 28, 1973 in Hollywood, Cal. He was noted for the innovative lighting of her productions. He left dancing in the early 1920's to work as a mining engineer. He later established the St. Denis Asia Bazaar in Hollywood. Two sons survive.

SAND, INGE, 45, soloist with the Royal Danish Ballet, died Feb. 8, 1974 of cancer in Copenhagen. During the 1951–52 season, she appeared with the Original Ballet Russe in England. She was a graduate of the Royal Danish Ballet School, and a recipient of the Order of Dannebrog. Her American debut was 1954 at Jacob's Pillow.

SCHONBERG, ROSALYN KROKOVER, writer, and former dancer and dance critic, died June 14, 1973 in Greenport, NY. She had danced with the Pavley-Oukrainsky Ballet, and the Chicago Opera Ballet. For many years she was dance editor and critic for the Musical Courier. She is survived by her husband, NY Times music critic, Harold C. Schonberg.

SOKOLOVA, LYDIA, 77, teacher, and former dancer, died at her home in Kent, Eng., Feb. 2, 1974. Born Hilda Munnings, she made her debut in 1911 with Mikhal Mordkin's company using her real name. She joined the Diaghilev Ballets Russes, and changed her name. She became the company's leading character dancer, and had parts written for her by both Fokine and Massine. She danced with Nijinsky in "Le Spectre de la Rose." She retired from the company after Diaghilev's death in 1929. In 1962 she appeared in the Royal Ballet's revival of "The Good-Humored Ladies," re-creating her original role. No reported survivors.

WIGMAN, MARY, 86, dancer, choreographer, teacher, and pioneer of modern dance in Europe, died Sept. 18, 1973 in Berlin, Ger. after a prolonged illness. She studied with Jacques-Dalcroze and later with Rudolf von Laban, becoming his assistant in 1914. In 1918 she created "The Seven Dances of Life" and began her career on the concert stage. In 1920 in Dresden, she established her own school to train dancers and experiment with choreography. Her U.S. debut in 1930 was a triumph, but controversial, and she returned for her third and last tour in 1933. During WWII she taught in Leipzig as a virtual prisoner of the Nazis. In 1950 she opened a school in West Berlin where she taught until ill health forced her to retire. She continued to choreograph for dance and opera groups in Germany. West Berlin honored her in a special celebration on her 80th birthday in 1966.

WOOD, MOLLY, 63, former dancer with the Ballet Russe de Monte Carlo, died Nov. 25, 1973 of a heart attack in her NYC home. She leaves a brother and a sister.

204

207

216

219